U.S. AGRICULTURAL POLICY: THE 1985 FARM LEGISLATION

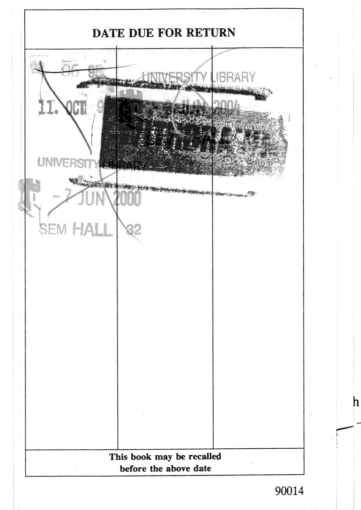

h

Library of Congress Cataloging-in-Publication Data
Main entry under title:

U.S. agricultural policy.

"A conference sponsored by the American Enterprise
Institute for Public Policy Research."
  Includes bibliographies.
    1. Agriculture and state—United States—Congresses.
2. Agricultural laws and legislation—United States—
Congresses. I. Gardner, Bruce L. II. American
Enterprise Institute for Public Policy Research.
HD1755.U17 1985   338.1'873   85-16820
ISBN 0-8447-2256-1 (alk. paper)
ISBN 0-8447-2255-3 (pbk. : alk. paper)

1 3 5 7 9 10 8 6 4 2

AEI Symposia 85C

Printed in the United States of America

Contents

Part Three
Issues In Policy Design

Foreword

The expiration of agricultural commodity legislation in 1985 and the resulting debate on a new "farm bill" provide an excellent opportunity for evaluation of U.S. governmental activity in this industry. The combination of financial stress and low farm income at the same time that about $15 billion per year is being spent on commodity programs indicates that the time is ripe for substantive policy changes.

This volume is devoted to papers and discussion addressed to the issues and policy options. They constitute the proceedings of a conference on U.S. Agricultural Policies held at AEI in January 1985. It is the third in a series of conferences, the first two of which were held on the occasions of the 1977 and 1981 farm legislation. These conferences, together with a number of studies we have published over a period of almost twenty years, reflect AEI's continuing interest in economic analysis of policy issues in this important area.

The conference papers assess the current state of U.S. farming, the causes of this situation, and the prospects for improving matters by means of reforms in federal farm programs. Three themes come through strongly. One is that current problems in agriculture are related to macroeconomic events, notably the federal budget deficit, inflation, interest rates, and exchange rates. The second is that the extensive integration of U.S. agriculture with the world economy that has occurred since 1970 has fundamentally altered the market situation of farmers and placed new constraints upon farm policy. The third is that it is now more crucial than ever to have commodity programs consistent with market realities. This means that support prices must be flexible and responsive to market conditions, including macroeconomic and international factors. Attempts to maintain unrealistically high support prices now lead to unsustainably large budgetary costs and resource misallocations (such as the idling of some 80 million acres of cropland in 1983), without really solving the financial problems of farmers, as recent experience demonstrates.

This volume addresses the complexities of these and other assessments and arguments and considers many issues in how reasonable policy reforms may be achieved. We hope that it will be a constructive element in the farm policy debate in 1985 and beyond.

WILLIAM J. BAROODY, JR.
President
American Enterprise Institute

Participants

Robert G. Chambers
University of Maryland

Bruce L. Gardner
University of Maryland

D. Gale Johnson
University of Chicago

Stanley R. Johnson
University of Missouri

Timothy Josling
Stanford University

Richard E. Just
University of California, Berkeley

Alex F. McCalla
University of California, Davis

Emanuel Melichar
Federal Reserve System

Eric Monke
University of Arizona

Patrick M. O'Brien
U.S. Department of Agriculture

Anne E. Peck
Stanford University

J. B. Penn
Economic Perspectives, Inc.

Todd E. Petzel
New York Coffee, Sugar and Cocoa Exchange, Inc.

Alan J. Randall
University of Kentucky

Gordon C. Rausser
University of California, Berkeley

Larry Salathe
U.S. Department of Agriculture

John A. Schnittker
Schnittker Associates

G. Edward Schuh
World Bank

Bernard F. Stanton
Cornell University

Daniel A. Sumner
North Carolina State University

Stefan Tangermann
University of Göttingen

Luther Tweeten
Oklahoma State University

Abner W. Womack
University of Missouri

Brian D. Wright
Yale University

This conference was held at the
American Enterprise Institute for Public Policy Research
in Washington, D.C., on January 28-29, 1985

Introduction

Bruce L. Gardner

On January 27, 1985, a front-page story in the *Washington Post* carried the headline "Farm Failures Threaten to Reshape Rural U.S.: Long-predicted Crisis Seems at Hand." On January 28 and 29, 1985, the American Enterprise Institute held a conference on U.S. agricultural policy at its facilities in Washington, D.C., the proceedings of which are contained in this volume. The sequential timing is not an illustration of the power of the press but is mentioned to give a sense of the atmosphere in which the early debate on the 1985 farm legislation took place. The economic problems of U.S. farmers, following a period in which $10 to $15 billion per year were already being spent by the federal government to aid farmers, set the stage for an especially difficult period of policy making. It is also an interesting period both for economic analysis and for political maneuvering and a period whose policy outcome could well be pivotal for the future of U.S. agriculture and the role of government in farming.

The occasion for the AEI conference, as for two earlier conferences held in 1977 and 1980, was the expiration of existing legislation for the major commodities.[1] The Agriculture and Food Act of 1981 expires with the 1985 crops. The conference participants were almost all professionals in agricultural economics—from universities, the federal government, and agribusiness.

This introduction offers an overview of the conference papers and discussion, which are presented in full in the remainder of the volume. Sessions were held on each of three subject areas, and the volume is divided accordingly into three parts: (1) the state of U.S. and world agriculture, (2) policy options for 1985, and (3) issues in policy design.

The overview is followed by my own assessment of the main themes of the sessions and of the overall tenor of the discussion. There is undoubtedly some element of idiosyncrasy in this, and the reader should in the last analysis let the authors speak for themselves by reading the papers.

The conference was part of a larger project, which included the preparation of eighteen detailed studies of agricultural policy issues. Several of the conference papers were drawn from the studies, which should be useful for readers seeking a fuller treatment of key issues. These are being published

1

separately but are available from AEI as Occasional Papers. Their titles are listed at the back of this volume.

The State of U.S. and World Agriculture

The *Washington Post* story on farm failures stated that "at least 40 percent of the farmers of the North Central region" have such burdensome debt that they are headed for insolvency. This kind of alarming picture has been painted often before but seldom as intensely and by such normally moderate sources as in the past few months. Consequently, the state of farmers' balance sheets and the number of prospective business failures were much discussed at the conference.

Luther Tweeten and his discussant, Emanuel Melichar, provide a detailed picture of the asset, debt, and equity situation in U.S. agriculture. Their data do not suggest anything approaching a crisis for U.S. agriculture as a whole. But a subset of farms have dangerously high ratios of debts to assets and insufficient income to cover debt service comfortably. Tweeten estimates that 22 percent of farmers are experiencing severe financial stress. Melichar sees the greatest risk for highly leveraged farms with between $40,000 and $200,000 in sales, which make up 8.8 percent of all farms. The question is, How many of these are likely to run their equity down to zero and leave agriculture as business failures? On this we have no reliable evidence, but Tweeten ventures a guess that up to half of his 22 percent at risk will fail in the next three years if present trends continue. Given the unprecedented (post–World War II) four-year decline in land prices, high real interest rates, and the maintenance on the books of financial institutions of loans to shaky farm enterprises kept afloat by emergency credit programs since 1978, it would be surprising if we did not see an unprecedentedly high rate of farm failures in the absence of policy action to forestall it.

It should be noted that the preceding list of causes does not include low commodity prices. Farm commodity prices have indeed fallen in relation to input costs in the past four years, but Tweeten provides evidence that commercial-scale farms would be able and willing to produce indefinitely at current price-cost relationships, that is, that 1984–1985 prices are not below long-term equilibrium levels.

A corollary is that an increase in support prices to increase the income and wealth of all farms is not an attractive policy response. Not only are commercial-scale farms viable without such increases, but they are as a group already quite wealthy. On January 1, 1985, the 660,000 farms having $40,000 or more in sales had an average net worth of close to $800,000. They form an unlikely target group for federal aid, despite the severe financial stress facing some of them.

2

Two of the three papers in the first part, those of D. Gale Johnson and G. Edward Schuh, are addressed to international economic issues. The international context of U.S. agriculture is a key to understanding events in the past twenty years and under the Agriculture and Food Act of 1981.

Johnson reviews the startling errors of many experts up to 1980 in forecasting world food supply and demand. Their overoptimism contributed to acceptance of support prices that have been proved mischievously high. It may also have influenced farmers' overoptimism, which led them to pay prices for cropland that proved unsustainable. Johnson, reviewing the evidence now available, sees no reason to expect world food demand to increase in relation to supply. He sees no reason to expect any systematic departure from the many-decade trends of gradually lower prices for grains. This carries the more weight in that he was saying the same thing in the 1970s when many others were not. Johnson warns against the tendency to replace the unrealistic bullish sentiment of the 1970s with a mirrored bearish sentiment today; but his main point for policy making is that the commodity programs should not be structured so as to depend for success on the accuracy of any forecast of market trends. He thus is the first of many at the conference to stress the necessity of flexibility in farm programs. A final important point of Johnson's is that a trend toward lower farm prices has no implication of a trend toward chronically lower farm incomes. The price declines will, as in the past, reflect productivity gains and lower resource costs; and returns to labor and capital devoted to farming will over the long term equal their (opportunity) returns in nonfarm activities.

Schuh discusses several broader international issues that are harder to grasp as causal factors in the current weakness of U.S. agricultural export demand. The most straightforward of these is the value of the dollar in terms of foreign currencies. It is intuitive that a strong dollar makes U.S. commodities cost more in foreign countries. With quasi-flexible exchange rates, one has to be careful to account for depreciation of each country's currency in terms of its own goods, that is, inflation, but the dollar has strengthened in real terms, too, during the 1980s. The more difficult analytical issue is how much real effect on U.S. farm product prices we can expect a fall in the foreign exchange value of the dollar to have. Schuh reviews the evidence and finds evidence of a substantial effect, perhaps a 6 percent rise in U.S. grain prices for a 10 percent fall in the (trade-weighted) dollar.

Schuh devotes much of his discussion to policies for a more stable and efficient international financial system. He then integrates this issue with consideration of international trade policies and U.S. commodity and export policy. He identifies many areas in which the world could do better, but particularly important are his recommendations for the United States to eschew tendencies toward protectionism and to consider the international context of U.S. commodity policy carefully. We are quick to criticize the import

3

restraints and export subsidies of others, but our own policies have also been protectionist when our domestic agricultural interests needed protecting. Schuh emphasizes the importance of strengthening the technological base of U.S. agriculture through research and development as a key element for the success of U.S. agriculture in the world economy. Many now speak of over-production in the United States, suggesting that we should not seek to expand output further. But if we do not maintain our agricultural productivity growth, the market for U.S. products at prices that cover costs will shrink further.

Policy Options for 1985

Given the situation and outlook as described, what should be done about it through governmental action? The authors and discussants in the first part provide many suggestions. The second part of the proceedings is a more systematic examination of policy options for 1985. Being systematic could well start with a statement of what policy is supposed to accomplish. Alex McCalla lists policy goals, and a more detailed itemization and discussion is available in the AEI Occasional Papers.[2] It is difficult, however, to say with confidence what the goals either ought to be or are in fact. Most observers of farm policy agree that an important goal is the improvement of the economic well-being of farm people. In commodity policy this has been translated as the support of prices received by farmers for their products. Whether this ought to be a goal of policy is an important question, but it was not addressed in this conference. Instead, the participants for the most part simply attempted to analyze the consequences of policy alternatives.

In September 1984 the authors of the four papers conferred on which of the virtually limitless set of policy alternatives it would be most illuminating to analyze. It was decided not to consider radical departures from the traditional form of commodity programs but to study modifications of the current (1981 act) programs along the lines listed by McCalla as "AEI options": The "market option" is radical in largely ending U.S. government involvement in the commodity markets but is still conventional as analyzed in keeping the structure of the programs constant and changing policy variables to generate the "market" outcome. Here a gradual change is just a fraction of the radical change.

The paper by Stanley Johnson, Abner Womack, William Meyers, Robert Young, and Jon Brandt is the product of a large policy simulation model developed jointly at the University of Missouri and Iowa State University. The authors attempt the difficult task of providing quantitative estimates of the results of policy options. Their approach can be viewed as a quantitative treatment of supply-demand interrelationships among commodity markets and the macroeconomic influences upon agriculture, using the best econometric specifications of the relevant equations that the authors can muster. Congressional deliberations will have to rely on some judgments of what will happen in the next four years under the alternatives being considered, and it is unlikely that they will have any better analysis to go on than that provided in these simulations. J. B. Penn questioned the lack of response of demand and supply to price changes in the market option. If either supply or demand is more responsive than the simulations assume, the farm income effects of the market option will be less and the export expansion results greater than Johnson and his colleagues project.

While Johnson et al. present much data on what happens under policy options, they do not attempt to provide a full bottom line. Following up on the earlier statement that a purpose, in my view the prime purpose, of farm policy is to improve farm income, the first bottom line statistic on a policy option is the effect on net farm income. This is provided by Johnson and his colleagues for each policy option. Since these policies do not constitute a "free lunch" (in the model, and presumably also in reality), someone is paying for whatever the farmers gain. The authors itemize a key element of these costs, budgetary costs of deficiency and other program payments. They do not, however, summarize the effects on buyers of program commodities (livestock producers and food consumers). Assuming that any changes in crop prices are passed on to one or the other of these groups, I calculate the net redistributional consequences of the policy options, using the Johnson et al. simulation, as follows. In moving from continuation of the 1981 act to the market option, average net farm income falls by $7.2 billion, taxpayers' costs fall by $4.6 billion, and domestic users' expenditures on supported commodities fall by $2.9 billion. The bottom line is thus a net gain from moving to the market option of $300 million per year. This gain is really quite small, providing no support for the idea that the 1981 act programs are a disaster from the point of view of the national interest. Some important aspects of policy are omitted, however, as McCalla and Penn discuss—administrative costs, some resource allocation effects, and the maintenance of the dairy, sugar, peanut, tobacco, wool, import restriction, and marketing order programs.

It should be noted that the $300 million gain is not a measure of total loss from the 1981 act programs, even within the confines of the Johnson et al. model, because there is another set of gainers in moving to the market option. These are the foreign buyers of U.S. exports, who gain $1.9 billion from lower prices of wheat, corn, soybeans, cotton, and rice, based on tables 3 to 7 in the paper by Johnson et al. This implies total worldwide gains from moving to the market option as follows: U.S. consumers and taxpayers, +$7.5 billion; U.S. farmers, −$7.2 billion; and foreign buyers, +$1.9 billion, total loss of $2.2 billion under the 1981 act as compared to the market option. This total loss is an approximation of "deadweight loss" as the term is used in applied welfare economics.

These user losses are calculated as price change times *market option* quantity for each commodity. This gives an upper limit for the consumer losses. A lower limit is obtained by using the 1981 act quantities, which give a total cost of 1981 act programs of $2.3 billion instead of $2.2 billion using market-option weights.[3]

In discussion the question was raised why Johnson and his colleagues find the market option generating more farm output at lower farm prices. The answer is that, given the supply-side equations in the econometric model, the output-reducing effects of acreage diversion offset the supply response to target-price guarantees. Moving to the market option shifts product supply functions to the right. Thus the market option result of lower price and higher output has no implication of a downward-sloping supply curve.

The finding that 1981 act programs reduce U.S. farm output compared with the market option implies that the EEC objection that current U.S. policy constitutes an implicit export subsidy is mistaken; instead, U.S. policy provides an enlarged market for foreign producers. It is more like an implicit export tax. It is not of course certain, however, that the Johnson et al. model captures the net effect of 1981 act programs on U.S. farm output. The existence of price guarantees may have induced investment in agriculture that the authors' supply functions omit. If so, the 1981 act programs had supply-increasing consequences that are not accounted for in the preceding discussion. Moreover, the elements of U.S. policy beyond the 1981 act programs—farm credit programs, crop insurance subsidies, federal income tax provisions, research and extension programs—all tend to increase U.S. agricultural output.

John Schnittker, in his synthesizing paper, suggests a variation of the 1981 act (base-line) option that reduces loan rates and maintains target price payments but ties them to acreage reduction and limits payments to perhaps $20,000 per farm by 1990. It may be viewed as a practical compromise between continuing the 1981 act programs and the market option. Schnittker also suggests reduction as currently scheduled in the support price for milk, followed by a market-related formula for adjusting the support price. But he does not see reducing sugar, peanut, and tobacco price supports as urgent since only small budgetary savings would be achieved by such cuts.

Although the papers were not expected to make the case for any particular policy option in 1985 legislation, the discussion indicated that none of the participants felt uncomfortable with the synthesis option. There was a general sense that some change from the 1981 act programs was not only warranted but important to achieve and that the change should be in the direction of greater market orientation.

Issues in Policy Design

Apart from the general issues in farm policy for 1985, a number of specific problem areas require attention. The third and longest part of this volume contains papers addressed to some of these problems. These issues involve particular objectives of policy, such as market stabilization (Wright) and the economic organization or "structure" of agriculture (Sumner); particular constraints or influences on farm policy, such as the macroeconomic situation (Rausser) or the policies of other countries (Tangermann); and issues of policy management and transition from current to new policies (Just, Petzel).

The paper by Gordon Rausser considers the interaction of the macroeconomy with the agricultural sector. Throughout the 1980s experts inside and outside the government have been saying that variables such as interest rates, the foreign exchange value of the dollar, the inflation rate—generally, the macroeconomic environment—have become as important as, or even more important than, farm programs or other commodity market variables in determining the economic health of the farm sector. The scientific basis for judgments in this area is not strong, however. Rausser develops a model designed to estimate the macroeconomic linkages to agriculture and implications for agricultural policy. He finds that the overinvestment in agriculture and unsustainable land prices of the late 1970s are attributable at least in part to the characteristics of the nonfarm economy and its linkages to agriculture. In particular, because of the U.S. monetary response to unexpected shocks of the 1970s and the changes in monetary policy from 1979 on, in the context of (short-run) fixed prices in the nonfarm sector and flexible prices for agricultural commodities, "the U.S. agricultural sector has been subjected to a vicious roller coaster ride; the valleys and peaks of which have been defined largely by external linkages to the U.S. macroeconomy and the international economy." Some questions were raised about the model in discussion. To what extent can agricultural asset values and commodity prices still be understood in terms of traditional factors of supply and demand, in the United States and abroad, in agricultural commodity markets? Johnson et al. find farm prices and incomes to be not very sensitive to stronger export demand. Although their model omits some of the linkages (through interest rates) and the feedback from agriculture to nonagriculture that Rausser incorporates, it seems likely that the traditional factors must dominate the longer-term price and income trends in agriculture. It is in understanding the current financial crunch and the dynamics of commodity and asset price movements in recent years that the macroeconomic linkages become crucial.

What are the implications of macroeconomic linkages for 1985 legislation? The general point is that, as Luther Tweeten emphasized perhaps more forcefully than anyone else at the conference, traditional commodity policy is rendered relatively impotent by the dominance of macroeconomic disturbances. True, commodity programs could conceivably cushion farmers from the effects of a strong dollar and high interest rates; but accomplishing this becomes so costly as to be impractical. After all, the federal government spent an average of about $12 billion annually under the 1981 act, and we still end up with net farm income and asset values in a depressed state. Much more would have been required to maintain the returns and asset values of 1975–1980, and if commodity programs had undertaken this effort, the maladjustment in the farm sector in 1985 would have been even worse. Still, many policy questions are left unaddressed if we focus on macroeconomic issues. It would be risky to refocus the agricultural policy agenda on macroeconomic policy because, first, it is not clear what the appropriate macroeconomic policies are to place interest rates and the foreign exchange value of the dollar at the "right" levels and, second, even if the agricultural community could convince itself of what the appropriate policies are, it has too little expertise to be taken seriously as objective macroeconomic advisers and too little political influence to be effective as an interest-group lobby. Nonetheless, several conference participants emphasized Rausser's point that the farm sector is more sensitive than most other parts of the economy to macroeconomic instability and that agriculture therefore has a special stake in our avoiding policy-induced macroeconomic instability.

Within our narrower role as agricultural economists, how does the macroeconomic situation change our message? An approach that some policy makers might be glad to see is this: since macroeconomic considerations dominate anyway, it does not matter much what we do with the traditional programs; so let us do whatever is politically expedient. This is, however, a dangerous view, because a reduction in export demand for U.S. commodities can greatly increase the budgetary cost and resource misallocation caused by inflexible price supports. Thus Rausser's main conclusion about commodity policy is that it should be adaptable to changing macroeconomic circumstances.

The paper by Brian Wright analyzes recent attempts to achieve the stabilization of objectives of farm policy. Market stabilization is accepted as a rationale for intervention by many economists who are quite skeptical of farm programs on other grounds. The reason is that the case is strongest for market failure in this area in the absence of intervention.[4] Wright's paper, however, is sobering in concluding that the grain price stabilization programs in the 1977 and 1981 acts have been quite ineffective. Drawing on past experience, he has several suggestions for stabilization programs, including a positive assessment of acreage controls as a stabilization device. But he recommends primary reliance on market risk transfer and storage institutions. The comments by Larry Salathe illustrate the difficulties of obtaining agreement on appropriate analytical methods in this area.

The paper by Daniel Sumner addresses the often expressed concern for the "family farm" and related structural aspects of policy. He finds the family farm concept not very well thought out in much policy discussion and structural effects of farm policy generally not possible to detect. As in Wright's paper, the main lessons are ones of fact, and analysis of details is often given short shrift or overconfident assertion (or both); both Wright's and Sumner's papers should be required reading for anyone serious about using farm commodity programs in pursuit of the ostensible policy goals of market stabilization and support of the family farm.

The paper by Stefan Tangermann considers how the European Economic Community (EEC) is likely to respond to U.S. commodity policy alternatives and what policies would best serve the joint interests of the United States and the EEC. It is salutary to have a detailed picture of how our present and prospective policies look from the European point of view. The strong dollar, for example, means that U.S. support prices have become very high, even exceeding for a time the EEC intervention price for wheat, which we had come to take as a paradigm of overpricing farm products.

The paper by Richard Just examines the rationale for support prices that vary according to a prespecified rule with market conditions. He shows that if a price support is optimal under a set of initial conditions, it is optimal to change the support price when conditions change. This may seem obvious, but the view that policy should be stabilizing might be taken to imply that farm programs should cushion the domestic economy from shocks, as the EEC does with its variable levy and related measures. Just's contribution is to show how to specify the appropriate amount of cushioning, if one takes the goal of policy as primarily redistributional in response to given social welfare or political preferences. Since it seems that commodity policy really is primarily redistributional, it is important, though too often neglected, to couch policy analysis in these terms.

The paper by Todd Petzel considers an alternative approach to some elements of farm policy, consisting of market-provided price insurance through commodity options. This is probably not a live alternative in 1985, but it is worth serious consideration for the longer term. And as Alan Randall states, it is useful to think about policy in terms of commodity options since the target price–deficiency payment approach is essentially the writing of put options by government, which have substantial value but are given away to farmers.

Overview of the Conference

Two final topics are the conclusions coming out of the conference and what was left out of the conference. The second is the larger topic.

The conclusions consist of judgments about the state of our knowledge in four areas: (1) the economic situation in U.S. agriculture today, (2) the economic outlook, (3) the causes of current problems, and (4) what can and should be done about them.

1. While financial stress is widespread, particularly in the western Corn

9

Belt, evidence on the extent and depth of the problem is soft. It seems clear, however, that the situation does not constitute a crisis. The commercial farm sector, dominated by large farms (over $100,000 in sales) that are nonetheless family farms, is not economically endangered. The U.S. farm sector can continue to produce at roughly current levels without substantial commodity price increases. It is true that the sector as a whole has suffered substantial losses in asset values and reduced rates of return on investment since 1980, but these constitute a cyclical correction from unusually high prices and returns of the 1970s.

In postconference events and debate about farm legislation, it has become ever clearer that the complexities of the situation and the lack of hard data are causing controversy even on matters of fact. Consider the following *Washington Post* report on a March 1985 Agriculture Department estimate that 93,000 family-size farms are under extreme financial stress or are technically insolvent:

> The figure, amounting to 13.7 percent of farms that form the backbone [of] U.S. commercial agriculture, is considerably higher than that which President Reagan cited last week when he vetoed legislation intended to provide emergency credit to farmers.
>
> Then, Reagan said, "The truth of the matter is, in need of immediate help are less than 4 percent or around 4 percent at best of all the farmers in the United States." Agriculture Secretary John R. Block, questioned later about the president's statement, said Reagan "misspoke" and knows the situation is far worse.

Since 93,000 is 3.9 percent of the estimated 2.4 million U.S. farms, Reagan did not misspeak. The *Post*'s 13.7 percent is obtained by dividing 93,000 by the 679,000 farms in the Agriculture Department's "family-size" sales categories. The difficulty of keeping even such simple facts straight does not bode well for reasoned debate on public policy.

2. The long-term trend toward lower real commodity prices is expected to continue. Prospects for an export-led upswing in prices are dim in either the short or the intermediate term, that is, in the period of the next farm bill. Still, once asset values have adjusted to these realities, it is expected that real returns to capital and labor in agriculture will be comparable to those in the nonfarm economy, with price trends reflecting technical advances and farm income reflecting nonfarm opportunity returns. Farms in the $40,000–$100,000 sales range will be less economically viable as full-time enterprises. The scale of the operation will have to grow, or the operators will have to become part-time farmers, leave farming, or subsist on substandard returns to their labor and invested capital.

3. Causes of the weakened market for U.S. farm commodities since 1980 were identified as expanded production abroad, other countries' protec-

tionism and export subsidies, reduced export demand due to the strong dollar, overexpansion of U.S. production, and high support prices that reduce our competitiveness in world markets. These causes overdetermine the observed events, in the following sense. What we observe is lower (real) commodity prices in the 1980s than in the 1970s, with excess supply at the support level. The support prices keep market prices from being even lower, especially for wheat and dairy products, and if prices were even lower, we would export more. But it does not seem right to attribute the weak markets to the support prices for the grains. In dairy products it looks more like a case of imposing unrealistic support levels on a relatively stable supply-demand situation, with the support price then calling forth more output than can be sold at the support level. Here it makes sense to call the support program the cause of the surplus.

Several participants went further to identify causes of the strong dollar: reduced U.S. inflation and high real interest rates. The high interest rates were attributed in part at least to the large U.S. budget deficit. Similarly, it was argued that we have to look deeper to explain the trade policies of other countries that have reduced the market for U.S. exports. We have helped to create the climate for this protectionism by our own protection of U.S. industrial products and agricultural products like sugar, dairy products, and meat. In addition, the U.S. export restrictions of the mid-1970s and 1980 and the payment-in-kind acreage controls of 1983 were cited as reasons for the expansion of foreign agricultural output.

Causes of the financial disaster facing some farmers were cited as the substantial decline in asset values for those who borrowed heavily to buy land or used land as security for heavy capital investment in 1975–1980, high interest rates, and reduced cash flows. The unfortunate debtor is thus unable to service the existing debt while the deteriorated balance sheet makes it impossible to postpone payment by borrowing more. Farmers in this situation who experienced inadequately insured crop failures at the same time, as occurred in some areas, are fairly sure to be doomed financially if they were highly levered. A cause of trouble in some instances, mentioned in passing, is an initial high leverage due to emergency Farmers Home Administration credit provided to precarious farm enterprises under the Emergency Agriculture Credit Act of 1978. Farmers in danger of bankruptcy now include not only victims of the current downturn but also some who would normally have gone out of business in the earlier downturns of 1978 and 1982.

4. Appropriate policy responses to agriculture's problems might be thought to follow readily from the preceding discussion. Having identified the causes, what we should do, roughly, is to undo them. We might weaken the dollar, undertake other activities to boost export demand, or reduce U.S. output. Is it a surprise then to find that the essentially unanimous view of the conference participants who expressed a view was that we should move toward

greater market orientation? The finding of Johnson and his colleagues that placed them on the front page of the *New York Times* (January 29, 1985, the day after their paper was presented) was their estimate of a 30 percent decline in net farm income under the "cold turkey" market option. John Schnittker's more gradual "warm turkey" option would differ mainly in magnitude. It is difficult to see how farmers could view any move toward market orientation as a solution of their problems.

Why the support for market orientation? It is not really a matter of responding to the disappointments of the 1980s. Many economists, most of them perhaps at this conference, would have given the same policy recommendation four, eight, or twenty years ago. But now the support is broader. One reason is surely that the current situation did not develop in the absence of attempts to aid farmers. Federal budget expenditures have averaged $12 billion per year under the 1981 act, along with the largest acreage control program ever in 1983. Yet we find agriculture in 1985 in the straits described. This makes it hard to argue for further cushioning of farmers from the effects of weak markets.

When it comes to attacking the causes of weak markets, the conference participants heard recommendations for reducing the federal deficit, liberalizing trade, reforming the international monetary system, and continuing research and development. Programs to promote exports in various ways have also been discussed.[5] Two problems with these remedies are that, first, there is some doubt about their efficacy and, second and more fundamentally, proposals that might do some good for farmers, such as spending a few hundred million dollars on export promotion, would inevitably tax consumers and the general public to aid farmers. Market orientation, which fits in well with trade liberalization and is consistent with deficit reduction too, should not be seen as a means to help farmers specifically but as a means to improve the agricultural economy from the viewpoint of society as a whole.

The preceding remarks point to a conceptual omission, or at least ambiguity, in much of the discussion at the conference. A great deal of the discussion dealt with problems of U.S. agriculture, the implied role of policy being to provide remedies. The government is to act as a physician curing ills. Yet, as is clear implicitly in the papers of Petzel and Johnson et al. and explicitly in the paper by Just, policy is mainly or at least significantly a matter of redistribution between interest groups. In this light government can solve one group's problems only by creating problems for another.

Some subjects were largely left out of the conference discussion. There were omitted topics and a lack of hard evidence on key issues.

An omitted topic that has received much attention elsewhere is soil conservation and its relation to farm policy.[6] Other omissions include water policy and other issues related to input use and production techniques. The food and fiber marketing sector, indeed agribusiness generally and its regulatory environment, were omitted. We had no discussion of farmers' bargaining power or of cooperatives, marketing orders, and other policies to enhance farmers' power in the marketplace. Food safety and health issues and food aid programs were ignored. No one even mentioned the key term thought so important in broadening our agenda only a few years ago, national food policy. Federal income tax provisions, particularly the sheltering from taxation of much agricultural investment, were touched on in discussion but not given the detailed attention they deserve. Finally, the discussion was mostly directed to the entire sector, and the only particular commodities treated were the grains, except in the papers by Sumner and Johnson et al. We had no detailed analysis of the programs for dairy products, sugar, cotton, tobacco, peanuts, rice, or wool. The justification for these omissions is that serious issues more central to discussion of the 1985 farm bill required the full attention of the conference to address adequately.

An important issue unresolved in this conference is the proper role of acreage control programs. Some saw these as the best way to handle current and prospective surpluses, while others were strongly against them. Arguments against acreage controls are that, if effective, they drive up consumer prices and hence constitute a hidden tax and that they help maintain a world price umbrella under which foreign competitors can expand. This seems to have been the predominant view among conference participants—it was an implied view at least of all three of the first-session speakers. Yet there are reasonable arguments in favor of moderate but effective acreage controls. The first is that as long as the demand for U.S. exports is not perfectly elastic, foreign buyers will pay some of the cost of supporting U.S. farm income. The Johnson et al. simulations have foreigners transferring almost $2 billion to the United States under the 1981 act as compared with the market option; this is the principal reason why the estimated net cost to U.S. consumers, producers, and taxpayers jointly of the 1981 act programs as compared with the market is so small. Penn, McCalla, and the first-session speakers all give more emphasis to market responsiveness, particularly in the long run, suggesting a substantially more elastic demand function for U.S. exports than Johnson et al. assume. This means that any substantial production cutback could well be counterproductive; but as long as the export demand function is less than perfectly elastic, some production control, though perhaps quite small, increases the joint income of U.S. producers and consumers. Second, if we are going to maintain prices above the no-program level for political reasons, acreage controls can be part of a second-best program package because they help offset target price incentives to overproduce. This supports the Schnittker synthesis option. Wright's persuasive discussion of acreage controls as an efficient stabilization instrument given inflexible support prices is also relevant.

The lack of hard evidence on many hypotheses about effects of past policy and options for 1985 is a reminder of the factual and analytical constraints we are operating under. It was a little disquieting in the conference discussion that the more an author revealed about details of his evidence and inferences, the more he was criticized. Thus Robert Chambers questioned some of Gordon Rausser's estimated coefficients, but Johnson et al. could not be so criticized because they did not reveal their coefficients. They did, however, explain the methods used in their policy simulations, and this in itself provoked some criticism. Their approach was essentially to estimate commodity supply and demand functions and then find new price-quantity equilibria caused by changes in policy parameters *given these estimated functions*. In discussion the point was raised at several points, particularly by John Antle, that these estimated functions might be sensitive to the existence of a policy regime as well as to parameter values for support prices and related variables. This is a well-known criticism of certain econometric macroeconomic models but might be thought less relevant to supply and demand functions, which are based largely on technology and tastes, which should be invariant to policy. Yet it is surely the case that the demand for speculative stocks can be dramatically affected by a public storage regime, even if no public stocks have yet been accumulated under that regime. Tangermann's paper provides a practical example of the problem with reference to the demand function for U.S. grain exports. He makes a reasonable argument that the choice of U.S. policy regime itself influences EEC policy. But this in turn changes the U.S. export demand function. So the structural model we really need is one in which the export demand function for U.S. grains incorporates the response of foreign commodity policy parameters to U.S. policy parameters. This is of course not in the cards for practical econometric modeling.

This conference was probably not the appropriate place for detailed scholarly argument. It is important to note, however, that many of the issues that remain unresolved are precisely issues that require scholarly argument, and more research, to resolve.

Often one hears gatherings of mainstream professionals criticized for failure to offer new ideas. This demand for new ideas reveals not so much a shortage of intellectual fertility on the supply side as a pipe-dream mentality on the demand side. The real shortage is of hard analysis of the hypotheses and proposals already before us. It is sobering to note the dubious notions that spring every week from the grass roots and from newly inspired professionals. An instance is provided by the *Wall Street Journal* letter from a Wisconsin farmer that John Daly cited at length at the round table discussion. The author has many fresh and thoughtful things to say about farming and agriculture in the United States today. When it comes to policy, however, he states:

> We need new initiatives that will recognize farming's importance as
> an integral part of America's past and future. One would be to
> extend the system of zoning blocks of land for exclusively agricul-

tural use; this is already practiced in many states. If it were sensitive to regional differences, such a policy could minimize conflict between urban and rural values by curbing speculation and the soaring land values that drive so many farmers off the soil.[7]

The irony of this proposal is that on this same date the *Washington Post* reported on demonstrations by farmers opposing a quite tentative step in the recommended direction by Howard County, Maryland. The *Post* reported: "Although the measure is supposed to protect farmers from the pressures of development, many at tonight's protest said that its restrictions would ruin them if it is adopted by the County Council."[8] What is truly needed, again, is analysis. What really is the economic impact of this kind of policy?

For a final dash of cold water on policy reforms, we may turn to congressional politics, an abundant source of such frigidity. The distress of farm state legislators in response to the Reagan administration's attempt to embrace the market option is telling, though unsurprising since it follows the scenario predicted in Schnittker's paper. On a particular issue, advocates of the market found encouraging the views of Senator Jesse Helms, expressed last November, that the tobacco program has become counterproductive. Yet as the time for action approached, with the Reagan administration actually proposing to phase out the program, Helms was among those referred to in a *Washington Post* article headlined, "Proposal to End Tobacco Program Has Congressional Backers Smoking."[9] This situation makes relevant Alan Randall's remark, in his discussion, that the economics of "second best" involves appropriate dealing with immovable objects. We might even elevate the situation to first best, following the dictum attributed to Frank Knight that whatever is inevitable is optimal.

Such consideration may moderate the hopes of economists that policy would be shaped by recommendations of conferences. I believe that the opportunity exists to shape policy through analysis; for Congress, however motivated, wants to know the consequences of its actions (although it may not want them all published). The value of this conference in this view rests in the accuracy of the papers in laying out the facts about the current situation, in analyzing the reasons why we are in this situation, and in assessing the probable consequences of various policy alternatives intended to improve matters.

Notes

1. Comparison with the earlier conferences shows some interesting evolution in the policy agenda and views about desirable action by government, as the economic situation in agriculture changed. See *Food and Agricultural Policy* (Washington, D.C.: American Enterprise Institute, 1977); and D. Gale Johnson, ed., *Food and Agricultural Policy for the 1980s* (Washington, D.C.: American Enterprise Institute, 1981).

2. Don Paarlberg and Donald D. Knutson, "Two Papers on the Goals of Agricultural Policy," AEI Occasional Paper, December 1984.

3. The "Harberger-triangle" estimate of deadweight loss using consumers' surplus calculations lies between these figures, which are compensating and equivalent variation measures in standard welfare economics terminology. This shows the triviality, for normative analysis of current farm programs, of questions raised about the applicability of applied welfare economics based on consumer surplus calculations.

4. For a theoretical discussion, see D. M. G. Newbery and J. E. Stiglitz, *The Theory of Commodity Price Stabilization* (Oxford: Oxford University Press, 1981).

5. See Philip Abbott, "An Assessment of the Effects of Programs to Promote U.S. Agricultural Exports," AEI Occasional Paper, December 1984.

6. See Sandra Batie, "Agricultural Policy and Soil Erosion," AEI Occasional Paper, December 1984.

7. *Wall Street Journal*, January 23, 1985.

8. *Washington Post*, January 23, 1985.

9. *Washington Post*, February 5, 1985.

Part One
The State of U.S. and
World Agriculture

World Commodity Market Situation and Outlook

D. Gale Johnson

In an important sense the topic of my paper should be irrelevant to the objectives of this conference and to the legislation that will be the new farm bill. The new legislation should have sufficient flexibility to permit adaptation to changes in the economic circumstances that will prevail. In other words, there should be sufficient flexibility in the administration of farm programs, given the agreed upon objectives, that modifications can be made in the policy instruments to reflect the particular circumstances of supply and demand.

This, of course, is a tall order, in terms of politics and economics. Our ability to predict, even for the short run, leaves something to be desired. A recent report of the Congressional Budget Office on the errors in the estimates of the outlays of the Commodity Credit Corporation for fiscal years 1980, 1981, and 1982 is a sobering document.[1] The errors in estimating outlays a few months in advance of the beginning of the fiscal year were large, variable, and exhibited no particular pattern within a year with respect to the magnitude of the error. In other words, the second estimate was not always better than the first; in fact, in two cases out of three it was worse.

That the outlays were incorrectly estimated is of only limited significance. What is of great significance is that these errors meant that in two of the three years, government's intervention in agricultural markets was much greater than anticipated. In 1982, for example, the error was large, and the consequences of the error were great indeed. The actual expenditures by the Commodity Credit Corporation were $9 billion in excess of the first projection. Actual expenditures were more than five times the projected expenditures.

I will discuss what might be called the medium-term economic climate within which agriculture is likely to operate. By "medium-term" I mean a period longer than two or three years but not much longer than a decade. I believe that, at best, we can indicate probable trends over a period of years; certainly I do not feel competent to project economic variables for a given year. We do know that, given the nature of agricultural production and the policies of the countries of the world, the relevant variables will vary around

19

the trend, sometimes greatly. I hope we have learned from the 1970s that variations lasting one or two years cannot be extrapolated into the future. This seems like an unnecessary warning, but one must only go back to the popular press and government pronouncements—and by some very prominent agricultural economists—from 1973 through 1980 to find that there is a lot to learn.

False Perceptions

At the end of the 1970s there were those who described future developments in the demand and supply of world food in terms of a more rapid growth of demand and supply. This conclusion had several implications. One was that low-income countries would have greater difficulties improving their nutritional situation; some experts suggested that the outcome would be mass starvation. The outlook for American agriculture, however, was optimistic; as the world's largest exporter of agricultural products, it would be difficult to increase supply at a sufficient rate to keep up with the growth in demand. If this were true, additional resources would need to be drawn into agriculture, and the real prices of farm products would increase.

One set of projections, that of *The Global 2000 Report to the President*, put the increase in real food prices in international markets between 1970 and 2000 at 45 percent, if real oil prices stayed the same as they were in 1973–1975.[2] Oil prices have, however, been higher than they were in 1973-1975, and so remain; yet real food prices have not increased even though the period of the projection is half completed. The smallest of the price projections was for a 30 percent increase in real food prices; the largest was for an increase of 115 percent.

In spite of a few dissenting voices, the farm legislation enacted in 1981 was based upon the view that demand would grow more rapidly than supply. The following is one description of the beliefs that helped to frame the legislation that resulted in massive accumulations of commodities in just two years:

> Observing the explosion of agricultural exports and implosion of productivity in the 1970s, experts from government, industry and academia predicted an upward trend in real agricultural price and incomes during the 1980s. Consequently, farmers and politicians decried the Agricultural and Food Act of 1981 as being wholly inadequate and suggested it be renamed the 'Farm Bankruptcy Act of 1981.'[3]

William Lesher, assistant secretary of agriculture, stated in early 1984:

> At the time the 1981 Farm Bill was formulated, the main concern was that world food needs would outpace production. Many believed—inside and outside of government—that *the* agricultural issue of the 1980's was going to be how to produce enough for a

starving world rather than surpluses. Many also believed that the United States was the only country that possessed the potential to expand food production enough to meet world needs.[4]

A further example of the false perceptions that were held in high places at the end of the 1970s and the beginning of the 1980s is the following excerpt from a speech made by Secretary of Agriculture Bob Bergland in mid-July 1980. The excerpt is rather long, but I include it because of the absurdity of its several parts:

At the very time when we have come to depend on agriculture to bolster our economy, the nature of agriculture has changed. The era of chronic overproduction, surplus disposal problems and a seemingly infinite supply of resources is over. We have moved into a new era—one in which food supplies are tighter, more food is being consumed, and the resources which produce that food are becoming depleted.

Writing for the current issue of *Atlantic*, Dan Morgan describes this era—and what might follow:

". . . the resources required to produce grain in modern agriculture are decidedly not renewable. When they run out, grain production will be unimaginably more difficult. Agriculture requires oil and natural gas to run diesel tractors, to power irrigation pumps, to dry grain, and to produce chemical fertilizers, herbicides. These fuels are finite, and are getting much more expensive. The underground water that irrigates crops in the western wheat belt in Colorado, Kansas and Nebraska will not last forever . . . food is produced on agricultural land that is shrinking as cities, highways, airports, and rights-of-way for pipeline and transmissions claim more and more of it."

Morgan concludes this description by saying, "Some gloomy predictions have American food exports ending by the year 2000 as a result of environmental, energy and economic constraints."[5]

There were, however, other voices, apparently neglected, that presented the view that the developments of the mid-1970s in the supply and demand of world food were short-term aberrations; the trend for most of the twentieth century had been toward declining real prices of the cereals. I was one of those voices, and I ask for your indulgence for a summary of the views that I expressed at the time.

In late 1973 I wrote a brief article titled "Are High Food Prices Here to Stay?" My answer was, "Not for very long." The reasons for that answer were developed at length in a monograph published by the American Enterprise Institute in 1975, *World Food Problems and Prospects*. I summarized my results, in part, as follows:

There is a real concern that the world has entered a period of

21

permanently increased food prices. Higher prices for energy, the return of diverted cropland to production in the United States, high rates of population growth in the developing countries, and rising per capita incomes throughout the world are given as reasons for the reversal in the long-term decline in real farm prices. But in this study I conclude that high farm prices are not here to stay, except insofar as farm prices reflect the effects of inflation. Energy costs do not constitute a large fraction of the costs of producing food, and the return of diverted land had only a small effect on total grain production in the United States in the early 1970s. I expect that the long-term decline in real grain prices will reassert itself. One factor delaying this decline is the devaluation of the American dollar. The overvaluation of the dollar during the 1960s and early 1970s probably depressed grain prices in international markets by 10 to 15 percent. In terms of the combined interests of taxpayers and consumers in the United States, the effect of the devaluation of the dollar is likely to be small since government payments to farmers largely compensated for the effects of the overvaluation.

There are no reasons based on limitations of resources or on the technology and biology of food production that will prevent the population of the world from being more adequately fed a decade hence than in the years immediately before 1972. I believe that the world's population will be better fed a decade hence, although I am less confident about the realization of the potential for increased food production than I am about the potential itself, even if current population growth rates continue.[6]

While the views expressed above were in the minority, at least one other analysis supported the position that the world did not face a crisis of food shortages and rising real prices; there were not many others. *The World Food Situation and Prospects to 1985*, published by the Economic Research Service, U.S. Department of Agriculture, in December 1974, has stood the test of time very well. The study hedged its conclusions somewhat: "While this study does not support the judgments that world food supplies per capita are likely to decline or that the growth of the world food supply is likely to lag behind growth in demand, these possibilities cannot be ruled out."[7]

Four years ago a conference on agricultural policy similar to this one was sponsored by the American Enterprise Institute. Then, as now, there was discussion of the prospective trend of farm prices. Significant disagreement was expressed, and perhaps the majority opinion was that real farm prices would increase in the 1980s. Others, including G. Edward Schuh and myself, argued the contrary. I concluded the paper I presented at that conference as follows:

> It is appropriate to close by making explicit my assumption concerning the future course of real or deflated prices of the major grains

and soybeans. The process of eliminating excess resources from U.S. agriculture was largely completed by 1972. Thus the source of more or less regular excess production capacity, such as existed during the 1960s, no longer exists. I expect that during the 1980s the growth rates of supply and of demand for agricultural output of the United States will be approximately the same. This means that, on average, the real or deflated prices of grain and soybeans will be approximately constant, and I would not be surprised if the long-term trend of a small rate of decline in the prices of these products continued throughout the 1980s.

The fact that I expect approximate equality of growth rates for supply and demand does not rule out significant variability of prices in international and domestic markets. To a large extent such price variability is a consequence of the national agricultural and food policies of many countries that prevent their internal prices from reflecting variations in world supply and demand.

In the context of these assumptions I believe that the 1981 agricultural legislation should continue the process of increasing the market orientation of our agricultural programs, a path followed for at least two decades. I also believe that the agricultural policy issues for the 1980s will continue to be the traditional ones of price supports, target prices, storage and reserves, export policies and disaster or insurance programs. It should not be assumed that the price increases occurring in 1980 negate the need to be concerned about setting support prices that will not interfere with the functioning of the market, if farm prices return to the real levels of, say, 1979.

If I am wrong and real farm prices increase during the 1980s, little will have been lost by continuing to be concerned about market-oriented agricultural programs. If farm prices were to increase significantly, the prices of some or most of the grains would move above target levels and the release and perhaps call prices. The holding of grain reserved would then be entirely in the private sector, as it was very largely from 1973 through 1976. For the 1981 agricultural legislation, which will extend through the middle part of the decade, we must be concerned with the traditional components of our agricultural policy. No evidence can be accumulated between October 1980 and early 1981 that will definitively delineate the trend of real farm prices for the 1980s.[8]

Even though there were disagreements about the future course of farm prices, it may be noted that none of the conference participants argued that the appropriate policy response was to increase loan and target prices.

I have presented this rather long and, some might argue, self-serving discussion of the perceptions of the outlook for agriculture during the 1970s and the beginning of the 1980s for a reason other than to show that I was correct all along. My reason is simply this: I fear the present gloomy perceptions of the future of farm prices will influence the farm legislation in 1985 to an undue extent and will lead to inappropriate decisions, just as the apparent opposite view resulted in erroneous actions in 1981. One possible outcome is that the new farm bill will attempt to use governmental actions to increase farm prices and incomes in ways that will inhibit the resource adjustments that must be made in the next few years if U.S. agriculture is to remain competitive in world markets and if farmers are to be independent business people instead of large-scale welfare recipients.

The Balance in Supply and Demand: How Poor Countries Have Fared

From the viewpoint of American agriculture the most relevant aspect of the prospective balance in supply and demand for food in the world is the price path that emerges. Real prices can be increasing with slow demand growth if supply growth is even slower. Thus, even if there is little or no improvement in nutrition in the low-income countries during the next decade, real prices can rise. Also, even if there is significant improvement in nutrition in low-income countries, real food prices could fall.

My understanding of the values of American farm people, however, is that they are interested not only in the prices of their products, but also in the nutrition of the world's poorer people. I shall, therefore, discuss indicators of changes in nutrition for the past few decades and prospects for the next decade.

We have but a limited number of indicators of changes in the nutritional status of populations in low-income countries. We have data of varying accuracy on food availability for entire populations but relatively few data on the distribution among or within families of actual food consumption. We do, however, have data on vital statistics—life expectancy, infant mortality, child mortality—that provide some evidence of changes in nutritional status. My colleague Robert Fogel has brought together a large amount of relevant evidence on the relationships between nutrition and the decline in mortality during the past three centuries. While much of the evidence is for the countries of Western Europe and North America, some data are from the Caribbean low-income areas. Using data on average adult stature as a measure of nutritional status, the preliminary conclusion is that improvements in nutritional status may have caused as much as 40 percent of the decline in mortality rates, but nearly all of this effect was concentrated in the reduction of infant mortality.[9] Life expectancy at birth in England at the beginning of the eighteenth century was thirty-five years, approximately the same as in the low-income countries in 1950.

If one accepts the conclusion that there is a relationship between declines in infant mortality and improvements in nutrition, the data in table 1 indicate a

TABLE 1

LIFE EXPECTANCY AT BIRTH AND INFANT MORTALITY RATES,
1960 AND 1982

	Life Expectancy at Birth		Infant Mortality Rates		GNP per Capita
	1960	1982	1960	1982	1982($)
Low-income economies	42	59	165	87	280
China	41	69	165	67	310
India	42	54	165	94	260
All other	43	51	163	114	250
Middle-income economies	51	62	126	76	1,520
Lower middle-income economies	46	57	144	89	840
Upper middle-income economies	56	65	101	58	2,490
Industrial market economies	70	75	29	10	11,070

SOURCE: World Bank, *World Development Report 1984*, pp. 262–63.

substantial improvement in the nutritional status of populations in many low-income countries during the past two or three decades.

Table 2 gives some of the available data on changes in the availability of food per capita since World War II. For many countries these data are subject to considerable error. The data for Africa may raise as many questions as they answer; the improvements in life expectancy and the declines in infant mortality have been impressive in the period 1960–1981. It is possible, of course, that neither the data on the availability of food nor the data on mortality are anything more than the figments of many imaginations. For those areas of the world where we have some reasonable confidence in the data, however, nutrition has gradually improved while infant mortality has decreased and life expectancy has increased.

The improvement in food supplies per capita in the developing countries has been due, in part, to increased imports of grains and other sources of calories. This source of improvement is often viewed with alarm rather than

25

TABLE 2

AVERAGE ANNUAL PERCENTAGE CHANGE IN FOOD PRODUCTION
PER CAPITA, 1951–1981

Country/Region	1951–53 to 1959–61	1959–61 to 1969–71	1969–71 to 1979–81	1951–53 to 1979–81	1959–61 to 1979–81
United States	0.75	0.73	1.56	1.03	1.14
Canada	−3.36	1.44	0.87	−0.16	1.15
Japan	2.34	−0.89	−1.34	−0.14	−1.12
Republic of South Africa	1.01	1.03	1.47	1.18	1.23
Oceania	0.64	1.52	0	0.72	0.76
Western Europe	1.85	1.59	1.46	1.62	1.53
Developed world	1.47	0.98	1.05	1.15	1.01
South and Central America	0.28	1.03	1.14	0.85	1.08
East Asia[a]	1.47	0.98	1.92	1.46	1.45
South Asia	1.28	0.41	−0.13	0.46	0.14
Middle East	0.13	0.10	0.89	0.50	0.50
Africa[b]	0.04	−0.10	−1.16	−0.44	−0.63
Less-developed world	0.91	0.47	0.33	0.55	0.40
Eastern Europe	1.47	2.07	1.11	1.56	1.59
USSR	4.64	1.41	0.16	1.87	0.78
China	−2.72[c]	2.92	0.53[d]	0.46[c,d]	1.94[d]
Centrally planned economies[e]	3.07	1.80	0.65	1.75	1.22
World[e]	1.42	0.62	0.23	0.71	0.42

a. Excludes Japan.
b. Excludes Republic of South Africa.
c. Series begins in 1952. Agricultural output reported for 1959–61 was considerably below the preceding and ensuing years.
d. Data available to 1976–77 only.
e. Excludes People's Republic of China.

SOURCE: Glenn Fox and Vernon H. Ruttan, "A Guide to Some Projections of LDC Food Security toward the End of the Twentieth Century," Hubert H. Humphrey Institute of Public Affairs, University of Minnesota, Working Paper, September 1983, table 2, p. 6. Underlying data are from U.S. Department of Agriculture.

considered as one of the important alternatives available to low-income countries to provide adequate food supplies. The developing countries, including China, imported 69 million tons of grain (net) during 1980 and 1981. If all of this grain were used for food, it would provide, after processing, 500 calories per day for a billion people. It may be noted that the developing countries exported $70 billion in agricultural products while importing $71 billion. Thus imports and exports of agricultural products were in approximate balance.

Recent Projections

I have undertaken no projections of the quantities of various agricultural products produced, consumed, and traded. My views concerning the future trends of supply and demand have been and are based on more impressionistic analysis of past trends in certain critical variables, especially real prices as related to the underlying trends in consumption, production, trade, and the available measures of productivity trends. I am one who believes that the types of projections presented in *Global 2000* or in *Agriculture: Toward 2000* by the Food and Agriculture Organization (FAO) are of significant value, if properly understood and analyzed.[10] In fact, both of the projections are consistent with the view that world food supply would grow at least as fast as world food demand for the rest of this century and thus that real food prices would be stationary or declining during that period. Furthermore, both projections in their least robust form indicated an increase in the availability of food per capita in the low-income areas. The fact that both sets of projections were differently interpreted, even by those who wrote the texts of the reports, is largely beside the point. As Fred Sanderson said in an unpublished memorandum dated December 13, 1983, both *Global 2000* and *Agriculture: Toward 2000* were political documents, and the startling conclusions either presented in the reports or attributed by others to the reports are unreasonable interpretations of the underlying projections of supply and demand and productivity growth. In comparing these projections with the ones recently completed by Economic Perspectives, Inc. (EPI) in cooperation with Resources for the Future (RFF), Sanderson noted: "Surprisingly, these differences in slant or tone cannot be explained by significant differences in the basic projections."

The EPI/RFF projections were in a report prepared for the U.S. Department of Agriculture.[11] The projections were made for the world, and then the demands for the U.S. farm output were derived as a residual after taking into account demand and supply in the rest of the world. Table 3 summarizes the projections of demand for major groups of U.S. agricultural commodities with a comparison to the growth of demand for the 1970s. Three projections were made for the past two decades of this century—baseline, high, and low.

TABLE 3

HISTORIC AND PROJECTED GLOBAL DEMAND FOR U.S. AGRICULTURAL PRODUCTS, 1969–2000

(in millions of metric tons)

Commodity	1969–1971 Domestic	1969–1971 Net trade	1969–1971 Total	1979–1981 Domestic	1979–1981 Net trade	1979–1981 Total	2000 Domestic	2000 Net trade	2000 Baseline Total	2000 High Total	2000 Low Total
Cereals[a]	171.0	39.0	210.0	192.7	109.6	302.3	227.0	168.2	395.3	405.3	378.6
Oilseeds[b]	20.2	17.0	37.2	31.5	33.3	64.8	38.1	53.9	92.0	92.9	91.0
Meat	21.9	−0.6	21.3	24.5	0	24.5	29.2	0.1	29.3	30.6	28.4
Milk	53.4	−0.2	53.2	59.0	−0.8	58.2	71.1	−0.9	70.2	70.8	70.2
Cotton	1.71	0.51	2.22	1.47	1.54	3.01	1.42	2.20	3.62	3.70	3.6

a. Includes food, feed, seed, industrial use and waste.
b. Includes oilseed trade, in oilseed equivalent.

SOURCE: Resources for the Future, *Resources*, no. 76 (Spring 1984), p. 12.

TABLE 4

HISTORIC AND PROJECTED ANNUAL RATES OF GROWTH OF
TOTAL PRODUCTION, UNITED STATES, 1969–2000
(percent)

	Growth Rate	
Commodity	1969–71 to 1979–81	1979–81 to 2000
Cereals	3.7	1.3
Oilseed	5.7	1.6
Meat	1.4	0.9
Milk	0.9	0.9
Cotton	3.1	0.9

SOURCE: Resources for the Future, *Resources*, no. 76 (Spring 1984), table 8, p. 12.

Comparisons of the demand growth rates projected for 1980–2000 with the actual growth rates of production for the 1970s show a sharp difference (see table 4). Only for milk are the projected demand growth rates the same as in the recent past, and the exception must have been due to the assumption that recent programs for price support and disposal of surplus would be continued for the rest of the century. Growth rates for cereals are projected to decline by more than 60 percent, and for oilseeds by more than two-thirds, and for cotton by even somewhat more. The decline in projected growth rate for meat compared to the recent past reflects a slowing in the anticipated growth of domestic demand since net trade is presumed to be unchanged.

These projections, to belabor the obvious, point to a sharp slowdown in demand growth. The meaning of these projections for price trends turns on the prospects for growth of supply at constant real output prices.

Agriculture: Toward 2000, the FAO publication, included projections of the prospective growths of demand and supply for grains consistent with the EPI/RFF projections. The major conclusions were stated as follows:

A continuation of production and demand trends world-wide implies large global surpluses in some commodities, despite the growing millions of seriously undernourished, and deficits in other, mainly livestock products. Thus the net surplus of cereals of the developed countries would tend to stand at 213 million tonnes at a time when the developing countries would have a deficit of 165 million tonnes. Projected net availabilities from the developing countries of such competing products as sugar, citrus fruit and

29

vegetable oils and oilseeds would substantially outstrip import demand in the developed countries, whose protectionism would limit severely any expansion in their imports of these products.

All in all, the tendency is for global surpluses worth roughly $20 billion in 1975.

The projected imbalances will not actually materialize; spontaneous or policy-induced adjustments will bring balance. The policy issue is how orderly adjustments can be brought about. They should increase rather than reduce trade—the developing countries should be able to import and consume more of the cereals produced in the developed countries and help to pay for them with increased exports of the commodities they are best suited to produce. Such an evolution would eliminate the irony in the situation of a world afflicted with undernutrition, but where there is a danger of global surpluses. [12]

Other projections will be referred to later in this paper. At this point it need only be said that the three projections, each made since 1981, are in general agreement that demand growth will be much slower in the next decade or so than during the past decade.

Price Projections

The potential implications for prices of the demand projections can be drawn from table 5, taken from Sanderson. To meet the baseline projected demand for cereals requires a very modest area expansion for the last two decades of the century—0.3 percent annually—and a yield increase of 1.0 percent annually or only slightly more than half the increase for the 1970s. Assuming a very sharp reduction in the increase in area devoted to soybeans—from a 5 percent growth rate for the 1970s to 0.7 percent during the remainder of the century—the yield growth for soybeans would need to increase very slightly from 0.9 percent annually to 1.0 percent annually. Growth in cotton production needed to meet the projected demand is less than a third of the actual growth during the 1970s.

My interpretation of the projected small increases in harvested area associated with rates of yield increases generally well below rates of the 1970s points to probable significant downward pressure upon real farm prices. In fact, one could argue that these projections have given little attention to some potential sources of increasing production. Between 1978 and 1982, for example, the area of double-cropped soybeans increased more than three-fold—from 3.2 million acres to 11.5 million acres. [13] The projected increase in soybean area for the twenty years (1980–2000) comes to 10 million acres; with rather modest reductions in the required growing period for soybeans either through varietal modifications or the use of growth regulators, it is likely that such an increase in area could be met without increasing the total amount of land in cultivation.

TABLE 5

HISTORIC AND PROJECTED ANNUAL RATES OF GROWTH OF AREA, YIELD, AND PRODUCTION, FOR MAJOR AGRICULTURAL COMMODITIES, UNITED STATES, 1969–2000

(percent)

Commodity	Area		Yield		Production	
	1969–71 to 1979–81	1979–81 to 2000	1969–71 to 1979–81	1979–81 to 2000	1969–71 to 1979–81	1979–81 to 2000
Cereals	1.8	0.3	1.9	1.0	3.7	1.3
Wheat	4.5	0	0.7	0.2	5.2	0.2
Corn	2.3	1.0	2.3	1.0	4.6	2.0
Oilseeds	4.4	0.7	1.2	1.1	5.7	1.8
Soybeans	5.0	0.7	0.9	1.0	5.9	1.7
Cotton lint	1.7	0.3	1.3	0.6	3.1	0.9

SOURCE: Resources for the Future, *Resources*, no. 76 (Spring 1984), table 8, p. 12.

FIGURE 1
Wheat Prices Received by Farmers, 1870–1980

Dollars per bushel

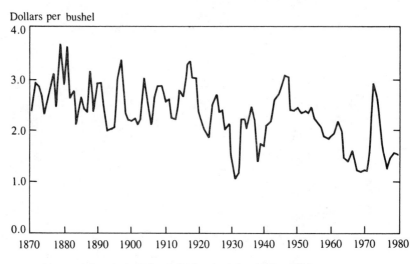

NOTE: The price deflator is the U.S. wholesale price index, 1967 = 100.
SOURCE: U.S. Department of Agriculture.

FIGURE 2
Rice Prices Received by Farmers, 1870–1980

Dollars per 100 pounds

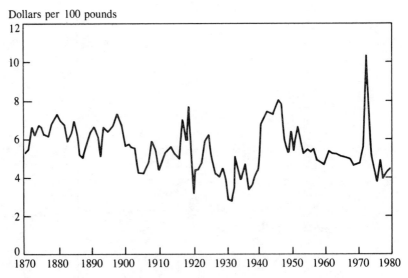

NOTE: The price deflator is the U.S. wholesale price index, 1967 = 100.
SOURCE: U.S. Department of Agriculture.

32

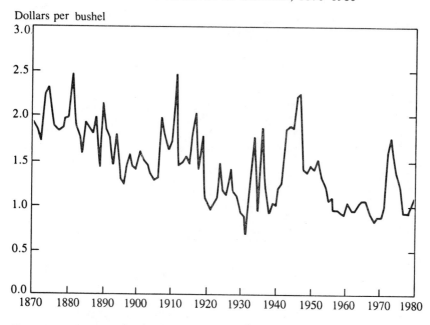

FIGURE 3

BARLEY PRICES RECEIVED BY FARMERS, 1870–1980

Dollars per bushel

NOTE: The price deflator is the U.S. wholesale price index, 1967 = 100.
SOURCE: U.S. Department of Agriculture.

Earlier I noted that the long-run trend of grain prices, adjusted for changes in prices had been declining during the twentieth century. Actually, on the basis of U.S. farm prices of grains, the declines started as early as 1970 for wheat, barley, and rice (see figures 1, 2, and 3). For corn the decline did not start until the early part of this century (see figure 4). The graphs of deflated prices show the declines quite clearly.

Table 6 presents the real export prices for wheat and corn for the United States for selected years from 1910 to 1959 and then annually since. As will be seen, the real prices for recent years are below those of the years of the Great Depression for both wheat and corn. The 1982 export price of corn was at a low of $39 in 1967 prices; this was probably the lowest price in the twentieth century.

The World Bank has presented annual data on export prices for various grains from 1950 to date (1984).[14] The World Bank has used a different deflator, namely the index of c.i.f. (cost insurance freight) unit values of manufactured products of the developed countries imported by developing countries. Since 1960 the c.i.f. index has risen somewhat more than the U.S.

33

FIGURE 4
Corn Prices Received by Farmers, 1870–1980

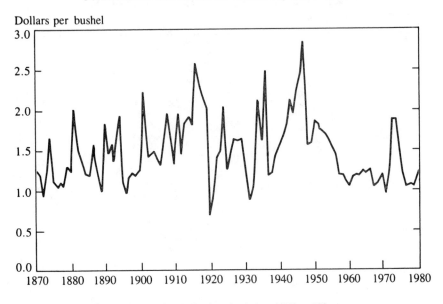

NOTE: The price deflator is the U.S. wholesale price index, 1967 = 100.
SOURCE: U.S. Department of Agriculture.

wholesale price index; consequently the real prices of the major grains have declined more since 1960 according to the World Bank estimates than those given in table 6. The other difference between the World Bank estimates and those in table 6 is that the World Bank has used the prices of given grades rather than average export unit values. Still, the results reveal a very similar picture. Between 1950–1954 and 1978–1982 the real price of U.S. corn in table 6 declined by 40 percent; the World Bank measure of the real price of Argentine corn fell by 50 percent and its measure of the U.S. export price by slightly more (52.2 percent). For wheat the comparisons are similar. The measure I used declined by 34 percent; the World Bank measure of the real export price of Canadian wheat declined by 40 percent and its measure of the U.S. real export price by 43 percent. The data in table 6 do not exaggerate the decline in real grain prices over the past three decades.

The frequent emphasis upon the instability of grain prices during the 1970s and early 1980s, so strikingly shown in the graphs and tables, often diverts attention from the remarkable growth in world trade in grain that occurred without a significant increase in the real prices of grain. Between 1969–1971 and 1980–1982, world exports of grain more than doubled. For the same period of time, world trade in all agricultural products increased by

TABLE 6

REAL EXPORT PRICES FOR WHEAT AND CORN, UNITED STATES, 1910–1983
(1967 $ per ton)

Calendar Year	Wheat	Corn	Calendar Year	Wheat	Corn
1910–1914	100	74	1969	57	48
1925–1929	103	76	1970	53	52
1930–1934	66	68	1971	54	50
1935–1939	79	85	1972	54	46
1945–1949	122	94	1973	80	63
1950–1954	95	80	1974	110	79
1955–1959	69	61	1975	95	76
1960	65	53	1976	80	64
1961	69	52	1977	58	52
1962	70	52	1978	61	50
1963	69	56	1979	67	50
1964	69	57	1980	66	50
1965	62	57	1981	62	50
1966	62	56	1982	56	39
1967	64	54	1983	54	45
1968	60	48			

NOTE: The export prices are export unit values; the price deflator is the U.S. wholesale price index.
SOURCE: U.S. Department of Commerce, *Statistical Abstract of the United States*, various issues.

about 60 percent. The capacity of grain producers to accommodate such a large increase in exports was an important contribution to world food availability and security.

As one looks at the remainder of this century, however, there seems little reason to expect a growth in world or U.S. grain trade at the same rate as was true of the 1970s. In fact, a more reasonable expectation is that annual growth for the remainder of the century would be less than half of the 7.5 percent realized from 1969–1971 to 1980–1982. *Long-Term Grain Outlook*, by the secretariat of the International Wheat Council, presents a series of informed judgments about prospective developments in the demand and supply of grains in five economic groupings.[15] While eschewing the concept of projections, their analysis of each group's likely production and consumption indicates a significant likelihood that between 1980 and 2000 world grain trade would increase by about 27 percent or an annual growth rate of but 1.2 percent. One hopes that this is a very pessimistic expectation. The U.S. Department of Agriculture has presented a more optimistic view, namely that during the 1980s world grain trade might increase at an annual rate of 2.7 percent.[16] This estimate is consistent with my analysis that a growth rate of 3.0 percent is a realistic expectation. Even if this rate were exceeded by half, the result would be a much slower growth than occurred during the 1970s.

If one analyzes the sources of growth in grain imports during the 1970s, it becomes obvious that such a high rate of growth cannot be sustained into the future (see table 7). The centrally planned economies accounted for almost half of the world import growth of 125 million tons between 1969–1971 and 1980–1982. Their grain imports grew at the remarkable annual rate of 25 percent. The next most important source of growth was the middle-income developing countries. The low-income developing countries had almost no net increase in grain imports during the period. As of the early and mid-1970s, many expected the low-income developing countries to become such a drain on world food supplies that drastic steps, such as limiting their right of access to world grain supplies, would be required. The capital surplus oil exporters had a very high growth rate, but these countries have such a small population that further substantial growth cannot be expected.

The high growth rates of grain imports by the centrally planned economies resulted from several factors. These included the relatively poor performance of Soviet agriculture after 1975, the rapid growth of meat production and consumption in Eastern Europe during the 1970s, decisions taken in the People's Republic of China to improve the living standards of its citizens, and adherence to the policy of keeping consumer prices of food constant in nominal terms.[17] Fixed nominal prices of food in the face of inflation and rising money wages cause demand to grow faster than supply unless extraordinary measures are taken to increase supplies. One of the measures used to increase meat and milk supplies was to increase sharply net imports of grain and feeding materials.

The fixed nominal prices of food have been made possible by the payment of large and increasing subsidies to make up the difference between the prices paid by consumers and the prices paid to producers. To increase domestic production, producer prices have been raised. These policies remain in most of the centrally planned economies. Subsidies have been largely eliminated in Poland and substantially reduced in Hungary, but large subsidies continue in other Eastern European economies.

Very large food subsidies exist in the Soviet Union. In 1983 such subsidies probably equaled 50 billion rubles and exceeded the value of retail sales of meat, milk, and potatoes—the primary products that are subsidized. The price policy that has resulted in such large subsidies, namely keeping the nominal prices of the major food products constant, has been one reason for the large-scale grain imports by the Soviet Union. The unwillingness of the Soviet government to use prices to equate supply and demand for meat and milk has resulted in large unmet demands for these products, which has put pressure upon policy makers to import large quantities of grain and other feeding materials. Recent quite modest crops of grain are another reason; but even if grain crops increase, Soviet imports will continue to be an important factor in world grain markets for years to come.[18]

There is, however, almost no prospect that the strong growth in grain imports of the 1970s resulting from policies and performance of agricultures in Eastern Europe and the Soviet Union will be repeated in the next decade. Eastern Europe would be unlikely to go into debt once again to buy feed, even if there were institutions willing to lend for that purpose. Unless governments of grain-exporting countries are willing to guarantee such loans, it is unlikely that financial institutions would make loans with as little concern about the use of the funds as they did during the 1970s. It is my view, therefore, that grain imports by Eastern European economies and the Soviet Union of the past few years will at best be maintained. In fact, imports will, most probably, decline.

China is one of the world's largest grain importers at approximately 18 million tons annually. While it would not be wholly unexpected for Chinese imports to increase to 22–25 million tons within the next decade, it is also possible that they could decline to 10 million tons. Recent radical changes in rural policy that have, in effect, abolished the commune as both an economic and political unit and reinstated a fairly liberal form of the family farm with collective ownership of the land have resulted in significant increases in output. Numerous other policy changes have also resulted in large increases in incomes in rural areas. Thus, demand as well as output has increased in the farm areas. Meat production has been increasing at a rapid rate. Further, China also has a system of food price subsidies for grains and vegetables oils for the urban population. Chinese population growth is slowing down and is likely to continue a downward growth trend for the rest of this century. Growth in income and greater freedom of the people to spend their income as they see fit are, however, likely to keep demand for grain and other foods growing apace with production. I conclude that the most likely prospect is for little or no change in China's imports of grain.

The middle-income developing countries will have a relatively high annual growth of grain use, and their exports will continue to increase, perhaps at nearly the same rate as that of the 1970s. This increase is, however, almost the only bright spot in the worldwide prospect for growth in the demand for grain. Use of grain for feed in the industrial countries will increase slowly, perhaps only slightly more than 1.0 percent annually, and use for food will increase hardly at all. Per capita incomes are now so high in the developed countries that per capita meat consumption may have reached a maximum in several developed countries. Use of grain for food may well fail to keep pace with population growth, and population growth will be slow indeed, at well under 1 percent.

TABLE 7

INTERNATIONAL TRADE IN CEREALS BY ECONOMIC GROUPS, 1960–1982

(millions of metric tons)

Country Group	1960–1962			1969–1971			1977–1979			1980–1982		
	Export	Import	Net	Export	Import	Net	Export	Import	Net	Export	Import	Net
Industrial countries	53.8	37.1	16.7	77.6	52.1	25.5	148.4	63.1	85.3	191.9	73.4	118.5
United States	31.4	0.6	30.8	36.3	0.4	35.9	90.9	0.2	90.7	109.0	0.3	108.7
Canada	10.2	0.7	9.5	13.7	0.5	13.2	18.5	0.7	17.8	23.8	1.2	22.6
Australia	5.9	—	5.9	8.8	—	8.8	11.7	—	11.7	15.8	0.1	15.7
France	3.4	1.0	2.4	11.4	1.0	10.4	14.3	1.9	12.4	20.4	1.9	18.5
Japan	0.1	5.0	−4.9	0.7	14.7	−14.0	0.3	23.3	−23.0	0.8	24.4	−23.4
Centrally planned economies	9.8	12.4	−2.6	12.4	17.5	−5.2	9.3	50.0	−40.7	7.7	73.1	−65.4
USSR	7.6	0.6	7.0	8.2	2.7	5.5	3.7	20.7	−17.0	2.4	39.3	−36.9
Eastern Europe	1.3	8.3	−7.0	2.2	9.7	−7.5	4.1	16.6	−12.5	4.0	13.5	−9.5
China	0.9	3.5	−2.6	2.0	5.2	−3.2	1.5	12.7	−11.2	1.0	18.6	−17.6

Low-income countries	2.4	7.3	−4.9	2.1	10.9	−8.8	2.8	11.7	−8.9	3.0	13.5	−10.5
India	—	4.1	−4.1	—	3.6	−3.6	0.8	0.6	0.2	0.8	1.0	−0.7
Indonesia	—	1.2	−1.2	0.2	1.3	−1.1	—	2.8	−2.8	—	2.5	−2.4
Middle-income countries	9.6	10.9	−1.3	17.6	24.2	−6.6	26.1	49.2	−23.1	23.8	57.3	−33.5
Korea	—	0.5	−0.5	—	2.6	2.6	—	4.1	−4.1	—	6.1	−6.1
Argentina	5.6	—	5.6	3.5	0.1	3.4	14.6	—	14.6	14.3	—	14.3
Brazil	0.1	2.1	−2.0	1.2	2.1	0.9	0.7	4.8	−4.1	—	5.6	−5.6
Mexico	0.2	0.1	0.1	0.5	0.4	0.1	0.1	4.0	−3.9	—	5.5	−5.5
South Africa	1.3	0.2	1.1	0.3	1.2	0.9	2.6	0.2	2.4	4.1	0.3	3.8
Thailand	1.9	—	1.9	2.9	0.1	2.8	4.4	0.1	4.3	6.0	0.2	5.8
Capital surplus oil exporters	—	0.7	−0.7	0.1	2.0	−1.9	0.1	6.8	−6.7	0.1	11.6	−11.5
Total	75.6	68.4	—a	109.8	103.9	—a	186.9	183.3	—a	226.5	228.9	—a

a. Statistical discrepancy.

SOURCE: FAO. *FAO Trade Yearbook*. various issues.

Consequently, there is little basis to assume that the long-term slow downward trend in real grain prices will be interrupted in the next decade or so. In fact, unless the resources devoted to grain production in the major exporting countries are substantially reduced, there is a strong probability that real prices of grains will decline at an accelerated rate.

I see nothing in these projections that could result in more than a temporary interruption in the long-term downward trend in real prices of grains. There could, of course, be circumstances that lead to higher real prices for grains; but projections in recent years based on different assumptions and by different groups contain no significant evidence that the price trends of the past half century are likely to be reversed within the next decade.

Looking ahead at the rest of the 1980s, one sees a number of short-run factors that will affect real grain prices. World grain stocks, including those held by the United States, are large; the United States could produce more grain than it produced in either 1983 or 1984, and the production and consumption trends in the European Community are likely to result in an increase in net exports of grain. As argued earlier, there appears little basis for projecting a robust international market for grains and other important farm crops for the rest of this decade. Were it not for the continued mismanagement of Soviet agriculture, grain prices now would be lower and U.S. stocks larger than they are. The debt situation in Eastern Europe and in numerous developing countries will continue to have an adverse effect upon imports of farm products until substantial adjustments occur. There seems little possibility that most of these adjustments will have occurred by the end of this decade.

Some Alternative Scenarios

My conclusions that the most likely prospects for American agriculture are for continuing gradual declines in real farm prices and a significant adjustment in the quantities of resources employed in agriculture can be described as rather gloomy. A reduction in resources will be required if the returns to the mobile factors used in agriculture—labor and capital—are to be approximately the same as for similar resources elsewhere in the economy. The adjustment is already under way. Farm employment has been declining at the long-run rate of several percent since 1981, after several years of very slow rates of decline. As any one familiar with the farm machinery business knows, farmers are gradually reducing the amount of capital devoted to farming.

Although I believe that the scenario I have portrayed is highly probable, some alternative scenarios should be mentioned. Some changes in the environment could soften the downward drift in farm prices and reduce resources required for withdrawal. The developments that might have some ameliorating effect upon the demand-supply balance for U.S. agriculture include devaluation of the U.S. dollar, substantial liberalization of world trade, and a decline in productivity growth in agriculture.

More research is required before we know how much effect a decline in the foreign exchange value of the dollar would have upon U.S. farm prices. From the available research it seems reasonable to assume that nominal U.S. prices would rise by approximately half as much as the decline in the value of the dollar. This is probably a minimum estimate; some studies would put the elasticity as high as 0.75.[19] True, this would be the change in nominal prices. It is probable that if the foreign exchange value fell, the general level of domestic prices would rise since the monetary authorities would be likely to accommodate to the increase in the dollar prices of tradable goods by increasing the money supply rather than forcing a contraction in economic activity. Thus, real prices of farm products would probably increase by less than the nominal prices, but there can be little doubt that a, say, 20 percent decline in the value of the dollar would mean that the market clearing level of prices during the next two or three years would be noticeably higher than would be true with the current value of the dollar.

A second possibility would be a significant move toward more liberal international trade regimes for both agricultural products and for labor-intensive manufactured products. A liberalization of trade in grains could result in an increase in international prices of wheat and corn of 10 percent with much larger increases in dairy products and sugar.[20] The demand for soybeans would probably decline, though soybean prices seem almost fully determined by production alternatives; demand determines quantity produced on a highly elastic supply curve.

The liberalization of imports for labor-intensive manufactured products by the members of the Organization for Economic Cooperation and Development (OECD) would increase the foreign exchange earnings of countries that have a high income elasticity of demand for food. As a result, a significant percentage of the increased real income that would result from expanded trade opportunities would be spent on food, and a considerable part of the additional food for consumption would be imported. Agriculture bears a significant part of the cost of very expensively protecting a small number of jobs in labor-intensive manufacturing.

A third possibility that could reduce the downward pressure of real farm prices would be a slowdown in productivity growth, not only in North America but in Western Europe and other major producing areas. What reason is there to expect such a slowdown? There were those who thought such a slowdown in productivity growth occurred in the United States after the mid-1960s and the 1970s. Apparently the slowdown was an illusion, as argued recently by Edwards and Harrington:

> During the 70s, the growth in productivity appeared to slow. This slowdown occurred during a decade in which total output was expanding to fill export markets. The slowdown raised questions whether technological advance in agriculture was approaching a limit at the same time that cropland harvested was approaching its

41

TABLE 8

Per Capita Household Expenditures of Farm Households and Wage-earning Households, Japan, 1970–1982

(wage-earning households = 100)

Fiscal Year	Nationwide	Cities, Towns and Villages, Population Less Than 50,000	Towns and Villages Only
		Average of All Farm Households	
1970	95.3	103.5	103.4
1975	107.1	109.1	108.1
1980	113.4	119.4	119.7
1981	111.4	116.7	117.6
1982	110.6	112.8	111.9
1982			
Full-time farm households (with a core male full-time farmer)	88.8	90.6	89.9
Class-I part-time farm households (with a temporary wage earner)	91.8	93.7	92.9
Class-II part-time farm households (with a permanent wage earner)	116.2	118.6	117.7

Source: Japan. Ministry of Agriculture and Forestry. The State of Japan's Agriculture 1983. A Summary Report. April 1984.

historical high. However, the slowdown was not substantiated for various disaggregations of the aggregate measure. For example, trends for corn yields did not change in either the Cornbelt or the South, but an increase in corn acreage in the lower-yielding South resulted in a reduction in the weighted-average national corn yield. And trends in livestock and crop productivity were little changed, but an increase in purchased inputs for the rapidly expanding crop enterprise changed the weighted average ratio of crop plus livestock outputs to all inputs. Therefore, what appeared to be a change in productivity may, instead, have been regional and commodity shifts in production.[21]

As one looks at the agricultural and biological research underway, there seems little reason to assume that productivity change will be slower in the coming years than it has been in the past. There is reason to assume that productivity will grow more rapidly in the years ahead than it has in the recent past.

The Irrelevance of Output Prices

For those families who will be engaged in farming during the first half of the 1990s, the rate of growth of demand for farm output or of farm prices will be of little importance. True, the number of farm families who will devote their own energies and other·valuable resources to farming will be a function of demand growth, productivity change, and farm prices. The incomes of those families who remain in agriculture will be determined by the alternative incomes that they could earn if they were not devoting some or all of their resources to agriculture.

One lesson that we should be able to learn from observation of the world is that the absolute incomes earned by farm families in various countries have no relationship to farm prices. Even stronger, the relative incomes of farm families have no relationship to farm prices, except as benefits of higher prices have been capitalized into the value of land and land has been acquired by gift or inheritance.

In support of these statements, it may be noted that the excellent incomes of Japanese farm families are not due to the high farm output prices that prevail in Japan. Full-time farm households constitute 12.5 percent of all farms. These are households in which either the farm operator or members of the household devote all or almost all of their time to farming. There are two classifications of part-time farms. In the first, one or more members of the household has a nonfarm job, but the net income from farming exceeds the nonagricultural income. These households constitute 18 percent of the total farm households. In the second category of part-time farms, households receive more income from nonagricultural sources than from farm sources. This

43

TABLE 9
Net Farm Income and Off-farm Income of Farm Operator Families, 1960–1982

Year	Net Farm Income (millions of dollars)	Off-farm Income (millions of dollars)	Total Income (millions of dollars)	Net Farm Income as Percentage of Total Income
1960	11,518	8,482	20,000	57.6
1961	11,957	9,163	21,120	56.6
1962	12,064	9,904	21,968	54.9
1963	11,770	11,020	22,790	51.6
1964	10,492	11,637	22,129	47.4
1965	12,899	12,727	25,626	50.3
1966	13,960	13,882	27,842	50.1
1967	12,339	14,495	26,834	46.0
1968	12,322	15,466	27,788	44.3
1969	14,293	16,612	30,905	46.2
1970	14,381	17,617	31,998	44.9
1971	15,043	19,110	34,153	44.0
1972	19,507	21,265	40,772	47.8
1973	34,435	24,714	59,149	58.2
1974	27,309	28,135	55,444	49.3
1975	25,555	23,901	49,456	51.7
1976	20,132	26,681	46,813	43.0
1977	19,821	26,120	45,941	43.1

	Net Farm Income per Farm (dollars)	Off-farm Income per Farm (dollars)	Total Income per Farm (dollars)	Net Farm Income as Percentage of Total Income
1978	27,651	29,704	57,355	48.2
1979	32,251	35,267	67,518	47.8
1980	21,505	37,660	59,165	36.3
1981	30,057	39,877	69,935	43.0
1982	22,051	39,431	61,482	35.9
Value of Sales, 1982 (dollars)	**Net Farm Income per Farm (dollars)**	**Off-farm Income per Farm (dollars)**	**Total Income per Farm (dollars)**	**Net Farm Income as Percentage of Total Income**
500,000 and over	571,097	26,831	597,929	95.5
200,000–499,999	53,461	13,720	67,180	79.6
100,000–199,999	19,786	11,074	30,861	64.1
40,000–99,000	5,539	10,615	16,155	34.3
20,000–39,999	504	12,887	13,391	3.7
10,000–19,999	–728	17,208	16,479	–4.4
5,000–9,999	–881	19,146	18,265	–4.8
2,500–4,999	–998	19,328	18,330	–5.4
Less than 2,500	–465	20,758	20,292	–2.3
All farms	9,959	16,430	26,386	37.7

SOURCE: U.S. Department of Agriculture. *Economic Indicators of the Farm Sector*, 1982.

group accounts for 68 percent of all households.

Even though crop prices in Japan in recent years have been as much as four times international prices, the number of full-time farms decreased by 80 percent from 1950 to 1980 while the number of part-time farm households increased by a third. Of the part-time households, the second category more than doubled while the first category decreased by more than two-fifths over the same period of time.

Table 8 presents information on the relative income position of Japanese farm families. Income is measured by household expenditures, which removes a significant part of the transitory component in farm incomes. The top part of the table indicates that, per capita, farm households have had higher expenditures since 1970 than wage-earning households in smaller cities, towns, and villages and higher expenditures than all wage-earner households from 1975 through 1982. In FY 1980, of the total income of all farm households only 21 percent came from agriculture. This was down from 33 percent in FY 1975 and 36 percent in FY 1970.

The bottom part of the table shows relative per capita expenditures by the households' reliance upon agriculture for employment. Farm households with a male full-time worker had per capita expenditures in FY 1982 some 24 percent below the part-time farm households that had a permanent nonfarm wage earner and approximately the same expenditures as the part-time households that had a temporary wage earner. Differences in age and sex composition of the labor forces, as well as in education levels, among the types of farm households probably explain some of the differences in per capita expenditures. Adjustment for these factors would reduce the expenditure differentials somewhat, but the major point would remain—the incomes of farm families depend upon alternative opportunities in the nonfarm economies. Between 1970 and 1982 the real per capita living expenditures of farm families increased by about 35 percent, more than for all Japanese families. For all Japanese families the increase was about 25 percent. During this period prices received by farmers showed no significant trend in real terms.

Table 9 provides somewhat similar data on the sources of income of farm families in the United States. The top part of the table indicates that net farm income as a percentage of family income declined from 55 percent or more in the early 1960s to an average of less than 40 percent in the early 1980s. The bottom part of the table indicates that only on farms with sales in excess of $100,000 did net farm income exceed off-farm income. Only some 12 percent of the farms had sales in excess of $100,000 in 1982.

It is quite remarkable that the percentage of the farms that obtain half or more of their income from agriculture is greater in Japan at about 30 percent than in the United States at about 12 percent. Even with the very high prices for many farm products in Japan, especially rice, wheat, barley, soybeans, beef, and milk, 70 percent of the farm families receive almost 90 percent of

TABLE 10

PRICES RECEIVED BY FARMERS IN MAJOR INDUSTRIAL COUNTRIES,
1970 AND 1979

($ per metric ton)

	1970		1979	
	Wheat	Coarse Grain	Wheat	Coarse Grain
Belgium	100	86	212	214
Denmark	—	62	224	214
France	84	75	232	214
Germany	99	89	274	247
Italy	110	93	231	210
Netherlands	102	—	212[a]	202[a]
United Kingdom	74	68	160	—
Ireland	76	—	—	181
Canada	61	—	117	100
Japan	162	131	770	582
United States	48	52	118	95

a. 1978.
SOURCE: OECD publications.

TABLE 11

ANNUAL RATES OF DECLINE IN FARM EMPLOYMENT, 1955–1979

(percent per year)

	1955–1960	1960–1970	1970–1979
European Community	−3.2	−4.6	−3.4
Belgium	−3.7	−4.9	−4.6
Denmark	−2.1	−3.1	−2.7
France	−3.7	−3.7	−4.6
Germany	−3.3	−4.6	−4.8
Ireland	−2.5	−3.0	−3.1
Italy	−3.2	−5.8	−2.2
Netherlands	−2.7	−3.4	−1.8
United Kingdom	−2.5	−3.8	−1.0
Canada	−3.6	−2.7	−0.7
Japan	−2.6	−4.0	−4.1
United States	−3.3	−4.5	−0.5

SOURCE: OECD publications.

their net income from nonagricultural sources.

Although output prices have some influence upon the number of people engaged in farming, evidence from a number of industrial countries indicates that other factors may largely mask the effect of prices. Tables 10 and 11 present such evidence for several industrial countries. The countries with high grain prices—the original six in the European Community and Japan—had approximately the same rates of reduction of farm employment as Canada and the United States. This was true for 1955–1960 and 1960–1970. For the 1970s, however, the three countries with the lowest rates of decline in farm employment were the three countries with the lowest grain prices in both 1970 and 1979. Thus high prices, including the very high prices in Japan, were not sufficient to halt or reduce significantly the outflow of labor from agriculture.

Conclusion

The available evidence indicates that real farm prices will probably decline slowly. For the United States the decline might be interrupted for a brief period by a fall in the foreign exchange value of the dollar. The rise in the dollar prices of grain and other internationally traded farm products that we export would encourage increased output both in the United States and in the major exporters whose currencies are fairly closely tied to the dollar. This includes all of our major competitors except the European Community. While it is true that a fall in the value of the dollar would reduce the local currency price of our exports in a number of importing countries, the effect on demand after a period of time would be outweighed by the effect on supply.

The decline in the value of the dollar, if and when it comes, cannot be expected, however, to return our farm prices to more than their real value of the late 1970s. This would mean real prices no higher than the low prices of the early 1970s, which would likely be a short-term effect, merely delaying the reemergence of the long-run decline in real prices.

As I hope I made clear, however, price projections should be irrelevant to the formulation of the 1985 farm bill. If price supports and target prices continue to be major policy instruments, ways must be found to adjust them to minimize their effect on production and marketing. My most important point is that the returns to farm labor, management, and capital depend very little, if at all, upon output prices. Far more important are general economic conditions that determine returns on resources in the rest of the economy—the alternatives that farm people have for nonagricultural uses of their resources.

Notes

1. Congressional Budget Office, *An Analysis of Congressional Budget Estimates for Fiscal Years 1980–82*, Special Study, June 1984.

2. Gerald O. Barney, study director, *The Global 2000 Report to the President* (Report prepared by the Council on Environmental Policy and the U.S. Department of State) (New York: Penguin Books, 1982).

3. Daryll E. Ray, James W. Richardson, and Elton Li, "The 1981 Agriculture and Food Act: Implications for Farm Prices, Incomes, and Government Outlays to Farmers," *American Journal of Agricultural Economics*, vol. 64, no. 5 (December 1982), p. 957.

4. William G. Lesher, "Future Agricultural Policy—A Challenge for All" (Paper presented at the Conference on Alternative Agricultural and Food Policies and the 1985 Farm Bill, Berkeley, California, June 11, 1984).

5. Bob Bergland, remarks prepared for delivery by the secretary of agriculture before the Conservation Foundation Conference, Washington, D.C., July 14, 1980, U.S. Department of Agriculture, Speeches and Major Policy Releases, July 14–18, 1980.

6. D. Gale Johnson, *World Food Problems and Prospects* (Washington, D.C.: American Enterprise Institute, 1975), pp. 3–4.

7. U.S. Department of Agriculture, Economic Research Service, *The World Food Situation and Prospects to 1985*, Agricultural Economics Report no. 98 (Washington, D.C., December 1974).

8. D. Gale Johnson, "Agricultural Policy Alternatives for the 1980s," in D. Gale Johnson, ed., *Food and Agricultural Policy for the 1980s* (Washington, D.C.: American Enterprise Institute, 1981), pp. 208–9.

9. Robert W. Fogel, "Nutrition and the Decline in Mortality since 1700: Some Preliminary Findings" (Copyright by Robert W. Fogel, 1984).

10. Barney, *Global 2000 Report*; and Food and Agriculture Organization, *Agriculture: Toward 2000* (Rome: FAO, 1981).

11. Resources for the Future, "Feeding a Hungry World," *Resources*, no. 76 (Spring 1984).

12. FAO, *Agriculture: Toward 2000*, pp. 24–25.

13. Lesher, "Future Agricultural Policy."

14. World Bank, *Commodity Trade and Price Trends*, 1983–84 ed. (Baltimore: Johns Hopkins University Press, 1983).

15. International Wheat Council, *Long-Term Grain Outlook*, Secretariat Paper no. 14, August 1984.

16. U.S. Department of Agriculture, *World Agriculture: Outlook and Situation*, WAS-30, December 1982.

17. D. Gale Johnson and Karen M. Brooks, *Prospects for Soviet Agriculture in the 1980s* (Bloomington: Indiana University Press, 1983); Johnson, "Agricultural Policy Alternatives"; and D. Gale Johnson, "Agriculture in the Centrally Planned Economies," Office of Agricultural Economics Research, University of Chicago, Paper no. 82-15, July 21, 1982.

18. Johnson and Brooks, *Prospects for Soviet Agriculture*.

19. Jim Longmire and Art Morey, *Exchange Rates, U.S. Agricultural Export*

Prices, and U.S. Farm Program Stocks (Washington, D.C.: Department of Agriculture, Economic Research Service, 1982).

20. Rodney Tyers, "Agricultural Protection and Insulations," Pacific Economic Paper no. 111, Australia-Japan Research Centre, Canberra, Australia; Kim Anderson and Rodney Tyers, "European Community Grain and Meat Policies: Effects on International Prices, Trade and Welfare," *European Rev. Agr. Econ.* 11 (1984), pp. 366–394.

21. Clark Edwards and David J. Harrington, "The Future Productive Capacity of U.S. Agriculture: Economic, Technological, Resource, and Institutional Determinants" (Paper presented at meeting of American Agricultural Economics Association, Ithaca, New York, August 1984), p. 70.

Commentary

Patrick M. O'Brien

I appreciate the opportunity to comment on Gale Johnson's paper and on the broader issue of the medium-term world commodity outlook. I agree with what I see as the two main thrusts of the Johnson paper—namely, the direction in which the world market for farm products is *likely* to move during the remainder of the 1980s and the implications of that direction for the upcoming debate on the U.S. farm bill. I will comment on these points but from a somewhat different perspective from that taken by the author.

World Commodity Market Prospects

The outlook for the world market for farm products during the remainder of the decade can probably best be described as "lackluster." Johnson cites an impressive catalogue of factors likely to push world growth in grain, oilseed, cotton, and livestock production above trend but keep growth in demand at or below trend.

On the supply side, two factors strike me as particularly important. Much of the investment in agriculture—particularly land and water development projects—made in a wide range of countries during the tight supplies and high prices of the 1970s has reached or is reaching maturity. Growth in productivity also appears to be accelerating in many countries as new technology is developed and the pace of adoption picks up. Given these and other factors, including more agricultural and trade policies oriented toward greater self-sufficiency, growth in world production of farm products could average 2.75 to 3.25 percent per year through 1990 without a significant increase in investment or improvement in product prices or producer returns. This compares with a postwar average of 2.5 to 3 percent.

Conversely, while the demographic and macroeconomic base for a rebound in demand from the stagnation of the early 1980s is in place, lags are likely to keep demand growth below trend until late in the decade. Given the relatively low price elasticities of demand in effect in much of the world, low commodity prices should help to boost growth in demand, but not sufficiently to reach the 2.5 to 3 percent postwar trend.

Given changes in production and use in individual countries, this global supply-demand combination is likely to generate stronger growth in world agricultural trade than experienced during the past five years. Growth in trade, however, would quite likely lag below the unusually fast pace of the 1970s and average near or somewhat below the longer-term postwar trend. Given what is likely to be a world buyer's market, the adjustment to slower growth in demand for farm products will probably be concentrated in the exporting countries.

Should the United States continue in its traditional role of residual supplier, slow growth in world trade could translate into the continuation of the export malaise the United States has experienced since 1980. Using postwar growth rates as a backdrop, growth in U.S. exports could average 3 to 5 percent for the second half of the decade compared to 7 to 9 percent during the 1970s and an average for 1950–1960 of 4 to 6 percent.

What does this export environment imply for U.S. agriculture? Given the sector's existing productive capacity, likely growth in that capacity, and the limited potential for growth in domestic demand, export growth of 3 to 5 percent implies significant financial and resource adjustment problems for the sector. A quick look at the farm sector's technology base suggests productivity growth could well continue at or above the postwar rate of 1.75 to 2 percent per year. This growth in productivity, combined with fuller use of agriculture's land base, could support growth in output of 2 to 3 percent per year without any significant improvement in producer returns. Conversely, growth in domestic demand for farm products appears likely to continue slowing from the 1 percent per year of the 1970s as per capita consumption levels approach saturation and population growth slips below 0.5 percent per year.

Should these projections for domestic supply, domestic demand, and export demand materialize, the farm sector would face serious pressure to idle—eventually to eliminate—excess productive capacity and considerable downward pressure on commodity prices and farm incomes. At commodity prices near the support levels provided in the 1981 farm bill, as much as a quarter of the sector's productive capacity would not be needed. In other words, commodity prices would have to fall as much as a third below target prices for the market to clear with the sector producing at full capacity.

Implications for the Debate on the 1985 Farm Bill

What does this perspective for the farm sector imply for the 1985 policy debate? Many analysts, including Johnson, suggest that more, rather than less, market orientation in farm policy is necessary if the sector is to adjust without large-scale resource transfers from the rest of the economy. Market orientation in this context is probably best measured by the responsiveness of farm prices and incomes (and in turn operator production and marketing decisions) to changes in supply and demand here and abroad. It can also be gauged, however, by the extent to which the risks involved in producing and marketing farm products are borne by taxpayers, shared between taxpayers and farm operators, or borne more or less completely by farm operators.

One can arrive at a bias in favor of more market orientation from at least two perspectives—a public cost perspective and a farm structure perspective. The agricultural sector has grown large enough (particularly with its expansion from a closed economy in the 1950s to an open economy with a large foreign market in the 1980s) and the commodity market has grown volatile enough that setting prices and returns that are at odds with the dictates of the market has become extremely costly. The cost of supporting even declining real farm incomes for the sector has grown sharply, from an average of $2–4 billion in the 1950s and 1960s to $9–11 billion in the 1980s.

This rising cost of farm programs—particularly price and income programs—is due in part to the types of support used in agriculture since the 1930s. Existing programs work to enhance incomes by manipulating market prices; equally important, they generally link the extent of support to the volume of output. Current support programs put the U.S. government in the position of buying up enough "surplus" wheat, corn, cotton, and other program commodities to short the market and raise commodity prices and producer returns above what would otherwise be market-clearing levels. Acreage reduction programs work in theory to restrict production and to minimize the volume of products the government has to buy to enhance prices and incomes. Problems with the design of supply control programs (for example, slippage and cross-compliance) and with the administration of the programs often minimize their effectiveness in limiting surplus output and reducing program costs.

The rising cost of public intervention also relates to the price and income stabilization provisions of the farm programs and the increasingly volatile nature of the market for farm products. Simply stated, the programs currently in place skew the distribution of the risks involved in producing and marketing program commodities heavily in the direction of taxpayers. In this setting, the increased market volatility of the 1970s and 1980s (whether related to weather, policy, or macroeconomic and financial developments here or abroad) have helped to raise public costs substantially. It is worth noting, moreover, that even with the current programs in place, swings in farm incomes have widened to the extent that fluctuations of 25 percent or more from year to year have become the norm rather than the exception.

Rising farm program costs also relate to a third set of longer-term considerations. With supports working through the market to raise prices and returns above equilibrium levels, they often touch off counterproductive supply and demand adjustments. With supply and demand elasticities of possibly $+0.3/-0.3$ in the short term and $+1/-1$ in the longer term, support programs that set returns above market-clearing levels generate consistently more output than the market can absorb. They also work to discourage growth in demand.

These secondary effects ultimately worsen the oversupply problem and raise the cost of public intervention over time to support a given level of income.

In the market setting forecast in Johnson's paper, continuing the price and income supports called for in the current program would involve even larger costs. With market forces signaling the need for resource outflows and lower farm returns to keep supply and demand in balance, public programs to the contrary would put the government even more in the position of residual adjuster. Moreover, continued skewed risk sharing in an increasingly volatile setting would work simultaneously both to increase program costs and to make forecasting public costs an increasingly difficult task.

These forces combined could push the public costs of price and income supports in the second half of the 1980s up to $8-12 billion per year with highs of possibly $14-16 billion and lows of $1 billion or less.

The need for more, rather than less, market orientation can also be argued from a farm structure perspective. More and more of the analysis suggests that support programs can actually undermine farm incomes over the longer run. Program benefits are generally capitalized into asset values and work to raise production costs. In many cases, the capitalization and cost changes involved can eventually cancel out any real income benefits they might have involved initially. In this sense, a more market-oriented farm economy is quite likely over the longer run to be a lower-cost agriculture. If cost structures do shift upward over time in response to program provisions as many analysts suggest, it is difficult to identify any significant program-related improvement in net farm incomes—particularly any improvement proportionate to program costs.

To the extent that it works to strengthen the competitive position of the United States in the world market by minimizing production costs, a more market-oriented farm policy can also be a higher-return agriculture. While the forces at play are less clear cut, analysis suggests that the expanded exports possible with more market-oriented farm policies could allow producers to use their plants at higher capacity utilization rates that: (1) take greater advantage of economies of scale, (2) lower unit costs of production, and (3) keep a larger share of their gross receipts as net income.

In the environment of slow demand growth that Johnson describes, strengthening the competitive position of the United States in the world market may be necessary simply to keep the sector from slipping to even lower capacity utilization rates and from facing added cost pressures on returns.

Caveats and Conclusions

From my perspective as a reviewer, Johnson makes a strong case for a lackluster outlook for the farm sector over the next several years. He also makes a strong case for more market-orientation in farm policy, although his work over the past two decades suggests his biases are clearly in favor of more market orientation regardless of market outlook. At least two key concerns need to be kept in mind, however, in deciding on just how much more or how much less market orientation in farm policy is advisable.

The first of my caveats relates to the question of linking farm policy to a single view of market prospects. Dr. Johnson recognizes in several places that, while there is considerable support for his outlook, the possibility of a dramatically different market environment is very real. Macroeconomic, financial, agricultural, and trade policy, and even weather factors, could work individually or collectively to generate strong demand for farm products, tight supplies, and prices well above support levels. In fact, the probability of the Johnson scenario, while larger than for any other scenario, may be 0.5 or less.

What does this uncertainty suggest for the farm bill debate? It suggests that the sector and the general economy would be poorly served by a set of farm policies—particularly an inflexible set of farm policies—geared to a single view of the future. In short, a farm policy legislating a sharp move toward more or less market orientation on the basis of a single view of the future is likely to be badly out of focus as the market environment changes from year to year.

The second caveat is equally important. While Johnson makes a strong argument in favor of more market orientation—if only to facilitate what he sees as more or less inevitable adjustments in the sector—it is difficult to identify how much market orientation is in the best interest of the sector and of the general economy.

It is clearly undesirable to leave farmers isolated from the market—particularly to the extent that they react contrary to market signals. Given the volatility experience of the past ten years, however, it is equally undesirable to leave the sector subject to wide, possibly short-lived, fluctuations in the market. In the extreme case, reaction to short-term fluctuations can be counterproductive. The issue, then, becomes one of allowing farmers to "hear" the market without being "deafened" by market noise.

This concern with overreacting and underreacting to market signals is particularly critical if Johnson's perspective on the next several years proves valid. With the limited funds available for farm programs, it is clearly in the public's interest for the sector to proceed with the resource and structural adjustments necessary to keep the sector healthy—and to proceed with all deliberate speed. Given the costs involved in these adjustments, it is equally critical that the sector not overadjust in a manner that weakens agriculture's capacity to meet future needs of the United States and of the world for food, feed, and fiber.

International Agriculture
and Trade Policies:
Implications for the United States

G. Edward Schuh

This paper is divided into three parts. The first part is a discussion of international monetary developments and issues and their effect on agricultural trade. The second part discusses developments in international trade policies. The third part outlines the main elements of an agricultural export policy for the United States.

This obviously is a much broader set of issues than the title of my paper suggests. I have broadened the perspective by design, for in my judgment some of the issues outside of international agriculture and trade policies are more important than factors inside it. This is a reflection of the dramatic changes in the international economy over the past twenty years and in how the U.S. economy relates to that international economy. As I have argued elsewhere,[1] there are four components to those changes: (1) the significant growth in U.S. dependence on trade, which means that it makes little sense for us to devise agricultural policies based on the assumptions of a closed model, as we have done in the past; (2) the emergence of a well-integrated capital market, which brings monetary issues to the fore; (3) the shift from a fixed exchange rate system to a system of bloc floating, which introduced a significant new price into our trade calculus, and which creates third-country effects of major significance;[2] and (4) the emergence of a great deal of monetary instability, which is an important new source of instability to international commodities, and also something we did not have to contend with in the past.

These developments have greatly changed the economics of agriculture, and in turn the basis of policy toward the sector. It is difficult to overstate just how dramatic and how significant the changes are. It is worth noting that most of the policies now on the books were developed when the United States either essentially had a closed economy or, for all practical purposes, assumed it had

---

G. Edward Schuh is director of agriculture and rural development at the World Bank. The views expressed are those of the author and do not necessarily reflect the opinion of the World Bank.

a closed economy, even though it did not. Similarly, there is little reflection in their design that currency exchange rates can fluctuate widely and thus cause domestic commodity programs to have even more deleterious effects than they have in a closed economy. There is little reflection in present policies that things as distantly removed from agricultural policy as monetary and fiscal policy and developments in the international petroleum sector can have major effects on the export performance of U.S. agriculture and thus on the welfare of U.S. farmers.

These *novidades* are further complicated by other developments in the international economy that are changing both comparative and competitive advantages. These developments make our general trade posture as important as our agricultural trade policies and require that both policy makers and private decision makers significantly extend this list of events and developments they must take into account in managing their particular affairs.

International Monetary Developments and Issues

The key issue for agriculture when policy makers consider international monetary developments is the value of the dollar in foreign exchange markets. There is much less disagreement today about the role of the exchange rate than there was some eleven years ago when I first raised the issue. It is interesting that rising exports had many parents, and nobody wanted to hear about the value of the currency. A decline in exports, however, was a fatherless child, and thus the sire was obviously that dastardly rise in the value of the U.S. dollar.

For those interested in visual evidence of the relationship between the value of the dollar and our export performance, figure 1 provides a plot of the trade-weighted value of the dollar and the value of U.S. agricultural exports. One could hardly find a closer relationship between two economic variables that economic theory predicts will be related than these two series, but ample statistical evidence has been developed over the years that supports the same relationship.[3]

Although this relationship is now reasonably well accepted, some remaining issues in my judgment are not as well understood as they might be. First, the extent to which changes in the exchange rate are translated into changes in relative prices in trading countries is not widely recognized. There can, of course, be changes in the prices of traded commodities before there are changes in the trade flows. For goods with a high degree of price flexibility, that would be the expected case.

Second, a change in the value of U.S. currency has an effect in other trading countries as well, so long as the United States is a sufficiently large exporter to affect world prices. A rise in the value of the U.S. dollar not only lowers the domestic prices of our agricultural exports, it also raises them in

FIGURE 1
Exchange Value of the Dollar and U.S. Agricultural Exports, 1967–1984

SOURCE: Exchange rate data from the Federal Reserve Board; export data from the U.S. Department of Commerce.

other countries. This rise in the price in the international market not only chokes off import demand for countries that let the world price be reflected domestically, it also increases the supply in other countries. Hence, both blades of the scissors cut, and the effect on our own exports can be large.

These effects are exacerbated when our domestic commodity programs limit the amount of price change that is possible here at home. When the rise in the value of the dollar causes the domestic prices of our export commodities to decline to the loan price, it can go no further. Consequently, further rises in the value of the dollar are reflected only in higher prices of our exports abroad. That has been a major problem in the 1980s, as Longmire and Morey have noted.[4] Our exports declined rapidly, and to sustain the loan price, ever larger quantities of output have to be moved into stocks, within the Farmer Owned Reserve or as direct acquisition by the Commodity Credit Corporation. This is what made the payment-in-kind (PIK) program necessary.

Another neglected aspect of exchange rate realignments is what I choose to call third-country effects.[5] These are in large part a consequence of the prevailing system being one of bloc-floating and not individual country floating. In other words, a large number of countries (especially less-developed countries) tie the value of their currency to the value of the dollar; others tie their currency to the British pound sterling, and still others to the French franc. Consequently, when the value of the dollar changes relative to the value of the French franc, for instance, it is not just the trade between the two countries that is affected. When the value of the dollar rises, the value of the currencies of all countries tied to the value of the dollar also change vis-à-vis the other blocs. This can have very important trade effects. Moreover, it explains why approximately 85 percent of international trade takes place across flexible exchange rates, even though the predominant *number* of countries have their currency fixed relative to the currency of one country or another.

It is precisely these third-country effects that exacerbated the international debt crisis when the value of the U.S. dollar rose so dramatically in the early 1980s. It was not by chance that the most serious crises were with Latin American countries—countries that tied their currencies to the dollar. Even countries such as Brazil, which used the exchange rate policy of the crawling peg, were using principles of purchasing power parity to fix the value of the cruzeiro relative to the dollar in real terms. Consequently, these countries saw their export performance relative to other countries decline as the value of the dollar rose. Moreover, they were not able to capitalize on the rise in the value of the dollar in their own trade with the United States because the value of their currency was pegged to the dollar.

It is important to recognize that even if these countries had floated their currencies rather than pegging them to the dollar, they would still have experienced significant shocks to their economies. Imports of raw materials and capital goods from the United States would have become more expensive, thus disrupting development programs, and a shift of resources into the export sector would have been required. Such adjustments are not costless.

The final point that appears to be insufficiently understood about exchange rate issues is the extent to which the value of the dollar and of other currencies is being dominated by the international capital market, and not by the trade account. The total amount of credit outstanding at the beginning of the 1980s was approximately $1.7 trillion, an amount commensurate with the total amount of international trade. Moreover, it is in the capital market where large shifts are occurring, not in the trade accounts.

This particular problem is reflected in the frequent comment in the U.S. press and elsewhere that the dollar should soon fall because the U.S. trade deficit is burgeoning. Such a statement in the 1950s would have been correct, but after the emergence of the international capital market in the 1960s and 1970s, it misses the main component of the foreign exchange markets. The point, of course, is that we have a large trade deficit because the dollar is strong, and the dollar is strong because there is a large capital inflow into the United States. Capital inflow can be offset only if the United States runs a large trade deficit. One is the obverse of the other. Under present circumstances, it is the capital market that is driving things, not the trade account.

In the final part of this section, I will discuss why the dollar is so strong. Probably no issue is more important to U.S. agriculture than this. The enormous rise in the value of the dollar since 1980—approximately 70 percent in nominal terms—has imposed an enormous shock on U.S. agriculture and literally swamped the effects of domestic commodity programs. The inability of the commodity programs to deal with the consequences of this large monetary disturbance is probably no better reflected than in the withdrawal of some 70 million acres of land from production in 1983 and the exhorbitant costs of commodity programs that year.

The question is, what caused the value of the dollar to rise so much, and what, if anything, can be done about it? In my judgment there is no single cause of the "problem"[6] and hence no single policy measure that will help turn it around. Still, those concerned about the welfare of U.S. agriculture have a vital interest in changing the present situation and in creating a more competitive environment for agricultural exports. The desired changes will also be in the best interests of the nation as a whole, for the effects of the factors causing the strong dollar and the strong dollar itself go far beyond agriculture.

The major factor behind the rise in the value of the dollar is the net inflow of capital into this country, now at an annual rate of approximately $130 billion. If this rate continues into the near future—and there is little reason to expect it not to—the United States will become a net debtor about June 1985. If it continues beyond that critical point, the United States will be the world's largest net debtor country by the end of 1985.

This capital inflow is motivated by interest rates that in real terms are unprecedentedly high. Longer-term real rates of interest are approximately 8-10 percent, despite the recent decline in nominal rates of interest. The decline in nominal rates has been offset by a decline in domestic price inflation, which helps to sustain the real value of the interest rate.

Why are interest rates so high? Among the most important reasons is the large deficit on the federal budget, especially in light of prevailing monetary policy. In 1979 the Federal Reserve decided it would no longer monetize the deficit on the federal budget. Once that decision was made, interest rates had to increase to a level that would induce the savings necessary to finance that debt. This factor alone has resulted in very high interest rates and played a significant role in causing the value of the dollar to be so strong. In effect, the United States is borrowing from abroad to finance its budget deficit.

In addition, this nation is a notoriously low-saving country. A higher savings rate would engender a larger flow of savings, and interest rates would not have to go so high to attract the required amount of funds to finance the deficit and other investments.

This low savings rate may create a situation in which strong exports in one sector, such as petroleum or minerals, give rise to a strong currency, thus making it difficult for other sectors to compete either with exports or with imports. Australia has long had periodic difficulties with this problem when there have been mineral booms.[7] In the United States, however, a strong currency might exist even if the budget were balanced, unless savings were sufficient to satisfy investment demands at interest rates comparable to those in other countries.

A high marginal productivity of capital in the United States may also be contributing to the strong dollar. The rapid recovery of the U.S. economy while the rest of the world lags behind adds credence to that argument, but the fact that the United States is drawing capital away from the rest of the world makes it difficult to know which is cause and which is effect. Proponents of the high productivity view argue that deregulation started by the previous administration has made our economy much more productive, thus creating a strong demand for loan funds.

The computer and communication revolutions also are creating a strong demand for investment funds from the private sector, as are developments in other high technology industries. My own judgment is that high productivity plays an important part in our recent high interest rates but is not the major factor. In other words, high productivity may account for a rise in the real interest rate from the long-term rate of 2 percent, which has prevailed in the past, to something like 4 percent, but certainly not anything like 8 percent.

Closely related, of course, is the frequently heard safe-haven argument. This theory is that political instability and economic uncertainty in other countries causes capital naturally to shift into dollar assets as a safe haven, thus bidding up the value of the dollar.

I believe this issue is overdone. The real attraction of capital funds from other countries is the higher rates of return in the United States. Those who want to make the safe-haven argument should recall that in the latter half of the 1970s the dollar was literally in a free fall. The United States was not such a safe haven at that time.

One of the more neglected explanations of both the previous fall and the recent rise in the value of the dollar is the enormous disturbances in the international petroleum industry. It is again difficult to disentangle cause from effect on this issue,[8] but it is clear that U.S. energy policy has played a major role in the events of the last decade. Implicit import subsidies, for example, created by our failure to let domestic prices rise to international (border price) levels obviously helped sustain the cartel. Burgeoning international prices, together with the U.S. import subsidy, made U.S. petroleum imports escalate rapidly, contributing to a weak dollar in the 1970s.

One of the first things President Reagan did upon coming into office in 1981 was to deregulate the domestic petroleum industry. This caused domestic prices to rise, leading to strong conservation measures, increases in domestic supplies, pressure on the cartel, and a large decline in U.S. import bill. This decline helped strengthen the dollar.

Given the institutional arrangements in the petroleum industry, a rise in the value of the dollar has more than a direct effect in the foreign exchange markets. Other countries pay for petroleum in dollars. The rise in the value of the dollar imposes severe foreign exchange demands on petroleum importers since their petroleum bill grows in terms of their domestic currency. This causes their currency to weaken even further.

The analysis so far has focused on the effects on the trade account. Developments in the petroleum industry caused large transfer problems, which affect the capital market. Perhaps the best way to recognize this is to recall the problems of the petrodollars at the peak of the petroleum boom. National governments and international agencies were calling on the commercial banks to recycle those petrodollars to keep the international economy from collapsing. This they did—to a fault. The international debt crisis of recent years has been the result.

Despite the contribution of the above items to the recent strength in the value of the dollar, I believe there is still a more important factor—the present international monetary arrangements and the role of the U.S. dollar in that system. The international economy is experiencing a liquidity crisis of a rather high order, revealed in the rapid growth in barter and counter-trade. The system does not have sufficient liquidity to finance the growth in trade and financial operations, and traders have to resort to barter.

The significance of the liquidity crisis to the U.S. dollar is that the international economy is essentially on a dollar standard.[9] U.S. monetary policy has created a severe scarcity of dollars as the Federal Reserve has attempted to squeeze inflation out of the U.S. system and, given the prevailing international monetary system, out of the international economy. At the same time, the United States and the other industrialized countries have starved the International Monetary Fund (IMF) for resources, thus giving an even greater role to the dollar.

A similar situation existed in the early post–World War II period. Because we were on the fixed exchange rate system of Bretton Woods at that time, the monetary conditions were reflected as a dollar shortage. Currently, however, with a flexible exchange rate system, the dollar is strong and rapidly rising.

The problem, in my view, is that the United States is managing its money supply and monetary policy on domestic considerations alone, yet the country is, in effect, the central banker for the world. It should be managing its money supply and monetary policy on conditions in the international economy. If the United States were to do so, it would be better for agriculture, for our smokestack industries, and for the international economy as a whole.

This misguided policy of the United States is creating serious problems for our trade sector (both export- and import-competing) and for the international economy. U.S. policies could hardly be more self-centered, nor impose a larger burden on the rest of the world. We create a situation of very high interest rates that raises the debt burden of other countries, then decline to provide the IMF with adequate funding. The high interest rates create a strong dollar, causing other countries to pay more in domestic resources to service and repay their debt. The United States is running a large fiscal deficit to offset the deleterious effects of the tight monetary policy on the U.S. economy. To add insult to injury, we piously lecture other governments on their mismanagement of their economies! The marvel of this is that other countries let us get by with it. It would be difficult to imagine a more effective set of policies for exploiting the international economy, especially if one is indifferent to the problems of agriculture and other trade sectors.

It is true, of course, that the strong dollar provides a strong stimulus to the export sectors of other countries, from which many of them have benefited. It takes time, however, for other countries to shift resources into their export sectors. Moreover, if their flow of exports becomes too large, the United States can always restrict the imports by tariffs or other means.

My main point is not to argue for other countries but to argue for the United States. These policies are not in *our* best interests. Agriculture and other trade sectors have certainly paid a high price; but if the debtor nations are stretched so thin that they renounce their debt and send our banking and financial system into collapse, the United States will have paid a very high price indeed for its policies.

The United States is rapidly getting into a situation in which it will either impose another large monetary convulsion on the international economy or place itself in a position of policy paralysis.

Consider the present situation. If we remain on our present course, by the end of 1985 the United States will be the world's largest debtor nation. As our domestic deficit continues to grow, so will our foreign debt. Once we become a net debtor country, we have to service that debt. For a while we might be able to do as the Brazilians did and borrow more to pay our interest bill. But that cannot go on for long. At some point we will need to run a trade surplus to service the foreign debt, which will require a dramatic fall in the value of the dollar.

The mechanism by which that will come about is not hard to imagine: a flight from dollar assets or a reversal of the capital flow. We then need to think about the consequences of a net outflow of, say, $130 billion a year on our capital markets, in contrast to the present inflow of that amount. Even higher real rates of interest will be the likely result, until we have choked off the economy to reduce the demand for investment funds. Since the consequence of a rise in the value of the dollar will be an increase in the rate of domestic inflation, the Federal Reserve will likely exacerbate the problem by pursuing even more restrictive monetary policies. Although agriculture would do well from a falling dollar, the loss in real income to the rest of the economy, and the possible economic wreckage from high interest rates, could be quite large.

As central banker for the world, the United States has one course of action not open to other countries. It can always inflate its way out over the top, repaying the debt with cheaper dollars. Such action would lead to a significant decline in the value of the dollar and another export boom for agriculture.

I would like to make three points in closing this section. First, the chances are quite good that in the not too distant future the dollar will decline—and decline significantly. This decline will improve the export performance of agriculture and the welfare of farmers. Second, whether the United States imposes another large recession on its domestic and on the international economies or inflates itself out over the top, the country will be imposing another large monetary disturbance and significant realignment in currency values on the international economy. Finally, we desperately need to recognize that we can no longer manage either our agricultural sector or the economy as a whole on premises of a closed economy. Doing so has already created a great deal of mischief for ourselves and others.

International Trade Developments

In addition to the significant developments in the international monetary arena, which have the potential for a great deal of economic change and uncertainty, there are also significant developments in trade. We are already witnessing shifts in competitive and comparative advantages on the international scene. In my judgment, we are likely to see further changes on an unprecedented scale. In this section, I will highlight a few of these.

The European Community. Two years ago, there was a great deal of economic pressure on the European Community (EC) to modify its agricultural policies. The costs of export subsidies to dispose of accumulating stocks abroad were about to break the budget. Today, that pressure has diminished significantly. The combination of rigid U.S. price supports and the dramatic rise in the value of the dollar has brought U.S. and world prices almost to the border price of the community. Consequently, the need for export restitutions has declined, and the pressure has been taken off the budget.

If the United States puts more flexibility into its support levels, and the dollar declines as I expect, we could put considerable pressure on the EC to change its policies. It will undoubtedly take economic pressures of this kind, and not the exhortations of the past, to bring about reform of EC policies. I expect these reforms to come about in the future, but only gradually.

The United States gives far more attention to the EC than it deserves in terms of trade potential. There would probably be some modest gains from trade liberalization on the part of the EC, but liberalization would probably have a greater effect on the composition of U.S. trade than on the total amount. U.S. exports of soybeans would probably decline and exports of feed grains increase.

The Centrally Planned Economies. China and the Soviet Union are the key countries, although possible developments in Eastern Europe are not insignificant. The rapid liberalization of the Chinese economy is perhaps the most significant single development among these countries. Liberalization of the system has led to significant increases in agricultural output. This has caused a decline in imports of wheat and the surprising emergence of China as an exporter of corn.

China is realizing cheap, once-for-all gains as it moves from a highly distorted agricultural sector to one that is more rationally organized. Once the once-for-all gains are realized, the output path will probably resume its previous direction. It is not an easy task to say what these developments mean for the long term. My own judgment is that a continuation of the present liberal policies will result in a sustained increase in per capita income and that this in turn will lead to a significant upgrading in diet. That upgrading could lead to needs for imports of feed grains, from which the United States could benefit.

Significant changes in the agriculture of the Soviet Union are unlikely in the near future.[10] Stagnant production is as much an organizational problem as a weather problem, and there is little reason to expect a major reform of the system. The Soviet Union has been investing heavily in its agricultural sector, but to little avail. Consequently, exports are likely to continue at the level of recent years into the foreseeable future.

The Newly Industrialized Countries. Since the mid-1960s a small group of third world nations has joined the ranks of significant exporters of manufactured products. These countries, which include Hong Kong, Singapore, South Korea, Taiwan, Brazil, Mexico, and sometimes Argentina and India, have been termed "newly industrialized countries" (NICs). Their emergence has changed the relationships not only between the industrialized North and the developing South, but also among countries of the South.[11]

Some of these countries, particularly the smaller ones in Asia, have,

TABLE 1

EXPORTS OF MANUFACTURED GOODS FROM THE LDCs AND NICs, 1965–1980

	Value (billions of current $U.S.)				Percentage of LDCs	
	1965	1975	1979	1980	1965	1979
LDCs	4.6	35.3	82.9	n.a.	100	100
NICs[a]	2.7	22.0	61.1	n.a.	59	74
Hong Kong[b]	1.0	5.6	14.0	18.0	22	17
Singapore	0.3	2.2	6.4	9.0	7	8
South Korea	0.1	4.1	13.4	15.7	2	16
Taiwan	0.2	4.3	14.6[c]	18.0[c]	4	18
Argentina	0.1	0.7	1.7[d]	n.a.	2	2
Brazil	0.1	2.2	5.7	n.a.	2	7
Mexico	0.1	0.9	7.6	1.7	2	2
India	0.8	2.0	3.7[d]	n.a.	17	4

a. Totals sometimes include data for years other than those indicated.
b. Includes reexports.
c. Taiwan became a noncountry in most international statistical series after 1977. Source for subsequent data is Council for Economic Planning and Development, *Taiwan Statistical Data Book* (Republic of China, 1981).
d. 1978 data.
SOURCES: Donald B. Keesing, *World Trade and Output of Manufactures: Structural Trends and Developing Countries' Exports*, World Bank Staff Working Paper No. 316 (Washington, D.C.: World Bank, January 1979); and *U.N. 1980 International Trade Statistics*, vol. 1 (1981).

within a relatively short time, transformed their societies and overcome much of their poverty. Their success has shown that less-developed countries can obtain rapid economic growth, while introducing a great deal of heterogeneity.

Data on the exports of manufactured products from these countries are presented in table 1. From 1965 to 1980 the exports of the six commonly identified NICs grew from $2.7 billion to $65 billion. About 40 percent of U.S. imports of manufactured products now come from these countries. In a short time they have displaced Japan as the source of labor-intensive manufactured products. Perhaps more important, they already are moving up the economic ladder to the manufacture of more capital-intensive products, in the process being followed by a new group of NICs comprising India, China, Malaysia, Sri Lanka, and the Philippines.

The significance of these developments is that they illustrate how comparative advantage and the division of labor is changing on the international scene. Four of these countries are resource-poor Asian countries. They are never likely to have strong agricultural capacity, but they have the capacity to compete with the U.S. manufacturing sector and to increase their per capita incomes and effect significant improvements in their diets. They, and similar countries that follow their development path, thus have the potential to be strong markets for U.S. agricultural exports. The key will be whether the United States will accept imports of manufactured products from these countries.

New Production Technology for Tropical Agriculture. Not many years ago, there was virtually no modern technology for agriculture in the tropical, less-developed countries of the world. U.S. investments in the capacity to produce a steady flow of new production technology for its agriculture thus helped give it a comparative advantage in agricultural products, especially the cereals, and today agriculture is one of the few remaining internationally competitive sectors in the U.S. economy.

The technological edge of the United States is, however, rapidly eroding as the capacity to produce production technology for tropical agriculture is rapidly developing. An important component of that capacity is the emerging system of International Agricultural Research Centers. The beginnings of this system were the International Rice Research Institute and the International Center for Maize and Wheat, established in the late 1960s and the source of the so-called miracle wheats and rice. This system has evolved to include thirteen centers and is supported by the international donor community with an annual budget of approximately $180 million per year.

This system is rapidly coming of age. It is working with national research systems in the less-developed countries and has established worldwide research networks for the major food commodities. Moreover, most of the centers have been established long enough to be producing a flow of new knowledge and technology. Among the new developments are tropical soybeans, improved rice for upland conditions, new soybeans and millets, and improved root crops and tubers. Perhaps more important, many developing countries have taken significant steps to strengthen their own agricultural research capability. Brazil is an outstanding example, as is India.

One of the unknowns in this changing picture is the role new biotechnology will play in the developing countries. It might be the ace-in-the-hole for the industrialized countries such as the United States. By the same token, it appears that much of the technology created by these new methodologies may be highly transferable, thus enabling the developing countries to close the gap with the United States at a rapid rate.

The importance of the growing capacity to produce new technology for tropical agriculture is two-fold. First, it suggests that the United States has no reason to be complacent about its comparative technological advantage or its

67

ability to compete in international commodity markets. Second, the capacity to produce and diffuse new production technology for agriculture is the key to the economic development of most of the developing countries. It provides the basis for rapid, broadbased increases in per capita incomes in these countries, and it is these increases in per capita incomes that ultimately generate markets for U.S. agricultural exports. Hence, these developments are not be be feared, but encouraged and supported.

Changing Economic Policies in the Developing Countries. The developing countries were a major component of the rapidly expanding markets for U.S. agricultural exports during the 1970s. U.S. exports to those countries grew as rapidly as exports to the centrally planned economies, and by the end of the decade they were of the same order of magnitude.

What has not been sufficiently recognized is that the imports of these countries grew so rapidly because of their widespread use of food subsidies and economic policies that discriminate against their agricultural sector. Trade and exchange rate policies have been the main instruments of such discrimination, which directly influence their trade performance. Explicit export taxes, quotas, and embargos have been used to help keep domestic prices of food products low, while high effective protection was provided to the manufacturing sector. As a result, domestic terms of trade shifted severely against agriculture, undervaluing and squeezing resources out of the sector and stimulating the rapid migration of rural populations to urban centers.

Similarly, currencies were consistently overvalued in foreign exchange markets. In fact, this was probably the most widespread form of discrimination against agriculture. An overvalued exchange rate constitutes an implicit export tax for export sectors and an implicit import subsidy for import sectors. Moreover, in many countries, sectors that would otherwise have been net exporters were transformed into net importers. The degree of distortion in the exchange rates was in many cases quite large.

In order to help fix magnitudes, data in table 2 constitute estimates of the subsidy provided to consumers of wheat in Brazil from 1973 through 1982. The subsidy was more than half a billion dollars (in constant value 1977 dollars) in three of the ten years. In one year it was more than a billion dollars, and in two years it was more than three-quarters of a billion dollars. At the same time, despite the existence of large direct subsidies to producers in the form of a price support program, the distortion in the value of the cruzeiro was such that wheat producers experienced a sizable net tax, with that tax taken entirely in the form of a distortion in the relative price of wheat (see table 2). Wheat producers were taxed in seven of the ten years, with the tax being well over $200 in 1974. This combination of a large consumption subsidy and significant export taxes helped make Brazil a major importer of U.S. wheat.

The case of soybeans in Brazil is another important example because

TABLE 2

CONSUMPTION AND PRODUCTION SUBSIDIES, WHEAT SECTOR, BRAZIL,
1973–1982

(millions of 1977 $U.S.)

Year	Consumption Subsidy	Producer Subsidy
1973	375	−91
1974	830	−239
1975	596	−41
1976	670	−58
1977	374	79
1978	499	105
1979	753	−77
1980	1,062	−150
1981	672	−39
1982	464	19

SOURCE: Geraldo Calagan, "Brazilian Wheat Policy and Its Income Distribution and Trade Effects: A Case Study" (Ph.D. diss., University of Minnesota, 1985).

TABLE 3

PRICE DISTORTIONS IN THE SOYBEAN SECTOR, BRAZIL, 1977–1983

(percent)

Years	Nominal Rate of Protection	Effective Rate of Protection
1977–1978	−42	−53
1978–1979	−37	−44
1979–1980	−41	−38
1980–1981	−39	−40
1981–1982	−26	−26
1982–1983	−18	24

NOTE: Both estimates of protection take account of distortions in the exchange rate.

SOURCE: Carlos Santana, "The Impact of Economic Policies on the Soybean Sector of Brazil: An Effective Protection Analysis (Ph.D. diss., University of Minnesota, 1985).

Brazil became a major competitor of the United States in the international soybean market in the 1970s. Moreover, the United States has repeatedly accused Brazil of using subsidies for its exports of soybean meal.

Carlos Santana has made a careful estimate of the nominal and effective

69

protection provided the Brazilian soybean industry. Some of the results, which take account of the distortion in the exchange rate, are provided in table 3. These data show that rather than being protected or subsidized, the Brazilian soybean sector was severely taxed throughout the period considered. Moreover, the taxation was large.

The nominal rate of protection shows how much domestic prices were distorted below international border prices evaluated at an estimated shadow price of foreign exchange. In four of the six years this distortion was over 35 percent.

The effective rate of protection takes account of the fact that an overvalued cruzeiro provided subsidies for modern imports such as fertilizers and also takes account of the sizable subsidy provided by cheap credit policies. Despite taking account of these important forms of subsidy, the taxation or discrimination was still large. In fact, in some years it was even larger than the nominal protection because of direct domestic taxes. Only in the 1982–83 crop year was the relationship reversed, and that was because the credit subsidy grew out of control because of a rapid increase in the rate of domestic inflation.

By far the major source of this distortion or taxation was due to the distortion in the exchange rate. This distortion directly affects Brazil's ability to compete in international trade. Despite this discrimination, Brazil became an ever stronger competitor of the United States.

Examples of such subsidies to food consumption and such discrimination against agricultural producers are widespread. Mexico's discrimination against its corn and wheat sectors throughout the 1970s and into the early 1980s played a major role in that country being a major importer of U.S. feed grains and wheat.[12] Egypt has provided huge consumption subsidies for food, while discriminating against its producer sector.[13] The evidence on other countries is rapidly accumulating.[14]

The important point for U.S. producers and for U.S. agricultural and trade policies is that the developing countries are changing their policies. The motivation for these changes is twofold. First, the outward-looking, export-based policies that have contributed so much to the success of the NICs is being widely emulated. Second, the international debt crisis that has dominated the news so much these past three years is having a salutary effect on trade and exchange rate policies in many of these countries. Some of the changes are induced by conditions enforced by the IMF and the World Bank. In addition, many countries are recognizing that they have little alternative but to improve their overall economic and export performance.

The significance of the debt problem as a source of weakened capacity to import has been recognized by many observers. The effect of the crisis is inducing more rational trade and exchange rate policies has received less attention. The latter may be by far the more important development over the longer term.

Two examples close to home provide ready examples. Brazil and Mexico have both undertaken massive realignments in the real values of their currencies over the past two years. In fact, until recently the Mexican peso was undervalued instead of overvalued, and the Brazilian cruzeiro is now undervalued by a significant amount. That means that the exchange rate is now an export subsidy and no longer an export tax. If Brazil makes this realignment stick and does not impose other forms of export restrictions, it may well take away the U.S. soybean market. It has developed new improved varieties, is working to introduce the new tropical soybean, and obviously has an enormous latent production capacity.

How one views these developments is again a rather mixed bag. The elimination of restrictions against exports and the removal of the discrimination against agriculture will make many of the less-developed countries more competitive in international markets. At the same time, this rationalization of economic policy will further strengthen the broadbased economic development already being engendered by technological advances. The net effect on demand, especially for feed grains and livestock products, may far outpace the capacity of agriculture to respond in many countries. Hence, the net effect on trade may well be positive, even though certain sectors in U.S. agriculture, such as soybeans, may well face serious adjustment problems. The important point is that both comparative and competitive advantages are undergoing rapid change on the international scene.

Emergence of a New Protectionism. One of the most significant developments on the international scene this past decade is the emergence of new forms of protectionism.[15] Much attention has been given to the growing use of nontariff barriers[16] and export subsidies. Perhaps, however, the more important developments are much more subtle. These include the growing use of selective protection that focuses on one country (usually Japan) or a group of countries (the NICs), of cartel-like arrangements that divide up the market (voluntary export agreements on automobiles, the textile agreements, the steel agreement), and of domestic subsidies as a trade distortion.

These developments also have diverse implications. On the one hand, they have been beneficial in that they have provided limited protection in lieu of a complete closing of the borders. On the other hand, perhaps their most damaging aspect is that they have eroded the principle of equal treatment, which has characterized trade arrangements in the post–World War II period and which has been the basis of a great deal of trade liberalization.

Summary. The environment for international trade is undergoing far-reaching and profound changes. International comparative and competitive advantages are rapidly changing, with significant changes in the international division of labor. The basis for strong competitive pressures in agricultural trade from other countries is strengthening rapidly. At the same time, so is the basis for rapid economic development in the less-developed countries, the part of the world where the greatest potential for U.S. agricultural markets lies. U.S. agricultural commodity and trade policies must enable the United States to remain competitive and to compete over the longer term.

Policies to Strengthen the Export Performance of U.S. Agriculture

U.S. policies have themselves become a barrier to improved trade perform-ance. These policies need to change if we are to have a vigorous agriculture and a reduced government role in the sector. It is a mistake to think, however, that our domestic commodity programs and our agricultural trade policies are the only issue. The United States needs to give more attention to reforming international trade and monetary arrangements and to the development of third world countries. We need to do these things not out of any sense of benevolence, but because it is in the best interests of the nation and especially of its agriculture.[17]

This review of policies for an improved trade performance is of necessity schematic,[18] but I hope it focuses on the key issues.

Reforming Domestic Commodity Programs. There seems to be little doubt that U.S. domestic commodity programs have become a serious barrier to export performance. The dramatic rise in the value of the dollar translated international prices into the domestic economy at increasingly lower levels. At some point domestic prices settled on the loan rate. From that point on, as the dollar rose even further, our domestic prices were translated into the value of foreign currencies at increasingly higher levels. This not only reduced the demand for our exports, it provided strong incentives for producers in other countries to increase their production.[19] Moreover, our support programs pro-vided an umbrella over the market so that exporters in other countries could undersell us. It would be difficult to find a better means of shooting oneself in the foot!

U.S. stocks programs then accumulated the unmarketable domestic sup-plies, and U.S. reserves grew out of control. The result was the costly PIK program, which resulted in the idling of approximately 70 million acres of this nation's agricultural land.

If the U.S. is to remain competitive internationally in the face of a strong dollar, and to avoid major intervention in the agricultural sector and the forced idling of large blocks of its rich agricultural land, it will have to devise commodity programs that are more sensitive to economic focus. That means more flexibility in both the loan and target prices.

Getting such flexibility need not mean the abandonment of present commodity programs. In fact, present programs are a means to provide subsidies to agriculture in a fashion consistent with making most efficient use of the nation's resources. Other sectors of the economy, and especially the manufacturing sector, are to some extent protected from international economic forces. (The current tariff protection of the manufacturing sector is about 5 percent,[20] and the new forms of protection may provide about another 5 percent.) To make most efficient use of the nation's resources, it is standard proposition of economics that equal protection should be provided to all sectors.

The optimal form of such protection to an export sector is an export subsidy in the form of a deficiency payment to producers, with the subsidy equal to the protection provided to other sectors. Interestingly enough, the United States was using such a subsidy for the wheat sector until the dollar became so strong as to cancel its effects. The target price for wheat was set above the market-clearing price, thus inducing an expansion of output, lower prices in the domestic market, and an implicit export subsidy. The loan level, however, provided a floor under the market, and when the dollar continued to rise the effect of the subsidy was lost.

Adjusting the programs to provide such an ideal subsidy would require a significant adjustment in present loan and target price levels. Consider the case of wheat. There is some consensus that market-clearing prices would be about $3.30 per bushel. If the protection to be matched is 10 percent, as suggested above, then the target price should be about $3.65 per bushel. If the export subsidy is to take effect, then the loan level should be below what otherwise would be the market-clearing level. At 10 percent below the market-clearing level, for example, or at $3.00 per bushel, the loan level should be $3.00 and the target price $3.65. Both of these are obviously below present levels. Moreover, if there are other taxes or subsidies, these should be taken into account in fixing the levels.

It should be noted this is not an argument for equity or income distribution. Instead, it is the policy that will cause the nation to make most efficient use of its resources. Because of that, there should be no cap on the deficiency payments. Such a cap is justified now primarily on equity grounds, although budget considerations are starting to creep in.

I find that many students of U.S. agricultural policy are horrified at this suggestion and believe it takes us away from market-oriented principles. That just is not the case, however. In fact, the prescription is designed to move toward a more rational use of the nation's resources, not away from it. A more serious criticism is that we compromise our principles in advocating free trade. As I will note in a later section of this paper, however, we did that long ago, and to argue to the contrary is to lack credibility.

The EC will not like such policies because they will increase the burden of its export subsidies. That is, however, precisely what we should want to do. Moreover, the EC is hardly in a position to criticize others for using trade distortions.

There is one final point. If the foreign import demand for U.S. exports is as large as I believe it to be, the total demand elasticity from major exports is greater than one. Hence, such a policy will increase total revenue to those respective sectors. It is time we began to take this point into consideration when setting our price policy as well.

U.S. Trade Policies. U.S. trade policies need significant changes if we are to develop a more rational policy for agriculture and have a satisfactory export performance. Rhetoric notwithstanding, the United States is rather protectionist of its agriculture. Domestic sugar prices are protected at about 21 cents per pound when the world price is about 5 cents. Tariffs protect the dairy sector with prices above those of the EC. The livestock (beef) sector is protected with what amounts to a variable levy.

Moreover, United States has insisted on a waiver from the General Agreement on Tariffs and Trade (GATT) to use tariff measures to protect domestic commodity programs. It surely must have a hollow ring to the EC when we threaten to take them to the GATT for using the very interventions we insist we have a right to use.

Surely it is time we phased out our protection of the domestic sugar industry. The growing use of high-fructose corn sweeteners is making any remaining protection a hollow victory. These artificial sweeteners have already cut into the use of domestic sugar cane and beets by 40 percent. Now, Pepsi Cola and Coca Cola have announced that henceforth they will use 100 percent high-fructose corn sweeteners in their soft drink formulations. Some analysts anticipate that up to 600,000 metric tons of sugar will be displaced by this one decision.[21]

The sugar industry is rapidly following the route of the tobacco producers—self-destruction. The protection for them is ultimately a protection for their strongest competitors. There is no way to win the game, but U.S. consumers in the interim pay a very high price.

Similarly, it is not clear how much longer this nation can afford the continued protection of the dairy industry. A more sensible policy would appear to be to negotiate with the EC and Canada a mutual reduction in protection, stretched out over a period of years. The United States would undoubtedly retain a viable dairy industry, especially if it were to deregulate the domestic industry so as to take advantage of available technology.

As a nation we need to develop a greater sense of trade-offs on our trade issues. This is as true of our agricultural trade policies as it is of our nonagricultural trade policies. U.S. sugar policy, for example, works a significant hardship on many less-developed countries that have a comparative advantage in that sector. If we were to provide expanded markets for that product, they might well provide expanded markets for our exports. Moreover, we probably would not need such programs as the Caribbean Initiative. The same applies to dairy and beef.

There are similar issues on the side of trade in manufactured products. We desperately need to recognize that trade is a two-way street and to stop the folly of sectoral negotiations. If we expect China and other developing countries to be the growing market for us that they can be, we will have to accept their exports of labor-intensive manufactured products. Moreover, we ought to do a great deal more horse trading on trade issues, making concessions on our side in exchange for concessions on the other side. Such an approach has a great deal of merit with the developing countries.

Adjustment Policies. If the United States is to benefit from the international economy of which it is now such an important part, it must develop and use more effective adjustment policies. The present problems of agriculture are the result of overcommitments of resources and inflated asset values that resulted from bad policies in the 1970s. The export boom (motivated by a weak dollar), the Malthusian rhetoric, and large negative real rates of interest in the late 1970s not only induced a net flow of resources into agriculture for the first time in fifty years, but also resulted in highly inflated land values. The disinflation that has followed in the 1980s, the collapse of the export boom, and the shift to unprecedentedly high real rates of interest have created an enormous adjustment problem, exacerbated by the collapse of the land market.

Unfortunately, the commodity programs have not been changed to reflect the changed conditions. Instead, they continue to send signals to producers for a market that does not exist. Moreover, the costly PIK program did not bring us one iota of longer-term adjustment. It would have been much more sensible to have used the $28 billion of program costs in 1983 for adjustment policies that would have helped get the problem behind us. It is long past time that we develop and use policies to that end.

International Monetary Reform. In my judgment, reforming our international monetary arrangements ought to be our highest priority. The deficiencies in this system are the source of most of our present problems. The main source of shocks to international commodity markets has been monetary disturbances, not weather disturbances.

There are two routes that we can go. First, the United States could strengthen the IMF so as to give it many of the attributes of an international central bank and phase out its role as central banker for the world. Second, we could accept our role as central banker for the world and manage our monetary policy accordingly, so as to provide ample liquidity for expansion of trade and finance. At present, we fail to manage our monetary policy so as to recognize our international responsibilities, while resisting any attempts to give the IMF either the resources or the autonomy it needs.

My preference is to reform the international system and provide the IMF with the resources it needs. It is no longer in our best interests to serve as central banker for the world, for the costs to our economy are too great and far outweigh any seigniorage gains.

The needed reforms of the system are fairly simple, First, the Special Drawing Right (SDR) needs to be revitalized so it serves as a respectable reserve asset. This can be done by giving it a market-determined rate of interest so national governments would want to hold it. The IMF should be given the right to issue SDRs as they are needed and, more specifically, to increase their number at a constant rate commensurate with the expected growth of international trade and finance.

Such a reform would see the dollar gradually phase out over time and the SDR gradually become more important. All countries could retain their domestic currency, but the United States would be free to manage its monetary policy according to the dictates of its domestic economy. The rest of the world, as well as our own exports and import-competing sectors, would be protected from the lurches of U.S. monetary and fiscal policies.

One of the great ironies of our day has been our approach to the IMF. The United States and the other industrial countries have never provided the IMF with the capital resources that were envisaged at the time it was created. The reason for such stringency has been a fear that the Fund would launch into a spree of profligate spending. When the surge of petrodollars came upon us, however, the commercial banking system launched into a lending spree to the developing countries that inflated the system almost out of control, and it did that with no conditions. It would have been much more sensible to have had the resources channeled through the Fund with its attendant conditions.

Reforming the International Trading System. The needs of highest priority are to broaden the sectoral coverage to include agriculture and the service sector and to broaden the coverage of trade interventions. The GATT has focused primarily on tariffs and on the manufacturing sector. These are now only a small portion of the trade instruments used, and trade in agriculture and services is growing rapidly. A broader set of codes is badly needed.

Strengthening Our Technological Base. The U.S. agricultural research system has come under increasing criticism and attacks in recent years.[22] The irony of this could not be greater. Productivity growth in the sector has outpaced that in almost all other sectors of the economy, and from a trade standpoint, agriculture is almost the only world-class industry the United States now has.

It is vital that we sustain and strengthen the capacity to produce a flow of new production technology for agriculture. Perhaps the greatest change that is needed is in the financing of agricultural research. Over the years a larger and larger share of the financial support has come from state governments, with federal support having stagnated for some time. Many of the benefits of agricultural research are now reflected in improved foreign exchange earnings. Those are national benefits that affect the economy as a whole. Hence, the case for stronger federal support is even greater.

In addition, the priorities for agricultural research need to reflect our international setting. They do not at this time adequately reflect those considerations.

Concluding Comments

I want to conclude by reiterating a point that I made earlier in my paper. U.S. agriculture is now an integral part of the international economy. The design of agricultural policies needs to reflect that change in economic setting. The economics of agriculture in an open, trading economy is vastly different from that of the closed economy we had in the past. In addition, a well-integrated international capital market is an important component of the new system. It offers important opportunities while imposing both shocks and constraints to domestic policies.

I have no doubt that U.S. agriculture can compete in the international economy. To do so, however, it will have to abandon and modify the policies of the past and to devise new ones consistent with its new economic setting.

Notes

1. G. Edward Schuh, "U.S. Agricultural Policy in an Open World Economy," testimony presented before the Joint Economic Committee, U.S. Congress, May 26, 1983.

2. See, for example, G. Edward Schuh, "Third Country Marketing Distortions in a Changed International Economy: The Case of Brazil and Mexico" (paper prepared for the 75th American Colloquium of the Harvard Business School, April 8–11, 1984).

3. For a review and evaluation of this literature, see David Orden, "Exchange Rate and Agricultural Commodity Markets: A General Equilibrium Perspective" (Department of Agricultural Economics, Virginia Polytechnic Institute, July 1984, mimeographed).

4. Jim Longmire and Art Morey, *Strong Dollar Dampens Demand for U.S. Farm Exports*, Foreign Agricultural Economic Report Number 193, ERS-USDA, Washington, D.C., December 1983.

5. See Schuh, "Third Country Marketing Distortions."

6. I put "problem" in quotation marks because it has become common to refer to it

in this way, despite the advantage of a strong currency is for the economy as a whole.

7. See, for example, R.G. Gregory, "Some Implications of Growth of the Mineral Sector," *Australian Journal of Agricultural Economics*, vol. 20, no. 2 (August 1976), pp. 71–91.

8. David Orden has made a careful attempt to report the effects of these two factors in the international market for corn. See "Capital Flows, the Exchange Rate, and Agricultural Commodity Markets" (Ph.D. diss., University of Minnesota, St. Paul, 1984).

9. Ronald I. McKinnon, "Currency Substitution and Instability in World Dollar Standard," *American Journal of Agricultural Economics*, vol. 72 (1982), pp. 320–33.

10. For a recent study of Soviet agriculture, see Gale Johnson and Karen McConnel Brooks, *Prospects for Soviet Agriculture in the 1980s* (Bloomington: Indiana University Press, 1983).

11. For an overview, see Neil McMullen, *The Newly Industrialized Countries: Adjusting to Success* (Washington, D.C.: National Planning Association, British-North American Committee, 1982).

12. Jeronimo Ramos S. Pardo, "An Economic Evaluation of Government Intervention in the Mexican Agriculture Sector: The Corn and Wheat Sectors" (Ph.D. diss., University of Minnesota, 1984).

13. Joachim von Braun and Hartwing de Haen, *The Effects of Food Prices and Subsidy Policies on Egyptian Agriculture*, Research Report No. 42 (Washington, D.C., IFPRI, November 1983).

14. See, for example, Malcolm D. Bale and E. Lutz, "Price Distortions in Agriculture and Their Effects: An International Comparison," *American Journal of Agricultural Economics*, vol. 63, no. 1 (February 1981), pp. 8–22.

15. An analysis of these new forms of protectionism can be found in Peter Morici, *The Global Competitive Struggle and Canadian-American Relations* (Washington, D.C.: National Planning Association, 1984).

16. Jimmye Hillman, "Non-Tariff Barriers: New Types of Agricultural Protection" (paper presented at AAEA Macroeconomic Workshop, Cornell University, August 1984).

17. See G. Edward Schuh, *The United States and the Developing Countries: An Economic Perspective* (Paper prepared for the National Planning Association, Washington, D.C., October 1984).

18. For a more comprehensive treatment, see *Policy Options for Developing the Trade Performance of U.S. Agriculture* (Paper prepared for the National Agricultural Forum, Washington, D.C., January 1984).

19. For an empirical analysis, see Jim Longmire and Art Morey, *Strong Dollar Dampens Demand for U.S. Farm Exports*, Foreign Agricultural Economic Report Number 193 (Washington, D.C.: ERS-USDA, December 1983).

20. Personal communication from Peter Morici, National Planning Association.

21. *World Agribusiness Report*, vol. 1, no. 6 (December 1984).

22. For an in-depth discussion of the issues, see Vernon W. Ruttan, "Public Investment in Agricultural Research: How Much Bang for the Buck (Paper presented to Lecture Series on Issues in Agricultural and Life Sciences, University of Wisconsin, December 6, 1984).

Commentary

Eric Monke

Schuh argues that the integration of U.S. agriculture into the international economy, the introduction of flexible exchange rate regimes, and the liberalization of international capital markets require that U.S. agriculture abandon and modify the policies of the past and devise new ones consistent with its new economic setting. Schuh recommends six policy changes: reforming the target price system to provide a uniform degree of export subsidy to all agricultural exports; phasing out the protection of particular agricultural sectors, such as sugar; reforming the international monetary system by expanding the role of the Special Drawing Right (SDR); expanding the coverage of provisions of the General Agreement on Tariffs and Trade (GATT) to include agriculture and service sector industries; strengthening the agricultural technology base through increased federal support of research and development; and introducing adjustment policies to facilitate the transfer of resources from agriculture. My remarks are concentrated on the first three suggestions, and I will argue that these proposals are internally inconsistent or are unlikely to have desirable effects. The latter three reforms are desirable irrespective of agriculture's "new" status in the international economy, and the merits and difficulties in realizing these policy changes have been widely discussed elsewhere.

It is perhaps worth reiterating the argument that the U.S. economy and the agricultural sector are better off with flexible exchange rates and liberal international capital flows than with the alternative environment of fixed exchange rates and immobile capital flows. The problem with fixed exchange rates has been their tendency to engender long-run resource misallocation. Fixed rates that were too low made balance of payments management an overwhelming preoccupation of macroeconomic policy. In most countries, the responses of policy makers to these imbalances involved, first, running down foreign exchange reserves and, second, imposing import restrictions and foreign currency controls. None of the these policies worked in the long-run, and ultimately governments were forced to make large discrete revaluations of their currency, resulting in large readjustment in the relative domestic prices of tradable commodities and nontradable goods. These shocks are eliminated in a flexible exchange rate system. While flexible exchange rates show more fluctuation than fixed rates (by definition), the possibility that increased short-run fluctuations have major implications for long-run resource misallocation

79

has yet to be demonstrated. It seems doubtful that agriculturalists, automobile producers, and television set manufacturers would flee their respective industries for dry cleaning businesses, government service, and other types of nontraded activities just because the price variability of traded goods is increased by flexible exchange rates.

If the U.S. capital market was isolated from that of the rest of the world and if the government continued to finance the deficit by borrowing, interest rates would be higher than they are currently. If Americans have "notoriously" low propensities to save, as Schuh suggests, interest rates could be much higher than they are now. Capital is a prominent input in American agriculture, and working capital costs, fixed capital equipment costs, and land debt servicing would all be directly affected by increases in interest rates. In short, agricultural producers are unlikely to find larger profit margins with alternative balance of payments policies. Higher input costs from increased interest rates could more than offset the gains from dollar-denominated output prices that would be higher because foreign capital was no longer flowing into the economy.[1]

If the current system is better than the alternatives, what is the role for agricultural policy? Schuh suggests a "second-best" efficiency argument that all export industries should receive a subsidy equal to the average level of protection provided currently to import-competing industries (estimated at 10 percent). For some agricultural commodities, the target price system could be reformed to reflect this subsidy by setting target prices 10 percent above market-clearing prices. For export crops outside the traditional programs, export subsidies would have to be introduced. Import-competing agricultural industries would also receive protection. Rather than dismantling protection policies for agriculture, as Schuh suggests, realization of the second-best optimum would require expanded protection for some import-competing agricultural commodities and at most a reduction in the level of protection given to currently protected agricultural commodities (sugar, beef, and dairy products).

Serious problems arise with this approach. First, flexible exchange rates will operate to nullify some of the protective effect of a subsidy *cum* tariff policy. To see this result, assume that import tariffs are extended to previously unprotected commodities and provide a uniform protective level of 10 percent to domestic value-added. The value of aggregate imports will decline from current levels. The introduction of a 10 percent rate of subsidization to export industries will cause exports to increase. The trade balance (imports minus exports, or $M-X$) increases. Capital account balances are unaffected, as international capital flows are dictated by cross-country differentials in real interest rates. Because the balance on the capital account must offset the trade balance, the exchange rate must appreciate. Imports expand and exports decline until balance of payments is restored. The appreciation-induced decline in $(M-X)$ must exactly offset the initial increase in $(M-X)$. Dollar-denominated prices of tradable commodities must decline, as does the magnitude of domestic value-added.

Thus the gains from the initial level of protection have been spread across industries, because previously unprotected industries have altered their prices relative to the initially protected industries. Newly protected industries will be better off with the subsidy *cum* tariff policy, but previously protected import industries will experience a profits squeeze. If these industries lobby for increased protection, however, the exchange rate will adjust to neutralize fully all effects of changes in the subsidy/tariff rate. Given the balance in the capital account, the value of $(M-X)$ cannot change. Exports cannot increase, and imports cannot decline. Attempts to expand tradable goods industries with subsidies and tariffs must be completely offset by appreciation in the exchange rate.[2]

The apparent fixity of the level of protection under subsidy *cum* tariff policies raises a set of political economy problems with second-best policies.[3] The experience of the postwar economy suggests that protection is variable rather than fixed, and protective rates appear amenable to changes in economic conditions and concerted negotiation. The agricultural sector may have more to gain by lobbying for the elimination of current protection provided to manufacturing rather than an expansion of protection for agriculture. For the economy as a whole, there is little doubt as to the superiority of a free trade posture.[4] Further, the extension of tariffs and subsidies to previously unprotected industries is certain to encourage protectionist responses among trading partners, and economic outcomes under retaliation could be decidedly inferior to present conditions.

A second policy reform suggested by Schuh comprises revitalization of the SDR to replace the dollar as the standard international currency. Schuh states that in this event, "the United States would be free to manage its monetary policy according to dictates of its domestic economy. The rest of the world, as well as our own exports and import-competing sectors, would be protected from the lurches of U.S. monetary and fiscal policies." This assertion is false. Replacement of the dollar as an international currency would have a once-and-for-all effect on the U.S. exchange rate. Foreigners would dishoard dollars from their asset portfolios because dollars would no longer have value as a transaction medium, but domestic macropolicies would still create fluctuations in the U.S. exchange rate. A fiscal deficit financed by borrowing, for example, would still require increases in domestic interest rates, would still encourage foreign capital inflows, and would still result in appreciation of the dollar relative to other currencies (including the SDR).

What are the policy implications of agriculture's integration into the international economy? The new international environment for agriculture has introduced additional sources of price variability to international markets. The

81

appropriate policy response has, however, nothing to do with making price supports more flexible or more responsive to exchange rate changes. It involves instead the encouragement of institutions that can help stabilize farm incomes in an unstable price environment, such as futures markets and insurance programs. Options markets may be particularly significant in this context, as they allow farmers to share both price risk and the returns that may accrue to risk bearing. A second effect of the new international environment is to place agricultural interest groups squarely behind efforts to reduce the federal deficit. As Schuh points out, deficit growth is probably the most important factor behind current high real interest rates and high exchange rates. Agricultural commodity groups, along with all other producers of tradable goods, have a clear incentive to convince the government that the magnitude of resource transfer implied by current fiscal policy—from tradable goods industries to federally financed industries, and from future consumers to current consumers—is not in the national interest. A final policy implication relates to expected changes in agricultural prices. If prices continue on a downward trend, as D. Gale Johnson argues, then agriculture must continue trying to produce with fewer inputs per unit of output. As Schuh suggests, a continuation of support for research and development remains an essential ingredient in sustaining the long-run viability of U.S. agriculture.

Notes

1. Other options for policy could be imagined. The government might choose to finance the deficit by printing additional money. This policy would create an inflationary spiral. Again, agriculture is not a clear gainer in this environment.

2. A further problem arises when nontraded goods industries are considered. Realization of the second-best position requires that these industries be subsidized as well, in order to maintain the relative price of traded and nontraded goods at its efficiency-maximizing level. This policy implies subsidies for, among others, government civil servants and university professors.

3. I would like to thank Tim Josling and Stephen Tangermann for helpful discussions on this topic.

4. Where optimal tariff arguments apply, the economy may benefit from protection to specific industries.

Farm Financial Stress, Structure of Agriculture, and Public Policy

Luther Tweeten

The economy reads like *A Tale of Two Cities*. For consumers it is the best of times, their record prosperity sustained by massive low-cost imports purchased on credit. For many producers it is the worst of times. A farm debt crisis stalks the land like the fifth horseman of the apocalypse, its poignancy dramatized in newspaper, television, and movie accounts of family farm bankruptcy. The effects of the farm debt crisis extend well beyond the farm. Agribusiness firms are affected, especially banks.[1] Of the thirty-seven banks liquidated in the second half of 1984, eighteen were banks with at least 25 percent of their loan volume to agriculture.

At issue is the extent of current and prospective future farm financial stress, its sources, and the appropriate public policy response. This paper deals with these issues. The conclusion of this paper is that the paradox of consumer prosperity and producer distress is the predictable product of Reaganomics, an economic policy followed against the best advice of the nation's most respected economists.

Farm Financial Situation

The farming industry entered the 1980s in robust financial condition. The late 1970s were good years for farmers. On January 1, 1980, the debt-asset ratio was 16.3 percent for the farming industry, and ranged from 32 percent for large farms to 10 percent for the smallest farms (see table 1). By January 1, 1984, the debt-asset ratio had risen to 21 percent for the farming industry, and ranged from 38 percent for large farms to 12 percent for the smallest farms. Although rising, these debt-asset ratios are low by nonfarm business and industry standards. No debt crisis is apparent from the data in table 1.[2]

Neither is the farm debt crisis apparent from nominal farm income and expense accounts for 1979 and 1983 in table 2. Net farm income, gross income less production expenses, averaged $11,749 per farm in 1983 com-

This is a professional paper of the Oklahoma Agricultural Experiment Station. Comments of Ross Love and Daryll Ray are much appreciated.

TABLE 1
BALANCE SHEET OF THE FARMING SECTOR BY VALUE OF SALES CLASS, JANUARY 1, 1980 AND 1984
(dollars per farm)

	Large Farms		Medium Farms		Small Farms		All Farms
	$500,000 and over	$200,000 to $499,999	$100,000 to $199,999	$40,000 to $99,999	$20,000 to $39,999	Less than $20,000	
Physical assets							
Real estate							
1980	2,887.337	1,312.192	813.249	472.338	285.219	117.731	311.329
1984	2,971.146	1,350.299	836.824	485.951	293.384	111.928	322.624
Non-real estate							
1980	931.841	358.276	225.498	135.195	75.081	29.923	86.042
1984	950.444	289.227	242.313	147.632	81.900	32.163	91.373
Financial assets							
1980	295.139	62.707	32.668	19.528	13.420	7.851	16.774
1984	410.298	82.144	42.256	24.292	15.722	8.274	21.123
Total assets							
1980	4,114.317	1,733.175	1,071.415	627.061	373.720	155.505	414.145
1984	4,331.889	1,721.670	1,121.393	657.875	391.006	152.365	435.120
Liabilities							
Real estate debt							
1980	526.248	186.860	97.781	49.644	23.770	9.643	35.184
1984	698.372	247.981	129.758	65.869	31.533	11.822	47.108

Non–real estate debt							
1980	776,105	166,582	84,045	45,055	22,580	6,324	33,109
1984	954,004	226,231	114,326	60,108	28,255	7,153	43,483
Total liabilities							
1980	1,302,353	353,442	181,826	94,699	46,351	15,967	68,293
1984	1,652,376	474,212	244,084	125,976	59,788	18,975	90,591
Proprietors' equity							
1980	2,811,964	1,379,733	889,589	532,362	327,369	139,538	345,852
1984	2,679,513	1,247,458	877,309	531,899	331,217	133,390	344,529
Total							
1980	4,114,317	1,733,175	1,071,415	627,061	373,720	155,505	414,145
1984	4,331,889	1,721,670	1,121,393	657,875	391,006	152,365	435,120
Debt/asset ratio (%)							
1980	31.7	20.4	17.0	15.1	12.4	10.3	16.3
1984	38.1	27.5	21.8	19.1	15.3	12.5	20.8

Note: Data include farm households.

Source: U.S. Department of Agriculture, *Economic Indicators of the Farm Sector: Income and Balance Sheet Statistics*, ECIS 3–3 (Washington, D.C., September 1984), pp. 127, 131.

TABLE 2

PRODUCTION EXPENSES AND INCOME, BEFORE INVENTORY ADJUSTMENT, BY VALUE OF SALES CLASS, 1979 AND 1983

(dollars per farm)

	Large Farms		Medium Farms		Small Farms		All Farms
	$500,000 and over	$200,000 to $499,999	$100,000 to $199,999	$40,000 to $99,999	$20,000 to $39,999	Less than $20,000	
Gross farm income							
1979	1,813,851	331,533	159,520	76,484	36,354	10,160	59,842
1983	1,835,918	347,623	170,996	84,564	40,405	12,021	68,853
Production expenses							
1979	1,256,528	260,228	129,179	65,216	33,019	10,424	48,583
1983	1,268,333	285,389	144,315	73,910	37,459	12,302	57,097
Net farm income							
1979	557,324	71,305	30,342	11,268	3,335	−264	11,237
1983	567,585	62,233	26,681	10,654	2,945	−281	11,749
Off-farm income							
1979	22,368	11,500	9,417	9,161	11,196	16,992	14,472
1983	28,603	14,610	11,793	11,253	13,547	20,269	17,299
Total income from farm and off-farm sources							
1979	579,692	82,805	39,759	20,429	14,531	16,728	25,709
1983	596,187	76,844	38,474	21,907	16,493	19,988	29,048

NOTE: Data include farm households.

SOURCE: Department of Agriculture, Economic Indicators, pp. 91–93.

pared to $11,237 in 1979. Adding off-farm income, total income of farm operator families from all sources averaged $29,048 in 1983 compared to $25,709 in 1979. The lowest income from all sources was $16,493 in 1983 on farms with sales of $20,000 to $39,999, a figure up from $14,531 in 1979.

In 1983, farm disposable income per capita averaged 69 percent that of nonfarm families. This figure was down from the unusually high figure of 98 percent in 1979. After adjusting for the cost of living and the money income farm people forgo to realize a farm way of life, the ratio of per capita income of farmers to nonfarmers in 1983 was not far out of line with a long-term equilibrium.

Several observations are apparent from figure 1 showing farm debt per dollar of selected economic indicators:

• Farm debt per dollar of net farm income rose sharply in recent years. That measure, perhaps the most widely used to dramatize farm financial stress, is misleading, however, because the ratio can be high even when farmers are prospering, as in the 1970s.[3]

• Farm debt per dollar of gross farm income and per dollar of net farm income before interest payments increased but not as dramatically as debt per dollar of net farm income. This illustrates that high interest rates and expenses have played a key role in creating financial stress.

• Off-farm income is an increasing source of cash to service farm debt. Debt per dollar of total farm income from all sources before interest payments increased only modestly from the late 1960s to 1983.

• Debt per dollar of assets was comparatively low over the period shown in figure 1. Assets provided a rate of return in excess of the interest rate on debt on the average for the 1960–1979 period, hence debt was a source of real wealth gains. Nonetheless, debt was a source of cash-flow problems in the 1970s, for reasons given elsewhere in this paper.

It is essential to dig deeper into the data to understand more fully the dimensions of the farm debt crisis. A high ratio of debt to assets becomes a low return problem when interest rates exceed total rates of return on assets for an extended period. Since the 1930s, total rates of return on assets exceeded rates of interest, on the average. The cash-flow problem turned into a real return problem in the 1980s as interest rates remained high while disinflation removed capital gains as a compensating return. The estimated rates of farm income return to assets (where income return is measured by gross income less nonasset expenses, including a return to operator and family labor and management) as a percentage of assets, are shown in table 3 to range from 18.2 percent for the largest farms to a negative amount for small farms in 1983.[4] Small farms had considerable off-farm income, however, to offset their farm losses.

Farms with sales of $500,000 and over received significant proportions

FIGURE 1
FARM DEBT PER DOLLAR OF SELECTED ECONOMIC INDICATORS, 1960–1984

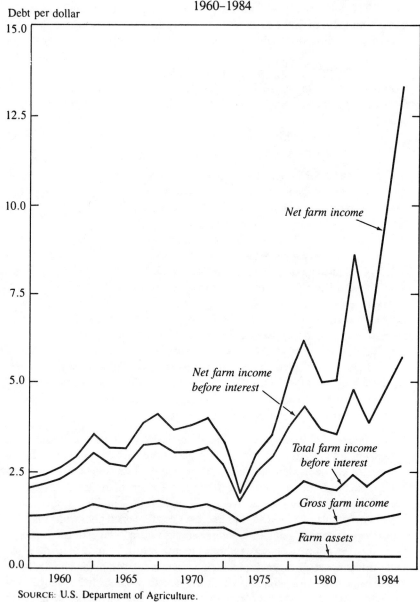

Debt per dollar

Net farm income

Net farm income before interest

Total farm income before interest

Gross farm income

Farm assets

SOURCE: U.S. Department of Agriculture.

TABLE 3

ESTIMATED RATE OF INCOME AND CASH-FLOW RETURN TO ASSETS AND TOLERABLE DEBT-ASSET RATIOS, BY VALUE OF SALES CLASS

Size of Farm, Annual Sales ($1,000)	Rate of Farm Income Return to Assets[a] (percent)	Rate of Total Cash Flow to Assets[b] (percent)	Tolerable Debt-Asset Ratio for Income to Pay Interest (percent)	
			Farm only[c]	Total cash flow[d]
500 and over	18.2	16.6	over 100	over 100
200 to 499	6.3	6.1	63	61
100 to 199	4.2	4.1	42	41
40 to 99	1.7	2.7	17	27
20 to 39	neg.	1.8	neg.	18
10 to 19	neg.	2.4	neg.	24
5 to 9	neg.	4.0	neg.	40
2.5 to 4.9	neg.	4.0	neg.	40
Under 2.5	neg.	8.0	neg.	80

a. Farm income return computed as gross income less production expenses including cost of operator labor ($10,000) and management (5 percent of gross cash farm income) divided by value of assets January 1, 1984, as computed by Melichar ("Incidence of Financial Stress," p. 13).
b. Net farm income before interest payments plus off-farm income less $15,000 family living allowance divided by value of assets January 1, 1984.
c. Computed from data as defined in footnote a, assuming 10 percent annual interest rate, the average interest rate paid in 1983.
d. Computed from data as defined in footnote b, assuming 10 percent annual interest rate.

of receipts from production of fruits and vegetables for processing, fed cattle, poultry, and other commodities under contractual or marketing-order arrangements providing more favorable prices than on smaller farms. Larger farms achieved sufficient economies in production and marketing to earn a high rate of return on assets in 1983, hence on the average experienced no financial crisis at current interest rates even with full indebtedness. The average farm paid approximately 10 percent interest, hence returns to assets failed to cover all interest on smaller farms even with low debt-asset ratios.

At 10 percent interest, asset returns were sufficient to cover interest payments on farms with $200,000 to $499,999 of annual sales up to a 63 percent debt-asset ratio (see table 3). Farms with sales of $100,000 to $199,999 broke even on interest payments up to a debt-asset ratio of 42 percent, and farms with sales of $40,000 to $99,999 broke even only at a debt-asset ratio 17 percent or less. Smaller farms could not break even with any debt.

The average small farm has considerable off-farm income to service debt; indeed, it could not survive financially from farm earnings alone. Because of their high ratio of off-farm to farm income and for other reasons, Melichar did not consider small farms to be experiencing financial stress.[5] Consequently, he confined the farm debt crisis to the mid-size commercial farms with sales of $40,000 to $200,000. He concluded that 8.8 percent of farms, 13.8 percent of farm assets, and 39.2 percent of farm debt were in financial stress. This is probably a lower limit.

I calculate a more realistic magnitude of farm financial stress using a cash-flow approach. Off-farm income plus net farm income before interest payments less a $15,000 family living allowance is expressed as a percent of assets in table 3 and labeled the rate of cash flow to assets. If this income flow is used to service debt at 10 percent average interest paid in 1983, tolerable debt-asset ratios are shown by economic class of farms in the last column of table 3. The ratio ranges from 18 percent for farms with sales of $20,000 to $39,999 to 80–100 percent for the very largest and smallest farms in 1983. This tolerable debt-asset ratio is applied to actual debt-asset ratios by farm size in table 4 to calculate the magnitude of financial stress. By this measure, 22 percent of farms and assets and half of farm debt experienced financial stress in 1983. The incidence of financial stress, measured by the proportion of farms in each sales class with debt-asset ratios in excess of tolerable limits, is shown in tabular form at the top of the next page. Proportions ranged from near zero for the largest and smallest farms to nearly half of all farms with sales of $40,000 to $99,999. An estimated 24 percent of farm output as measured by cash income was produced by farms in financial stress in 1983. When such farms fail, output does not necessarily fall because the assets usually are acquired by others with stronger farm and financial management.

These data have many limitations. The $15,000 consumption allowance

Size of farm ($1,000 of annual sales)	Percentage of farms in each class experiencing financial stress	Percentage of all output accounted for by:	
		Financial stress farms	All farms
500 and over	0	0	29
200 to 499	24	4.6	19
100 to 199	36	6.8	19
40 to 99	46	9.2	20
20 to 39	41	2.5	6
10 to 19	29	0.9	3
5 to 9	14	0.3	2
2.5 to 4.9	11	0.1	1
under 2.5	1	0	1
		24.4	100

is arbitrary. Principal payments were not included in the analysis, and many farms with newly acquired short-term debt paid 15 percent interest rather than the 10 percent assumed. Financial stress has deepened since the above data were assembled. Assumptions can be faulted, but I conclude that farm financial stress is severe for at least 22 percent of all farms, 22 percent of all farm assets, and 51 percent of all farm debt. Up to half of such stressed farms will fail in the next three years if current trends continue. This projection is subject to more than usual error because public policies and other conditions are likely to change.

Although the largest farms are most leveraged on the average, failure rates probably will be highest among mid-size commercial farms. On smaller farms, cash flow and low returns on assets constrain investment and explain why they have low leverage ratios of debt to assets. Leveraging that was tolerable and supported by rising land values in the 1970s has become a major source of financial stress in the 1980s as real land values and collateral declined.

Although financial stress is felt most acutely by highly leveraged debtors, the decline in real wealth is shared widely by asset owners, many of whom have little or no debt. Real capital losses in the four years from 1980 through 1983 totaled $164 billion, an average of $68,000 per farm. Real wealth losses were closely related to assets owned and were therefore essentially proportional to the asset distribution among farm sizes, as shown in table 4.

Sources of Financial Stress

In this section, the origins of financial stress are divided into proximate and primary sources. Proximate sources are discussed first.

TABLE 4

ESTIMATED PERCENTAGE DISTRIBUTION OF ALL FARM OPERATORS, THEIR DEBT AND ASSETS, BY RELATIVE DEBT LEVEL AND SIZE GROUPS, JANUARY 1, 1984

Size of Farm, Annual Sales ($1,000)	Ratio of Farm Operator Debt to Assets (%)[a]					Sum of Farms, Assets, & Debt in Financial Stress[b] (%)
	Total	0–10	11–40	41–70	71 and over	
Operators						
500 and over	1.1	0.2	0.4	0.3	0.2	0
200 to 499	3.3	0.7	1.2	0.8	0.6	0.8
100 to 199	7.4	1.9	2.8	1.5	1.2	2.7
40 to 99	16.0	6.0	5.2	2.7	2.1	7.4
20 to 39	10.9	5.4	3.2	1.3	1.0	4.5
10 to 19	11.5	6.9	2.6	1.1	0.9	3.3
5 to 9	12.9	9.0	2.1	1.1	0.7	1.8
2.5 to 4.9	13.9	10.1	2.3	0.9	0.6	1.5
Under 2.5	23.3	17.4	3.7	1.5	0.7	0.3
Total	100.0[c]	57.6	23.5	11.2	8.0	22.3
Assets						
500 and over	10.2	2.3	3.8	2.3	1.8	0
200 to 499	12.9	3.7	4.9	2.7	1.6	2.4
100 to 199	16.3	4.9	6.9	2.9	1.6	4.5
40 to 99	21.9	9.6	7.4	3.2	1.7	8.6
20 to 39	9.7	5.5	2.8	0.9	0.5	3.4
10 to 19	7.8	5.1	1.8	0.6	0.3	1.8
5 to 9	6.4	4.6	1.1	0.5	0.2	0.7
2.5 to 4.9	6.1	4.7	1.0	0.3	0.1	0.4
Under 2.5	8.4	6.1	1.6	0.5	0.2	0.1
Total	100.0[c]	46.5	31.3	13.9	8.0	21.9
Debt						
500 and over	17.7	0.4	4.0	5.2	8.1	0
200 to 499	18.1	0.5	5.2	6.1	6.3	8.1
100 to 199	20.7	0.8	7.1	6.5	6.3	12.8
40 to 99	22.4	1.2	7.2	7.2	6.8	17.6
20 to 39	7.1	0.5	2.7	2.0	1.9	5.8
10 to 19	4.7	0.4	1.6	1.4	1.3	3.5
5 to 9	3.3	0.3	1.0	1.0	1.0	2.0
2.5 to 4.9	2.5	0.2	0.9	0.8	0.6	1.4
Under 2.5	3.7	0.3	1.5	1.2	0.7	0.3
Total	100.0[c]	4.6	31.2	31.4	33.0	51.5

a. Data from Melichar, "Incidence of Financial Stress," p. 15.
b. Estimated from criteria shown in table 3 based on total cash-flow return.
c. Totals not exact because of rounding.

Proximate Sources of Financial Stress. Possible proximate sources of financial stress include farm prices, receipts, expenses, interest rates, debts, and assets. Although each of these has contributed, commodity prices, receipts, or earnings are not the major sources.

Prices and income returns. As shown by Melichar, gross farm income and net farm income before interest in the four years 1980–1983 averaged approximately the 1976 and 1977 average levels, somewhat below levels of 1972–1975 and 1978–1979 but well above 1970 and 1971 average nominal levels.

The current income return on farm assets averaged 1.6 percent for the four years 1980–1983. Excluding the boom of 1972–1975, this rate of return conforms closely to current rates of return on farm assets since the Korean conflict. Prices received by farmers relative to prices paid by farmers averaged only 57 percent of the 1910–1914 average in each of the years 1982, 1983, and 1984. A strong case can be made that these seemingly low prices and current rates of return on farm assets are near an equilibrium and are unlikely to average higher in the future. To understand why, it is useful to digress and examine the cost structure of the farming industry.

Figure 2, taken from an earlier study, is constructed by dividing all resource costs by all returns (gross farm income) for each of eight economic classes of farms in 1982.[6] Long-term resource costs include production expenses plus a cost for operator and family inputs—labor hours times the hired labor wage rate, 5 percent of receipts for management—and an 8 percent real interest rate on short-term capital and a 5 percent real interest rate on long-term capital.[7] Costs were a little less than $1 to produce $1 of output on farms with sales of over $500,000 in 1982. As noted earlier, these farms have an atypical commodity and market configuration and cannot be compared directly with smaller farms. The commodity structure of farms with sales of $200,000 to $499,999 is more typical of other farms; these farms approximately broke even under the assumptions used to construct figure 2. Small farms operated at a substantial loss when all resources are valued at long-term opportunity cost.

Because farms that account for over half of all farm output normally cover all costs at 1982–1984 prices, there is no reason to expect the market to bring higher prices to assure production. An increase in prices and returns could cause well-managed farms of adequate size to bid up land values; the long-term pattern shown in figure 1 can therefore be expected to hold even with sustained higher commodity prices, given time for asset price adjustments. If large farms are breaking even on the average and smaller farms are losing money, it follows that an average of all farms will show a rate of return on assets well below opportunity cost levels in equilibrium.

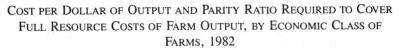

FIGURE 2

COST PER DOLLAR OF OUTPUT AND PARITY RATIO REQUIRED TO COVER
FULL RESOURCE COSTS OF FARM OUTPUT, BY ECONOMIC CLASS OF
FARMS, 1982

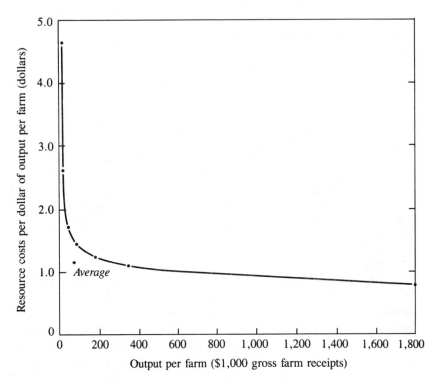

Output per farm ($1,000 gross farm receipts)

SOURCE: Tweeten, "Diagnosing and Treating," p. 33.

This analysis begs the question of why most farms (mainly smaller farms) continue to operate when returns are negative—it costs them well over $1 to produce $1 of output. The number of smaller part-time farmers has increased sharply, and it is difficult to conclude that they are irrational. Their behavior is primarily explained by the value they place on rural living and the tax advantages of farm residence. Given current tax incentives, they have no incentives to make adjustments, though not in economic equilibrium in the absence of tax incentives. A higher proportion of mid-sized family farmers are there by accident of birth and miscalculations of the future profitability of agriculture, based on favorable expectations formed in the 1970s, which turned out to be incorrect. Many will not survive financially or will require substantial transfer payments from relatives or taxpayers.

94

TABLE 5

SELECTED MEASURES OF INTEREST RATES AND INFLATION, 1970 to 1983

(percent)

	Prime Rate, Large Banks		Federal Land Banks		Rural Banks, Non-Real Estate Production Loans		Change in Consumer Price Index[a]
	Nominal	Real[b]	Nominal	Real[b]	Nominal	Real[b]	
1970	7.9	2.4	8.7	3.2	8.3	2.8	5.5
1971	5.7	2.3	7.8	4.4	8.2	4.8	3.4
1972	5.2	1.8	7.4	4.0	8.0	4.6	3.4
Average	6.3	2.2	8.0	3.9	8.2	4.1	4.1
1973	8.0	−0.8	7.5	−1.3	8.2	−0.6	8.8
1974	10.8	−1.4	8.1	−4.1	8.7	−3.5	12.2
1975	7.9	0.9	8.7	1.7	9.0	2.0	7.0
1976	6.8	2.0	8.7	3.9	9.1	4.3	4.8
1977	6.8	0	8.4	1.6	9.2	2.4	6.8
1978	9.1	0.1	8.4	−0.6	9.3	0.3	9.0
1979	12.7	−0.6	9.1	−4.2	10.8	−2.5	13.3
1980	15.2	2.8	10.4	−2.0	14.8	2.4	12.4
1981	18.9	10.0	11.3	2.4	17.9	9.0	8.9
Average	10.7	1.4	9.0	−0.3	10.8	1.8	9.2
1982	14.9	11.0	12.3	8.4	17.1	13.2	3.9
1983	10.8	7.0	11.6	7.8	14.3	10.5	3.8
Average	12.8	9.0	11.9	8.1	15.7	11.8	3.8

a. Change from December to December.
b. The real rate is the nominal rate less the inflation rate as measured by the consumer price index.

SOURCE: George Amols and Wilson Kaiser, "Agricultural Finance Statistics, 1960–1983," *Statistical Bulletin* no. 706 (Washington, D.C.: Economic Research Service, Department of Agriculture, 1984); and Council of Economic Advisers, *Economic Report of the President* (Washington, D.C., 1984).

Interest rates. The foregoing analysis shows that commodity prices and current income cover all costs on well-managed farms of adequate size at historically normal real interest rates. The major proximate cause of the farm financial crisis is interest rates.

Table 5 shows trends in real and nominal interest rates on new loans, the prime rate of large banks, and the inflation rate. Of the three periods in table 5, the 1970–1972 period was least abnormal for interest rates. The increase in inflation rates in subsequent years was unanticipated. Nominal interest rates

95

increased but did not keep pace with inflation, so that real interest rates were negative on loans made by federal land banks in the 1973–1981 period. By the early 1980s, inflation rates expected to remain high coupled with competition of federal deficit funding for savings drove real interest rates historically high.

The financial structure of the farming industry has been built around real interest rates of 3 or 4 percent. Few enterprises on the majority of farms yield returns sufficient to cover real interest rates in 1984 double or triple the historic rates. Astute financial management can reduce farm losses but treats symptoms rather than causes.[8] High real interest rates are felt through higher interest expenses and through asset depreciation (discussed in the section "Asset Depreciation").

Interest expenses. Farm interest payments increased from $3.4 billion in 1970 to $21.4 billion in 1983, or at an annual compound rate of 15 percent. To gain some insight into future interest payments, the gain for 1970–1983 is disaggregated into its components below.[9]

	Annual compound increase, 1970–1983 (%)	Share of increased interest payments (%)
Interest rate (r)	3.7	25
Real assets (A)	1.6	11
Inflation (i)	7.5	52
Debt-asset ratio (L)	1.7	12
Interest payment (I)	14.5	100

More than half of the increased interest expense is associated directly with inflation as measured by the consumer price index. Inflation raised land returns, which were quickly capitalized into land values. Buyers increased debt for purchases; owners monetized appreciated assets to obtain cash. Thus much of the increased interest cost to which farmers object so strongly stems from asset appreciation from which many farmers benefited in the 1970s.

Increased leverage L accounted for only 12 percent of the growth in interest payments. Some of the increased leverage L may be attributed indirectly to financial problems caused by high interest rates.

Real asset growth A from 1970 to 1983 was modest, though more substantial in the perspective of a constant real volume of farm inputs. Substitution of capital for labor is expected in a progressive industry. If real interest rates decline to more normal levels, the real volume of assets and debt will increase if current leverage is maintained.

A notable conclusion from the above estimates is that up to 90 percent of the growth in interest payments from 1970 to 1983 is associated with monetary-fiscal policy—assuming only real asset growth is excluded. The above data indicate that restoration of the 1970 debt-asset ratio of 17 percent would reduce interest payments relatively little, but restoration of interest rates to the 1970 level would be a major help.

Asset depreciation. High real interest rates cause financial stress by causing farm assets, especially land, to decline in real value. The result is losses in real wealth and declining collateral for loans. At issue is whether the market process for valuing assets from discounted future earnings is arbitrary and capricious. Did participants in the land market behave rationally, or did speculation in the 1970s and panic in the 1980s aggravate an already difficult situation?

To explain the behavior of land prices, it is well to review briefly the theory of rational land pricing in a well-functioning land market.[10] The land price P_t in year t is a function of current land earnings or rent, R_t, capitalized at a rate $b - i'$ where b is the desired real rate of return and i' is the expected real rate of increase in future earnings R.

$$P_t = R_t / (b - i') \qquad \text{(general)}$$

Assume that b is 0.05 or 5 percent, the average real rate of return on farm equity from current earnings and real capital gains since 1949. If land earnings per acre behave like a bond paying a constant nominal return of $100 per year in perpetuity and if inflation i is expected to average 6 percent, then $i' = -.06$ and

$$P_t = R_t / (b + i) = \$100/0.11 = \$909 \qquad \text{(bond)}$$

Thus the current rate of return on farmland in this example is $(R_t/P_t) = \$100/\$909 = 0.11$ or 11 percent. Land earnings are capitalized at a rate $b + i$ if earnings are expected to remain constant in nominal dollars.

If land returns are expected to remain constant in real terms and hence just keep pace with inflation so $i' = 0$, a reasonable expectation for the future, as I later contend, is

$$P_t = R_t / b = \$100/0.05 = \$2,000 \qquad \text{(land)}$$

and the current rate of return on land (R_t/P_t) is $\$100/\$2000 = 0.05 = 5$ percent. Land earnings are capitalized at the real return b if earnings are expected to remain constant in real value. Capital gain compensates for the inflation premium in interest rates.

If land returns are expected to increase at a real rate $i' = 0.02$ or 2 percent per year as seemed likely based on expectations in the 1970s then

$$P_t = R_t / (b - i') = \$100/0.03 = \$3,333 \qquad \text{(growth stock)}$$

and the current rate of return on land (R_t/P_t) is $\$100/\$3,333 = 0.03$ or 3 percent per year.[11]

As the expected real rate of increase in land earnings approaches the real discount rate b, land values become very large relative to earnings, the current rate of return becomes very small, and cash flow problems become severe for this growth stock scenario. The real rate of return b remains the same, however, in each scenario above.

Given current land earnings of $100 per acre, expected inflation at 6 percent, and a desired real return of 5 percent, the present value of land could fall from $3,333 per acre to $909 per acre because expectations of future earnings shift from real growth of 2 percent per year to no future growth in nominal earnings. In summary, the value of farm real estate is influenced by the expected trend in real earnings i', which is in turn influenced by expected inflation and nominal land earnings. Land value also is influenced by the real discount rate b, which is in turn influenced by time preferences for income, by rates of return on alternative investments, and by interest rates paid on farmland debt.

With this background, we analyze the behavior of land values in the eight states where prices fell most sharply in the United States from 1980 to 1984 (see table 6). The analysis uses Ohio as an example because that state experienced the largest price decline, 26 percent, in the nation. Similar inferences can be drawn from data for other states. At issue is whether land prices behaved rationally.

Net cash rents in Ohio increased from $62.44 per acre in 1980 to $70.71 in 1984; declining land prices are hardly explained, therefore, by declining nominal land earnings. Investors' discount rates are influenced by real mortgage interest rates, which for the federal land banks averaged near zero in the 1970s, as noted in table 5. Investors would, however, be expected to desire a real return of at least 5 percent; hence assume $b=0.05$ for 1980. Real land rents increased an average of 6.9 percent annually in Ohio in the 1970s. If investors perceived this trend to be permanent, the capitalization rate $b-i'$ would approach zero and the land price infinity. If $b=0.05$, the actual land price was consistent with expectations in 1980 that land earnings would increase at 1.3 percent per year—a conservative expectation based on past history, even the 1960s when real land rents in Ohio increased 1.7 percent per year. Land was not overpriced in Ohio in 1980 based on reasonable expectations formed from information available in the 1970s.

Of course, economic conditions and expectations changed in the 1980s. What land values were justified based on expectations in 1984? Real interest rates of the federal land banks averaged 8.1 percent in 1982 and 1983. If future real rents are expected to be constant so $i'=0$ but the discount rate is raised from 5 percent to 8 percent, land rents in 1984 would have justified a land price of only $884, a drop of 47 percent from the 1980 value. Such expectations would call for a further drop of 40 percent from the 1984 land price.

If future land rents in Ohio are expected to keep pace with inflation, the 1984 land prices and rents will provide a real return of 5.6 percent as shown

TABLE 6

LAND VALUE, NET CASH RENT, AND RATIO OF NET RENT TO LAND VALUE
PER ACRE, SELECTED STATES, 1980 AND 1984

State	Land Value/Acre (dollars)		Net Cash Rent/Acre[a] (dollars)		Net Rent to Value Ratio/Acre (percent)			
	1980	1984	1980	1984	1980	1984	1960–69	1970–79
Minnesota	1,061	990	54.30	65.35	5.12	6.60	6.25	6.00
Ohio	1,678	1,245	62.44	70.71	3.72	5.68	4.48	4.17
Indiana	1,833	1,477	85.38	91.96	4.66	6.23	5.84	5.74
Illinois	2,013	1,692	84.71	102.09	4.21	6.03	4.61	4.56
Iowa	1,811	1,396	87.31	99.10	4.82	7.09	5.43	5.71
Missouri	878	759	47.52	48.52	5.41	6.39	6.15	5.88
Nebraska[b]	600	495	40.84	47.50	6.80	9.59	6.86	8.68
Kansas	573	528	27.79	31.21	4.85	5.91	5.29	5.07

a. Net rent is cash rent on farms rented for cash less property taxes.
b. Nonirrigated land.
SOURCE: U.S. Department of Agriculture, "Farm Real Estate Market Developments," CD-89, Economic Research Service (August 1984 and earlier issues).

by the net rent/value ratio in table 6. If inflation is 4 percent, this is consistent with a normal nominal interest rate of 10 percent. Such expectations for longer-term interest rates and land earnings (as well be argued later) do not suggest irrationality in the land market.

Other states in table 6 show patterns not unlike those in Ohio. Nominal net land rents increased in each state from 1980 to 1984. In 1980, each state had a lower ratio of net rent to land price than in the 1960–1969 or the 1970–1979 periods. The 1980 ratio by no means reflected the capitalization rate that would have been apparent if the trends of 1970–1979 in real land rents and real interest rates had been perceived as permanent.

Ratios of land rent to land prices in 1984 were in each state higher than the averages for the 1960–1969 or 1970–1979 periods. The ratios represent rather strong earnings relative to historic rates, but fell well short of reflecting the full reduction in land values that would be warranted if the real interest rates of 1984 were perceived to be permanent.

In summary, several observations are drawn from the above and from other analysis:[12]

• Farmland prices in the 1970s were not built on speculation that inflation would push real estate values upward without regard to land earnings. If the

99

price structure had been a "house of cards" or "giant pyramid scheme" as many, including some agricultural economists, claimed, it would surely have tumbled down in the financial earthquake of the 1980s. Land values declined as new information emerged in the 1980s, but panic was not evident. Farm real estate appears to be an efficient market; participants showed good judgment in using available information to establish land prices. Farmland was not overpriced in 1980 in relation to reasonable expectations available from the 1970s and earlier years; neither was farmland underpriced in 1984 in relation to reasonable expectations for the future. Expectations will change with new information, of course. The most vital new information will be decisions regarding monetary-fiscal policy, to be discussed later.

• If currently high real interest rates and the slow increase or decline in land earnings persist for several more years, the potential is great for expectations to change in a manner causing massive land price reductions and decapitalization of farming assets. The value of farm assets could fall to half current levels, causing huge capital losses and financial failures.

• Finally, it is important to note that data and analysis from table 6 have several limitations. Land prices and land rents are not measured without error. Cash rents are contractual obligations in part reflecting expectations and therefore are not exact measures of current land earnings. Other measures such as residual income to land could be used but entail arbitrary measures of operator labor and other costs, which can be measured very imperfectly. Net cash rents are not an exact measure of land earnings either on farms rented for cash or on farms that are owner-operated or rented on shares. Farm cash receipts fell from 1980 to 1983 in each of the eight states in table 6. Cash rents will fall if receipts continue to fall.

Primary Sources of Financial Stress. High interest rates have been the core of farm problems for a decade. High nominal interest rates from 1974 to 1981 created cash-flow problems but not necessarily low returns because land value appreciated with the inflation that attended high nominal interest rates for farmers.[13] High nominal interest rates arise from excessive expansion in money supply, which begets inflation, which in turn begets a demand by investors for an inflation premium in interest rates. Inflation raises immediate costs and defers returns, which in the case of farm real estate are realized only when land is sold. Unanticipated inflation transfers real wealth from creditors to debtors but does not have a large effect on total real wealth.

Financial stress caused by high real interest rates from 1982 to 1985 has had effects on farms similar to high nominal interest rates, except that land values do not appreciate and hence do not provide collateral from which to borrow to service cash-flow needs. High real interest rates not only reduce aggregate real wealth, they also transfer wealth from debtors to creditors—a special disadvantage to farmers who on the average are net debtors. In 1970, farm operators had $43 of financial claims on others for each $100 of claims on them. This ratio fell to $23 in 1980 and 1984.

Domestic monetary and fiscal policy have become an increasing source of economic instability.[14] From 1973 to 1981, the difficulty was excessive and erratic money supply. Since 1981, monetary policy has been more enlightened and inflation rates accordingly low, but the legacy of earlier years lingers. The credibility of the Federal Reserve's commitment to control money supply is in doubt. Investors are reluctant to commit their savings at nominal interest rates that might result in negative real interest rates if inflation revives. As shown in the appendix, investors demand an interest premium when interest rates are unstable. The principal source of high real interest rates in recent years is fiscal policy (see the appendix). Massive federal deficits compete for savings in financial markets and drive up real interest rates. Unanticipated high real interest rates are problems enough in themselves to producers, but some of the most insidious effects come through foreign linkages. High real interest rates attract investments from abroad, creating a foreign demand for dollars relative to supply and driving up the value of the dollar in international exchange. The high value of the dollar in relation to purchasing power parity of the dollar in turn has increased U.S. imports and reduced exports. Domestic industries such as steel, auto, and textiles that compete with foreign imports have been hurt and have acquired some protection from imports. Such action provokes foreign reactions that restrain trade in farm products. Another indirect effect of high real interest rates is the financial crisis in Latin America and elsewhere, which slows demand for U.S. farm exports. Off-farm employment so important to today's farmers has been reduced by competition from low-cost imports in lumber, mining, and textiles, industries prominent in rural areas.

Projected Future Financial Situation for Agriculture

As indicated earlier, market participants do not expect unfavorable conditions in agriculture to persist. At issue is what are reasonable expectations for the future of farm income, land earnings, interest, and discount rates.

Trends in Farm Prices and Incomes. Excess capacity, defined as output in excess of what the market will absorb at current prices, is approximately 5 percent under normal weather and is largely concentrated in grains and dairy.[15] Assuming a short-run price elasticity of demand for farm output of $-.25$, release of the excess capacity on the market by removing government supply control and other income support programs would reduce farm prices 20 percent and farm receipts 15 percent in the short run.[16] A shift toward greater market orientation in the 1985 farm legislation would reduce land earning in the short run. In the long term, commodity programs, whether market oriented or not, cannot be expected to maintain farm and land earn-

101

ings. Instead, earnings will be determined by long-term trends in supply and demand for farm output.

A number of recent studies project future prices and earnings in agriculture.[17] These studies anticipate slightly faster rates of increase in supply (because of productivity growth) than in demand for the next decade or two. No strong downward trend in real farm prices is projected, but there will be considerable variation around the long-term trend.

Returns to land increased somewhat faster than farm income from 1960 to 1977.[18] In the eight states shown in table 6, real land earnings approximately doubled from 1960 to 1984—hence land earnings more than kept pace with inflation except in the 1980s. Given only modest projected declines in real farm prices and real farm income, the tendency for land earnings to decline less than farm income and for inflation to be fully reflected in land earnings, it seems reasonable to expect that land earnings will keep pace with inflation in the long run. In short, land earnings can be expected to maintain their real value in the next decade or two after adjusting to a greater market orientation in commodity programs.

Trends in Interest Rates and Macroeconomic Variables. The twin economic villains of agriculture, high real interest and exchange rates, are in turn associated with twin deficits—budget and balance of payments. Neither twin set is sustainable, and the decision when to reduce the federal deficit is political and unpredictable. It is possible, however, to predict the effect of a balanced budget on real interest rates. Analysis in the appendix predicts that a balanced government budget will reduce real interest rates approximately four percentage points, though more than a year is required to achieve that adjustment.

A drop of four percentage points in the interest rate could drop the federal land banks' rate of 12 percent in 1983 (see table 5) to 8 percent and the rural bank production loan rate from 16 percent in 1983 to 12 percent—rates more in line with past real rates if inflation is 4 percent. Each reduction of one percentage point in the average interest rate would reduce interest expenses by approximately $2 billion. Average interest rates equal to the 1970 rate would therefore reduce farm interest costs approximately $8 billion and add a similar amount to net farm income.

A more nearly balanced federal budget and attendant lower real interest rate would reduce the value of the dollar by at least 20 percent.[19] Each 1 percent decline in the value of the dollar is expected to increase farm exports about 0.5 percent in one to two years and by 1 percent in a longer period.[20] Thus decisive action to move toward a balanced federal budget would increase exports 10 percent in one to two years and by 20 percent over a longer period, other things equal. Lower U.S. interest rates would reduce foreign financial stress and promote economic growth abroad, further adding to U.S. farm exports. Export demand could expand to alleviate the current 5 percent excess capacity and attendant supply control necessary to maintain farm income. Thus, convincing the federal government to move toward a balanced budget would go far to alleviate the two major current farm economic problems—financial stress and excess capacity.

The window of opportunity for sound fiscal policy to restore economic vitality to agriculture is rapidly closing. The current economic expansion may last only another year. Even if Congress acted quickly, the more nearly balanced budget achieved through spending cuts and tax increases, or both, might come at an inopportune time when the economy is beginning a recession. The result would be to increase the magnitude of the recession by reducing aggregate demand. Still, farmers might be better off than with the current policy of large full-employment (structural) deficits. Farmers would fare better with lower interest and exchange rates, but domestic demand for farm products would be depressed slightly by lower income. Although domestic income has little direct effect, foreign linkages are important. Reducing imports into the United States would slow income growth abroad, which in turn would slow U.S. farm exports, other things equal.

U.S. consumers have been living well beyond their collective means since 1983. Domestic consumption has been able to exceed domestic production because the trade deficit has been financed by capital imports. As a result, foreigners have built large financial claims on the United States. The nation is shifting from a major net world creditor to a net debtor, a situation unlikely to persist in the long run for a highly developed industrialized country. More normal real interest and exchange rates will reverse the recent capital flows. U.S. farmers and other producers will play a major role in redressing past trade and financial imbalances through increased exports. Thus a turnaround in fiscal policy would be expected to benefit producers relative to consumers in the next decade—a reversal of the current situation.

An ideal macroeconomic policy would counter business cycles and promote sustained economic progress with little inflation. Such a policy would entail federal deficits during recession and a balanced or surplus budget during expansionary phases of the cycle. Monetary policy would be slightly expansionary in recessions and neutral or contractionary during boom times. Such fine tuning is too much to hope for.

It is well to review briefly what various combinations of loose and tight monetary and fiscal policies would mean to the farming industry. The earlier scenario of more sound fiscal policy relieving financial stress and excess capacity assumed action taken in a period of U.S. and world economic recovery. If action is taken instead to balance the budget when the U.S. economy is faltering, as now seems more and more likely, what will be the effect on the farming industry?

Under a scenario of continued tight monetary policy and large deficits, inflation will be low, and real interest and exchange rates higher than normal but trending downward. Continuing large federal deficits will stimulate the economy less and less because increased imports, reduced exports, and high real interest rates will eventually erode domestic industries. The burden of financing the debt will further strain the economy. The eventual result will be higher than normal unemployment, idle industry capacity, and continued financial crises in agriculture. The policy will not persist, however, because continued large budget deficits and international payment deficits are not sustainable in the long run.

The administration is placing considerable pressure on the Federal Reserve to expand the money supply to reduce interest rates. In the face of continued loose fiscal policy, the initial result of an expansionary monetary policy might be to reduce interest rates. The economy would expand, reducing unemployment and excess industrial capacity. Inflation rates would increase. Financial markets would quickly perceive the consequences for inflation of this policy, and nominal interest rates would climb. Because farmers are better off with high nominal than with high real interest rates, they might be better off with this policy than with the current policy. This scenario too is unsustainable because the Federal Reserve would eventually restrict the growth in the money supply to reduce inflation. Recession would follow.

Near-Term Policy Options to Relieve Financial Stress

Policy options ranked most to least desirable to alleviate financial stress in agriculture are summarized below.

Monetary-Fiscal Policy. Monetary policy was erratic and overly expansionary in the 1970s but has performed well since 1981. In its role of restraining inflation, monetary policy has been helped by the high value of the dollar in international exchange. As real interest rates fall and the dollar rises in value, money supply management will become more difficult as inflationary pressures build.

The principal immediate problem is fiscal policy. The federal government must give convincing evidence that it is capable of moving toward a balanced full-employment budget. Doing so would reduce real interest rates and farm expenses and would raise exports and asset values—hence relieve financial stress and excess capacity in agriculture. Immediate action on fiscal policy is necessary to avoid timing fiscal restraint with an economy going into recession. Farmers might be better off with fiscal restraint even in a depressed economy, but consumers and service industries would be worse off. One cost of the current irresponsible fiscal policy is fewer options to stimulate the economy during a recession.

Targeted Credit Assistance. If the first-best solution of responsible fiscal policy is rejected, the second-best solution to farm financial stress is to target limited federal funds to those most disadvantaged by high real interest rates. Farmers will need some credit assistance to relieve stress while benefits of fiscal restraint take time to work their way through the system. Although most farmers have been hurt by high real interest rates, the acute problem is with highly leveraged borrowers. Federal action to share some of the cost of debt restructuring with private lenders and to allow the Farmers Home Administration greater flexibility is a form of triage, targeting assistance to salvageable borrowers in serious financial stress. Such a solution requires less Treasury outlay than would more general assistance but treats symptoms rather than causes.

Targeted Commodity Programs. As shown earlier, farming is not uniformly a low-return industry. Many well-managed farms of adequate size are making an adequate return on investment. Many part-time small farms are not in farming to make a profit and can handle farm losses with off-farm income. Mid-size family farms are most in jeopardy. If society wishes to reduce financial stress through commodity programs, preserve family farms, and exercise budget restraint, then a case can be made to target a higher proportion of benefits to such farms. Such targeting requires greater emphasis on direct payments. Production is difficult to control with any voluntary program, but it is nearly impossible to do so if benefits are targeted to mid-size farms. Targeted assistance therefore means less emphasis on supply control, and forgoing supply control requires market-oriented loan rates that do not build surpluses by encouraging production and pricing output out of export markets.

General Commodity Programs. Alleviating financial stress in farming by increasing supports under commodity programs used for a half-century is the least economically desirable of the policy options considered here. One billion more dollars of Treasury outlay go far in relieving financial stress if carefully targeted but do little to reduce financial stress if distributed under conventional commodity programs. A transition program to a market orientation is necessary; sudden termination of supports would turn financial stress into a financial debacle.

Summary and Conclusions

The principal proximate source of farm financial stress is high real interest rates. High real interest rates are caused mainly by large continuing structural federal deficits. The farming industry is especially disadvantaged by high real interest rates because it is highly capitalized (the capital-labor ratio is double that of other industries), is highly dependent on exports, and is a net debtor.

High real interest rates add to farm expenses and reduce real wealth by increasing the rate of discount on future earnings of durable farm resources. High real interest rates cause high exchange rates, which reduce export demand for farm products. It is not by chance that the eight states with the largest decline in land values shown in table 6 depend heavily on export markets, which have been sharply constrained by fiscal policy.

The farming economy is experiencing its greatest financial problems since the Great Depression, but unlike the 1930s the source of the problem is not low farm prices. The current ratio of prices received to prices paid by farmers appears to be near or even above a long-term equilibrium. Current prices and gross farm income have been supported by government commodity programs—an expected greater market orientation in such programs is likely to reduce farm income in the short run. For other reasons also the near-term outlook for relieving farm financial stress is not favorable. Responsible fiscal policy remains elusive. The timing of federal action may be quite wrong.

The farming industry has considerable capacity to make adjustments. It is capable of adjusting, albeit with much trauma, to current high real interest rates and a greater market orientation. Food supplies would not be threatened, but many family farms would be casualties. Capital losses would be massive. The warnings, however, that a few large corporations then would take over agriculture and run up food prices are without substance. Current macroeconomic policies are unsustainable, and a turnaround is inevitable if unpredictable. After an adjustment period of perhaps five years, the farming industry would be positioned for a major comeback and could experience a boom. The average utility of farmers over a boom and bust cycle is, however, much less than the utility gained from the same average economic outcomes realized with greater stability. Many farmers and markets lost in the bust are not retrieved in the boom.

While the case for responsible fiscal policy is strong, the case for more generous federal credit or commodity program assistance is less strong. The principal argument for federal assistance is that macroeconomic policy caused the financial crises, therefore the federal government is obligated to redress the wrongs perpetrated thereby. The counterargument is that farmers in earlier times reaped windfall gains from macroeconomic policies; should plungers, many of whom handsomely profited in the previous half-century from leverage, now be bailed out? Will not a federal bailout signal that plunging pays because gains are retained while losses are forgiven? Injecting more credit would encourage speculation in land values, increase output, and reduce rates of return on farming assets in the long run. If all farmers receive assistance, why not assist all businesses and others hurt by current policies? If the federal government is generous in redressing wrongs, will not the federal deficit become even more burdensome?

Although high real interest and exchange rates are the proximate cause and outsized structural deficits the primary economic cause of financial woes, the root cause of financial stress is a breakdown of the political process.[21] Conservatives traditionally have given fiscal responsibility higher priority than tax reductions. President Reagan, however, whose support is essential for fiscal responsibility, has given tax cuts and increased military spending priority over a balanced federal budget. Democrats in Congress have given social program spending priority over a balanced full-employment budget. Until adversaries rearrange their priorities, chances for fiscal responsibility remain slim. Reforms are also needed in legislative processes—a topic too complex to treat here but discussed with insight by Bonnen.[22]

Because it depends on biological processes and on nature, agriculture is especially buffeted by natural phenomena. Agriculture can be expected to accept risk from nature without subsidies. In an age when the nation presumably has better information, analysis, and tools to control instability, it is disturbing that in the 1970s and 1980s so much of the instability facing farmers has come from public policy. Manmade sources of economic ills can be reduced or avoided, and agricultural interests need to be at the forefront of corrective action. It makes sense for farmers and the organizations representing them to turn some of their attention from commodity programs to macroeconomic policies that will continue to devastate agriculture in the absence of stronger political pressures for reform.

In formulating a political strategy, farmers have a dilemma. On the one hand, if they and others make sacrifices that restore fiscal responsibility, all will be better off in the long run despite short-run dislocations. On the other hand, if current fiscal policy continues, farmers have a case for continued compensation for the "tax" imposed on them by high real interest and exchange rates. Farmers get the worst of all outcomes if they sacrifice subsidies to promote fiscal responsibility while others do not so that high real interest and exchange rates continue.

Appendix

Effect of the Government Deficit on Interest Rates

Table A-1 shows results of ordinary least squares regressions of various interest rates (percent) in year T on the inflation rate (percent) in year T, total government (state and federal) deficit as a percentage of gross investment in year T and year $T - 1$, and the coefficient of variation (percent) for Aaa corporate bonds in the past five years. The theory is that nominal interest rates are increased by inflation, by greater variation in past interest rates, and by the deficit in relation to gross investment.

Of special interest is the effect of the deficit on interest rates. The deficit-investment ratio was 30 percent in 1983. The reductions in interest rates predicted respectively from the equations in table A-1 with the deficit-investment ratio zero (no deficit) are as follows:

Dependent variable and equation	Reduction in interest rate with zero deficit (percentage points)
Aaa corporate bonds	
1	4.2
2 (T and T − 1)	6.0
3	3.6
Federal Land Bank	
1	3.0
2	4.5
3	3.0
Production credit associations	
1	3.0
2	3.6
3	2.1
Rural bank production loans	
1	3.9
2	5.1
3	3.0

Estimates vary depending on the specification, but equations containing current and lagged deficit variables suggest that elimination of the deficit could subtract approximately four percentage points from nominal interest rates when inflation and other variables are held constant. Because the equations are linear, reductions in the deficit of less than 100 percent are merely proportional to those shown above.

As shown by the probability of a greater t value $(P > t)$ in table A-1, nearly all coefficients except those on the lagged deficit are statistically significant and display signs predicted by economic theory. The Durbin-Watson (D-W) d statistic indicates significant positive autocorrelation in the residuals.

The positive autocorrelation suggests that relevant variables are omitted. Several variables were added including the proportion of industry capacity utilized, unemployment rate, a lagged dependent variable to allow longer-term adjustments, and lagged independent variables to reflect expectations. Equations also were estimated from data divided into 1950–1966 and 1967–1983 periods. None of these formulations improved results. Other functional forms, interactions, and estimates using autoregressive least squares and ac-

TABLE A-1

ORDINARY LEAST SQUARES REGRESSIONS OF INTEREST RATES ON THE INFLATION RATE, GOVERNMENT DEFICIT-INVESTMENT RATIO, AND THE VARIATION IN INTEREST RATES. U.S. ANNUAL DATA, 1950–1983

Dependent Variable and Equation	Intercept		Inflation rate (%)		Deficit-investment ratio (%) T		Deficit-investment ratio (%) T = 1		Coef. of variation (%)		R^2	D-W
	Coef.	($P>t$)	Coef.	($P>t$)	Coef.	($P>t$)	Coef.	($P>t$)	Coef.	($P>t$)		
Aaa corporate bond yield												
1	3.14	<.01	.61	<.01	.14	<.01					.72	1.01
2	2.71	<.01	.66	<.01	.10	<.01	.10	<.01			.79	.83
3	1.27	.01	.64	<.01	.05	.04	.07	.01	.44	<.01	.87	.99
Federal Land Banks												
1	4.72	<.01	.40	<.01	.10	<.01					.68	.92
2	4.39	<.01	.44	<.01	.07	<.01	.08	<.01			.77	.78
3	3.22	<.01	.42	<.01	.04	.03	.06	<.01	.36	<.01	.88	.96
Production credit associations												
1	5.80	<.01	.41	<.01	.10	<.01					.67	.81
2	5.65	<.01	.43	<.01	.08	<.01	.04	.23			.68	.73
3	4.55	<.01	.42	<.01	.05	.05	.02	.53	.34	<.01	.78	.75

Independent Variable

TABLE A-1 (Continued)

Dependent Variable and Equation	Intercept		Inflation rate (%)		Deficit-investment ratio (%)				Coef. of variation (%)		R^2	D-W
					T		$T=1$					
	Coef.	(P>t)	Coef.	(P>t)	Coef.	(P>t)	Coef.	(P>t)	Coef.	(P>t)		
Rural bank production loans												
1	5.80	<.01	.48	<.01	.13	<.01					.57	.70
2	5.47	<.01	.52	<.01	.10	<.02	.07	.08			.61	.56
3	5.83	<.01	.51	<.01	.05	.15	.19	.05	.43	.01	.70	.49

SOURCE: See appendix text for data description. Data from Council of Economic Advisers, *Economic Report*; Amols and Kaiser, "Agricultural Finance Statistics"; and Emanuel Melichar, *Agricultural Finance Databook* (Board of Governors of the Federal Reserve System) (September 1984 and earlier issues).

counting for changes in monetary structure (banking deregulation, Fed targeting of money supply rather than interest rates) might improve results but were not considered in the equations of table A-1.

Notes

1. See Emanuel Melichar, "An Overview of Agricultural Banking Experience" (Paper presented at Financial Stress in Agriculture Workshop, Kansas City, Missouri) (Washington, D.C.: Board of Governors of the Federal Reserve System, 1984); and Peter Barry, "Impacts of Financial Stress and Regulatory Forces on Financial Markets for Agriculture," NPA Report 204 (Washington, D.C.: National Planning Association, 1984).

2. Changes beiure 1980 influenced the ability of farmers to adjust to financial stress in the 1980s (see Michael Boehlje and Vernon Eidman, "Financial Stress in Agriculture: Implications for Producers," *American Journal of Agricultural Economics*, vol. 65 [December 1983], p. 937). Real estate debt raised flexibility but increased interest payments on debt, other things equal. Asset liquidity declined, as measured by the drop from 11 percent in 1970 to 7 percent in 1980 for financial assets and crop storage as a proportion of all farm assets.

3. I have shown elsewhere that a high ratio of debt to net income is normal in an inflationary economy such as that of the 1970s. A high ratio reveals a cash flow squeeze but not necessarily a low return, because much of the total return comes as capital gain rather than as current income. See Luther Tweeten, "Farmland Pricing and Cash Flow in an Inflationary Economy," Research Report P-811 (Stillwater: Agricultural Experiment Station, Oklahoma State University, 1981).

4. Emanuel Melichar, "The Incidence of Financial Stress in Agriculture" (Paper presented at Agricultural Seminar, Congressional Budget Office) (Washington, D.C.: Board of Governors of the Federal Reserve System, 1984).

5. Ibid.

6. Luther Tweeten, "Diagnosing and Treating Farm Problems," in Jimmye Hillman, ed., *United States Agricultural Policy, 1985 and Beyond* (Tucson: University of Arizona, Department of Agricultural Economics, 1984), pp. 19–52.

7. The real interest rate is the nominal (observed) interest rate less the inflation rate.

8. John Brake, "Short-Term Credit Policies for Dealing with Farm Financial Stress and Their Impacts on Structure and Adoption of Technology (Paper presented at Financial Stress in Agriculture Workshop, Kansas City Federal Reserve Bank, October 1984).

9. Computed from the formula $I = r\,A\,i\,L$, where terms are defined in the text table. The percentage increase in I is the sum of the percentage increase in each component.

10. Tweeten, "Farmland Pricing and Cash Flow."

11. See ibid.

12. Ibid.

13. Ibid.

14. Instability from weather and from business and commodity cycles has long been a problem to farmers. Shifting from high nominal to high real interest rates is another episode in the continuing saga of instability. High real interest rates raise costs

of holding buffer stocks, hence increase instability because the market holds less stocks to reduce commodity supply and price variation between periods. Shifting from one inflation rate to another causes real price and income instability to agriculture because prices paid to farmers tend to change more rapidly than prices paid by farmers. See Luther Tweeten, "Impact of Federal Fiscal-Monetary Policies on Farm Structure," *Southern Journal of Agricultural Economics,* vol. 15, no. 1 (July 1983), pp. 61–68. In the long run, however, real prices paid and received by farmers seem not to be influenced significantly by inflation rates. High real interest rates also contribute to other problems, such as soil erosion—high discount rates reduce benefit-cost ratios for soil conservation measures.

15. Tweeten, "Diagnosing and Treating."

16. Ibid., p. 22.

17. Patrick O'Brien, "World Market Trends and Prospects: Implications for U.ʊ. Agricultural Policy," in *Agriculture, Stability and Growth* (Port Washington, N.Y.: Associated Faculty Press, 1984); Resources for the Future, "Feeding a Hungry World," *Resources,* vol. 76 (Spring 1984), pp. 1–20; and Winrock International, "World Agriculture, Review and Prospects into the 1990's" (Morrilton, Ark.: Winrock International Research and Training Center, 1983).

18. Tweeten, "Farmland Pricing and Cash Flow," p. 36.

19. The calculation was made by extending to 1985 the estimates of purchasing power parity by Dallas Batten and Michael Belongia, "The Recent Decline in Agricultural Exports," *Federal Reserve Bank of St. Louis Review,* vol. 66, no. 8 (October 1984), p. 10. The presumption is that lower real interest rates would trigger the fall in the dollar.

20. The short-run exchange rate elasticity is from John Dunmore and James Longmire, "Sources of Recent Changes in U.S. Agricultural Exports" (Washington, D.C.: International Economics Division, Economic Research Service, Department of Agriculture, 1984), p. 28. The long-run estimate is from unpublished estimates of Tom Barclay, Department of Agricultural Economics, Oklahoma State University.

21. Markets fail when private discount rates (because of need for consumption *now*) well exceed social discount rates and where private incentives sharply deviate from social incentives (disassociation of private from social marginal costs). These same difficulties have become a growing cause of public policy failure in recent years. Decline of party discipline, opening of legislative processes in congressional committees and elsewhere to special interests, and other sources of divergence between private and social political costs (or benefits) have seriously distracted from serving the public interest. Also the short planning horizons of Congress and the president place high priority on consumption now at the expense of future growth. Consequently, political failure has been as widespread as market failure. It is increasingly naive to assume that the invisible hand of the political process leads government to serve the public interest.

22. James Bonnen, "U.S. Agriculture, Instability and National Political Implications," in Hillman, *United States Agricultural Policy,* pp. 53–84.

Commentary

Emanuel Melichar

I agree with many of the points made by Tweeten. In particular, his message concerning fiscal policy is one that we should heed.

The foreign trade deficit and the federal budget deficit are two related and unsustainable trends. At some point, it will become financially painful to service the debt that is being incurred, especially the foreign debt. Servicing the debt will force reduction of government spending or of the quality of private living. The real debt service burden may also be reduced through price inflation.

It would be ironic if, at some future date, national defense is weakened in the course of coping with debt service burdens that arose, in part, because improved defense was financed by borrowing. Instead of raising taxes to pay for improved defense, large tax cuts were simultaneously voted. Tax rates were reduced, and additional opportunities were provided for the accumulation of tax-deferred wealth. Investors are locking in double-digit nominal interest rates, to compound tax deferred for up to four decades.

The public at large must service the public debt accumulating in these accounts. In nominal terms, the future obligations are mind-boggling and can perhaps be most readily understood by looking at data on issues of zero-coupon bonds. The Student Loan Marketing Association, for example, raised $72.5 million in 1984 by selling zero-coupon bonds with a value of $2 billion at maturity in 2014. Then it raised $127.5 million by selling zero-coupon bonds with a redemption value of over $5 billion in 2022. As such debt service burdens of our present spending tend to depress future spending, there may be great pressure for stimulative measures that coincidentally produce inflation that reduces the real burden of debt.

One other comment on macroeconomic policy. Both Tweeten and preceding speakers criticized the monetary policy of the 1970s. They seem to believe that lower and more stable money growth could have prevented inflation and "stagflation." They might rethink that conclusion, particularly because agriculture contributed to the price shocks of that decade.

When farm commodity prices soared (wheat tripled, corn tripled, and

---

The analyses and conclusions are solely those of the author and do not necessarily reflect the views of the Board of Governors of the Federal Reserve System or of other members of its staff.

113

soybeans quadrupled from the spring of 1972 to the fall of 1973), transferring real income from the general public to the farm sector, should money growth have been held steady, so that other prices and wages would on average have to fall as necessary to keep average prices stable? Clearly, an immediate recession would have resulted if that type of adjustment had been forced. Rather than accepting their reduced real income, other sectors react by seeking price and wage increases in vain (on average) attempts to maintain real profits and income. So alternatively, should money growth have accommodated this inflationary spiral?

Neither of these alternatives is a tenable policy response to a major price shock. Rather, secondary and later price and wage increases must be accommodated as necessary to prevent depression, but then must be dampened to prevent runaway inflation and gradually restore price stability. Sectors losing the most real income to other sectors experience recession. The result of this policy was called stagflation. Those who lament the stagflation following the major price shocks of 1972–1974 (farm and oil) and 1980 (oil) should ponder the alternatives. The timing and degree of monetary restraint could have been better, as is always the case in retrospect, but some variety of stagflation had to occur.

The remainder of my comments deals with estimating the incidence of financial stress among farmers.

First, I have no problem with Tweeten's building on the estimates I made in November 1984, in the paper "The Incidence of Financial Stress in Agriculture." In presenting his results, however, he contrasted his estimate of the proportion of farmers in financial stress with my estimate of that proportion on all "farms," which is lower, rather than with my estimate of that proportion on family-sized commercial farms, which is higher. Thus he casts me, unfairly, as underestimating or minimizing the problem of farm financial stress.

Using, as the base, all 2.4 million operators whose units meet the Census Bureau's definition of a farm, I estimated, as Tweeten described, that 9 percent of them are financially stressed and that the stressed group owns 14 percent of operators' farm assets and owes 39 percent of operators' farm debt. I had also shown, however, that most of the operators with farm financial stress must be those with farms producing annual sales between $40,000 and $499,999. On average, the smaller farms have little or no net farm income, and did not have any during the farm boom. And, on average, the small number of very large farms with sales of $500,000 or more have remained highly profitable, and so not many can be financially stressed. Thus, I concluded, about one-third of the operators of the remaining farms are relatively heavily indebted and likely to be experiencing financial stress. This is a very significant proportion, higher than Tweeten's 22 percent. Furthermore, I estimated that this third owes nearly two-thirds of the total debt of the operators of this group of farms. My estimates certainly did not minimize the incidence or importance of financial stress.

Among possible policy responses to farm financial stress, Tweeten listed targeted credit assistance. On their face, such programs appear to be efficient ways to get assistance to those who need it the most. Providing money directly and only to those farmers in financial distress seems more efficient than attempting to raise farm income generally by amounts that would be meaningful to those in distress.

Experience with such credits extended in the late 1970s, however, indicates the problems they present. In particular, those farmers who made the most ill-advised or, in retrospect, uneconomic investments, or who are lacking in technical, managerial, or marketing skills, will appear to be the most in need. They will be at the top of the list for targeted assistance and will be difficult or impossible to sort out.

In addition, some of the farm investments made during the boom are not only uneconomic now, but have undesirable environmental aspects that, while tolerable during a period of acute need for more food, are now unsupportable. Farmers who plowed grassland subject to wind erosion or drilled wells to tap an irreplaceable aquifer now appear among the most needy, but these investments need to be reversed rather than perpetuated.

I will close with several comments on our perceptions and analyses, as researchers, of the financial potential and condition of farms. Reading Tweeten's paper reinforced my belief that we need to rethink our characterization of farms by size. Our classifications by gross sales tend to mislead in that many farms seem larger than they really are in terms of the net income they are capable of producing; in addition, we need to adjust our classifications to reflect the general price inflation that has occurred.

Net income averages about 20 to 25 percent of gross sales. Sixty-two percent of all farms have gross sales under $20,000. On the very largest of these farms, therefore, one can net $5,000 per year, or $100 per week, $15 per day. The earning potential of this enterprise is equal to that of a motorized paper route or some other way of earning $15 per day—and this is the largest of this group. Twenty years ago, we were employing a useful category called noncommercial farms, which was based on multiple criteria involving the amount of off-farm work as well as the amount of farm sales. A category like that is still needed. In banking, there is now a category called nonbank banks. Perhaps these farms should be called nonfarm farms.

If $15 per day is an appropriate lower limit for small farm-farms, where might we draw the line between small and mid-sized farm-farms? Perhaps at a net income equal to starting salaries for college graduates, say, $20,000 to $25,000 per year? So $100,000 in annual gross sales is where we might reasonably separate small farms from mid-sized farms.

If that sounds too high, think again. That is gross sales of $2,000 a week, $300 a day. The earning potential of that farm is equal to that of a little newstand in a hotel that also grosses $300 per day and nets $75 in labor and capital income. To avoid misleading ourselves as well as those who use our analyses, we need to use classifications that are consistent with modern connotations of the adjectives that we employ.

My final point concerns the identification of farms with financial stress. In work done about a year ago, I classified farms by debt-asset ratio and showed that the debt-asset ratio was probably highly correlated with difficulty in servicing debt from farm income. I was using 1979 census data that did not include income and interest payments and thus used the debt-asset ratio as a proxy for such direct data on financial stress. These are the same data on debt and assets from which Tweeten has derived additional estimates of financial difficulties.

For the debt-asset ratio to provide useful indications of the incidence of financial stress, we need farms to have the same relative profitability, interest rate, and debt repayment schedule. Among these, the profitability assumption is the most unrealistic. Profitability differs by size of farm and by type of farming. Prices on some products are far better than on others. There are also regional differences because of drought, floods, and freezes.

If one has information on income and interest payments, financial stress is measured directly rather than inferred from debt-asset ratios. Then, the debt-asset ratio takes its place, alongside profitability, interest rate, and other factors, as one of the variables that are important in explaining the relative degree of financial stress.

Ideally, to measure the effect of debt, one has data on net income before interest payments and on income remaining after interest is paid. With such data, one can far more confidently assess and compare the relative incidence and severity of financial stress on different types and sizes of farms than if one has data only on debt-asset ratios. One can also measure the effect of debt service.

The U.S. Department of Agriculture (USDA) has recently improved an annual survey to produce such income data but nevertheless has continued to couch its analyses in terms of debt-asset ratios. Reports on farm finance surveys conducted by universities have also emphasized debt-asset ratios. As a result, the analytical content of these surveys has not been fully exploited. The USDA has pointed out, for example, that poultry farms have a relatively high average debt-asset ratio, that this may mean that they have more severe financial problems than other farms, but that they may not be stressed because they produce larger sales and income per dollar of assets. Both analyst and reader are left hanging. When analysts already have, or can obtain, information on income received and interest paid, they should use that as the primary indicator of financial stress and then investigate the relative degree to which debt-asset ratio and other factors are responsible for such stress.

Part Two
Policy Options for 1985

Options for the 1985 Farm Bill: An Analysis and Evaluation

*Stanley R. Johnson, Abner W. Womack, William H. Meyers,
Robert E. Young II, and Jon Brandt*

The 1985 farm bill will be drafted during a period for agriculture and the U.S. domestic and world economies quite different from that when the 1981 farm bill was enacted. In determining the policies and programs associated with these four-year agricultural legislative packages, there is a tendency to focus almost exclusively on specific commodity markets. This tendency has frequently resulted in legislation with outcomes for agriculture quite inconsistent with the intentions of the parties to the policy-making process. The 1981 farm bill, for example, set into motion policies designed to serve expanded export markets resulting from domestic and foreign economic growth and favorable exchange rates. Loan rates and target prices were indexed to expected inflation rates as well. If there is a lesson to be learned from this and previous experiences with farm legislation, it is that the effects of farm programs should be evaluated across commodity markets, for the agricultural sector, and under different sets of economic conditions for the United States and economies in major exporting and importing countries.

The importance of considering program options in a broadened context, abstracted from current economic and political pressures, is especially apparent for the 1985 farm bill. There is increasing evidence of significant financial stress in agriculture due to high interest rates, falling land prices, and commodity prices affected by slowed economic growth and high exchange rates. In addition, world commodity markets are being realigned as a result of technological change, the debt situation in developing countries, and responses of competitors to the relatively high U.S. commodity prices dictated by past farm legislation. It is the objective of this paper to contribute to the 1985 policy debate by providing complete and explicit quantitative evaluations of four major agricultural policy options.

Four 1985 Farm Bill Options

The four policy options evaluated are (1) the base line, (2) the market option, (3) the expanded export base line, and (4) the 80 percent of parity option:

- the base line: a continuation of the current policy under moderate to positive conditions for the U.S. and world economies with minimum loan and target rates set at 1984–1985 levels
- the market option: a policy of minimum government intervention under moderate to positive conditions for the U.S. and world economies and with loan rates moving more toward world market prices and an elimination of the target price
- the expanded export base line: a continuation of the current policy under more optimistic conditions for the U.S. and world economies and with minimum loan and target rates set at 1984–1985 levels
- the 80 percent of parity option: farm prices set at 80 percent of parity, production controls through a mandatory quota system to set retail prices consistent with farm price parity levels, and moderate to positive conditions for U.S. and world economies

These four options were evaluated with the large-scale econometric model of the Food and Agricultural Policy Research Institute (FAPRI). Specific sets of program parameters consistent with the general themes of the policy options are specified for each major commodity market. Implications of these policies are evaluated across commodity markets and for the livestock sector. Finally, the outcomes of these policies in major commodity markets are related to farm income, government costs, and the consumer price index. The evaluation includes an analysis of commodity program effects not only within the domestic U.S. economy but also in import and export markets.

The Policy Model

The FAPRI annual agricultural policy model has components for each of the major commodities. These include livestock (beef, pork, and poultry) and crops (feed grains—corn, sorghum, oats, and barley—soybeans, wheat, rice, and cotton). The econometric models for the commodity components include behavioral relationships for production, stocks, exports, imports, final consumption, and, if appropriate, consumption as intermediate products. Each commodity model can be operated on a "stand alone" basis or integrated into a larger system with other commodity components. Sketches of the structures of the hog and corn models are shown in figures 1 and 2.

The commodity components are linked for the policy analysis exercises as shown in figure 3. These links between the commodity markets are designed to reflect the simultaneity of price determination processes in U.S. agriculture. Livestock prices, for example, condition the demand for feed grains; feed grain prices, in turn, influence investment and production deci-

FIGURE 1
STRUCTURE OF THE HOG MODEL IN THE FAPRI POLICY MODELING SYSTEM

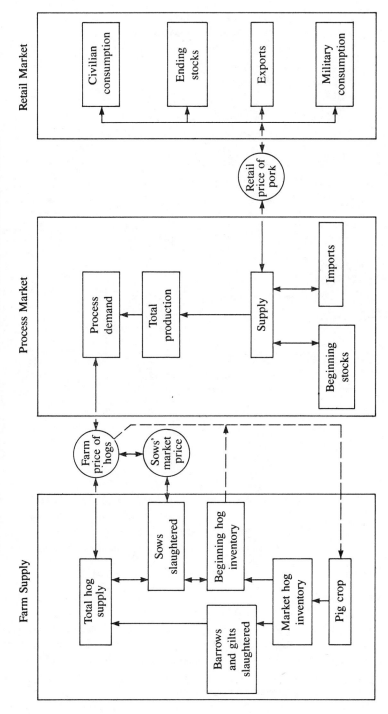

FIGURE 2
STRUCTURE OF THE CORN MODEL IN THE FAPRI POLICY
MODELING SYSTEM

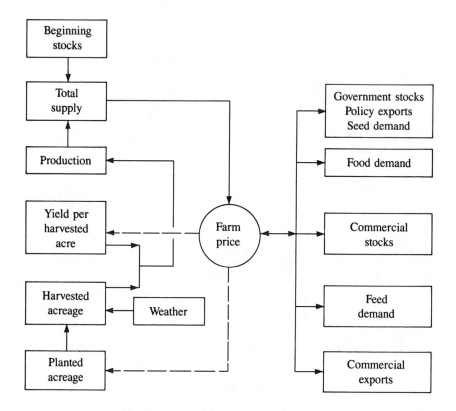

sions for livestock and, correspondingly, livestock prices. These links across commodity markets are especially important for policy evaluation. Government policies for the major commodity markets in the United States are only for crops. Thus, to evaluate the policies fully, links to the livestock markets must be included.

In addition to the commodity components, the FAPRI policy model has farm income and government components. The farm income component uses output for the major commodity components, along with simplified information on the specialized commodities and farm expenses, to generate estimates of gross farm income, net farm income, and other sectorwide performance measures. The government component estimates costs by commodity program and total budget exposure. It also calculates information reflecting the extent of government intervention in agriculture.

122

FIGURE 3
Links among Commodity Components in the FAPRI Policy Modeling System

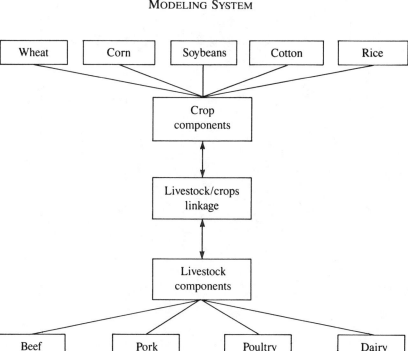

The dimensions of the FAPRI model are, by necessity, relatively large. First, the model rests on an extensive set of predetermined or exogenous variables. These variables reflect the U.S. domestic economy, the world economy, climatic conditions, and other determinants of prices in agricultural commodity markets. These conditioning or predetermined variables number over 1,100. The number of endogenous variables, or variables determined by the model, is 325: 130 for livestock, 110 for crops, and the rest for farm income and government cost. The model has 250 behavioral equations, and seventy-five identities. The pork model illustrated in figure 1 has seventeen behavioral equations, and the corn model illustrated in figure 2 has twelve. For the policy evaluation exercises subsequently reported, the model was estimated from annual data for the period 1961–1982.

The FAPRI agricultural policy model has a number of key structural parameters. A complete review of these and the model specification is not within the purview of this discussion, but parameters that will contribute to the transparency of subsequent analyses of policy options are provided in table

TABLE 1
REPRESENTATIVE STRUCTURAL ELASTICITIES FROM THE FAPRI AGRICULTURAL POLICY MODEL

Commodity	Feed Elasticity	Feed Share[a] (%)	Food Elasticity	Food Share[a] (%)	Exports Elasticity	Exports Share[a] (%)	Stocks Elasticity	Stocks Share[a] (%)	Total	Acreage Response Elasticity[b]
Corn	−0.19	51	−0.20	11	−0.28	25	−1.24	10	−0.32	0.13
Wheat	−1.47	9	−0.04	16	−0.16	36	−0.89	35	−0.51	0.18
Soybeans	−1.40[c]	50			−0.83	37	−0.08	9	−1.01	0.47
Soymeal	−0.58	75			−0.27	24			−0.50	
Rice			−0.10	21	−0.25	41	−0.80	27	−0.34	0.40
Cotton	−0.11	34			−0.35	38	−0.33	28	−0.26	0.15

Export Demand Own and Cross Price Elasticities

Commodity	Corn	Wheat	Soybeans	Soybean meal	Soybean oil	Rice	Cotton
Corn	−0.28						
Wheat		−0.16		0.49		0.01	
Soybeans	0.34		−0.83	0.39	0.23		
Rice						−0.25	
Cotton							−0.35

Retail Meat Price and Income Effects[e]

Commodity	Beef	Pork	Chicken	Income
Beef	-0.35	0.13	0.15	0.60
Pork	0.07	-0.79	0.40	0.42
Chicken	0.51	0.44	-0.67	0.35

a. Shares are computed at 1983–1984 levels for the indicated variables.
b. Foreign supply elasticities for major competitors: corn, Thailand, 0.40, South Africa, 0.06, Argentina, 0.10; soybeans, Brazil, 0.01, Argentina, 0.12; and wheat, Australia, 1.26, Canada, 0.47, Argentina, 0.20.
c. Bean crush demand.
d. Cotton mill demand.
e. Diagonal price effects and income effects are flexibilities. Off-diagonal effects are retail cross elasticities of price transmission.

125

1. Observe that the short-term export elasticities evaluated at mean 1961–1982 prices are relatively inelastic for the FAPRI model. Generally, short-term elasticities are under 1 in absolute value, and longer-term elasticities are near 1. Selected domestic retail demand elasticity estimates used in the model are also listed in table 1. Again, they are evaluated at the means for the sample period. Elasticity estimates are also presented for stocks, acreages, and income. Generally, the response estimates in the table are more conservative than those developed in less comprehensive models. Finally, these elasticity estimates should be regarded as indicators of the structure implicit in the model. We have taken liberties in defining "representative values" reported.

Policy Evaluation Process

The policy evaluation process is an exercise conducted with the estimated FAPRI agricultural policy model and additional information related to:

- initial conditions for the agricultural sector
- projections of conditioning factors for agriculture from the U.S. economy
- projections of factors affecting imports and exports
- assumptions on parameters for implementing the policies

The policy exercises are, of course, implicitly forward looking. For this reason, the conditioning factors for agriculture from the U.S. economy and for imports and exports and the parameters for the four policy options must be specified or projected over the evaluation period. For the present exercise, this period is 1984–1985 to 1989–1990, six years. Initial conditions are specified implicitly by calibrating the model to the 1983–1984 crop year. The sequences of policy parameters are constructed to specialize the four program options. It is shown in the next section that implementing these four policy options requires highly structured sets of assumptions on target prices, loan rates, stock levels, and other policy parameters.

Satellite Structure. The policy analysis with the FAPRI model incorporates a satellite hypothesis. Specifically, variables reflecting the general U.S. economy and foreign economies are taken as predetermined or determined outside the model. Policy parameters for the four alternatives are introduced in the period of reference. Then the agricultural policy model is solved annually and sequentially over the evaluation period. After the model is solved, performance variables of interest are calculated. These performance variables are in three general categories: market, government, and industry or sector. The satellite relationship of the FAPRI agricultural policy model, the implementation of the policy regimes, and the generation of the performance variables are illustrated in figure 4.

FIGURE 4
Policy Structure in the FAPRI Model

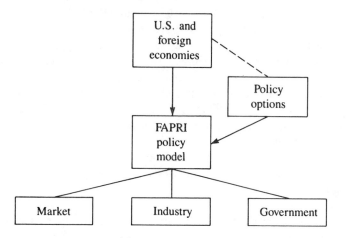

In implementing the policies government costs were calculated as a residual. Specifically, market prices dictated by the parameters for the policies were maintained by reduced acreage and paid diversion programs. Supply levels required to achieve prices consistent with the four policy options were obtained with these two policy instruments and government stocks. Government stocks targets were imposed, on the basis of long-term relation between domestic U.S. production and consumption levels. The assumption underlying the imposed stocks target was that the "system" had in the past been rational. When the policy instruments were implemented to achieve prices required by the program options, government costs were generated. The supply control instruments affect substitution relationships across commodities through the acreage equations. Program participation rates or acreage levels and supply levels were determined by using implied prices for participation in government programs as well as models external to the FAPRI model that generated break-even prices for representative firms.

The Process. The solution to the FAPRI policy model and the rolling of the annual solutions of the model through the policy evaluation period involve a sequence of steps. At each point in this sequence, temporally current information is introduced, the model is rolled forward, and the results are cross-checked with those from previous annual solutions. That is, there is cross-checking as the annual sequential solution progresses to determine whether the model is producing consistent and plausible results. This aspect of the

127

solution process necessarily requires judgment. Thus the evaluation exercise is not conducted within a "black box" or with a "push-button" model.

Step one in the process is to identify the general economic assumptions for the U.S. and foreign economies. These assumptions, for the present exercise, are drawn from other sources. Assumptions on exchange rates, economic growth, interest rates, and other factors must be implicitly consistent. That is, the values for the projection period must be consistent with relative values for these variables experienced in the past by the U.S. and world economies and with a particular model. The Congressional Budget Office, Wharton Econometrics, and other private and public groups produce sets of these projections. For this exercise projections from these two organizations were used. It is important to emphasize that using these projections as predetermined and the operation of the model on a satellite basis ignore potentially important feedback to general price levels and the general economy from agriculture.

Step two is to develop the foreign sector projections. This requires the use of both the external information driving the model and structural equations in the FAPRI model. For the major exporters and importers, assumptions on economies and projections for the future are from Wharton Econometrics. Partial reduced-form equations from the FAPRI model are then applied to estimate anticipated exports or imports. The result is a trade component in the model that is partly predetermined and partly from a partial reduced-form estimation.

Step three in the evaluation is to specify policy parameters for each commodity market, loan rates, target prices, government costs, reduced acreage programs, paid diversion parameters, and other factors. These factors are described in detail in the next section. Some tuning of the way the policies are implemented occurs as the evaluation exercise evolves. That is, it is difficult to specify the parameter values for a particular policy option several years into the future and attain required prices and other performance variables without first experimenting with alternative parameter values in the model.

Step four is to align the annual solutions to the FAPRI model. There are, in fact, three functions for this process. First the information on exports and imports is incorporated in the model. Then general economic assumptions are used to condition the demands for the livestock sector. The livestock sector demands for feed grains and the demands for wheat and other crop commodities are then determined provisionally for the U.S. and foreign markets. With these provisionally determined livestock demands and associated feed use requirements, the crops portion of the model is incorporated. That portion generates supplies of commodities consistent with the policy assumptions, the model structure, and effects of the exogenous conditioning variables. The policy parameters are then adjusted to achieve prices, stocks, and other market variables consistent with the policy prescriptions. The final solution is

FIGURE 5
Policy Evaluation Process with the FAPRI Model

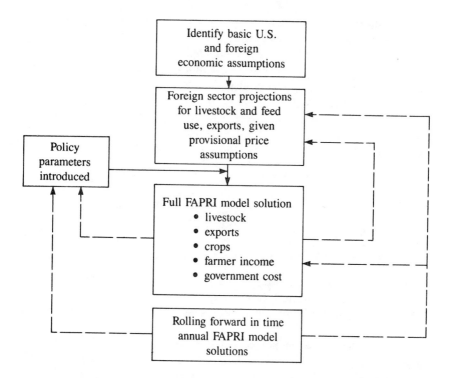

attained by iterating between the livestock and crops components, adjusting to achieve the parameters prescribed by the policy.

Step five of the evaluation is to iterate forward from the base year over the policy analysis period. Specifically, in each year a sequence indicated by the four steps above is repeated. For each year, consequences for the policy are evaluated in relation to the outcomes in previous years. Thus the "solution process" for the model is not simultaneous and does not involve a general optimization within the model. Instead, it is sequential, with judgment exercised to introduce policy parameters that "balance" effects across the years and maintain levels for performance variables that are consistent with those prescribed by the policy. This sequence of steps and the iterative process is illustrated in figure 5.

Policy Alternatives

The four policy options to be evaluated in this exercise were broadly identified above. This discussion compares and contrasts these options and relates them to more general policy goals and objectives for the agricultural sector. Implications are developed for three sets of performance measures: government, commodity markets, and the industry. Expanded analyses of these policies might be directed to assessments of income transfer, risk, food security, price levels, program adaptability, the structure of the agricultural sector, resource use and conservation, and political stability.

Details on the options for major agricultural commodity markets selected for analysis are listed below. The list contains highlights for comparing and contrasting the policies. A summary of the policy alternatives is presented in table 2. The entries in the table have been abstracted from the values used in the evaluations. Actual values for the parameters, loan rates, target prices, reductions in acreage, government costs, and other features are provided in the sections in which the policies are evaluated.

Base line. The base-line option through 1989–1990 requires parameters for program operation on loan and target rates, P.L. 480 shipments, government stocks, and acreage control instruments. The following criteria have been used in establishing the program parameters used to implement the base line:

- loan rates and target price minimums set at 1984–1985 levels
- upward adjustment in loan and target price to reflect five-year moving average farm price, with high-low prices removed for feed grains, wheat, and rice
- cotton loan rate set at the lower of 85 percent of the preceding three-year average domestic price or 90 percent of the average price in northern Europe, with a minimum of fifty-five cents a pound
- soybean loan established at 75 percent of the simple average of prices received by farmers over the preceding five marketing years—excluding the high and low years—with a minimum of $5.02 per bushel
- target prices at a constant percentage of loan rates, with 1984–1985 as the base
- reserve programs for feed grains and wheat with reserve entry price set at the loan rate; no limit on level of reserves; exit at current levels, plus a provision to allow grain to stay in the farmer-held reserve (FHR) and not default to the Commodity Credit Corporation (CCC)
- paid diversion and reduced acreage control programs implemented if stocks exceed long-term average levels
- base acreages for all crops maintained at 1984–1985 levels

Market Option. The market option maintains minimum government support and corresponding levels of market intervention. Loan rates are adjusted up or down according to a fixed percentage of a moving average market price. The

TABLE 2

VALUES FOR SELECTED POLICY PARAMETERS APPLIED IN THE EXERCISES EVALUATING FOR FOUR ALTERNATIVES, 1984–1985 TO 1989–1990

Crop/ Year	Base Line							Market Option						
	Loan rate	Target rate	Reserve entry	Reserve release	Set aside	Paid diversion	Payment rate	Loan rate	Target rate	Reserve entry	Reserve release	Set aside	Paid diversion	Payment rate
Corn[a]														
1984–85	2.55	3.03	2.55	3.25	10[b]	—[b]	—	2.55	3.03	2.55	3.25	10[b]	—	—
1985–86	2.55	3.03	2.55	3.25	10	—	—	2.55	3.03	2.55	3.25	10	—	—
1986–87	2.55	3.03	2.55	3.25	10	—	—	2.13	—	2.13	3.25	NAC	NAC	NAC
1987–88	2.55	3.03	2.55	3.25	10	10	1.50	2.13	—	2.13	3.25	NAC	NAC	NAC
1988–89	2.55	3.03	2.55	3.25	10	10	1.50	2.09	—	2.09	3.25	NAC	NAC	NAC
1989–90	2.55	3.03	2.55	3.25	10	10	1.50	2.04	—	2.04	3.25	NAC	NAC	NAC
Wheat[a]														
1984–85	3.30	4.38	3.30	4.45	30	10–20	PIK 80	3.30	4.38	3.30	4.45	30	10–20	PIK 80
1985–86	3.30	4.38	3.30	4.45	20	10	2.70	3.30	4.38	3.30	4.45	20	10	2.70
1986–87	3.30	4.38	3.30	4.45	20	10	2.70	2.79	—	2.79	4.45	NAC	NAC	—
1987–88	3.30	4.38	3.30	4.45	20	10	2.70	2.75	—	2.75	4.45	NAC	NAC	—
1988–89	3.30	4.38	3.30	4.45	20	10	2.70	2.68	—	2.68	4.45	NAC	NAC	—
1989–90	3.30	4.38	3.30	4.45	20	10	2.70	2.66	—	2.66	4.45	NAC	NAC	—
Cotton[c]														
1984–85	56	81	—	—	25	—	—	56	81	—	—	25	—	—
1985–86	56	81	—	—	15	10	30	56	81	—	—	15	10	30

(Table continues)

131

TABLE 2 (continued)

	Base Line							Market Option						
Crop/ Year	Loan rate	Target rate	Reserve entry	Reserve release	Set aside	Paid diversion	Payment rate	Loan rate	Target rate	Reserve entry	Reserve release	Set aside	Paid diversion	Payment rate
1986–87	56	81	—	—	15	10	30	46	—	—	—	NAC	NAC	—
1987–88	56	81	—	—	15	10	30	47	—	—	—	NAC	NAC	—
1988–89	56	81	—	—	20	—	—	50	—	—	—	NAC	NAC	—
1989–90	56	81	—	—	20	—	—	50	—	—	—	NAC	NAC	—
Rice[d]														
1984–85	8.14	11.90	—	—	25	—	—	8.14	11.90	—	—	25	—	—
1985–86	8.00	11.90	—	—	20	15	3.50	8.14	11.90	—	—	20	15	3.50
1986–87	8.00	11.90	—	—	20	15	3.50	6.73	—	—	—	NAC	NAC	—
1987–88	8.00	11.90	—	—	20	15	3.50	6.66	—	—	—	NAC	NAC	—
1988–89	8.00	11.90	—	—	25	—	—	6.41	—	—	—	NAC	NAC	—
1989–90	8.00	11.90	—	—	25	—	—	5.95	—	—	—	NAC	NAC	—

	Expanded Export Base Line							80 Percent of Parity						
Crop/ Year	Loan rate	Target rate	Reserve entry	Reserve release	Set aside	Paid diversion	Payment rate	Loan rate	Target rate	Reserve entry	Reserve release	Set aside	Paid diversion	Payment rate
Corn[a]														
1984–85	2.55	3.03	2.55	3.25	10[b]	—[b]	—	2.55	3.03	2.55	3.25	10	—	—
1985–86	2.55	3.03	2.55	3.25	10	—	—	2.55	3.03	2.55	3.25	10	—	—
1986–87	2.55	3.03	2.55	3.25	10	—	—	—	—	—	—	—	quota	—

	1	2	3	4	5	6	7	8	9	10	11	12	13	14
1987–88	2.55	3.03	2.55	3.25	10	—	—	—	—	—	—	—	quota	—
1988–89	2.55	3.03	2.55	3.25	10	10	1.50	—	—	—	—	—	quota	—
1989–90	2.55	3.03	2.55	3.25	10	—	—	—	—	—	—	—	quota	—
Wheat[a]														
1984–85	3.30	4.38	3.30	4.45	30	10–20	PIK 80	3.30	4.38	3.30	4.45	30	10–20	PIK 80
1985–86	3.30	4.38	3.30	4.45	20	10	2.70	3.30	4.38	3.30	4.45	20	10	2.70
1986–87	3.30	4.38	3.30	4.45	20	10	2.70	—	—	—	—	—	quota	—
1987–88	3.30	4.38	3.30	4.45	20	10	2.70	—	—	—	—	—	quota	—
1988–89	3.30	4.38	3.30	4.45	20	—	—	—	—	—	—	—	quota	—
1989–90	3.30	4.38	3.30	4.45	20	10	2.70	—	—	—	—	—	quota	—
Cotton[c]														
1984–85	56	81	—	—	25	—	—	56	81	—	—	25	—	—
1985–86	56	81	—	—	15	10	30	56	81	—	—	15	10	30
1986–87	56	81	—	—	15	10	30	—	—	—	—	—	quota	—
1987–88	56	81	—	—	20	—	—	—	—	—	—	—	quota	—
1988–89	56	81	—	—	20	—	—	—	—	—	—	—	quota	—
1989–90	56	81	—	—	20	—	—	—	—	—	—	—	quota	—
Rice[d]														
1984–85	8.14	11.90	—	—	25	—	—	8.14	11.90	—	—	25	—	—
1985–86	8.00	11.90	—	—	20	15	3.50	8.00	11.90	—	—	25	15	3.50
1986–87	8.00	11.90	—	—	20	15	3.50	—	—	—	—	—	quota	—
1987–88	8.00	11.90	—	—	25	—	—	—	—	—	—	—	quota	—
1988–89	8.00	11.90	—	—	25	—	—	—	—	—	—	—	quota	—
1989–90	8.00	11.90	—	—	25	—	—	—	—	—	—	—	quota	—

NOTE: NAC = no acreage control; PIK = payment in kind.
a. Dollars per bushel.
b. Percent.
c. Cents per pound.
d. Dollars per hundred weight.

price support is ensured by government acreage programs, when necessary; however, participants receive no deficiency or diversion payments. Government CCC stocks are released when market prices reach 105 percent of the floating loan rate for nonreserve commodities. Program participants have the option of defaulting CCC loans for bottom-side price protection.

- loan rates for feed grains, cotton, wheat, and rice set at 80 percent of the five-year average market price, excluding maximum and minimum years
- base acreage used for loans and supply control based on five-year moving average of actual planted acres
- target prices eliminated
- participants ensured the loan rate by access to the nine-month nonrecourse loan with the CCC
- P.L. 480 and food aid programs maintained, but not exceeding levels for the 1981 farm program

Expanded Exports Base Line. The expanded exports option is identical with the base line except in the assumptions on factors conditioning the export markets for agricultural commodities. That is, the policy parameters and instruments are the same as those for the base line. Export market possibilities are enhanced by an artificial assumption of lower exchange rates and higher economic growth in the developed foreign economies. Details of these external assumptions are provided below.

80 Percent of Parity. The 80 percent of parity option was implemented with mandatory quotas required to restrict supply at the retail level to ensure farm prices consistent with the parity assumptions. Import restrictions were assumed to be imposed as well. Government stocks existing at the imposition of the program were phased down to appropriate long-term levels.

- prices at 80 percent of parity mandatory for all livestock and crop commodities
- mandatory government supply controls with quotas or marketing certificates based on long-term historical production
- parity index adjusted according to input costs except for feeder cattle and feed prices
- import restrictions to prevent foreign producers from undercutting prices in U.S. markets
- production on any portion of the land base, that is, no long-term land retirement
- program implemented at the beginning of the 1986–1987 crop year, with immediate adjustments in all livestock and crop sectors

The Base Line Option

This program evaluation traces the continuation of the 1981 farm bill from 1984–1985 through 1989–1990. Commodity market results highlighted in this summary of the outcome for the base line option are for corn, soybeans, wheat, cotton, rice, beef, pork, and poultry. The sequence of the presentation of conditioning information and the analysis is as described in the section "Policy Evaluation Process."

General Economic Assumptions. Most of the assumptions align with the July 1984 Congressional Budget Office forecast. Key factors in this forecast that directly affect agriculture include the following:

• federal government deficit moving from $175 billion in fiscal year 1984 to $263 billion by fiscal year 1989
• growth in the nominal gross national product falling from a high of 11.5 percent in 1984 to a low of 7.9 percent in 1989; in real terms the GNP (in 1972 dollars) projected to grow at 7.3 percent in 1984, fall to 3.6 percent in 1985, and average about 3 percent per year through 1989
• Civilian unemployment declining from 7.3 percent in 1984 to 6.3 percent in 1989
• three-month T-bill rates declining from 10 percent in 1984 to 9.7 percent in 1985 and holding at 8.9 percent through 1989
• dollar devaluing in 1985, through the remainder of the projection period; total fall of 18 percent from current levels, with the biggest decline in 1986

Foreign Projections and Assumptions. Alignment with the international markets necessitates an evaluation of competitive production potential, growth of foreign demand, foreign farm programs, and political implications. For the base line, foreign economic growth is reflected in the expected movement of real gross domestic products of major developed, underdeveloped, and centrally planned economies. The average growth rates per year projected for the next five years are Japan, 3.6 percent; Europe, 2.0 percent; the developing countries, 3.9 percent; and the centrally planned economies, 3.1 percent.

Supply levels for major foreign production regions were generated from regression models designed to estimate planted areas. These equations include as explanatory variables internal prices, world market conditions, and rates of exchange. Yields were projected by simple trend analysis. This analysis, together with the consumption projections, shows that foreign export demand is not likely to expand sufficiently rapidly to sustain significant growth in U.S. commodity exports. The potential dollar devaluation may change these projections. Even with the projected economic expansion, however, it is unlikely that the current 1.5 to 2.5 percent per year growth of the livestock herd would increase significantly. Foreign production of competing grains will keep pace

135

with demand growth, increasing competition from other producers for traditional and nontraditional foreign markets for U.S. commodities.

U.S. Crop and Livestock Sector. These evaluations are based on the FAPRI agricultural policy model. International and domestic projections are fed into the model to determine livestock demands for feed grains. Policy parameters along with the model structure determine equilibrium prices and other market-related variables.

Wheat

• Strong government control programs are required throughout the forecast, moving acreage from a low of 78.8 million in 1985–1986 to a high of 83.1 million in 1989–1990 (see table 3).

• Domestic demand remains at about 1.0 billion bushels; the expected increase in food use is offset by declining feed use.

• Export demand reaches 1.82 billion bushels by 1989–1990, with year-over-year increases of approximately 50 million bushels. Commercial exports increase at about 20 million bushels per year from 1985–1986 on. The modest export growth is due to strong foreign supplies, a highly valued dollar, and the heavy debt load of underdeveloped countries. Exports to centrally planned economies increase by approximately 30 million bushels per year during the same period.

• Prices increase from $3.40 per bushel to $3.72 by 1989–1990.

• Returns to producers over variable production cost are around $50–55.

Corn

• Acreage control programs are required throughout the evaluation period; 10 percent reduced acreage in 1985–1986 and 1986–1987 with 10 percent reduced acreage and 10 percent paid diversion in 1987–1988, 1988–1989, and 1989–1990 (see table 4).

• Domestic use increases from 5.1 billion bushels in 1984–1985 to 5.8 billion in 1989–1990, or 2.7 percent per year, reflecting the 3 percent growth forecast for real GNP.

• Export demand increases moderately, from 2.1 billion bushels in 1984–1985 to about 2.3 billion in 1989–1990. Foreign grain competition, moderate growth in foreign livestock economies, a relatively strong dollar, and competition from the U.S. soybean industry are major factors contributing to this slow rate of growth.

• Prices are in the $2.60 range through 1986–1987 and increase to $2.92, reflecting the stronger acreage control programs in 1987–1988 to 1989–1990.

• Prices reach the release rates during the crop years 1988–1989 and 1989–1990.

• Returns to producers over variable production cost are around $110–130 per acre.

136

TABLE 3
FAPRI POLICY PROJECTIONS. WHEAT, 1985–1986 TO 1989–1990

Variable	Program Option	Agriculture Department			FAPRI			
		1983–84	1984–85	1985–86	1986–87	1987–88	1988–89	1989–90
Planted acres	B	76.4	79.5	78.8	80.1	80.8	81.9	83.1
(millions of acres)	M	—	—	—	82.8	83.6	84.6	85.5
	E	—	—	—	80.1	80.7	85.9	84.8
	P	—	—	—	48.5	41.6	39.5	39.6
Domestic use	B	1,112	1,067	1,031	1,030	999	1,027	1,038
(millions of bushels)	M	—	—	1,034	1,081	1,087	1,081	1,077
	E	—	—	1,031	1,030	989	1,025	1,028
	P	—	—	991	684	691	701	718
Total exports	B	1,429	1,602	1,583	1,657	1,708	1,749	1,820
(millions of bushels)	M	—	—	—	1,689	1,748	1,805	1,879
	E	—	—	—	1,663	1,743	1,823	1,903
	P	—	—	1,562	1,191	1,003	886	745
Total carry-over	B	1,398	1,302	1,306	1,273	1,271	1,268	1,255
(millions of bushels)	M	—	—	1,303	1,278	1,245	1,223	1,192
	E	—	—	1,306	1,267	1,239	1,302	1,273
	P	—	—	1,367	1,240	1,060	926	933

(Table continues)

137

TABLE 3 (continued)

Variable	Program Option	Agriculture Department		FAPRI				
		1983–84	1984–85	1985–86	1986–87	1987–88	1988–89	1989–90
Farm price	B	3.53	3.40	3.41	3.46	3.66	3.66	3.72
(dollars per bushel)	M	—	—	3.40	3.21	3.25	3.32	3.48
	E	—	—	3.41	3.49	3.71	3.64	3.81
	P	—	—	3.81	6.52	6.82	7.07	7.28
Loan rate	B	3.65	3.30	3.30	3.30	3.30	3.30	3.30
(dollars per bushel)	M	—	—	—	2.79	2.75	2.68	2.66
	E	—	—	—	3.30	3.30	3.30	3.30
	P	—	—	—				
Nonparticipant	B	74.93	63.59	51.86	50.91	55.16	53.69	54.51
returns over	M	—	—	51.49	41.53	39.80	40.94	45.17
variable costs	E	—	—	51.86	51.89	56.97	53.09	57.94
(dollars per acre)	P	—	—	66.95	184.22	194.43	204.68	212.99
Government cost[a]	B			2,858	2,520	2,200	2,094	1,890
($ millions)	M			—	654	627	627	627
	E			—	2,520	2,068	1,656	2,145
	P			—	380	264	138	−353

NOTE: B = 1981 farm program continuation; M = market option; E = expanded exports option with base-line parameters; P = 80 percent of parity prices with marketing quotas.

a. FAPRI estimates of crop year costs. Not consistent with Agricultural Stabilization and Conservation Service (ASCS) estimates of fiscal year costs.

TABLE 4
FAPRI Policy Projections, Corn, 1985–1986 to 1989–1990

Variable	Program Option	Agriculture Department			FAPRI			
		1983–84	1984–85	1985–86	1986–87	1987–88	1988–89	1989–90
Planted acres	B	60.2	79.8	81.9	82.0	78.0	76.9	76.3
(millions of acres)	M	—	—	—	81.8	81.7	81.5	81.3
	E	—	—	—	82.0	82.6	78.4	81.7
	P	—	—	—	57.0	57.0	57.3	58.0
Domestic use	B	4,691	5,074	5,443	5,604	5,512	5,622	5,774
(millions of bushels)	M	—	—	—	5,690	5,700	5,837	5,980
	E	—	—	—	5,674	5,556	5,614	5,746
	P	—	—	5,436	4,615	4,683	4,738	4,943
Total exports	B	1,856	2,121	2,081	2,135	2,151	2,224	2,264
(millions of bushels)	M	—	—	—	2,161	2,228	2,385	2,456
	E	—	—	—	2,261	2,441	2,621	2,801
	P	—	—	—	1,637	1,499	1,414	1,373
Total carry-over	B	740	1,073	1,384	1,614	1,657	1,524	1,255
(millions of bushels)	M	—	—	—	1,479	1,620	1,575	1,418
	E	—	—	—	1,417	1,577	1,205	977
	P	—	—	1,391	1,059	899	899	900

(Table continues)

TABLE 4 (continued)

Variable	Program Option	Agriculture Department				FAPRI		
		1983–84	1984–85	1985–86	1986–87	1987–88	1988–89	1989–90
Farm price	B	3.20	2.68	2.64	2.63	2.87	2.90	2.92
(dollars per bushel)	M	—	—	—	2.53	2.49	2.42	2.66
	E	—	—	—	2.67	2.86	2.94	2.95
	P	—	—	2.62	4.71	4.91	5.08	5.23
Loan rate	B	2.65	2.55	2.55	2.55	2.55	2.55	2.55
(dollars per bushel)	M	—	—	—	2.13	2.13	2.09	2.04
	E	—	—	—	2.55	2.55	2.55	2.55
	P	—	—	—				
Nonparticipant	B	101.47	119.65	117.18	108.52	130.25	129.83	128.72
returns over	M	—	—	—	96.83	87.86	75.24	98.75
variable costs	E	—	—	—	112.76	129.27	134.67	132.05
(dollars per acre)	P	—	—	114.52	373.50	397.55	419.23	438.39
Government cost[a]	B			1,791	2,265	2,157	1,365	1,446
($ millions)	M			—	601	601	601	601
	E			—	2,211	1,609	1,800	692
	P			—	351	211	111	−316

NOTE: B = 1981 farm program continuation; M = market option; E = expanded exports option with base-line parameters; P = 80 percent of parity prices with marketing quotas.

a. FAPRI estimates of crop year costs. Not consistent with ASCS estimates of fiscal year costs.

Soybeans

• Bean/corn price ratio holds soybean acreage below 70 million until 1989–1990 (see table 5).

• Domestic soybean demand increases at approximately 2 percent per year, from 1.1 billion bushels in 1984–1985 to 1.24 billion bushels in 1989–1990.

• Exports increase at about 5.1 percent per year, from 780 million bushels in 1984–1985 to around 1 billion in 1989–1990. Export levels reflect strong foreign competition for the soybean complex, a strong dollar, and a moderate rate of growth in foreign livestock economies.

• Prices at the lower $6.00 per bushel level increase to $6.63 per bushel by 1987–1988 and to $6.82 per bushel by 1989–1990.

• Returns to producers over variable production cost around $90–111 per acre.

Cotton

• Acreage is projected to remain at 11.5 million through 1987–1988, then increase to 12.5 million by 1989–1990. Strong acreage control programs are required (see table 6).

• Domestic use grows with the general economy, ranging from 2.7 to 3.7 percent per year, with total mill use at 6.40 million bales by 1989–1990.

• Export growth averages 2.5 percent per year, reaching 7.1 million bales by 1989–1990.

• Prices reflect the excess supply capacity, remaining near $0.60 per pound until 1987–1988 and increasing to about $0.70 per pound by 1988–1990.

Rice

• Production controls are necessary throughout the projection period, holding acreage between 2.8 and 3.0 million through 1989–1990, approximately 1.2 million below the 1984–1985 base of the Agricultural Stabilization and Conservation Service, or ASCS (see table 7).

• Domestic use follows economic and population growth, with both food and brewery use increasing by 2.2 percent per year.

• Export growth at about 1.5 to 1.6 percent per year reflects the growing competition from Thailand and the $5.00 to $7.00 per hundredweight U.S.-Thailand price difference. U.S. prices will have to drop sharply for export trade to increase. Rice price at Rotterdam averaged $527 per metric ton for U.S. exports in 1983, compared with $369 per metric ton for Thai exports, roughly a $7.20 per hundredweight difference.

• Rice prices increase moderately from $8.54 per hundredweight in 1985–1986 to $9.43 per hundredweight in 1989–1990. Most of the price strength is associated with production controls.

TABLE 5

FAPRI Policy Projections, Soybeans, 1985–1986 to 1989–1990

Variable	Program Option	Agriculture Department				FAPRI		
		1983–84	1984–85	1985–86	1986–87	1987–88	1988–89	1989–90
Planted acres (millions of acres)	B	63.1	68.2	67.6	67.0	67.2	67.8	71.5
	M	—	—	—	66.8	68.3	70.6	73.2
	E	—	—	—	67.0	67.7	71.3	72.9
	P	—	—	—	39.1	40.7	41.2	41.4
Domestic use (millions of bushels)	B	1,066	1,132	1,166	1,189	1,198	1,212	1,235
	M	—	—	—	1,194	1,216	1,239	1,254
	E	—	—	—	1,199	1,208	1,224	1,247
	P	—	—	1,123	823	829	840	856
Total exports (millions of bushels)	B	740	780	821	868	908	955	1,000
	M	—	—	—	870	928	986	1,029
	E	—	—	—	876	931	986	1,040
	P	—	—	806	555	513	520	532
Total carry-over (millions of bushels)	B	175	164	241	224	183	120	128
	M	—	—	—	209	165	133	146
	E	—	—	—	206	148	153	152
	P	—	—	300	198	198	208	210

Farm price (dollars per bushel)	B	7.75	6.27	5.98	6.13	6.63	6.97	6.82
	M	—	—	—	6.04	6.17	6.22	6.51
	E	—	—	—	6.20	6.74	7.42	7.45
	P	—	—	6.57	11.43	11.93	12.35	12.72
Loan rate (dollars per bushel)	B	5.02	5.02	5.02	5.02	5.02	5.02	5.02
	M	—	—	—	4.57	4.57	4.62	4.61
	E	—	—	—	5.02	5.02	5.02	5.02
	P	—	—	5.02	5.02	5.02	5.02	5.02
Nonparticipant returns over variable costs (dollars per acre)	B	119.98	91.80	95.59	93.23	105.13	112.63	105.54
	M	—	—	—	90.63	90.89	89.09	95.54
	E	—	—	—	95.48	108.69	126.89	125.48
	P	—	—	114.03	286.81	301.63	314.29	326.14
Government cost[a] ($ millions)	B	0	0	0	0	0	0	0
	M	—	—	—	—	—	—	—
	E	—	—	—	—	—	—	—
	P	—	—	—	—	—	—	—

NOTE: B = 1981 farm program continuation; M = market option; E = expanded exports option with base-line parameters; P = 80 percent of parity prices with marketing quotas.

a. FAPRI estimates of crop year costs. Not consistent with ASCS estimates of fiscal year costs.

TABLE 6
FAPRI Policy Projections, Cotton, 1985–1986 to 1989–1990

Variable	Program Option	Agriculture Department			FAPRI			
		1983–84	1984–85	1985–86	1986–87	1987–88	1988–89	1989–90
Planted acres (millions of acres)	B	7.90	11.10	11.00	11.50	11.50	12.00	12.50
	M	—	—	—	11.20	10.80	12.40	12.70
	E	—	—	—	11.50	12.10	12.20	12.80
	P	—	—	—	5.25	6.05	5.81	5.89
Domestic use (millions of bales)	B	5.90	5.30	5.65	5.80	6.00	6.22	6.40
	M	—	—	—	5.84	6.00	6.22	6.42
	E	—	—	—	5.80	5.63	5.46	5.29
	P	—	—	—	5.27	5.54	5.73	5.89
Total exports (millions of bales)	B	6.80	6.50	6.13	6.33	6.55	6.92	7.05
	M	—	—	—	6.60	6.55	7.00	7.15
	E	—	—	—	7.00	7.67	8.34	9.01
	P	—	—	—	3.22	2.34	1.90	1.97
Total carry-over (millions of bales)	B	3.00	4.58	4.27	4.29	3.99	3.79	3.97
	M	—	—	—	3.75	2.76	2.94	3.23
	E	—	—	—	3.62	3.25	2.62	2.30
	P	—	—	—	2.35	2.43	2.50	2.56

Farm price (dollars per pound)	B	0.66	0.60	0.67	0.60	0.67	0.69	0.71
	M	—	—	—	0.55	0.69	0.67	0.67
	E	—	—	—	0.67	0.72	0.75	0.85
	P	—	—	—	1.09	1.14	1.18	1.22
Loan rate (dollars per pound)	B	0.56	0.56	0.56	0.56	0.56	0.56	0.56
	M	—	—	—	0.47	0.48	0.52	0.52
	E	—	—	—	0.56	0.56	0.56	0.56
	P	—	—	—	0.56	0.56	0.56	0.56
Nonparticipant returns over variable costs (dollars per acre)	B	96.32	121.19	93.99	45.82	72.28	76.81	77.09
	M	—	—	—	21.14	88.26	65.74	59.12
	E	—	—	—	79.96	103.46	125.52	182.86
	P	—	—	—	385.33	423.72	445.92	470.14
Government cost[a] ($ millions)	B			1,805	1,290	955	648	561
	M			—	−491	0	0	0
	E			—	945	394	−88	0
	P			—	−1,046	0	0	0

NOTE: B = 1981 farm program continuation; M = market option; E = expanded exports option with base-line parameters; P = 80 percent of parity prices with marketing quotas.

a. FAPRI estimates of crop year costs. Not consistent with ASCS estimates of fiscal year costs.

TABLE 7
FAPRI Policy Projections, Rice, 1985–1986 to 1989–1990

Variable	Program Option	Agriculture Department			FAPRI			
		1983–84	1984–85	1985–86	1986–87	1987–88	1988–89	1989–90
Planted acres	B	2,190	2,850	2,850	2,850	2,850	3,000	3,000
(thousands of acres)	M	—	—	—	3,017	2,881	2,844	2,850
	E	—	—	—	2,850	3,000	3,250	3,500
	P	—	—	—	1,566	1,372	1,375	1,555
Domestic use	B	49.1	54.0	58.4	59.2	60.1	61.0	62.0
(millions of cwt)	M	—	—	—	60.8	62.2	63.1	64.3
	E	—	—	—	61.4	63.6	65.8	68.0
	P	—	—	—	53.3	54.1	54.4	55.4
Total exports	B	70.3	64.0	68.0	69.8	70.7	72.0	73.5
(millions of cwt)	M	—	—	—	71.0	72.2	73.6	75.1
	E	—	—	—	75.3	80.8	86.3	91.8
	P	—	—	—	26.3	15.3	13.6	11.6
Total carry-over	B	46.9	64.0	63.3	60.5	56.3	57.4	56.4
(millions of cwt)	M	—	—	—	65.5	59.2	49.2	37.2
	E	—	—	—	52.8	42.0	35.9	34.4
	P	—	—	—	50.9	40.1	31.5	30.4

Farm price (dollars per cwt)	B	8.79	8.57	8.54	8.90	9.34	9.23	9.43
	M	—	—	8.51	7.07	6.80	6.64	6.81
	E	—	—	8.54	9.14	9.38	9.39	9.85
	P	—	—	9.18	17.89	18.68	19.36	19.94
Loan rate (dollars per cwt)	B	8.14	8.00	8.00	8.00	8.00	8.00	8.00
	M	—	—	—	6.76	6.69	6.28	5.64
	E	—	—	—	8.00	8.00	8.00	8.00
	P	—	—	—	8.00	8.00	8.00	8.00
Nonparticipant returns over variable costs (dollars per acre)	B	160.93	176.71	132.84	136.90	144.68	125.99	121.99
	M	—	—	131.43	50.79	24.79	3.35	-2.47
	E	—	—	132.84	148.19	146.57	133.57	141.92
	P	—	—	162.93	576.87	609.81	637.59	621.21
Government cost ($ millions)[a]	B			571	512	447	387	367
	M			—	-52	-9	-40	-58
	E			—	442	273	189	243
	P			—	-296	-226	-233	0

NOTE: B = 1981 farm program continuation; M = market option; E = expanded exports option with base-line parameters; P = 80 percent of parity prices with marketing quotas.

a. FAPRI estimates of crop year costs. Not consistent with ASCS estimates of fiscal year costs.

Beef

• Beef production is projected to decline in 1985 and 1986 reflecting inventory increases, decreasing from 23.5 billion pounds in 1984 to around 22.2 billion in 1986 (see table 8). The expansion cycle reaches a peak of 23.5 billion pounds by 1990, regaining levels attained in 1983. Current demand projections imply little upward trend in this expected production cycle.

• Prices for Omaha steers should increase from $62.50 per hundredweight in 1983 to a peak of $72.00 in 1986. This supply-induced price strength will begin to moderate after 1986, dropping to $67.00 per hundredweight by 1989. With a movement away from beef at the retail market, the overall price trend remains low.

Pork

• Pork production enters a building phase in 1986 that terminates a steady decline from 15.9 billion pounds in 1981 to around 14.6 billion in 1985. Production peaks at around 16.1 billion by 1987 and then declines sharply through 1989 (see table 8).

• Prices should move opposite the supply cycle, with a peak of $53.00 per hundredweight in 1985. The low price year is 1987, at $45.00. This cyclical pattern occurs around a moderate upward trend, reflecting a moderate increase in consumer demand.

Broilers

• Supplies of broilers follow the longer-term trend, increasing at about 3 percent per year throughout the projection period (see table 8).

• Wholesale prices follow the pork price cycle, and to a lesser extent the beef price cycle, with highest prices in 1985 and 1989.

Farm Income

• The generally weaker agricultural market prices result in a significant eroding of farm income over the evaluation period (see table 9).

• The general forecast is for a weaker farm economy over the next six years, and a major agricultural downturn is projected for 1988, with farm income at $20.0 billion. In real terms this is $6.8 billion smaller than the level for 1984.

• An improvement in the agricultural economy is expected in both 1989 and 1990 with farm income levels of $22.4 billion and $25.7 billion.

• During 1986 total production expenses will exceed total farm cash receipts by $664 million. The difference between receipts and expenses has been declining over the past sixty years, but 1986 will be the first time in U.S. history that the difference has been negative.

• A major factor supporting farm incomes through 1989–1990 is the relative increase in nonmoney and other farm incomes.

TABLE 8
FAPRI Policy Projections, Livestock, 1984–1990

Commodity and Variable	Program Option	1984	1985	1986	1987	1988	1989	1990
Beef								
Omaha price ($/cwt)	B	$65.30	$69.20	$72.00	$69.50	$68.00	$67.00	$67.50
	M	—	—	—	$70.00	$69.50	$67.00	$66.50
	P	—	—	$75.34	$89.47	$93.23	$96.21	$99.01
Marketings (million pounds)	B	23,477	22,700	22,200	22,600	23,100	23,400	23,500
	M	—	—	—	22,450	22,690	23,200	23,570
	P	—	—	21,370	18,352	17,219	18,037	18,262
Per capita consumption (retail weight)	B	78.8	75.2	73.4	74.0	74.8	75.2	74.9
	M	—	—	—	73.5	73.6	74.6	75.1
	P	—	—	69.5	55.6	51.7	53.7	53.9
Retail price per pound	B	$2.40	$2.65	$2.80	$2.82	$2.87	$2.94	$3.06
	M	—	—	—	$2.84	$2.91	$2.94	$3.03
	P	—	—	$2.92	$3.35	$3.53	$3.69	$3.86
Expenditures	B	$189.12	$199.28	$205.21	$208.86	$215.11	$221.17	$228.98
	M	—	—	—	$208.45	$214.21	$219.43	$227.83
	P	—	—	$202.50	$186.46	$182.46	$198.12	$207.99

(Table continues)

TABLE 8 (continued)

Commodity and Variable	Program Option	1984	1985	1986	1987	1988	1989	1990
Pork								
Seven-city market price ($/cwt)	B	$47.50	$51.50	$49.50	$45.00	$49.00	$51.00	$51.00
	M	—	—	—	$42.50	$46.00	$47.50	$48.00
	P	—	—	$56.31	$80.46	$83.83	$86.52	$89.03
Marketings (million pounds)	B	14,636	14,575	15,500	16,100	15,500	15,200	15,700
	M	—	—	—	16,600	15,940	15,600	15,850
	P	—	—	14,782	12,823	13,040	13,253	13,366
Per capita consumption (retail weight)	B	61.0	60.4	61.5	63.2	60.4	58.9	60.2
	M	—	—	—	65.0	62.1	60.3	60.7
	P	—	—	58.0	47.7	48.1	48.5	48.5
Retail price per pound	B	$1.62	$1.71	$1.77	$1.74	$1.85	$1.93	$1.98
	M	—	—	—	$1.69	$1.80	$1.87	$1.93
	P	—	—	$1.91	$2.41	$2.51	$2.61	$2.70
Expenditures	B	$98.83	$103.32	$108.99	$109.87	$111.95	$113.78	$119.43
	M	—	—	—	$110.23	$111.66	$112.88	$117.30
	P	—	—	$110.86	$115.11	$120.91	$126.33	$130.96

Chicken

Farm price ($/cwt)	B	$34.10	$30.10	$27.60	$26.50	$29.40	$32.90	$27.90
	M	—	—	—	$22.90	$23.90	$24.90	$24.90
	P	—	—	$32.10	$47.42	$49.41	$51.00	$52.47
Marketings (million pounds)	B	13,457	14,153	14,624	15,181	15,514	15,800	16,253
	M	—	—	—	15,181	15,833	16,438	16,910
	P	—	—	—	13,672	14,232	14,660	15,018
Per capita consumption (retail weight)	B	54.8	57.3	58.6	60.3	61.1	61.7	62.9
	M	—	—	—	60.3	62.3	64.2	65.5
	P	—	—	57.6	56.3	58.1	59.3	60.2
Retail price per pound	B	$0.83	$0.75	$0.70	$0.68	$0.73	$0.78	$0.69
	M	—	—	—	$0.62	$0.63	$0.64	$0.63
	P	—	—	$0.78	$1.04	$1.07	$1.09	$1.11
Expenditures	B	$45.49	$42.95	$41.19	$41.06	$44.28	$47.99	$43.13
	M	—	—	—	$37.35	$39.35	$41.20	$41.56
	P	—	—	$44.97	$58.50	$61.98	$64.50	$66.58

NOTE: B = 1981 farm program continuation; M = market option; P = 80 percent of parity prices with marketing quotas.

151

TABLE 9
FAPRI Policy Projections, Farm Income and Government Cost, 1983–1990
(billions of dollars)

	Program Option	1983	1984	1985	1986	1987	1988	1989	1990
Total farm cash receipts	B	138.72	143.13	150.75	156.08	159.42	165.07	169.42	175.10
	M	—	—	—	155.56	156.40	159.78	164.25	171.93
	E	—	—	—	156.72	160.57	166.25	171.18	177.76
	P	—	—	—	157.68	200.45	202.99	211.37	220.38
Direct government payments	B	9.29	8.70	5.12	5.73	4.76	3.34	3.29	4.28
	M	—	—	—	0.00	0.00	0.00	0.00	0.00
	E	—	—	—	5.37	3.80	3.18	2.31	3.67
	P	—	—	—	4.48	0.00	0.00	0.00	0.00
Realized gross farm income	B	163.16	167.93	172.74	179.58	182.61	187.68	192.88	200.51
	M	—	—	—	173.36	175.02	179.24	184.63	193.16
	E	—	—	—	179.86	182.84	188.74	193.78	202.72
	P	—	—	—	178.76	217.75	220.89	230.07	241.51
Net farm income	B	16.10	31.81	25.73	25.64	24.58	20.04	22.39	25.66
	M	—	—	—	18.08	16.81	14.67	16.60	15.63
	E	—	—	—	26.02	24.90	21.01	22.75	26.97
	P	—	—	—	45.83	74.03	74.32	75.31	81.15

Net farm income (1972 dollars)

B	7.48	14.25	11.03	10.41	9.57	7.44	7.89	8.54
M	—	—	—	7.34	6.54	5.44	5.85	5.20
E	—	—	—	10.57	9.69	7.80	8.02	8.98
P	—	—	—	18.61	28.82	27.58	26.54	27.02

NOTE: B = 1981 farm program continuation; M = market option; E = expanded exports option with base-line parameters; P = 80 percent of parity prices with marketing quotas.

153

Government Cost

• Acreage control programs are required throughout the evaluation period (see table 10).

• The combination of deficiency, diversion, storage, and other costs requires from $7.3 billion in 1986–1987 to a low of $4.7 billion in 1989–1990 over the projection period for the crops sector alone.

Summary

Current factors in the agricultural industry:

• slow recovery of food demand in domestic and foreign economies
• strong dollar in world markets
• high debt load of underdeveloped countries
• increased production potential both in competing countries and in importing regions
• long-term agreements signed by Soviets with five competing export countries
• high interest rates putting stress on a capital-intensive agriculture with declining asset values
• moderate levels of net farm income declining from around $14.25 billion in 1972 dollars to around $8.54 billion in 1990
• potential severe cash flow problems for up to 20 percent of producers in $50,000 to $200,000 gross sales category.

Although it is difficult to rank these factors in degree of importance, the world growth rate seems to be most critical. With 2 to 2½ percent annual growth in the Japanese livestock industry and 1 to 1½ percent annual growth in other developed regions, exports of feed grains, soybeans, and soybean meal and oil will increase only moderately. The wheat sector is critically affected by the heavy debt load of underdeveloped countries. Rice and cotton will face strong competition, with exports reflecting moderate expansion in world importing economies.

The export situation is further complicated by stronger foreign production, coupled with slack demand. The U.S. is faced with a narrowing gap between foreign production and demand. For these reasons, it will be difficult to turn the slow export market around unless demand-side factors increase significantly over projected levels.

A final factor is the significance of the government program payments necessary to maintain the current supply-demand balance. With an ASCS base acreage of approximately 195 million for corn, wheat, cotton, and rice, strong program controls will be necessary. The planted area will have to be held to about 175 million acres, or 20 million acres below the ASCS base level, to balance the markets at existing loan and target prices.

The Market Option

General Economic and Foreign Sector Assumptions. This analysis uses the same general economic assumptions as for the base line. Foreign economic growth is also assumed to be identical with that in the base line. Production of grains and oilseeds by competitors and importers is allowed to adjust to U.S. price movements.

U.S. Crop and Livestock Sector

Wheat

• The planted area exceeds the base line by approximately 2 million acres for each year. No acreage controls are imposed (see table 3).
• Domestic demand exceeds that for the base line by 30–70 million bushels per year, with the majority of the growth in feed demand.
• Commercial exports increase approximately 3 percent per year over the base line. Further export market expansion is limited by the inelastic demand implicit in the FAPRI model and by the foreign supply response.
• Farm prices range from $0.20 to $0.40 per bushel below those for the base line, averaging approximately $3.30 per bushel.

Corn

• Acreage averages 3 million per year over the base line, or approximately 4 percent per year. No acreage control programs are applied during the evaluation period (see table 4).
• Domestic demand significantly increases over the base line because of an extension of the expansion phase of the livestock cycle. Lower feed grain prices provide the stimulus for livestock inventory building in excess of the base-line estimate, resulting in an approximately 3 percent year-over-year increase in feed demand.
• Export demand shows an increase of 190 million bushels over the base line in 1989–1990. This increase does take substantial time to occur, however. In the first year exports total less than 30 million bushels over the base line. With lower prices there are incentives to reduce foreign production, allowing the United States to capture a larger share of total world commercial corn exports.
• Prices range from $2.42 per bushel in 1988–1989 to $2.66 per bushel in 1989–1990. The price strength at the end of the period reflects the expansion in the livestock industry and an increase in exports.

155

TABLE 10

GOVERNMENT DIRECT FARM PAYMENTS AND OTHER COSTS FOR CROPS, CROP YEARS 1984–1985 TO 1989–1990

(millions of dollars)

	Program Option	1984–85	1985–86	1986–87	1987–88	1988–89	1989–90
Direct payments							
Total feed grains	B	1,798	1,122	2,177	1,928	980	1,235
	M	—	—	0	0	0	0
	E	—	—	2,177	1,364	1,687	528
	P	—	—	0	0	0	0
Total food grains	B	1,913	2,600	2,338	1,953	1,787	1,563
	M	—	—	0	0	0	0
	E	—	—	2,329	1,736	1,229	1,778
	P	—	—	0	0	0	0
Total cotton	B	1,088	1,193	1,216	881	574	487
	M	—	—	0	0	0	0
	E	—	—	871	702	267	0
	P	—	—	0	0	0	0
Total direct government payments	B	4,799	4,915	5,731	4,762	3,341	3,285
	M	—	—	0	0	0	0
	E	—	—	5,377	3,802	3,183	2,306
	P	—	—	0	0	0	0

Total other government nonrecoverable costs for crops	B	1,292	2,655	1,595	1,603	1,529	1,381
	M	—	—	869	1,376	1,345	1,327
	E	—	—	1,595	1,055	824	992
	P	—	—	−601	239	16	−609
Total nonrecoverable government costs for grains and cotton	B	6,091	7,570	7,325	6,365	4,870	4,666
	M	—	—	869	1,376	1,345	1,327
	E	—	7,276	6,972	4,857	4,007	3,299
	P	—	.	−601	239	16	−609

NOTE: B = 1981 farm program continuation; M = market option; E = expanded exports option with base-line parameters; P = 80 percent of parity prices with marketing quotas.

• Returns to producers over variable costs of production are lower than for the base line by about $45 per acre.

Soybeans

• Acreage is projected to average about 1.4 million above the base line (see table 5).
• Crush demand reflects the expansion in the U.S. livestock industry, primarily pork and poultry, averaging a year-over-year increase of about 20 million bushels.
• Exports respond to the lower price projections, with beans averaging about 20 million bushels annually over the base line.
• Prices range from $6.03 per bushel in 1985–1986 to $6.50 in 1989–1990, approximately 5 percent below the base line.
• Returns per acre to producers average 14 percent below those from the base-line design.

Cotton

• The planted area is initially below the base line but increases to slightly above the base line by the end of the evaluation period. A slight oversupply in 1986–1987 in relation to demand results in a low price incentive, with price and acreage realignment (see table 6).
• Only moderate increases in exports occur, in the face of lower domestic prices, because of strong foreign competition. The majority of the competition comes from the Soviet Union.
• Prices are near the base-line solution in all years except 1986–1987. Slight oversupply with lower support results in a $0.06 per pound drop in price in 1986–1987. These prices are low enough that per acre returns fall below the average variable cost of production. Acreage adjustments in following years produce a price path very near the base-line level. In general prices continue to reflect excess supply capacity.

Rice

• Lower prices result in lower acreage and an overall decrease in production (see table 7).
• Domestic use increases about 1 percent per year, reflecting food consumption trends.
• Exports increase about 1 percent per year, reflecting the noncompetitive position of U.S. rice exports in the world market, with domestic prices $3.00 to $5.00 per hundredweight higher than world prices.
• Inelastic demand and limited export demand result in a low price path, given U.S. potential supply capacity.
• Lower loan rates with reduced market price support have a significant effect on returns to rice producers. Projected returns will not cover average

variable production costs in the last year, implying further reductions in plantings in future years.

Beef

• Total supply averages 1 percent less than the base line each year until 1990, when the effects of the extended herd-building cycle begin to reach the market (see table 8).
• The price cycle is similar to the base line, with a peak in 1986. Prices run modestly above the base line until 1989.

Pork

• Pork production is 3 percent above the 16.1 billion pound base-line peak in 1987, remaining 2½ to 3 percent above the base line (see table 8).
• From 1987 through 1989 prices average about 6 percent below the base line.

Broilers

• Annual poultry production averages 1 percent higher than the base line.
• Wholesale prices average 4 to 6 percent lower than for the base line (see table 8).

Farm Income. Farm income is projected to average $16.4 billion per year from 1986 to 1990 under the free market scenario, a 30 percent decline from the base line (see table 9).

Government Cost. No acreage control programs in effect (see table 10). Program cost for the crops sector is approximately $1.3 billion per year. This cost is due to storage and forgone interest on government-controlled stocks. Sales of government-owned cotton and rice contribute to the lowering of government costs in 1986–1987.

Summary. U.S. agriculture has traditionally received income support through commodity programs. Moving in the direction of a market-oriented program with less price support demonstrates rather dramatically the current influence of these programs on the agricultural industry, especially in the present world market environment, which exhibits sluggish domestic and export demand.

This situation is further evident in the demand expansion associated with the overall price declines experienced in the market option. U.S. agriculture is traditionally characterized as an inelastic demand industry. Therefore, price declines, other things unchanged, result in declining total revenues for producers. Model parameters, indicated in the section "Policy Alternatives," reflect inelastic short-term domestic and foreign demand for all markets except soybeans. Thus results from this modeling system necessarily imply that

159

reductions in market prices will reduce revenues for crop producers. The simultaneous solution does show an expansion of exports from growth of the foreign livestock sector and foreign food use plus reductions in foreign supplies. This expansion will take time to occur, however, since foreign producers face problems of fixed assets similar to those of U.S. producers. Domestic use is projected to increase, with a corresponding expansion over the base line, in the U.S. livestock industry. Since the market-oriented policy alternative is initiated in a sluggish demand environment, however, the supply side of the crops sector takes up a considerable amount of the necessary slack. This occurs because the planted area is now substantially below the ASCS base acreage without production control programs.

All crops would be severely affected by the market program, especially rice and cotton. Declining rice prices would move to make the United States a stronger competitor in the world market, but the projected price decline would still not be low enough to offset the difference between Thailand and U.S. prices. For cotton the large stocks and initially higher prices would produce the same pattern of results.

Lower prices, limited expansion of domestic and export demand, and no government payments for acreage controls or target price supports will substantially reduce net farm income for U.S. agriculture, which will move down from about $25.7 billon in 1985 to $15.6 billion in 1990. At this level, current asset values in agriculture will have to adjust. The departure from current loan levels and the related 15 to 18 percent price support reduction imply that U.S. agriculture will initially have to absorb most of the adjustment cost associated with the movement to the more market-driven program.

If export expansion with a market-oriented agriculture becomes the objective of the U.S. agricultural industry, these results suggest investigating a more moderate strategy for approaching this goal than an immediate shift to the market-oriented program. Step-down strategies would allow more adjustment time for an industry with nonmobile assets. The choice of this program option was made to demonstrate the overall effect of an immediate move to a market-oriented agriculture. Results indicate that the demand side is not immediately responsive enough to compensate for the estimated price decline, especially with the world economy in its present condition.

Finally, in relation to the market-oriented loan rate strategy, examination of the simulated price paths over time suggests one- to two-year lags in responding to market conditions. A sequence of good or bad crops can distort the loan rate and the price protection signal to producers. Where should the focus be with regard to U.S. support prices? The rolling average loan rate is one alternative; however, given the lag time for response built into this loan rate formula, agriculture again becomes subject to the possibility of unbalanced supply response corresponding to support signals inconsistent with present market conditions.

The Expanded Exports with Base-Line Option

Farm Program Operation. Program parameters for the expanded growth option are identical with those for the base line. All loan and target prices are maintained at a minimum of the 1984–1985 levels; upward adjustments of loans and targets are governed by a moving average of market prices. No limit is placed on reserves, and acreage control programs are applied if expected carry-over exceeds long-term average levels.

General Economic Assumptions. The intent of this evaluation is to examine and contrast the base-line solution with a stronger general economic outlook. Values of conditioning variables selected for this scenario are based on previous growth periods in domestic and export demand. General economic indicators were imposed that reflect this more favorable economic situation:

- the federal government deficit moving from a high of 4 percent of GNP to a low of about 1 percent
- growth in real GNP averaging near 4.5 percent per year
- civilian unemployment averaging 6.7 percent per year
- lower interest rates, three-month T-bill averaging 6.8 percent
- lower exchange value of the dollar—an average devaluation rate of 3.75 percent per year

Foreign Projections and Assumptions. Annual real growth rates for the next five years are assumed to average 4 percent for the developed countries, 6 percent for the developing countries, and 4.5 percent for the centrally planned economies.

U.S. Crop and Livestock Sector. The general expansion of demand is exhibited more prominently in the export than in the domestic commodity markets. Export growth tends to raise overall crop prices, resulting in a relatively higher use of concentrates for feed in the livestock sector. The combination of higher input prices and increased growth of domestic demand tends to hold the domestic livestock herd at about the base-line level. The expanded economic growth is reflected more strongly in the export market.

Wheat

- The planted area is approximately the same as the base line in 1986–1987 and 1987–1988 but increases 2 to 4 million acres in 1988–1989 and 1989–1990 (see table 3). Even with the expanded economic growth, acreage controls are required in all years: 20 percent reduced acreage and 10 percent paid diversion in both 1986–1987 and 1987–1988 and 20 percent reduced acreage in 1988–1989 and 1989–1990.

• Domestic demand is approximately the same as in the base line. Acreage controls necessary to maintain supply-demand balance generate approximately the same domestic price path as in the base line.

• Total exports average approximately 50 million bushels per year over the base line, reaching 1.9 billion in 1989–1990, about 80 million above the corresponding base-line export level.

• Farm prices are likely to be about the same as for the base line, given the magnitude of the U.S. production potential.

• Returns average $55 per acre, the same as the base line.

Corn

• Acreage averages about 3 million per year over the base line (see table 4). Reduced acreage programs are required in 1986–1987 and 1987–1988. Set-aside and paid diversion programs are required in 1988–1989 and 1989–1990.

• Domestic use is slightly above that for the base line.

• Export demand averages year-over-year increases of about 180 million bushels, in contrast to about 40 million per year for the base line.

• Prices are slightly higher than the base line in 1987–1988 and 1988–1989. Price levels in 1988–1989 and 1989–1990 reflect the release of farmer-held reserves, holding the season average price at an upper bound of $3.25.

• Returns per acre average above those for the base line, the largest difference, of $5 per acre, occurring in 1988–1989 as a result of a paid diversion program.

Soybeans

• Acreage averages about 1.3 million per year over the base line (see table 5).

• Crush demand is slightly above the base line, reflecting limited change in U.S. livestock and moderate expansion of meal exports.

• Exports are projected to average 20 million bushels over the base line. The total growth for each year averages approximately 55 million bushels, in contrast to 45 million in the base line.

• Prices reach $0.60 per bushel above those for the base line in 1989–1990.

• Returns to producers average about $10 per acre over the base period.

Cotton

• Acreage averages 320,000 per year above the base line (see table 6).

• Domestic use trends downward, reflecting higher prices and competition from synthetics.

• Prices are slightly higher than the base line but are moderated by the release of CCC reserves and slightly higher acreage.

• Returns to producers average $122 per acre.

Rice

- Acreage averages about 250,000 above the base line; production controls are required in all years, but of relatively weaker design than the base line; participation is also less (see table 7).
- Domestic demand increases at about 4 percent per year, in contrast to 1.5 for the base-line evaluation.
- Commercial exports average an increase of 8.75 percent per year, compared with the base line figure of 2 percent per year.
- Prices are only about $0.20 to $0.30 per hundredweight higher than the base because of the relatively large CCC carry-over releases. These releases occur at 115 percent of the loan rate.
- Returns to producers average $8.00 per acre above the base line.

Livestock. Feed grain and high protein prices are very near base-line prices. For this reason, it is likely that the livestock industry will be unchanged from the base-line solution. Since the prices for livestock are nearly the same as in the base line, they are not repeated in table 8.

Government Cost. Total government costs will probably range between $3.3 and $6.8 billion (see table 10). Demand expansion because of the better world economic conditions is not sufficient to compensate completely for the U.S. current production potential.

Summary. This option was selected to demonstrate the possible effect of growth in world economies on U.S. agriculture. Imposed demand strength similar to previous growth periods for U.S. agriculture does increase prices and acreage and reduce government costs, resulting in slightly more strength in net farm income than exhibited by the base line.

An important consequence of investigating this option is the contrast it permits for commodity price paths in relation to the base line. Why, for example, are corn prices very nearly the same under both options? Increases in farmer-held reserves in 1984–1985 and 1985–1986 have a release price of $3.25 per bushel. This becomes a top-side constraint on the corn price. Export expansion could trigger the release of reserves, leaving prices at or near the same level for the base-line and enhanced export options.

For wheat the excess supply capacity is the deciding factor in holding price paths for this option. Acreage controls are necessary to maintain prices moderately above loan rates even with stronger domestic and foreign markets. The difference between the base line and this option is apparent, however, in less restrictive production controls and reduced government budget exposure.

This kind of economic boom period would be beneficial to crop producers in U.S. agriculture. The livestock sector, however, would eventually bear some of the pressure from an extended period with expected increases in crop prices. In this case, the cycle and evaluation period were not long enough to evaluate this kind of reduction fully. Even by 1989–1990 total planted area will be about 15 million below the current ASCS base for corn, wheat, cotton, and rice. Thus the expanded exports option was not sufficient to move U.S. agriculture out of an excess supply position and had some negative effects on the U.S. livestock sector.

The 80 Percent of Parity Option

General Economic and Foreign Sector Assumptions. This analysis uses the same general economic assumption as the base line, but alignment of the international trade sector was required. First, as U.S. market prices were increased to 80 percent of parity, trade restrictions were imposed, preventing imports of foreign agricultural commodities (see table 11). Second, as U.S. prices increased, production response patterns in foreign markets were different from the base line.

Analytical Process. The simultaneous agricultural model generates equilibrium prices and quantities. This analysis imposes prices from outside the system. Therefore, the initial task was to determine marketing quotas to meet demand at the imposed prices. A sequential or recursive process was used, first, to establish the magnitude of retail demand for implied retail prices passed from the farm sector at 80 percent of parity prices and, second, to determine the corresponding size of the domestic livestock industry.

Retail prices were derived from linear relationships reflecting historical spreads between farm and retail prices. Retail meat demand equations were used to estimate per capita consumption at retail prices driven by projected income and inflation and legislated 80 percent of parity. Finally, total meat consumption was converted into farm equivalent livestock units to calculate corresponding quota restrictions in the livestock sectors.

These livestock numbers were converted into grain-consuming-animal units (GCAU) to interface with the feed grain and soybean meal markets. Given this combination of domestic and estimated export demand at higher prices, acreage restrictions were deduced that also reflect carry-over objectives. The yield per harvested acre was also modified to reflect the effect of the reduced planted area. Farmers would most likely concentrate production on the better portion of the land base and perhaps use more nonland inputs or better cultivation practices at the higher output prices.

U.S. Crop and Livestock Sector

Wheat

• Acreage or quota controls required to balance the domestic, export, and

TABLE 11

PRICES AT 80 PERCENT OF PARITY, 1986–1990

(dollars)

	Per Bushel			Per Pound	Per Cwt
	Wheat	Corn	Soybeans	Cotton	Rice
1986–87	6.52	4.71	11.43	1.09	17.89
1988–89	6.82	4.91	11.93	1.14	18.68
1989–90	7.07	5.08	12.35	1.18	19.36
1990–91	7.28	5.23	12.72	1.22	19.94

	Livestock			
	Omaha ($/cwt)	Seven-city pork ($/cwt)	Broiler (farm price, $/cwt)	Farm prices paid index (1910–14 = 100)
1986	75.34	56.31	32.10	1,209
1987	89.34	80.46	47.42	1,267
1988	93.23	83.83	49.41	1,320
1989	96.21	86.52	51.00	1,362
1990	99.01	89.03	52.47	1,402

NOTE: 80 percent of parity to be imposed October 1, 1986, for livestock and feed grains, September 1, 1986, for soybeans.

carry-over objectives with farm prices at 80 percent of parity would decrease acreage from an estimated 78.8 million planted in 1985–1986 to 48.5 million in 1986–1987, a reduction of approximately 30.3 million acres (see table 3). Further realignment to reach carry-over objectives (reduce existing government stocks) in conjunction with declining exports results in about 40 million planted acres by 1989–1990. If current base areas are used as a reference, this adjustment implies about 43 percent utilization of the 93.7 million acres.

• Domestic food and feed utilization is estimated to decline about 34 percent from the base line, from approximately 1,030 million to 684 million bushels in 1986–1987. Most of this adjustment is associated with the movement of feed use from 275 million bushels in 1985–1986 to 25 million in 1986–1987.

• Exports are projected to decline from the 1986–1987 base line of 1,657 million bushels to 745 million by 1989–1990, a 55 percent reduction.

• Prices are mandatory at 80 percent of parity, increasing about 90 percent from current levels of $3.40 per bushel to $6.52 per bushel in 1986–1987.

165

• Returns per planted acre above variable cost are estimated to increase from about $50 to approximately $200.

Corn

• Production or quota restrictions imply a planted area of about 58 million acres (see table 4). This approximately 30 percent reduction in planted area leaves the land area planted lower than during the 1983 payment-in-kind (PIK) year. Part of this reduction is associated with higher average yields, projected to increase to 118 bushels per acre over the base level of 110.5 bushels.

• Domestic use reflects higher prices and the approximately 13 percent reduction in grain-consuming-animal units. Total use is estimated at 4.6 million bushels, about 18 percent below the corresponding base-line estimate in 1986–1987.

• Exports are projected to decline from the 2.1 billion base-line estimate in 1986–1987 to about 1.4 billion in 1989–1990. The relatively inelastic demand of −0.17 in conjunction with increased foreign supplies implies the total decline of 33 percent. The 1989–1990 export estimate is 900 million bushels below the corresponding base-line estimate.

• Prices are mandatory at 80 percent of parity, increasing about 82 percent from current prices of $2.60 per bushel to $4.71 per bushel in 1986–1987.

• Returns to producers over variable production costs increase from about $110 to $400 per acre.

Soybeans

• Mandatory controls on soybean production implied about 40 million planted acres by 1989–1990, about 27 million acres below current estimated planted acres for 1985–1986 (see table 5).

• Domestic soybean crush declines about 29 percent in 1986–1987, reflecting higher prices and a 13 percent reduction in grain-consuming animal units.

• Exports are projected to be at approximately one-half the base-line level of 1.0 billion bushels in 1989–1990. The 46 percent reduction reflects an elastic export demand response of −1.52 plus increased supply pressure from competitors.

• Prices are mandatory at 80 percent of parity, increasing about 80 percent from current levels of $6.00 per bushel to $11.43 per bushel in 1986–1987.

• Returns to producers over variable costs increase from about $110 to $300 per planted acre.

Cotton

• Mandatory supply controls require 5.2 to 6.1 million planted acres in the project period (see table 6). This is approximately one-third the current ASCS base of 15.6 million acres. The reduction is about 2.5 million acres below that for the PIK year—7.9 million planted acres in 1983–1984.

• Domestic mill use declines about 10 percent from the base estimate in 1986–1987 because of a fairly inelastic domestic mill demand.

• Total exports are estimated to be about 5 million bales below the 1989–1990 base estimate, declining from 7.05 million bales to 1.97 million bales, for an approximately 72 percent reduction by the end of the projection period.

• Prices are mandatory at 80 percent of parity, increasing about 82 percent from current levels of $0.60 per pound to $1.09 per pound in 1986–1987.

• Returns per acre over variable production costs are estimated to increase $120 to $400 per planted acre from the base line.

Rice

• Acreage is projected to decline from the 1985–1986 base of 2.85 million to about 1.6 million in 1986–1987 (see table 7). This reduction is approximately 40 percent of the current ASCS base of 4.2 million acres and about 600,000 acres below acreage planted in 1983 with the PIK program.

• Domestic use is estimated to decline about 9 percent from 1985–1986 to 1986–1987, reflecting an inelastic domestic demand market, particularly brewery demand.

• The price increase required by parity simply prices the United States out of foreign markets. U.S. prices are higher than those of foreign competitors. The parity price would worsen this situation, resulting in a steady decline in exports from around 55 million hundredweight to about 12 million hundredweight by 1989–1990.

• Prices are mandatory at 80 percent of parity, increasing about 95 percent from current levels of $9.00 per hundredweight to $17.89 per hundredweight in 1986–1987.

Beef

• Since the parity program design is implemented on a crop year basis, the full effect on livestock does not occur until 1987 (see table 8). The Omaha price of beef at 80 percent of parity in 1987 is $89.34 per hundredweight. This is about 30 percent above that of the base line for the corresponding year.

• Since all production is consumed, marketing is projected to decline from 22.6 billion pounds in the 1987 base line to 18.4 in the first full 80 percent of parity year, or approximately 18.5 percent.

• Corresponding per capita consumption will decline from about 75 pounds to 54 pounds.

Pork

• Market prices (seven-city) at 80 percent of parity increase from $45.00 in the 1987 base line to $80.46 per hundredweight in 1987 under parity, about 80 percent. The increase is at about 4 percent per year over the projection period (see table 8).

• Marketings decline from 16.1 billion pounds for the 1987 base line to

12.8 billion in 1987 under parity, about a 21 percent reduction.
• Per capita consumption declines about 17 pounds, from 64.2 estimated in 1985 to 47.7 pounds in 1987.

Poultry

• Parity prices are not calculated for poultry. This series was constructed by manufacturing an index based on average prices over a base period in relation to a base prices paid index (see table 8).
• Marketings are estimated to decline from the 1987 base of 15.2 billion pounds to 13.7 billion. The full effect of the price increase is modified by the competitive price advantage over beef and pork and exacerbated by the loss of export markets.
• Per capita consumption is projected to increase throughout the projection period. Total production, however, is estimated to fall about 2½ percent short of the base-line estimates in each of the forecast years.

Farm Income

• The approximate increase of $20 per hundredweight for livestock prices and 80 to 90 percent increases in crop commodity prices increase realized gross farm income from a base line of $183 billion in 1987 to about $217 billion for the same period under parity, an increase of 19 percent (see table 9).
• Production expenses are estimated at $140 billion, reflecting higher input costs, primarily in the livestock industry.
• Net farm income approximately triples over that for the base line, at about $74 billion compared with $20 to $25 billion.

Government Cost. Costs for this parity program reflect a phasing out of farmer-held reserves plus maintenance for CCC storage (see table 10). No estimates are made for regulation, program supervision, and administration. Given the nature of the parity program, these costs could be substantial. Considerable sampling and spot checking would be necessary, for example, to ensure that producers were in fact complying with program production quotas. With the level of excess supply capacity, strong incentives would exist for transactions to occur outside the quota structure.

Summary. This program requires strong government control to maintain the sharply reduced supplies of agricultural commodities that will generate 80 percent of parity prices for all major crops and livestock commodities. This is accomplished by regulatory quotas based on historical production. Agricultural imports are restricted to prevent potential undercutting by competitors.

Prices are predetermined at the farm level but seek a market equilibrium in the retail sector. This approach to pricing would require rather delicate actions on the part of the Agriculture Department to read retail demand signals correctly so that allocated quotas or supplies would not exceed levels necessary to sustain mandated parity prices. Without proper government operation, the program could generate disequilibrium, resulting in downside retail prices with farm prices below the preassigned parity level. Government intervention in this case would require purchases of excess supplies or deficiency payments to compensate farmers for the differential. Thus program operation would require considerable monitoring at the retail level to ensure an appropriate supply balance plus strict adherence to production controls at the farm level.

In short, this program forces consumers to support farm commodity prices at higher levels. The major mechanism for accomplishing the objective is control of supply. Reduction of supply is accomplished by idling about 120 million acres of the current 265-million base acreage for corn, soybeans, wheat, cotton, and rice, about a 45 percent reduction in current land bases. About 54 million acres of wheat, 27 million acres of corn, 10 million acres of cotton, 2.8 million acres of rice, and 27 million acres of soybeans would be idled under this program.

Red meat and poultry supplies would be reduced 35 to 40 pounds per capita to ensure prices at 80 percent of parity for livestock. Producers assigned quotas would receive a substantial increase in net income. Estimated total net farm income is about $74 billion, some $50 billion above base-line estimates.

In essence, this program would result in a domestically oriented U.S. agriculture. Prices at this level would induce increased foreign supplies and reduced demand by importers, with corresponding downside pressure on U.S. export demand. In the model, the short-term export demand elasticities imply this downside pressure on exports. Although these elasticities are relatively small for feed grains, cotton, and food grains, longer-term responses indicate a significant reduction in total U.S. exports by 1989-1990.

The total value of exports under parity increased by about $5 billion over the baseline in 1986-1987. By the end of the period, however, the pattern had reversed, with total value of exports at $3 billion below the base line, or 1981 farm program extension. The direction of year-over-year changes in the value of parity-priced exports also indicates that in the longer term this program will substantially reduce the U.S. market share.

Consumers allocated about 20 percent of personal consumption expenditures to food under the base line. This proposal would increase expenditures by approximately 25 percent and raise the consumer price index for food by about 20 percent over the base period. An additional effect would be felt in the general economy. Idling 120 to 125 million acres of cropland would reduce input use by $10 to $15 billion. Farmers would have an additional $50 billion in purchasing power.

169

A longer-term and more significant effect would be the incentive to buy up production quotas or corresponding land. If acreage continues to turn over in the real estate market at 3 percent per year, this would imply a significantly higher land price base for over 30 percent of the total planted area by 1996. These new producers buying the land at the higher prices could find themselves in a tight financial squeeze not dissimilar to that now experienced by agriculture.

Therefore, the advantages of the program would be quickly capitalized into land or quota prices. The result would be a significant wealth transfer, with higher entry costs but returns to labor and management seeking preparity equilibrium levels. The Agriculture Department would have to maintain a tight rein on supplies, conditioned on the level of retail and export demand that could sustain parity prices. This would require significant skills and refinement in quantifying and projecting these necessary components of the program management system. Strong incentives also exist to sell outside the program and to import at low prices. Government control and regulation would be an additional expense to society for the parity program.

The trade-offs for the parity program design are associated with whether society and the agricultural sector are best served by higher prices and restricted supplies or by a more moderate design that requires prices competitive in the domestic and world markets with an emphasis on production and export market shares. The major benefactor in the 80 percent of parity program is clearly the producer that owns the marketing quota or land: an additional $50 billion in net farm income. Some spillover into the general economy could be expected. But the reduction in acreage and livestock production would increase food prices by about 20 percent, requiring an additional 3 to 4 percent in consumer expenditures for food, a roughly $10 to $15 billion reduction in the import industry supplying agriculture, a loss of U.S. trade share, and a reduction in agricultural employment. In the longer term agricultural operations could be faced with a financial squeeze similar to that under the base line. Land prices would be bid up to the point that these initial profits could be extracted as windfalls by current holders.

Overview

How will the choices for U.S. agriculture and the performance of U.S. agriculture be governed by the 1985 farm bill? Four policy options have been examined:

- maintaining the current 1981 farm program
- moving toward a more market-oriented agriculture
- enhancing the export market
- 80 percent of parity

These policy options have been evaluated for market, government, and industry performance parameters. The major effects of three of the options in relation to the base line are summarized in table 12.

The situation for agriculture through the end of the decade as implied by these policy exercises is likely to be difficult. U.S. agriculture has important excess supply potential at current loan and target prices. World economic conditions, even if generously interpreted, appear insufficient to move agriculture from this condition of excess supply. Finally, there is increasing evidence of financial stress in agriculture. Agricultural debt is considerably higher than in the past and for many farms cannot be serviced at market prices consistent with the base-line loan and target rates. The consequence for three of the four policies evaluated—the exception being the 80 percent of parity option—could be a substantial reevaluation and restructuring of assets in agriculture.

These four policy exercises describe alternatives for addressing the high debt load and the excess supply situation caused by U.S. and world economic conditions and agricultural policies of the past. The base-line policy option requires large government costs to sustain loan and target rate prices at 1984–1985 levels. Moreover, under this option, the excess supply in U.S. agriculture continues through the end of the decade. Increased production levels of competitors, high exchange rates, relatively low growth in world economies, high debt in developing economies, and high interest rates are important contributors to a continuation of the excess capacity under the base line. In fact, the general economic conditions in the United States and the world, along with the increasing production technology, more than the farm program parameters dictate the outcome for agriculture under the base line.

The market-oriented option results in decreased government exposure. Under this option agriculture would absorb a large share of the adjustment costs in the transition toward more market-oriented prices. The FAPRI model structure, if correct, indicates that demand responses in domestic and international markets would not generate farm incomes consistent with those of the base line at the lower market prices for agricultural commodities. Prices for basic agricultural commodities would fall from 15 to 20 percent. Exports would increase, but the increase would take time. Foreign producers also have considerable assets in agriculture, and it would require more than a single year of low prices to move those assets out of agriculture. While the reductions in prices of crop commodities result in some improvement in the livestock sector, the general implication with sluggish domestic and foreign economic growth is for substantially reduced net farm income.

Possibly the starkest of the policy evaluation exercises is for the repetition of the base line but with an expanded export potential. Even with relatively generous assumptions about expanding exports, this exercise indicates that it would be difficult to move prices significantly above base-line levels.

171

TABLE 12

SUMMARY OF KEY FARM PROGRAM EFFECTS
IN RELATION TO THE BASE LINE
(percent)

Performance Criterion	Policy Options		
	Market	Enhanced export	80 percent of parity
Farm prices	−8 to −10	+1 to 3	+80 to 90
Net farm income	−30	+3	+196
Direct government cost	−80	−18	a
Administrative cost	−	No change	SR+ LR?
Land prices	SR− LR−+	+	SR+ LR?
Input prices	+−	+−	−
Meat consumption per capita (beef, pork, chicken)	+1.6	No change	−17.9
Price per pound, aggregate meat bundle	−3.0	No change	+25.7
Land use	+3	+2.6	−39.3
Export value[b]	+23	+42	−15
Excess acreage capacity in relation to ASCS base[c]	5.6	6.0	44.4

NOTE: SR = short run; LR = long run.
a. No cost once government stocks depleted.
b. Percentage change in 1989–1990 value from 1986–1987 value of policy option. Base-line change was +18 percent.
c. Corn, wheat, soybeans, cotton, and rice; current base is 265 million acres (assumes 68 million acres in soybean base).

The enhanced export situation results in a taking up of some but not all of the excess capacity in U.S. agriculture. The livestock industry would be more or less unaffected. Gross farm income levels would be similar to the base line. The result of the enhanced export situation is simply to reduce the government budget costs for maintaining current loan and target rates. The conclusion is that if policies similar to the 1981 farm bill are continued, it will take substantial growth in the world economic situation to provide enough demand strength to move prices of basic agricultural commodities significantly above the base-line projections. Additional growth takes up some of the excess supply capacity, but price strength is modified by projected growth in farmer-held and CCC carry-over in 1985 and 1986 that would enter the market in later years.

For the 80 percent of parity option, farm incomes increase significantly with associated mandatory supply controls. Under this policy option, the U.S. agricultural sector becomes essentially domestically oriented. Export potential at parity prices is quite limited, and the value of exports is trending further down at the end of the evaluation. The economic benefits of this program, if the quotas are tied to land, would be capitalized into land, creating a wealth redistribution toward agriculture and relief from financial stress. Production would be highly limited, however, administrative costs would be high, and the welfare of the agriculturally related industries and rural communities would be significantly affected.

Clearly, the evaluations of the four policy options suggest quite different results for U.S. agriculture, but some more general conclusions can be drawn. The excess supply in agriculture at current loan and target prices is substantial. Sharp reductions in supply are required to increase domestic prices under the parity option. Those reductions would substantially diminish the role of the United States in world agricultural markets and the resource requirements of U.S. agriculture. Alternatively, high government costs are required to sustain present agricultural prices and net farm incomes with current world and domestic economic conditions. Of course, the external domestic and world conditions could change. The enhanced export option indicates, however, that the change in these economic conditions would have to be significant, rapid, and of major magnitude to affect net farm income. The effects of the 1985 farm bill will be important for agriculture unless world economic conditions improve dramatically.

Assessment from Outside the Beltway

Alex F. McCalla

Probably no agricultural policy debate in any country at any time has ever received the attention of so many conferences, seminars, and analyses papers as the debate preceding the 1985 farm bill. In fact, some people have argued that the only growth node in the agricultural industry has been the demand for economists and policy pundits to discuss the 1985 bill. This presents a problem for someone who has to present yet another paper when at least fifteen conferences and hundreds of papers have preceded this one. This problem is serious enough, but today I am sharing this program with a $1-2 million computer model and two experts in the political economy of agriculture who can bring to bear insights on policy denied someone "from outside the beltway." What can a qualitative person from an isolated desert valley 3,000 miles away hope to add?

Having neither a model nor Washington savvy and being unwilling to expose myself naked with nothing but my own graf ic and "back of the envelope" capacity, I assigned the task given me to my graduate policy class in the fall 1984 term as their policy analysis project. This way I had access to the analytical talents of thirteen of Davis's brightest and best. Although these students should not be held responsible for what I say, I gratefully and fully acknowledge their considerable contribution.[1]

My analysis of the assigned policy options proceeds as follows. First I discuss some possible goals for food and agricultural policy, because the analysis of options requires something to compare the outcomes against. I believe that insufficient attention has been paid to goals in previous discussions. Next I review the options originally discussed and compare them with those analyzed in the Food and Agricultural Policy Research Institute (FAPRI) model.[2] What I want to do in subsequent sections is to take the analysis beyond that done quantitatively by Johnson et al., by adding more wrinkles and using a broader set of goals. My analysis is presented in three parts. First I present a simple graphic analysis of options in a world market context, which allows a

---

The author acknowledges helpful comments from his colleague Elmer Learn.

comparison of options in a decomposed fashion in relation to prices (farm, consumer, and world), output, exports and export earnings, and government costs. Next I present a qualitative analysis (in tabular form) of the options against a broader set of goals. I also have suggestions about how the FAPRI model could be even more useful. Third, I speculate on the likely sensitivity of the results to external macro conditions of fiscal and monetary policy and international markets. The paper concludes with a discussion of several points of interconnectedness: cross-commodity implications, especially for livestock and nonpolicy commodities; critical policy trade-offs; issues of short-term stress in agriculture versus longer-term issues; and some comments on still unanswered questions.

Policy Issues and Policy Goals

Goals are presumably formulated because the analysis of the current state of affairs identifies issues that are at variance with what groups in society judge to be desirable. But to pay attention only to the current situation makes us prisoners of our immediate past. A historical review of past policy debates suggests that, when policy has been based on the prevailing situation, it is more often than not wrong.[1] The history of the 1981 bill surely attests to this. If the 1985 legislation is designed only to solve the current severe malaise in U.S. production agriculture, our debate will focus on the "farm problem" of 1984–1985, namely, falling prices, rising costs, and lower net farm income presumably caused in the main by high interest rates, the strong dollar, global recession, and falling international market shares. But would "solution" of these problems eliminate the farm policy problem? Would it solve, for example, the issues of (1) the structure of farming; (2) the appropriate role of agriculture in contributing to national goals of growth, employment, and foreign exchange earnings; (3) environmental effects and the preservation of natural resources; and (4) consumer nutrition, safety, and the affordability of food.

Thus I believe that long-term policy analysis (for 1989 and beyond) should be concerned with a broader set of goals than are generally discussed— as, for example, by the FAPRI model. Limiting analysis to farm prices, costs, national net farm income, the quantity of exports, and government costs does reflect the full spectrum of food and agricultural concerns. Clearly, these objectives are tractable in quantitative models, but is that enough? I therefore list longer-term and broader goals for consideration in the 1985 debate.

Farm Income Goals. Here there are multiple candidates. The first is national average farm income versus nonfarm income. What is the appropriate measure—average net farm income versus median nonfarm income or average income of farm families versus average nonfarm income? This avoids the

175

critical question of how off-farm income of farm families should be treated in the policy debate. If off-farm income is included, farm families in virtually all gross sales categories do, on the average, relatively well compared with median off-farm income.[4] Thus there is a question whether the longstanding goal of "improving farm income vis-à-vis nonfarm income" is still relevant.

A second candidate for an income goal relates to the distribution of farm income within the sector. In earlier times, when it was perceived that agriculture was a homogeneous industry made up of small and medium-sized family farms, improving national net farm income was judged to improve the well-being of individual farmers. Given the current skewed distribution of farm size and income, however, distributional questions arise. Whom are we trying to help—all farms in proportion to their sales, family farms (however defined), intermediate-sized farms where farm families receive the majority of their income from farming, or small farms?

Two other possible income candidates are the regional or commodity distribution of income and the stability of farm income. It is not for me to decide which one or what combination is appropriate. All I can say is that to say a policy is good because it "improves farm income" is analytically incomplete.

Farm and Food Prices. Goals with respect to prices could also be multifaceted and potentially conflicting. Higher farm prices are presumably related to farm income goals; but, given constant or proportional marketing margins, they also contribute to reduced consumer welfare and inflation. What weighting should be applied? The stability of prices is also often stated as a farm policy goal, presumably on the grounds that unstable prices destabilize farm incomes and lead to misallocation of resources. But farmers prefer a particular kind of stability—on the downside only. This kind of stability may help mitigate sharp drops in income but makes a questionable contribution to intertemporal resource allocation if high prices lead to excess capacity, which may contribute to future low prices and incomes and ultimately threaten the viability of some farmers. What is the appropriate price goal?

Consumer Food Policy Goals. Recent pieces of farm legislation have included "food" in the title, presumably because we are concerned about consumers. What are our concerns? Do we have goals regarding nutritional quality, food safety, diversity of choice, and affordability? If so, how are they included in the policy calculus? Most policy analysis is silent on these issues.

Macro Goals. In our early history great concern was expressed about the importance of the health of agriculture to national income growth, employment, and trade balances.[5] Does the fact that production agriculture employs less than 3 percent of the labor force and adds about the same amount to the gross national product mean that macro goals are irrelevant? I doubt it. According to the Agriculture Department, the food and agriculture sector, in all its dimensions, accounts for more than 20 percent of GNP and employment.[6] Further, food prices are highly visible elements of the consumer price index, and rapid changes in food prices incite quick concerns. Thus at least subsidiary concerns remain about agriculture's effect on growth, employment, inflation, and economic stability. More recent macro concerns have related to trade balances and budget exposure. Trade balances are discussed below under international goals. Budget exposure, an important topic in periods of $200 billion deficits, has two dimensions. The first is the exposure that results from farm program variables in normal operation under the most likely scenario. Presumably this exposure is "predictable" given normal conditions, and the likely objective would be to minimize budget costs. The second exposure issue relates to potential variability in budget costs given a set of program parameters. Variability arises from at least three sources: weather, macro economic effects (for example, the value of the dollar), and policy changes in other countries (for example, Soviet policy changes in 1971–1972). The exposure is worse in an entitlement program with prices fixed in nominal terms. Thus an additional macro concern is variability in budget costs. Even if loan rates were indexed to the preceding five-year moving average, for example, a rapid fall in prices could greatly increase budgetary costs in the short run.

International Goals for Agriculture. Much conversation these days is focused on the "goal" of expanding agricultural exports. But is this a goal or a means to other goals? Expanding exports could result from stronger world commodity markets, which would suggest higher prices and higher farm incomes. In this context, expanded exports are a means to an income goal. Or do we want to expand exports to earn foreign exchange so as to limit the current account deficit caused in part by the U.S. fiscal deficit? This is a macro goal, the accomplishment of which may or may not contribute to farm policy goals. We also hear a lot of talk about improving our market share. This statement in itself has little substance. If we lower prices (say, by releasing stocks or subsidizing exports) to expand market share, whether or not we are better off depends on the elasticity of demand for our imports. So we need some clarity on the export goal question.

Resource Conservation and Productivity. The long-run capacity of U.S. agriculture to produce for domestic and international markets depends on our not letting our basic soil and water resources deteriorate and on maintaining a flow of yield-increasing technology that allows productivity to grow or at least be maintained. All of this must be done in an environmentally acceptable fashion. It seems almost too obvious to have to cite these goals. Often, however, policy encourages short-run expansion (as in 1973–1975) without paying attention to long-run consequences. It is crucial that conservation, environmental, and research goals be placed firmly in the debate.

The Structure of Agriculture. Last is the need for a statement of what kind of agriculture we want in the long run. If we are content to let the trends in farm size and concentration of production that have occurred in the past thirty years continue until the vast majority of output is produced by 200,000 large-scale farms, let us admit it and stop talking about millions of family farms. This would presumably be consistent with a goal that says we want the agricultural structure that produces our needs most efficiently. Surely that would be a radical departure from our past rhetoric, but a goal of "preserving the family farm" clearly has little meaning unless we are much more explicit about our structural and distributional goals. If the farmers in the sales range of $20,000 to $200,000 still depend on agriculture for a significant portion of income and are too large to have full-time off-farm employment and too small to be fully efficient and we want to preserve them for social, aesthetic, or environmental reasons, let us explicitly state that as a goal. Similarly, if we are concerned abut the current high rates of bankruptcy and the potential effect on the health of rural communities in America, let us explicitly say that we have a goal of maintaining a rural America populated by intermediate and small-sized farms and dotted with healthy small towns at frequent intervals.

My purpose in raising the structural issue and all the preceding ones is not to say that these are what the goals ought to be. Rather, I am sure people in the United States are concerned about one, some, or all of these goals and probably many more. Therefore, it is incumbent on all policy analysts and economists to indicate the implications of policy options for a broad set of possible goals stated explicitly. The first of a number of small quibbles I have with the FAPRI paper is that it is too indirect and too narrow in expressing what goals of agricultural policy it compares the options against. I sincerely hope the goal structure was not dictated by what was tractable in the model.

The Policy Options

Having discussed goals, I present two sets of the options being analyzed: the options discussed by the authors of this part before the conference and the FAPRI interpretation thereof.

Provided by AEI	*Analyzed by FAPRI*
A. Continuation of 1981 act with loan rates and target prices set at 1984 levels and presumably with options for acreage reduction	Same as AEI with acreage reduction programs triggered by desired stock levels

178

B. Gradual reduction of support levels by, say, a fixed percentage (5 percent) in each year of the act (though not specified, support would presumably eventually become indexed to market prices); target prices and loan rates retained as safety nets; whether there is supply control not stated

One-time reduction of loan rates to 80 percent of five-year market average, with minimum and maximum prices removed; no supply control or target prices—P.L. 480, Commodity Credit Corporation (CCC) credits, and so on retained at 1981 levels; the "cold turkey" option

C. "Farm prices" (target prices?) established at 1981 act target price level, loan rates 5 percent below target, and stocks kept manageable by expanded food aid, CCC credit, and export subsidies

Macro conditions altered by lowering value of the dollar and interest rates and assuming more favorable economic performance in the United States and abroad; otherwise, same program characteristics as option A (continuation)

D. Market prices raised to 1981 act target prices by means of permanent, mandatory supply control (acreage allotments or marketing quotas)

Prices at 80 percent of parity with mandatory supply control

The Analysis of Policy Options

Lacking a model, I resort, in this section, to graphic and qualitative analysis. I first present a simple graphic analysis of options in a large country–open economy partial equilibrium analysis that explicitly includes world markets. I then try to look at the implications of the options for a broader set of goals. The results are presented in qualitative terms in tabular form. Third, I ask how sensitive these results are to alternative macro scenarios.

Results by Options and Goals Using Graphic Analysis. Being neither an econometrician nor a mathematician, I resort to simple graphic analysis of the four options outlined. My intent is to show the effects of the policy options on variables that include (1) farm and retail prices and therefore effects on consumers, (2) net farm income (changes in producer surplus), (3) government costs, (4) exports and export earnings, and (5) effects on world markets.

Option A—continuation of current programs with 1984 prices given by 1981 act. Figure 1 presents the analysis of this option. The right side of the diagram depicts the rest of the world (*ROW*). The excess supply functions of all other exporters of a commodity are horizontally summed to get a world supply function (ΣEs_{ROW}). Similarly, the excess demand functions of all im-

FIGURE 1

OPTION A: CURRENT PROGRAM CONTINUES

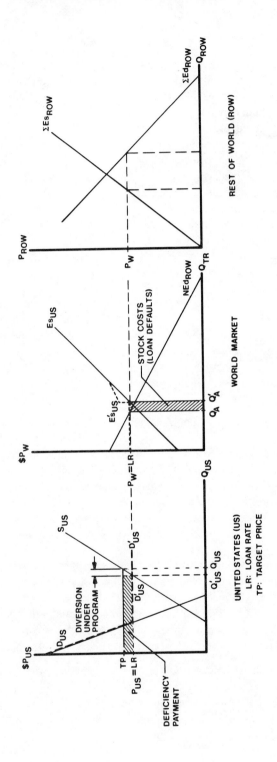

ALEX F. McCALLA

porters are horizontally summed to yield a world demand function (ΣEd_{ROW}).
$\Sigma Ed_{ROW} - \Sigma Es_{ROW}$ yields a world net import demand/export supply function,
which is NEd_{ROW} in the middle panel. The United States is depicted on the left
with domestic demand D_{US} and domestic supply S_{US}. The subtraction of D_{US}
from S_{US} yields the U.S. excess supply function Es_{US}, which is depicted in the
middle panel. The middle panel is the world market as seen by the United
States. Clearly, the United States faces a downward-sloping export demand
function because it is very large in world commodity markets for wheat, corn,
soybeans, rice, and cotton, for example. In the absence of any policy intervention, the world price would be determined by the intersection of Es_{US} and
NEd_{ROW}. (This free market solution is shown in figure 2, which is discussed
under option B.)

U.S. policy under the 1981 act has two relevant domestic prices, the
target price (TP) and the loan rate (LR). These are shown on the left of figure
1. Producers who participate are guaranteed TP for a reduced level of land
use, shown as Q'_{US}. Participating producers would plan to produce Q'_{US} regardless of world price. Participants can also place their crops under loan at
LR. The implications of this for world markets is to alter the U.S. excess
supply function. At TP it is less than Es_{US} because of land diversion (how
much depends on the amount of diversion). For world prices (denominated in
dollars) between TP and LR, U.S. excess supply is perfectly inelastic. For
world prices below the loan rate, U.S. excess supply drops to zero (in theory)
because U.S. domestic demand (because of the loan program) becomes perfectly elastic (D'_{US}). Thus at the loan rate U.S. excess supply is horizontal.
$E's_{US}$ is depicted in the figure as having a horizontal portion at LR; it is vertical
between LR and TP and would merge into Es_{US} at prices above TP. It might
have some slope if the United States held stocks that were dissipated as world
prices rose.

World prices are determined in the middle panel by the intersection of
NEd_{ROW} and $E's_{US}$, which yields world price, P_W, which is equal to the loan
rate. It is thus true that the loan rate puts a floor under world prices. At P_W the
world demands Q_A, which is less than the United States is willing to supply
(Q_A'). The difference ($Q_A' - Q_A$) enters U.S. stocks.

Program costs have three components: (1) deficiency payments of $TP - LR$ on Q'_{US} (shown as the hatched area); (2) stock costs of acquiring $Q_A' - Q_A$
at the loan rate LR, some of which may be recouped in subsequent years by
sale of stocks; and (3) the cost of any paid diversion to reduce U.S. output
from Q_{US} to Q'_{US}. Consumers pay P_W for domestic consumption.

The results of the program, then, are to raise domestic and world prices
(in relation to the free market), reduce exports (whether export earnings
increased or decreased would depend on the elasticity of NEd_{ROW}) and incur
the costs identified. This graphic depiction qualitatively confirms all the
FAPRI model results.

181

FIGURE 2

OPTION B: FREE MARKET

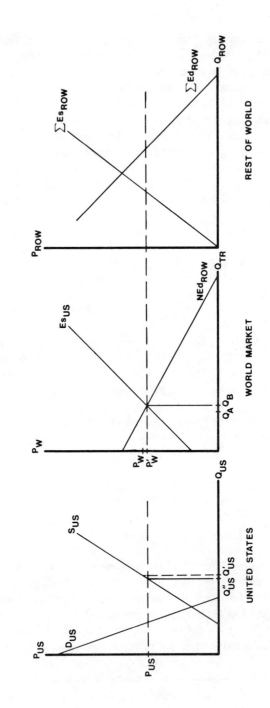

Option B—the free market. The free market option is shown in figure 2. Its simplicity is intrinsically appealing. The results in relation to the continuation option are as the model suggests. U.S. and world prices drop to P'_W ($P'_W = P_{US}$). What happens to U.S. production depends on whether producers produce more or less at the lower prices (P'_W) than they did with diversion programs in place. As drawn, U.S. production drops to Q''_{US}, which is less than Q'_{US}. The FAPRI model suggests that U.S. output increases. Either way world prices fall. U.S. consumers gain, and exports expand; but whether export earnings increase or decrease depends critically on whether NEd_{ROW} is elastic or inelastic at P'_W. This, of course, is G. Edward Schuh's point. If the elasticity of demand for U.S. exports is greater than one, we would be better off to reduce prices. In the absence of any programs, government costs fall to zero. Finally, what happens to net farm income depends critically on the combination of the elasticity of domestic demand and the elasticity of export demand. Even if export demand were elastic, gross returns could fall if domestic demand were inelastic and the weighted (by the proportion consumed domestically and the proportion exported) aggregate elasticity were less than one. This still does not tell us whether the critical policy variable— net farm income—rises or falls. The elasticity of the demand for U.S. exports is an important empirical question, which, if known, would greatly enlighten the current policy debate.

Option C—expanded exports. To this point, the graphic analyses of the AEI options and the FAPRI model options have been the same. For the last two options, however, the model deviated from the discussed options. I present graphically three variants of option C: first, the FAPRI dollar devaluation and improved economic growth option; second, the high-support price-export subsidy option; and third, the expanded credit, or P.L. 480, option.

1. Figure 3 presents a simplified version of the FAPRI expanded exports model. In that model target prices and loan rates remain at 1984 levels. The principal change from their base-line model is that the U.S. dollar is devalued and rates of economic growth in both the United States and the rest of the world improve. In figure 3 the devaluation of the dollar causes a rotation of net world demand upward to NEd'_{ROW}, because the devaluation makes domestic prices in the rest of the world rise in relation to U.S. prices, so that import demand expands at all prices. It is analytically equivalent to an ad valorem export subsidy. The result is that world prices rise to P''_W. As I have drawn it, P''_W rises above the loan rate (LR); thus stocks do not accumulate, and deficiency payments are less. The continued existence of the U.S. program changes the U.S. excess supply function to $E's_{US}$, which results in a world price lower than it would have been in the absence of the U.S. program.

This analysis clearly shows that if the U.S. dollar were devalued enough, world prices would rise above program levels, and supply control would be unnecessary. The model results suggest some rise in prices, but there would still be a need for acreage diversion.

183

FIGURE 3
OPTION C1: FAPRI MODEL

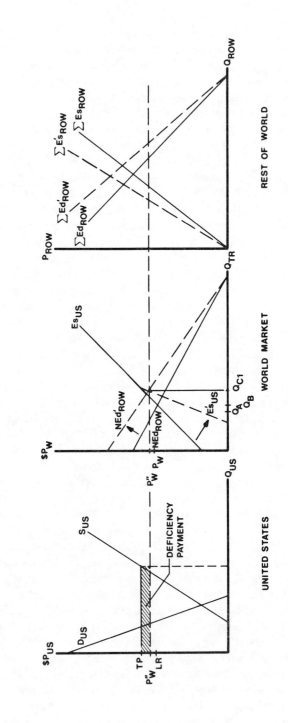

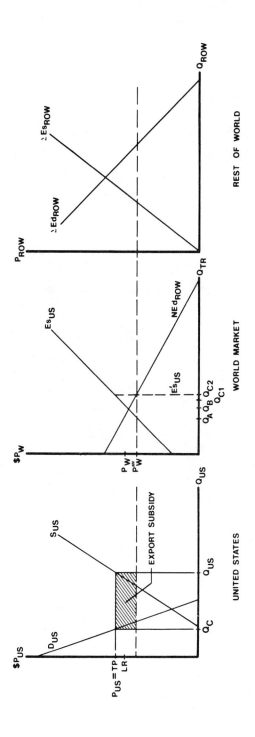

FIGURE 4

OPTION C2: AEI EXPORT SUBSIDY

185

FIGURE 5

Option C3: AEI P.L.480/Credit Expansion

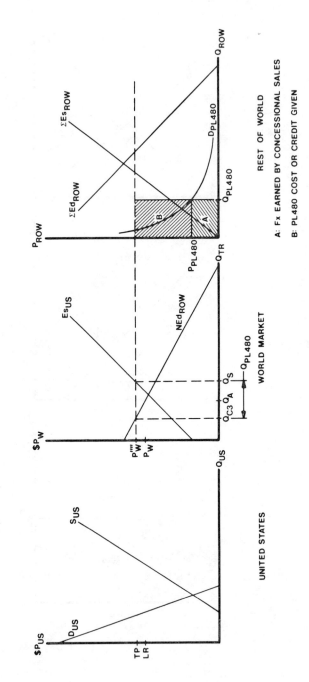

UNITED STATES

WORLD MARKET

REST OF WORLD

A: Fx EARNED BY CONCESSIONAL SALES

B: PL480 COST OR CREDIT GIVEN

2. The option discussed earlier was not really analyzed by the FAPRI model. It called for setting prices at or near 1984 target prices and disposing of excess supplies by the use of either an export subsidy or expanded credit and P.L. 480 sales. The export subsidy model is presented in figure 4. U.S. producers are guaranteed target price TP, which results in the production of Q_{US}. At TP U.S. consumers (made worse off by the policy) consume Q_C. The difference $(Q_{US} - Q_C)$ is sold on world markets (that is, U.S. excess supply becomes perfectly inelastic—$E's_{US}$). The excess supply $(Q_{US} - Q_C)$ is shown as Q_{C2} in the middle panel. This forces world price down to P_W''', and U.S. exports expand in relation to all previous options $(Q_{C2} > Q_{C1} > Q_B > Q_A)$. Again, foreign exchange earnings depend on the elasticity of export demand. U.S. producers are clearly better off than under all previous options because prices are higher and there is no supply control. U.S. consumers are worse off, and program costs are now the export subsidy shown as the hatched area, which is $(Q_{US} - Q_C)$ $(TP - P_W''')$. This case involves an explicit export subsidy; current policy has analytically the same effect, with the deficiency payment as an implicit export subsidy.

3. The notion that excess supplies could be dispersed with expanded P.L. 480 grants or expanded credit must be based on the assumption that there is additional demand in world markets that is constrained by the availability of foreign exchange or credit. Such a demand would have a unitary elastic character. This is shown in the right-hand panel of figure 5 as D_{PL480}. Thus the option suggests setting domestic prices at TP and selling on the commercial world market at that price (P_W''''). The commercial export market would buy Q_{C3}, leaving $Q_S - Q_{C3}$ (middle panel) in excess of commercial sales. This is shown as Q_{PL480} in the right panel $[Q_{PL480} = (Q_S - Q_{C3})]$. Given the foreign exchange constraint (or credit constraint) of importers, they would be able to pay only P_{PL480} for Q_{PL480} or A dollars. Either credit or a $PL480$ loan would have to be given for B dollars to allow the developing countries to buy at P_W''''. Thus the current government cost of this program is area B, but presumably some or all of this would be repaid. Obviously, an export expansion program could be a combination of export subsidies and credit. This could be analyzed by combining figures 4 and 5.

Option D—high prices and supply control. The graphic analysis presented in figure 6 attempts to model the option of mandatory supply control to achieve 1984 prices. Prices to farmers are guaranteed to producers at TP, and supply control is mandatory to reduce supply sufficiently to clear markets at that price. This would require U.S. supply to shift from S_{US} to S'_{US}. World and U.S. market prices would rise to $P_W'''' = TP$. U.S. producers would lose producer surplus on this commodity equal to the vertical hatched area. Net producer losses would be the difference between the loss in producer surplus and the returns from the transferred resources to the next best use (the opportunity cost of wheat production times the quantity of production on displaced

187

FIGURE 6
OPTION D: HIGH PRICES AND SUPPLY CONTROL

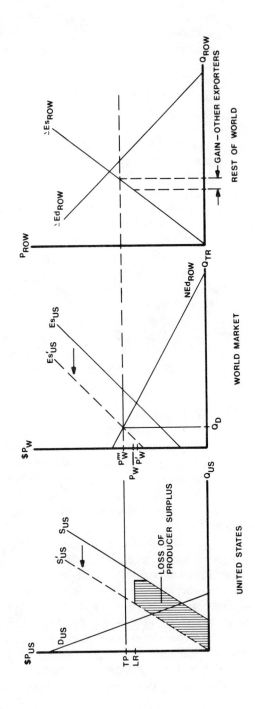

land). This would also be the minimum amount the government would have to pay if the supply control were by voluntary paid diversion rather than mandatory. Producers could be better off under this option only if the elasticities of both domestic and international demand were sufficiently low (that is, highly inelastic) that gross revenue and net farm income increased with reduced supplies. While it is plausible that domestic U.S. demand is highly inelastic for wheat, it is less likely for the other program commodities. For international demand to be sufficiently inelastic presupposes extensive fixed price intervention in all importing countries. The FAPRI model's analysis of 80 percent of parity is not strictly comparable, but, its results suggest significant increases in net farm income. This seems to follow directly in all cases except soybeans from their assumed elasticities of demand, which are low.

Summary of graphic analysis. This trip through elementary graphic analysis was made to look at the components of the farm policy puzzle that are simultaneously worked out in a model such as that used by Johnson et al. This is, in my judgment, the advantage of this intermediate stage. It allows us, for example, to look explicitly at policy trade-offs in prices, incomes, government costs, and world market effects. These are discussed later in more detail. It also allows us to look explicitly at the international dimension of policy choice in a large, export-oriented, open-economy country such as the United States.

Broader Qualitative Analysis. The graphic analysis just presented perhaps has the merit of being simpler and simultaneously more transparent and decomposable than the simultaneous system contained in the FAPRI model. Therefore, I think it is potentially useful in disentangling and identifying crucial variables in the policy debate, such as the critical importance of the elasticity of the demand for U.S. exports. It is also helpful in looking more explicitly at international market effects and at identifying the government expenditure trade-offs and could be used to explore alternative policy instruments beyond those contained in the four options. But, in fairness, it must be noted that it has serious deficiencies in relation to a simultaneous quantitative model. It deals with a single commodity and cannot deal easily with cross-commodity issues. It cannot give numerical estimates of the values of critical parameters. It does not allow for the inclusion of decision rules, such as desired stock levels that trigger further policy intervention. The two kinds of analysis are thus not competitive but rather potentially complementary and mutually reenforcing.

Neither approach does very well at dealing with discrete qualitative goals, such as structure or equity. But surely such goals must be addressed in the broader policy debate, even if nothing more than the direction of change is identified. This is what I have attempted in table 1. For each of the seven major possible goals (with subgoals in most cases), I try assess the effects

189

of the policy options. For example, using economic intuition, historical data, and models where relevant, I attempt to judge the effect of the various options on the preservation of intermediate-sized family farms. Options A, B, and C-1 seem likely to continue or accentuate the trend toward a bimodal agriculture, with a few very large farms producing most of the output and depending mainly on agriculture for income and many small farms depending almost exclusively on off-farm income. The reasoning runs as follows. All three options are market oriented in the sense that the most efficient (and probably the largest) producers benefit in proportion to output—thus the minus (−) entries, because if the goal is to have more viable intermediate-sized farms, these options would be counterproductive. Options C-2, C-3, D-1, and D-2, presumably by raising prices significantly with or without supply control, should slow the trend toward a bimodal agriculture—thus the plus (+) entries.

The entries should be interpreted as hypotheses about whether the option has a positive effect on the goal, a negative effect, no effect, or an unknown effect. Even a casual look at the table suggests that no policy option has positive effects on all goals (nor for that matter does any have all negative effects). Thus no option is dominant or is dominated. This should not be surprising because policy is, after all, involved with trade-offs and marginal choices.

This simple qualitative analysis has three important implications: (1) We, as economists, cannot say that one policy is "better" than another without further information. That additional information consists of (2) the quantitative magnitude of the effect (does option B have twice the negative effect of C-1 on, say, resource conservation?) and (3) the relative weights society attaches to each goal (that is, a social welfare function). Needless to say, neither this paper nor that by Johnson et al. can answer all these questions, but a crucial first step is to try to understand at least the direction of change and to be explicit about the trade-offs.

It is quite likely that models like the FAPRI model will go further toward better comprehensive policy analysis than simple graphics. Some comments about how I would have liked them to go further follow.

First, how sensitive are these model results to different elasticities of demand? For example, suppose they believed Edward Schuh and inserted international demand elasticities of greater than one in table 1. How different would the results be? My supposition is that options B, C-1, C-2, and C-3 would all look much better and option D would look much worse.

Second, what would happen if they modeled a gradual indexing of loan rates to market prices rather than the cold turkey approach of option B? This would be interesting for at least two reasons. First, the path of adjustment and its implications for farm viability may be of considerably more short-term interest to policy makers than finding long-run equilibrium. If, for example, that path is strewn with an enormous number of bankruptcies, the structural

TABLE 1

Summary of the Effects of the Options on a Broad Set of Possible Goals

Options	Farm Income		Farm Prices (relative to now)		Consumer Welfare		Macro Goals		International		Resource		Structure of Agriculture	
	Farm versus nonfarm	Distribution (more even)	Level	Stability	Quality	Diversity & prices	Budget exposure	Control of inflation	Foreign exchange earnings	Market share	Conservation	Efficiency	Efficiency	Family farm
Option A: Continue 1981 act	−	−	0	0	0	+	−	+	−	−	+	−	−	−
Option B: Free market	−	−	−	−	?	+	+	+	?	+	−	+	+	−
Option C: 1. FAPRI	+	−	+	+	0	−	+	−	+	+	−	+	+	−
2, 3. AEI	+	?	+	+	?	−	−	−	?	+	−	?	?	+
Option D: 1. FAPRI	+	+	+	+	?	−	+	−	−	−	+	−	−	+
2. AEI	?	+	+	+	?	−	+[a]	−	−	−	+	−	−	+

NOTE: + = contributes to improvement in the goal; − = detracts from the goal; 0 = no effect; ? = uncertain—depends on other factors, such as elasticity of export demand for foreign exchange earnings.

a. If mandatory; could be quite high if it was a paid diversion.

and political price may be too high. Second, to have some notion of the rate and costs of adjustment, given resource rigidities in the short run and lags in production adjustment, could be valuable in looking at transitional policies.

Third, I had hoped they would analyze option C as given and compute the costs of disposing of output through export subsidies, domestic and international give-away schemes, and greatly expanded credit. Further, would it be possible to pick an optimum combination of these policy tools, given some explicit goals for prices, net farm income, and budget costs? Clearly the model offers opportunities to put numbers on the costs identified in the figures and thus give government policy makers some notions of relative magnitudes. Going a step further, the model could be shocked by various exogenous factors—interest rates and exchange rates, weather, policy change, rate of economic growth—to determine the relative variability in budget exposure of each option or combination of options.

Similarly, the efficiency of alternative forms of supply control could be explored as a trade-off frontier between costs and net income, for example. I think it should be relatively easy to trace out policy trade-off frontiers.[7]

Macro Sensitivity of the Results. A fifth point would be to encourage Johnson et al. to explore the effects of a range of macro scenarios on the option results. In essence, they have done most of their analysis using 1984 conditions—high real interest rates, a strong dollar, slow economic growth, and high U.S. deficits. Most would argue that these are worst-scenario terms, but I doubt it because even their analysis has the dollar value coming down slowly. But what if it stays high or rises even further? At the other extreme, suppose the conditions of the middle 1970s returned—a falling dollar, negative real interest rates, rapid economic growth, expanding demand for agricultural products, and trade liberalization. Would we still have a policy problem? Option C-1 is a small step in that direction, but how far would macro conditions have to change to improve things materially? It would be nice to know whether, if macro and international variables were in the "right" constellation, the farm problem would be solved. My judgment is that it would not be, but to listen to many policy papers over the past year one would think it would. I could go on, but these questions are sufficient to illustrate how much further policy modeling could go in providing more rational analysis of complex interrelated policy problems.

Concluding Comments

I conclude with some issues and questions that I believe are critical to the policy debate and that have received inadequate attention from policy modelers, political pundits, and qualitative analysts alike.

Cross-commodity links are critical. The FAPRI model goes a long way by explicitly including the livestock sector. Clearly, what is good for the crop folks seems not so good for the livestock sector in terms of price level. But is this really true? If input costs rise and markets work, presumably a new set of livestock and grain prices will result that are in stable profitable equilibrium. A large poultry producer recently said that he did not care whether grain prices were high or low as long as they were reasonably stable and predictable. If grain prices rise, all meat prices rise, and consumption shifts toward poultry. It thus appears that the stochastic question is critical. But intercommodity effects go beyond program crops and the livestock subsector. In California, for example, if the cotton program were abolished and cotton prices fell twenty cents per pound, it would surely have huge effects on the acreage devoted to tomatoes, walnuts, almonds, grapes, pistachios, and alfafa, to name but a few commodities. The thinner the markets, the greater would be the price effects. I have been trying to tell California specialty crop producers that farm programs do matter to them, even if they do not produce wheat or corn or cotton or tobacco or rice or peanuts. Economists need to learn the same thing.

I really think multiple-goal, multiple-instrument policy trade-offs are a powerful tool of policy analysis that can potentially be estimated empirically. Yet we persist in single-instrument, single-goal analysis. In the options being discussed here, a large number of trade-offs are implicit: in options A and B between reduced budgetary costs and lower and unstable farm incomes or, as in comparing options A and C-2, between explicit or implicit export subsidies and higher farm incomes. Surely, the greatly increased interdependence of agriculture and of the national and international economies dictates a dynamic trade-off approach. Otherwise, how can we expect the policy process to succeed, first, in dealing with the complexity of trade-offs resulting from additional goals and, second, in designing policies to provide flexible options to adjust to changing external conditions? But clearly both are required, because picking somebody's best-guess scenario and locking policy parameters to it, as was done in 1981, is no longer acceptable.

Perhaps the most difficult problem is how we move toward a longer-term rational, comprehensive, coherent, and just policy when there is an immediate crisis in much of agriculture. Can the policy process put the bankruptcy prairie fire in proper perspective?

Finally, although it may be politically safe to limit the analysis of policy options to variations within a set of policy instruments we have used for over fifty years, is it really reasonable to think that a long-term set of instruments is contained in that set? In my judgment a long-term policy solution for U.S. agriculture in 2000 is unlikely to be found by tinkering with a policy framework now in its sixth decade. Across-the-board attempts to raise prices by reducing land inputs do not solve stability, equity, or budget problems. If equity remains a goal, targeting seems necessary. If stability remains a goal, insurance and futures options are live possibilities.

Because I did not have a model or the wisdom that results from continuous immersion in the policy hot tub of Washington, my contribution has been to try both to decompose and to simplify the policy puzzle with simple graphic and qualitative analysis while at the same time underlining the complexities of a multiple-goal, multiple-instrument policy situation. If I have done nothing more than to cause some of you to reflect more deeply on the complexities and the trade-offs, I will have been successful. Better yet, if I have disabused only one person of the notion that if we keep looking under enough rocks, the perfect policy solution will be found, I will have been very successful. Complex policy problems are unlikely to be solved by simple, yet undiscovered, policy instruments.

Notes

1. They are Ricardo Amon, David Bunn, Oscar Chaves, Russ Graeber, David Iyamah, Paula Mara, Raymond Olsson, Kyrre Rickertsen, Eduardo Rodriguez, Helen Roland, Richard Standiford, Richard Wayman, and Dennis Wichelns.

2. S. R. Johnson, Abner W. Womack, William H. Meyers, Robert E. Young II, and Jon Brandt, "Options for the 1985 Farm Bill: An Analysis and Evaluation," in this volume.

3. Alex F. McCalla and Elmer W. Learn, "Public Policies for Food, Agriculture, and Resources: Retrospect and Prospect" (Paper presented at the conference "Food, Agriculture, and Resources: Policy Choices 1985," organized by the National Center for Food and Agricultural Policy and the National Agricultural Forum, Washington, D.C., December 4, 1984).

4. Ibid.

5. W. W. Cochrane, *The Development of American Agriculture: A Historical Analysis* (Minneapolis: University of Minnesota Press, 1979).

6. U.S. Department of Agriculture, Economic Research Service, *Economic Indicators of the Farm Sector: Farm Sector Review, 1983* (Washington, D.C., 1984).

7. Nicole S. Ballenger, "Agricultural Policy Analysis for Mexico: Sectoral and Macro Impacts" (Ph.D. dissertation, University of California, Davis).

Assessment from
Inside the Beltway

J.B. Penn

Johnson and his colleagues have contributed a useful compendium of information to the farm bill debate. Their paper provides a comprehensive assessment
of the four options in a broad framework that reflects much of the dynamics of
agriculture. I certainly endorse their initial argument that farm policy must be
assessed in a broader context than we have typically used. They extend that
context from the single commodity to the broader crop and livestock sector.
We must keep in mind that the considerations now extend even far beyond
that—to the allied industries in the food system—inputs, processing, distribution, exporting, and others. Part of our dilemma today lies in the fact that farm
policy has been too parochial for too long.

One could question certain of the authors' assumptions and reasonably
argue about some of the model parameters. I suggest that two key areas
deserve more scrutiny. One, of course, is the question of the short- and long-
run price responsiveness of exports, around which there is already much
disagreement. The other is the domestic supply response. I was somewhat
surprised at the lack of responsiveness indicated by the model to the market
option.

My intent, however, is not to argue about specific results or procedures.
The results give us a very useful basis for advancing the policy discussion. For
all four of the options considered, they present a very somber picture indeed.
They do not immediately reveal any option that offers at once an effective and
a politically acceptable solution. This is in part because the causes of the
problems probably lie elsewhere, outside the farm sector, and the solutions
are probably there as well. Alteration of the commodity programs will not
answer the most vexing problems that face agriculture policy today.

Underlying Messages

The model results suggested several underlying messages that come through
quite clearly. The first of these is simply that agriculture must adjust. It must
make an adjustment on its own with great pain or with the assistance of
government—and even then not without considerable pain. With the slowed

195

foreign demand, there is again excess capacity in the sector that, as the model results suggest, is unlikely to disappear even with a resumption of reasonably strong rates of export growth. Recent attempts to use the programs to forestall this adjustment have become exceedingly expensive, much too costly to be politically palatable for very much longer.

A second message is that the present system, the present complex of programs, either managed more or managed less, will not lead us to a solution. Managed more—the continuation of current policy—they appear too costly ($23.3 billion over the four-year life of a bill) for the limited improvement in the farm economy. Managed much less—the abrupt reduction of the programs, the market option—they promise to be much less costly but are likely to cause too much dislocation too quickly to be politically acceptable.

A third message is that "good markets," as good as can reasonably be expected, will not bail us out. The farm sector's accumulated productivity gains continue to the point where even resumed export growth consistent with better world economic conditions does not offer a solution, at least not in the near term. As the model results clearly indicate, foreign market growth is unlikely to be strong enough to permit full use of resources (as in the 1970s), to allow greatly reduced government program costs, and to maintain incomes and earnings high enough to satisfy farmers (and their bankers). Hoping for a miracle—a return to the export boom of the 1970s—does not appear to be a practical answer.

Another message that seems both evident and persuasive is that we cannot turn inward again, as the 80 percent of parity option would require. The effects of that approach do not improve much with age; if we have learned nothing more in our experience of over fifty years with the programs, we should have learned that. A one-time transfer of wealth to one generation of farmers that adversely affects much of the rest of the food system, entails higher food prices and government costs for food-related and other indexed programs, and greatly reduces our presence in global food markets does not appear an acceptable answer. But, although most economists will readily disavow it, we cannot afford to overlook the appeal of high prices and low budget costs. The apparent equity of mandatory controls has some political appeal, especially in a crisis atmosphere laden with frustration. It is not without some strong supporters and will probably gain more, although I think there are far too many participants in today's debate to permit a resumption of those policies.

These messages suggest that none of the four options so widely discussed today is the answer. If so, where does that leave us?

What Must Be Done?

It appears to me that we are now confronted with two primary problems: (1) the design of acceptable means to facilitate the adjustment that is necessary in agriculture, moving to greater reliance on the market but in as orderly a manner as possible and perhaps with greater sensitivity to the dislocation involved; and (2) finding acceptable means of effectively addressing the farm debt problem, which appears to be looming larger each day. This is not a commodity program issue but threatens to overwhelm the farm bill debate and perhaps forestall the needed reforms in the commodity programs.

In addressing the first of these problems—finding acceptable means to facilitate necessary adjustment and greater reliance on the market—some obvious criteria or helpful guidelines might be suggested. These take the form of homilies that we have all heard but that bear repeating nonetheless, economic guidelines, and what might even be called exhortations.

- The programs, whatever they are, must work—the goals must be achievable and realistic. Some market stability can be added, but there are limits to how much. Some land conservation can be achieved. Some cushion against bad crops can be offered. Some help for farms in transition can be offered. But the policies and programs should not be asked to stop adjustment to market and technological forces.

- The programs must be less expensive. The realities of the deficit cannot be ignored and will probably mean defeat for any farm bill that attempts to ignore them.

- The programs must be fair, in their effect across farms and commodities and in the distribution of benefits.

- The programs can no longer be based on the myth of the small, poor family farm that requires large income transfers to correct a social problem. That is for the most part long behind us. The 700,000 commercial farms (those that depend primarily on farming for family income, have at least $40,000 in annual product sales, and produce 88 percent of the farm output) had an average net family income during 1980–1983 of $46,114, approaching twice the national average family income. The emphasis should be on viewing the units as farm businesses and on problems related to their business viability.

- The programs must recognize the tremendous changes that have occurred in the farming industry and its environment in just the past two decades. To pretend that these have not occurred will not solve anything and will only lead to even more problems later. Agriculture is now closely integrated into the national economy, affecting and being affected by it, and is closely linked to the international economy and world food markets.

- The programs must add stability to the market, but not too much. The changes have brought much greater potential instability, not so much instability in price movements within a year as longer-term wide swings that can produce enormous problems not only for the farm sector but also much more widely across the economy. The boom of the 1970s, for example, was followed by the sharp downturn of the 1980s that still persists. Designing a system that removes all safeguards against such swings only postpones the inevitable and probably leads to pressures for relief of immediate problems, pressures that Congress finds hard to resist.

• The programs must deal only with real problems. Much greater attention must be given to correct identification of the problems being addressed, while facilitating the adjustment to market forces to avoid resource allocation and production patterns so far out of line with the markets that dilemmas such as we now face continue to confront us.

• The programs must be based on reality, on real estimates of supply response and productivity. Here is where the paper by Johnson and his colleagues and others like it help a lot. We have underestimated future yields for the past thirty years. We have refused to recognize increasing milk yields at all. These change incentive responses, and Congress must build all that into the design of programs. We face a more protectionist world, and efforts to counter protectionism may only make it worse in the short run. Can we expect the new Export Commission to say that blended credits, let alone export subsidies, are self-defeating?

The second of the major problems confronting us provides ample evidence of the wide economic swings that can now occur. Because of the boom of the 1970s, a debt-restructuring, asset-ownership problem now exists that requires an approach separate from the commodity programs. The full extent of that problem is still unfolding, but estimates by Melichar and others provide notions of the overall magnitude.[1] Melichar has estimated that the real capital gains on farm assets from 1972 to 1979 totaled $447 billion (in 1983 dollars) and the subsequent real capital losses have reached $149 billion. This leaves about $300 billion of the gain still in existence along with the billions of dollars of debt incurred in transferring the assets at the higher prices.

The cash flow to the sector is now insufficient to support these higher asset values. One of two things must happen: the cash flow must be greatly increased, or the asset values must be written down to levels that the expected cash flow will support. Greatly increased cash flow appears a remote prospect from present forecasts of economic conditions, and achieving it through the commodity programs would require something as drastic as the 80 percent of parity option.

Recently reported Agriculture Department data provide some notion of the number of farms affected (table 1). Those data show almost one-fifth of all farms to have a debt-to-asset ratio greater than 40 percent, not a level that means imminent bankruptcy but an indicator of potential serious financial stress nonetheless. About one-fourth of the commercial farms are in this category, but they constitute only 8.1 percent of all farms. These farms collectively hold about 56 percent of the total indebtedness of the sector.

TABLE 1

DISTRIBUTION OF FARMS BY DEBT-ASSET RATIO, 1983

(percent)

Size in Sales ($ thousands)	40 to 70 Percent			Over 70 Percent		
	Sales class	All farms	Total debt	Sales class	All farms	Total debt
Less than 10	8.0	3.1	—	4.4	1.7	—
10–25	8.0	1.4	3.9	4.4	0.7	2.6
25–50	9.7	1.2	1.9	8.1	1.0	2.2
50–100	14.6	2.0	6.2	8.8	1.2	3.9
100–250	18.3	2.4	10.5	9.2	1.2	5.9
250–500	19.5	0.8	5.1	12.2	0.5	4.2
500 and over	22.2	0.3	4.8	22.3	0.3	4.9
Total		11.2	32.5		6.6	23.7

NOTE: Dash (—) means negligible.

SOURCE: U.S. Department of Agriculture, Economic Research Service.

These estimates suggest that from one-fourth to almost one-half of the farm debt outstanding is potentially in jeopardy. Although not all this stands to be lost, of course, even a potential write-off of 10 percent amounts to several billion dollars. These magnitudes clearly illustrate that any government assistance far-reaching enough to treat the problem effectively will probably be very expensive. Finding ways to address this problem directly without allowing it to interfere with the problems of the commodity programs is likely to be a tall order.

Some Other Matters

While the Johnson et al. approach incorporates much of agriculture, there are notable exceptions that are important, both as policy issues themselves and as they affect what is eventually done for the major commodity programs. I refer specifically to dairy products, sugar, peanuts, and tobacco. The increasing emphasis on consistent treatment of commodities suggests that including these sectors in the model for comprehensive assessment would be most helpful.

Another area that could usefully be incorporated is consideration of various designs of a long-term land reserve. This not only addresses the serious issue of soil conservation but meshes nicely with the need to address adjustment to the problem of excess capacity.

The available data suggest that the amount of cropland acreage that is most highly erosive and is now being cropped is not far different from the amount related to the excess capacity in the sector. Much of this fragile land came into production in the boom years of the 1970s. A long-term land conservation reserve could offer a cost-effective means of returning some of this acreage to less intensive uses. Estimates place the annual cost of buying this land out of crop production at from $30 to $50 per acre. Even at the higher figure and for 30 million acres, spending some $1.5 billion for this purpose could well preclude having to spend several times that amount on deficiency payments and acquisition of stocks. It would be very interesting to see the model results with such a scheme incorporated.

Finally, let me say again that the Johnson et al. paper is very useful and could be elaborated a bit to be made even more so. Such assessments will prove invaluable as we move from the options presented to mixtures of options that will emerge as the process of developing a farm bill progresses.

Note

1. Emanuel Melichar, "A Financial Perspective on Agriculture," *Federal Reserve Bulletin* (January 1984).

A Synthesis

John A. Schnittker

I want to congratulate the authors of the major paper. It is a landmark paper that will be well read and will be useful not only for what is in it but as a basing point from which to develop more practical approaches from the stylized models they have presented. There are plenty of things wrong with it, too, and I will get to some of those as I go along.

First, I must synthesize a slightly more valid and consistent set of economic assumptions, to guide Congress in its deliberations. Most of the assumptions of the paper can be adopted, but the basic model presented today incorporates both a rising federal budget deficit and a falling dollar, whereas the conventional wisdom is that the budget deficit must be reduced if we are to deflate the dollar in the next few years.

It is not appropriate or realistic, in my judgment, to build a major decline in the value of the U.S. dollar into a base-line projection in which most other variables have been frozen. Congress should certainly not do this. If the dollar does fall sharply, farm exports will increase somewhat, and farm policy will cost less and look better than we expect, but if Congress bases its program decisions on excessive export expectations, as in 1981, we will again be embarrassed by an unworkable and costly farm program.

Second, I wish to deal with all the stylized options presented in the paper, at least briefly, for they are well and seriously done.

• Option M (for market) is a drastic version of the draft farm program for 1986–1989 of the Agriculture Department and the Office of Management and Budget, which was prepared principally as a budget exercise and is being embedded in the printed 1986 budget. This proposal will appear for its brief and unhappy life on and after February 4, 1985 (budget day). Here is an option without a strategy, both in the paper and in real life. Relatively sharp reductions in support levels have been forced into the proposal, to achieve arbitrary cuts in budget expenditures. This option is essentially where farm policy is headed during the next five years if the federal deficit must be reduced, if the Reagan administration plays hardball, and if Congress is responsive, but it is not likely to go into effect in 1986.

• Option E (for accelerated exports) should largely be ignored in this discussion and by Congress. Somehow the modelers forgot that they had provided for accelerated exports by deflating the dollar in the base-line option. I consider this a wholly unrealistic basis for policy debate in 1985.

• Option P (for parity) should also be forgotten, even though it is valuable as an exercise. It is a parody of past mandatory programs, ostensibly designed for the late 1980s but providing only an interesting and flawed look at an impossible dream for American farmers. Option P is interesting because of its arithmetic demonstration that selling less at home and abroad could bring farmers more money—much more. It is flawed because the parity option has no chance of being adopted by Congress in 1985 and would be vetoed by the president if it were sent to him. The analysis also incorporates one extremely unrealistic assumption—that this option would raise world prices as well as U.S. prices for most commodities. Any realistic approach to this option would incorporate export subsidies and more reasonable domestic price objectives than have been assumed.

That takes us back to the base-line option (B), which, as it stands, is really E—an accelerated export option. Let us reconstruct B realistically, reduce its export potential a little, and take it through the 1985–1986 agricultural policy and budget policy process simultaneously.

This is useful in my judgment, because present law, not the administration's bill, is likely to become the starting point for bill drafting by the House and Senate committees. Thus in synthesizing a realistic option from the stylized options, we choose a vehicle that has a little momentum. In fact, the only serious possibilities for adoption of major administration proposals are in the Senate committee, since it is led by Republicans, or on the floor of either house, if members can be found knowledgeable enough about farm issues or angry enough about spending on farm programs to lead the way on major floor amendments. We should not forget, however, that action on the budget deficit will force policy decisions along the lines of the administration's proposals but carried out much more gradually.

My practical approach to the base-line option, which I shall call option 1, since it is now the leading political option as action shifts to Congress, goes as follows for the major features of our commodity programs.

Price Support Loans

• For grains and cotton, Congress should amend the very useful formula in the law (called the Findley amendment), permitting the secretary to reduce price support loan levels on the basis of the previous years' farm prices. Minimum loan levels now in the law for wheat, cotton, and rice should be cut about $2.75 per bushel, $0.50 per pound, and $6.00 per hundred weight beginning in 1986. The minimum loan for corn in the 1981 act, at $2.00 per bushel, is low enough for the next few years. Congress could also substitute the present soybean price support formula, instead of amending the language described above, while stepping down the minimum support levels for the commodities listed.

• For dairy products Congress should (1) allow the support level to decline as scheduled, to $12.10 per 100 pounds of milk on April 1 and $11.60 on July 1, and should amend the law to reduce the support level to $11.10 on October 1, 1985. This should be accompanied by a formula similar to the one now in the law for grains or soybeans, setting future support levels slightly below recent average farm prices.

• For sugar, peanuts, and tobacco, price supports should at least not be increased but need not be materially reduced in the public interest in 1985, since only limited budget savings would be achieved by such reductions. Price support stability or reductions are required here for consistency but not for budgetary relief.

Target Price Payments

• If agriculture must contribute $2-3 billion to the initial deficit reduction, much (but not all) of it must come out of target price payments on wheat, corn, cotton, and rice. I suggest that the necessary reduction on loan levels described above be associated with parallel cuts in target price payments. This would be enforced not by farm committees but by the Budget committees, Congress, the lobbyists for all nonfarm interests, and eventually, if necessary, by one or more vetoes by the president. Some farm groups that favor target price payments might go along with this move if they could get a payment standstill for 1986-1987. Congress seems likely to try to provide a brief standstill, by using the same kind of creative cost estimating that produced $12-16 billion cost estimates for the 1981 farm bill, which will have cost more than $50 billion when it has run its course on or about September 30, 1986.

• Target price payments should be progressively limited, to perhaps $20,000 per farm by 1990. Then if Congress wishes to target such payments to small, needy, full-time, and midsize farms, it could do so.

• While these payments continue and as long as commodity surpluses persist, the payments should be treated functionally as acreage diversion payments, so that their effect is to reduce production slightly rather than to serve as incentives to increased production. When payments end or get very low, say by 1990, annual acreage reductions would end.

Production Control. Clearly, this element of past and present farm policy is obsolete. It has demonstrably not been cost effective, especially since about 1981, and it is full of holes, carefully designed by commodity interests for passage by Congress. The program has been administered reluctantly and badly, in recent years adding many billions of dollars to program costs and thus to the federal deficit quite unnecessarily, while apparently doing little for farmers.

Even so, it is sensible, cost effective, familiar, and therefore realistic to continue this program for up to four or five years rather than end it abruptly with the 1986 crops. This should be done as long as target price payments are being made to farmers, independently of any congressional decision on acreage controls.

If Congress were to close program loopholes—end skip-row planting for cotton, the summer fallow provision for grain, and similar measures for rice and corn—and were successfully to direct the administration to run the program vigorously, money could be saved by continuing this feature temporarily.

Legislative Changes. Criticism of the 1981 act by me and others in the past year might lead one to believe that it is beyond redemption. That is not so: only limited word and number changes are required, and they will constitute the real battleground this year. Key changes include the following:

• Drop minimum price support loan levels by at least 5 percent per year until they are below market prices, and require these reductions by formula for each commodity, instead of permitting them at the discretion of the secretary, who acts politically rather than in response to economic circumstances.

• Forget the cost of production as a guide to setting target prices, and depend on the discipline (if any) invoked by Congress on the budget. In short, set target prices for the next crop year during the budget process in Congress each year. If Congress and the president will not limit the increase in defense spending and will not face up to the overall deficit, farm interests may well gain a standstill on federal payments for several years.

• Require that acreage reduction be proportional to target price payment eligibility, to avoid the kind of program administration we have recently had—simply giving away money to increase surplus production without using its limited potential for production adjustment.

• Substitute progressively $40,000, $30,000, and $20,000 for the present $50,000 payment limitation now in the law.

Out of this process, focusing on limited progress at the margin on price supports, payments, and production adjustment, including the elaborate fabric of legislated loopholes, we can hammer out a new agricultural policy from present law. In four or five years of intensive debate and struggle, aided by some discipline on federal spending across the board, we will be able to say in 1990 that we have achieved a new farm policy, built not on the illusion that political change can be made abruptly but on the solid rock of experience and necessity.

Part Three
Issues in Policy Design

Macroeconomics and U.S. Agricultural Policy

Gordon C. Rausser

Thus far in the 1980s, the agricultural sector in the United States has been greatly influenced by events in the domestic and international economies. Many of these events can be traced to the change in U.S. Federal Reserve policy in October 1979 and to the Reagan administration's fiscal policy. In October 1979, the Federal Reserve announced that it would attempt to control money supply directly and withdrew its previous policy of targeting interest rates. The Reagan administration, meanwhile, adopted a policy of reducing federal taxes and expenditures, but achieved significantly more success in reducing revenues. As a result, the federal government now has huge deficits, which the Federal Reserve has, on the whole, consciously avoided monetizing.

U.S. fiscal policy and monetary policy have driven real interest rates to all-time highs. The management of money supply and the relatively high interest rates in this country have reversed the decline that the U.S. dollar experienced throughout the 1970s. Interest rates have been largely responsible for enhancing the value of the U.S. dollar against other major currencies to a point where it recently exceeded the level reached before the introduction of flexible exchange rates. Given the dominant role of the Federal Reserve and the rapid appreciation in the value of the dollar, other central banks also maintained a tight rein on their money supply and attempted to manage the value of their currency vis-à-vis the dollar by selling dollars and buying their currencies. In doing so, they indirectly contracted their own respective money supplies.

The above monetary phenomena, along with the following factors, are responsible for the significant decreases in real agricultural prices and the

The author gratefully acknowledges financial support from the Giannini Foundation, the International Economic Division of the Economic Research Service of the U.S. Department of Agriculture, and Resources for the Future. He gives special thanks to James A. Chalfant, Kostas F. Stamoulis, and H. Alan Love for their comments and suggestions on an earlier draft of this manuscript and their collaborative assistance in the preparation of the section on "Model Validation and Simulation Experiments."

deflation in agricultural commodity markets since 1980:

• a steady increase in the value of the dollar, which has increased import competition in a number of economic sectors, including segments of U.S. agriculture, and in addition has decreased the inflation rate

• the reduction of some barriers to trade, which stimulated supply response and increased the liquidity of international markets for a number of commodities

• a significant decline in the rate of export growth in the United States (with respect to developing, industrialized, and Communist countries) due, in part, to the rapid increase in competitive supplies available from other agricultural exporting countries such as Brazil and Argentina

• the record crops in 1981 and 1982, which brought significant pressure on spot markets and led to market prices that enhanced the attractiveness of the farmer-owned reserve established by the Food and Agriculture Act of 1977 and continued under the act of 1981[1]

With the deflation in agricultural commodity markets and the increasing attractiveness of financial assets, the value of some agricultural assets, particularly land, has dropped sharply. Given the role of land resources as collateral for agricultural loans and credit lines, the apparent debt-absorption capacity of U.S. agriculture has decreased considerably, as is evident from the growing frequency of bankruptcies in the agricultural production sector and from what has come to be called the agricultural financial crisis of 1984.

Recent History of U.S. Agricultural Markets

In the 1970s, general conditions in the U.S. economy and the international economy were almost the exact opposite of what they have been since 1980. The magnitude of increases in farm product and food prices between 1972 and 1973 surprised even the most informed people within the public and private sectors. The move to flexible exchange rates, the rapid expansion of international markets, the emergence of a well-integrated international capital market, and the diminishing barriers between the agricultural economy and other domestic economic sectors in concert brought about significant changes in the agricultural sector. During this period, the Federal Reserve expanded the U.S. money supply in order to hold the real price of energy at basically the same level; other countries attempted to inflate their way out of the energy price shocks by increasing their money supplies. They also attempted to manage their exchange rates with the U.S. dollar by selling their currencies and buying dollars and thus indirectly increased their money supplies even more. These various measures helped to spark a rapid increase in agricultural commodity prices. The following factors also played an important role:

- the declining value of the U.S. dollar on international currency markets
- the barriers to trade that insulated many countries from the price-formation process on international markets and thus eliminated potential supply responses to the favorable prices and made international markets thinner than they otherwise would have been
- the real growth in export demand in a number of developing countries along with the improving or upgrading of diets in industrialized and Communist countries
- the elimination of the huge governmental stocks that had accumulated during the 1960s[2]

With the rise in commodity prices and the rapid increase in the rate of inflation during 1972-1974 and again in 1978-1980, the principal resource in agricultural production—namely, land—jumped in value. Indeed, land values increased more than almost all other assets in the U.S. economy. Because of the distinction between tax rates on earned income and on capital gain income, U.S. agricultural land prices rose more rapidly than the rate of inflation during much of the 1970s. Land, as noted earlier, was used as collateral for agricultural loans and credit lines, and thus the total absorption capacity of U.S. agriculture for debt appeared to be augmented by leaps and bounds during this period.

Since the early 1970s, then, the U.S. agricultural sector has been subjected to a roller-coaster ride, the valleys and peaks of which have been defined in part by the external linkages to the U.S. macroeconomy and the international economy. To be sure, these external linkages have made it clear that timing, with respect to entry and exit from U.S. agricultural production, is critical. Entrants into agricultural production prior to 1972 are doing quite nicely even though asset values and income levels have been dropping since 1980. If asset values alone are considered, such owners of agricultural land could be totally incompetent at farming and still have benefited substantially from their investment. Anyone who entered agricultural production between 1978 and 1980, however, is either on the verge of bankruptcy or has an independent source of income. How effective one is as a farming entrepreneur or manager has no bearing on the situation.

In addition to the external linkages, government commodity policies continue to play an important role in determining the course of development of the U.S. agricultural sector. The numerous surveys and evaluations of U.S. agricultural policy that have been conducted offer many views on the formal justification for governmental intervention.[3] Some have argued at length that the only market failure justification for government intervention is *excessive* uncertainty or unanticipated instability.[4]

Before 1972, this instability was commonly attributed to the inelastic nature of aggregate food demand, the low income elasticity of demand, and, on the supply side, weather patterns, rapid technological change, atomistic behavior (and, in some treatments, naive price expectations), and asset fixity.[5] These characteristics were said to exist in a closed, insulated representation of the U.S. agricultural sector. Many believed that, without governmental intervention, the inherent and unanticipated instability resulting from these characteristics would be unacceptable to all actors in the food and agricultural system: input suppliers, producers, assemblers, processors, distributors, and consumers.

According to John Maynard Keynes, the instability inherent in storable commodity markets leads to insufficient private stockholding.[6] Keynes believed that three factors in particular contribute to this outcome: the risks associated with price volatility, uncertainty about the ultimate "normal price," and the length of time that stocks have to be held. He argued, as others did later,[7] that government intervention is needed because of the divergence between social and private risks. One evaluation of this and a number of other justifications for government interventions to stabilize the prices of volatile commodities concludes that the divergence between social and private benefits provides the best justification.[8] Private stockholders, in particular, will not store for extreme contingencies because they do not expect to receive the true scarcity value of their stocks during such periods.

Since 1972, the conventional wisdom has placed less emphasis on the instability in commodity markets and more emphasis on external linkages with other markets. With the deregulation of the credit and banking system during this period, agriculture has been exposed more and more to conditions in the domestic money markets. Also, because of the shift from fixed exchange rates to flexible rates, commodity markets have become more exposed to international money markets and real trade among countries. Moreover, the well-integrated international capital market that has emerged during this period has forced agriculture, through domestic money and exchange rate markets, to become increasingly dependent on capital flows among countries.[9]

Government behavior has also contributed to commodity market instability. Prices increased sharply after the Soviet grain deal, for example, because there were no government-held stocks. Changes introduced in the commodity programs by the Food and Agriculture Act of 1977 permitted a wider fluctuation in prices. The export embargo in 1980, variations in the rules of the farmer-owned reserve program since 1980, and the payment-in-kind (PIK) program of 1983, to name but a few major changes in government agricultural programs, make it clear that policy uncertainty can lead to instability in the private commodity market. Moreover, the mere existence of governments is one of the main reasons why private stockholders may not store for extreme contingencies and thus provide needed price stabilization. History reveals that it is difficult for governments to resist taking actions that interfere with the market system during periods of shortage.[10]

The greater dependence on trade since 1972 has exposed U.S. agriculture to more shocks from foreign markets. With the increased dependence on trade worldwide, U.S. agriculture has become heavily dependent on exports. In the late 1970s, U.S. agricultural exports accounted for almost 40 percent of total U.S. output and approximately 20 percent of the total U.S. exports. Net agricultural exports consistently make a positive contribution to the balance of payments, whereas the nonagricultural sector is a net importer. To be sure, this increased dependence has made U.S. agriculture less stable, in part, because the Soviet Union, which has an unstable agriculture, has become a major importer and because barriers to trade cause changes in foreign markets to be borne by the United States and other exporting countries that practice relatively free trade.

The linkages between commodity markets and U.S. money markets are indeed pervasive. Since farming is extremely capital intensive[11] and debt-to-asset ratios have climbed over the past ten years, movements in real interest rates can have significant effects on the cost structure of agricultural production. Stock carrying in storable commodity systems is sensitive to changes in interest rates; and for nonstorable commodities (for example, live cattle and live hogs), breeding stocks are interest-rate sensitive. These effects, combined with the influence of interest rates on the value of the dollar, put pressure on grain products from both the demand side (for example, export demand, domestic livestock grain demand, and stockholding demand) and the cost side. The fact that agriculture is especially sensitive to interest rates suggests that it is vulnerable to monetary and fiscal policy changes. It has been argued that, since 1972 but particularly since 1980, the instabilities in monetary and fiscal policies have greatly added to the instabilities of commodity markets.[12]

There is ample evidence that, because of deregulation and the introduction of completely flexible exchange and interest rates, the U.S. agricultural sector has become more closely tied to the domestic and international economies. The instability in monetary and fiscal policies is thought to have imposed sizable shocks on commodity markets. If agricultural commodity markets behave as "flex-price" markets while others behave as "fixed-price" markets, "macroexternalities" will be imposed upon the agricultural sector. That is to say, overshooting will occur in agricultural sector markets even if expectations are formed rationally because of the spillover effects of monetary and fiscal policy on commodity markets.[13]

Overshooting can introduce further instabilities into a sector that is already inherently unstable. These overshooting externalities can assume the form of implicit taxes or subsidies. In the United States, for example, high and volatile interest and exchange rates work together with corresponding contractions in world income and agricultural export demand in calling for resources to move out of agricultural production. Only in this fashion will the agricultural sector reach an equilibrium with the balance of the U.S. economy. Without governmental intervention, however, farmers are faced with a painful adjustment tax because of agriculture's capital intensity and its dependence on international trade. Over the period from 1980 to 1983, this tax took the form of higher interest payments and lower commodity prices in cases where the supply of goods was not shrinking fast enough. An additional tax was imposed in the form of a significant drop in farmers' stock of wealth. Precisely the opposite situation occurred from 1973 to 1975. The externalities during this period assumed the form of subsidies, which led to the accumulation of wealth through large increases in land values.

A number of basic questions emerge from the above story: To begin with, is this story consistent with the facts? What are the principal linkages among the macroeconomy, international economy, and agricultural economy? What is the order of magnitude of the direct, indirect, and feedback effects of policy changes originating in agriculture, the macroeconomy, and the international economy? Given the importance of agriculture in the U.S. economy (food products contribute approximately 20 percent to the weight of the consumer price index [CPI]), what influence (inflationary or deflationary) have commodity markets had on general economy wages and prices? What is the differential impact of macroeconomic policies (fiscal and monetary) and agricultural sector policies on the performance of the U.S. agricultural sector? Should agricultural sector policies be conditional on shocks to macroeconomy and international economy emanating from U.S. fiscal and monetary policies?

The present study provides partial answers to these questions. Any empirical attempt to address such questions is constrained, however, by the lack of data on flexible exchange rates and interest rates facing the U.S. agricultural sector. The information that is available on these rates covers about ten and four years, respectively.

The analysis begins with a brief literature review followed by specification of the macroeconomy, the international economy, and the agricultural sector economy. (A complete list of all variables, endogenous and exogenous, in the specification of each of the three components and selected empirical equations can be found in my earlier paper.)[14] The following sections report some simulation experiments, the overall results, and some important implications for agricultural policy choices in 1985 and beyond.

Existing Conceptual Frameworks and Empirical Evidence

An earlier review of the available theoretical and empirical evidence on the three components under examination here has suggested that greater attention needs to be given to the combined role of (1) the general price level (inflation or deflation); (2) exchange rates; (3) the effect of sector versus general economic policies; and (4) the main linkages between the domestic macroeconomy, the international economy, and the agricultural economy.[15] Existing conceptual frameworks focus instead on one or another of these factors.

General Price Level and the Nonneutrality of Money. One of the first studies of food prices and inflation concluded that food prices rose in the early 1970s largely because of increased demand and production shortfalls. Another study attributed the large price increases in international markets primarily to the inability of consumers and producers to react to price changes because of governmental policies designed to stabilize domestic prices.[16] In this view, all of the adjustment to the production shortfalls and demand increases was imposed upon a rather limited segment of the worldwide market for commodities, as illustrated by the classic example of sugar prices from early 1974 through early 1975. Others have emphasized the role of speculators in this price explosion and have treated commodities both as assets and as inputs into consumption.[17] They reject the view that a rise in primary commodity prices represents solely a change in relative prices.

Some have argued that the rapid accumulation of international monetary reserves is a source of the disturbances. The transition mechanism between reserves and commodity prices has not been modeled adequately, however. The consequences of international monetary reserves on commodity market behavior, it has been pointed out, can be appreciated fully only when these markets are embedded in a general equilibrium model of a dualistic economy that has both auction (flex) and customer (fixed) markets.[18] A formal model of a dualistic economy that has been developed includes three markets: a money market, a primary commodity market that clears in the short run by price adjustments, and a manufactured goods market that clears in the short run by quantity adjustments. Because expectations are presumed to be rational, nominal changes are neutral in the long run; but, in the short run, unanticipated monetary disturbances affect relative commodity prices. Commodity booms may stem from monetary factors in addition to changes in the conventional determinants of supply and demand. Monetary changes are allowed to operate through channels other than those of interest rates and the level of aggregate demand. In this type of representation of a dualistic economy, macroeconomic externalities associated with commodity price fluctuations provide a rationale for direct governmental intervention.

In a frictionless classical framework with complete price flexibility, one-shot anticipated monetary disturbances will be neutral. Such frameworks have been referred to as monetarist-new classical models.[19] Other frameworks, however, imply different adjustment speeds in nominal variables and departures from money neutrality. In fact, investigations of the money neutrality proposition have empirically addressed the "stickiness" of prices in various markets. If prices are sticky, quite obviously the strict monetarist proposition—that money supply growth in excess of the growth in money demand

213

instantly translates into rapid inflation—*does not* hold.

The underlying forces that make some prices sticky do not, of course, hold to the same extent in all markets. An important distinction here is that between manufactured goods and services (or customer markets) and basic commodity markets (or auction markets).[20] Customer markets are said to be characterized by imperfect competition, noninstantaneous arbitrage, and differentiated products that make the adjustments of prices to economic demand and supply forces sluggish. In contrast, the homegeneity and the ease of arbitrage in auction markets allow prices to adjust to demand and supply forces instantaneously. Perhaps more important, it has been demonstrated that, in an economy with both sticky and flexible prices, a monetary shock that leaves sticky prices unchanged in the short run causes the flexible price markets to overshoot their long-run equilibrium until all prices reach an equilibrium reflecting the initial monetary shock.[21] This overshooting phenomenon has been referred to as a macroeconomic example of the Le Chatelier principle: "Because one variable in the system (manufactured good prices) is not free to adjust, the other variables in the system (commodity prices) must jump correspondingly further in order to compensate."[22]

Conceptual and empirical validation of the distinction between fixed and flex prices and of the overshooting phenomenon has been attempted in a number of studies. Generally, the question that is investigated is not whether commodity prices respond instantaneously and manufactured prices do not, but whether commodity prices adjust at a faster rate than do manufactured or noncommodity prices. A 1975 study of the effect of aggregate excess demand on price movements found that, although nonfood prices are responsive to changes in the ratio of actual to potential income (defined as the inflationary gap), they adjust very slowly. In contrast, food prices were found to adjust almost instantaneously.[23]

A subsequent empirical investigation of the Sargent-Wallace-Lucas (SWL) policy effectiveness argument attempted to isolate the forces that dictate price stickiness. This examination focused on adjustment costs, long-term contracts, and the decentralization of decision making.[24] Here, price changes were related to changes in the inflationary gap, lagged prices, and various forces representing supply shocks. Empirical results obtained unambiguously, it was concluded, reject the SWL proposition in favor of the notion of fixed-price markets. In particular, prices were found to respond slowly to changes in the ratio of current to natural output and only partly to expected money growth.

Another study concerned with the differential rates of adjustments of sectoral prices to monetary changes explains the pattern of industry and sectoral price response to monetary changes by implicit contract lengths.[25] In this case, it was assumed that the degree of price flexibility across sectors can be represented by price variability in that sector, and thus that commodities respond more rapidly than manufactured goods to monetary changes. The empirical results validate the distinction between the behavior of auction markets that are characterized by price flexibility and customer markets characterized by the use of long-term contracts and price inflexibility.

Some have recognized that internal inconsistencies arise when rational expectations are imposed on models with sticky prices. A price adjustment rule has therefore been developed to achieve consistency and to circumvent these theoretical difficulties.[26] The rule is derived from a microeconomic model in which there is an implicit cost in continuously changing prices; thus, it is optimal to adjust individual prices only at discrete intervals and by finite amounts. In essence, the rule provides for price changes at frequencies that make it possible to equate the marginal gains of reducing the losses from disequilibrium to the marginal costs of continuous price changes.

In a similar but more formal theoretical model that has been developed, fixed-price markets emerge naturally.[27] This is a dynamic model in which perceived costs of adjustments by firms play a dominant role. The empirical representations correspond to the fixed-price hypothesis. Empirical estimation of the theoretically derived price paths satisfy all the relevant theoretical constraints and appear to be robust. In other words, the empirical results support the fixed-price hypothesis and they reject a nested hypothesis of a "Walrasian adjustment" (instantaneous price adjustment to contemporaneous changes of money balances). The principal reasons for these results appear to be the small response of aggregate demand to changes in money balances and the high cost of changing prices. Of particular note is the significance obtained when food prices and fuel prices are removed from the price indexes (gross domestic product price deflator). This result further supports the separation of fixed and flex prices and the differential responses to monetary growth.

Overshooting of flex-price markets is an obvious result in theoretical models that incorporate price stickiness, yet few direct tests of overshooting have been conducted. To be sure, overshooting can only be tested in conjunction with a particular model. Thus, the results obtained depend in part on the assumptions imposed therein. Several models of exchange rate determination lend indirect support for the price stickiness hypothesis as well as exchange rate overshooting. One direct test of whether overshooting can be validated for exchange rates has shown that domestic and foreign prices for the United States, Germany, Japan, and the United Kingdom are predetermined with respect to the exchange rate.[28] These results are also consistent with exchange rate overshooting.

In another model of the fixed-price/flex-price variety of the inflation process, output is supply determined in the long run, and the inflation rate depends solely on the rate of growth of the nominal money stock.[29] In the short run, however, shocks to food prices can induce substantial and persistent

215

bursts of inflation even if the rate of growth of the money supply is fixed. This framework is used to test the hypothesis that consumers' expectations are biased in the sense that they place too much weight on the recent behavior of food prices. Under this hypothesis, shocks to food prices may be assumed to have magnified effects on subsequent rates of inflation. Since the empirical results do not support this hypothesis, it is argued that sectoral anti-inflation policies, such as agricultural export controls and meat price ceilings, are less effective and, hence, less justifiable than is generally presumed.

Still other studies have emphasized the effect of inflation on the performance of the agricultural sector. Those that have investigated prices paid to, and received by, farmers relative to the general price level incur possible specification errors by omitting other real factors determining prices received and paid.[30] Studies that have examined the effects of inflation on agricultural finance[31] and on farm assets and values in general support the view that inflation has real effects on the structure and performance of the agricultural production component and on income distribution.[32]

Some ad hoc relationships for agriculture during recessions and inflations have been proposed for the period 1976–1978. Not surprisingly, with only five years of data under a less regulated agricultural sector, the main explanatory variables have been recessions and the exchange rate.[33] A recent investigation of the dynamic relationship between an index of food prices and proxies representing monetary and fiscal policies has found, however, that money stock has a statistically significant cumulative effect on food prices, and that this effect increases quantitatively as we move from the farm to the retail level.[34]

Exchange Rates. The theory of exchange rate determination has evolved from the traditional Keynesian[35] model to the modern asset-market portfolio balance approach—a framework better suited to the analysis of inflation, expectations, and portfolio substitution. The role of the current account in influencing exchange rates has been integrated in a number of portfolio balance models,[36] and it has also been empirically tested.[37]

The shift to flexible exchange rates adds a new dimension to the interdependence between the agricultural and nonagricultural sectors. In a regime of floating exchange rates, the equilibrium rate of exchange is not a price that equilibrates one particular market, such as the market for foreign exchange, or a price that assures flow equilibrium (balance of payments), or the price of relative monies determined in the asset markets (stock equilibrium). Rather,

> The exchange rate is not in any rigorous sense determined either in a stock market or in the flow market. The exchange rate has an effect on many of the decisions of the economic agents in the model, decisions regarding both the stock and flow variables, and these decisions in turn affect a number of different markets.[38]

216

The effect of the exchange rate on U.S. agriculture is of considerable interest. As noted elsewhere, the exchange rate was overvalued during the 1960s and thus intensified the adjustment problems facing U.S. agriculture.[39] The subsequent devaluations and movement to flexible exchange rates during the 1970s led to significant structural changes. With the movement away from the fixed exchange rate, U.S. agriculture became more vulnerable to international economic events and policies, but, at the same time, was freed from the implicit export tax burden of the overvalued dollar in the latter days of the Bretton Woods Agreement.

The effects of exchange rates on agriculture have been simulated in a dynamic, quarterly model constructed to analyze the time path of the effects on prices received, quantities produced, consumption, exports, and inventory stocks for wheat, corn, and soybeans.[40] A similar analysis has been carried out for the wheat commodity system.[41] The results in both cases suggest that the exchange rate elasticity of price is greater than unity, that there is a complex time pattern of adjustment, and that the pattern differs across commodities. Such investigations are somewhat limited in their perspective, however, in that they ignore the effects of exchange rate changes on domestic price inflation and incomes that, in turn, affect agricultural input costs and output demand. Some have argued that the partial equilibrium approach overestimates the domestic price effect of a devaluation on agricultural prices by a substantial margin.[42]

The effects of monetary policy through its influence on the exchange rate have also been simulated in a model with an endogenous determination of exchange rates.[43] This empirical framework allows the monetary effects to work their way exclusively through the exchange rate, but it ignores the effects of changes in the monetary stock on interest rates, inventories, production costs, and so on.

A particularly controversial question today is whether exchange rates have both real and nominal effects. The answer depends in large part on the rigidities in the economy, expectation formations on prices and further exchange rate changes, and whether the initial state is one of equilibrium or disequilibrium. Now that market forces (rather than governmental decree) play a dominant role, the debate centers around the principal factors and causal mechanisms determining exchange rates. A growing body of theory and empirical studies focusing on the capital component of the balance of payments supports the view that monetary and fiscal policies affect capital flows.[44] This component, in turn, is an important causal force explaining short-term movements of exchange rates. These and other studies on the traded goods and services component suggest that the exchange rate and agriculture should be embedded in a model that recognizes economywide behavior along with monetary, fiscal, and official foreign reserves policies.

The specification of exchange rate determination is closely tied to the export demand relationships facing U.S. agricultural commodities. Most empirical studies to date have treated the exchange rate as exogenous and have omitted potential causal factors that are likely to bias estimates of export price elasticities downward,[45] but a few have specified a framework that allows for partial responses of domestic to world prices resulting from policy intrusions, transport cost, and product heterogeneity.[46] This work has been motivated by the controversy surrounding the price transmission elasticity for different countries due to national agriculture and trade policies and the sensitivity of these policies to market conditions. For these reasons, empirical estimates of the export demand elasticities for particular commodities vary widely. For aggregate net export demand in the United States, these estimates range from less than unity to approximately ten. Operationally, it is indeed likely that the time path of adjustment will depend on short-run inventories, lagged supply responses, and eventual policy reactions to market prices. Some studies that have investigated these issues conclude that foreign policies have exaggerated the instability of world excess demand for U.S. agricultural commodities.[47]

General Economic versus Sector Policies. Unfortunately, there has been little quantitative analysis of the effectiveness of general economic policies versus sector policies with respect to the performance of the U.S. agricultural sector. One empirical investigation points in the direction of the price and quantity interlinks among commodity policies, general inflation indexes, the exchange rate, and aggregate economic activity (aggregate economic activity is based on the Wharton macro and agricultural sector econometric models).[48] In this study, the "parity price" values for nineteen commodities were introduced into the Wharton agricultural model using inputs from the Wharton macroeconometric model. The resulting simulations of the Wharton agricultural model were fed into the Wharton macroeconometric model to generate revised general inflation levels, national income levels, world trade, and related magnitudes. These revised values were in turn fed into the agricultural models, and the effects were evaluated. The simulation indicated large increases in farm income, the CPI, and U.S. Treasury costs and significant reductions in domestic and export demand.

A short-run theoretical model of the interaction between the financial and agricultural sectors has been used to examine the effects of monetary policy on the agricultural sector.[49] The short-run effects are not neutral since agricultural prices are more flexible than nonagricultural prices. The theoretical results are explained by the effect of a restrictive monetary policy on commodity stockholding behavior and by the decreased competitiveness of agriculture in world markets due to an increase in the exchange rate.

An effort has also been made to describe the relationship between commodity markets and international liquidity, exchange rates, and money market interventions.[50] This work was based on the results of a study on currency

218

substitution that concluded commodity price declines are the result of a combination of tight monetary policy (which leads to revaluation of the dollar and a reduction in export demand) and international portfolio substitutions away from commodities.[51] Apart from the questions concerning currency substitutions per se, several hypotheses advanced in the study have to be tested before such explanations are given to commodity price variations.

Others have looked at the relationship between inflation and agriculture using a model that combines both structuralist and monetarist characteristics.[52] Here structural characteristics are taken to be the differential path of adjustment among sectors—agriculture being the flex-price part and manufacturing and services being the fixed-price part. As monetarist characteristics, they are considered to be the "autonomous" increases in prices caused by monetary increases. Although this model includes a number of the intersectoral linkages, it omits the effects of interest rates on private and public grain storage, most forms of agricultural policy instruments, and the dynamics of adjustment in the livestock component. Moreover, it treats the exchange rate as fixed.

Major Linkages. The differential effects of macro versus agricultural policies cannot be determined without first capturing a number of important linkages, some representing causal influences of the macroeconomic sector on the agricultural sector and some running from the international component to the agricultural sector. Both types of causal influences are defined as forward linkages. The opposite effects—that is, those that run from the agricultural component to the macroeconomic or the international economic components—are defined as backward linkages. In addition to forward and backward linkages, there are potentially important linkages between U.S. monetary policy and foreign monetary policies.

Forward linkages. Macroeconomic variables should be integrated into the agricultural sector wherever they are theoretically relevant. The most important linkages are observed in acreage, yield, demand, and inventory behavior. The macroeconomic variables included in these linkages are interest rates, personal income, nonfood and general inflation rates, and energy costs.

An increase in interest rates will have several direct effects on the agricultural sector. The most immediate impact will be on inventory behavior. Within the grain sector, rising interest rates will lead to the movement of grain from private positions into government positions, including the farmer-owned reserve and the Commodity Credit Corporation (CCC) inventories or the selling of grain on spot markets. Moving grain into government positions allows farmers to gain the benefit of subsidized interest rates offered by the CCC, and selling grain reduces interest costs to zero. Since some farmers may not be eligible for the benefits of the farmer-owned reserve or CCC nonrecourse loans, their only alternative may be to sell grain on the spot market.

Within the livestock sector, rising interest rates make it more costly for livestock producers to hold breeding animals. Therefore, in the short term, higher interest rates will lead producers to slaughter breeding inventories. Other short-term effects include (1) reduced feed demand, since it becomes more costly to hold livestock to heavier weights; (2) reduced acreage, since, all else constant, an increase in interest rates increases production costs and the implicit interest subsidy offered by the CCC and therefore increases the incentive to participate in any acreage reduction programs that may be offered; and (3) increased yield per planted acre, since increased participation in acreage reduction programs allows farmers to take their least productive land out of production.

The short-term effects of these changes include (1) movement of grain into the farmer-owned reserve, which "insulates" that grain from the market so that it has a less depressing effect on price; (2) pressure for lower grain prices, because higher interest rates may lead farmers who are not eligible for the government storage programs to sell more grain; and (3) pressure for lower meat prices, because increased slaughter of breeding animals will lead to higher meat supply and a lower price. Which of these effects will dominate depends on the current levels of all the variables and on the magnitude of the change in the interest rate. The crop production effect will probably be small, however, and, in most cases, the pressures for lower prices will outweigh the pressures for higher prices. If all else is constant, a sudden rise in interest rates will be followed by a fall in meat prices.

In the longer term, these changes will lead to pressure for higher grain prices. This will occur in the intermediate run because there will be less grain stored in private inventory positions than when interest rates are lower, and less grain will be in total inventories because larger quantities will have been consumed after the rise in interest rates. Later, pressure will be felt for lower grain prices because grain must be removed from the farmer-owned reserve if the market price reaches the call level (at least historically), or the government must take possession of the farmer-owned reserve grain at the end of three years. In either case, prices will be depressed. Pressure for higher meat prices will be felt in the longer run because there will be fewer breeding animals and therefore fewer animals will be placed on feed and the meat supply will be smaller.

An increase in the CPI will primarily affect the consumer market for agricultural commodities. In the short term, an increase in the CPI can have two possible effects, depending on the behavior of wages. If wages increase at the same rate as the general price level and no monetary illusion exists, then an increase in the CPI will have no impact on the demand for agricultural commodities. If wages increase at a slower rate than the CPI, then the demand for agricultural commodities, particularly beef, will fall. In general, only changes in relative prices will affect the demand for agricultural commodities over both the short and long runs.

If the demand for beef does fall as a result of a decrease in real wages, beef prices will decline, and possibly pork and broiler prices because these are substitutable commodities. Previous studies suggest, however, that a decrease in real income may cause a greater expansion in demand for pork and broilers than the increase in demand caused by the substitution effect away from beef. The price of pork and broilers may therefore fall or rise from an increase in the general price level when wages do not keep up. These ambiguous results hold for both the short and the long terms.

When the nonfood CPI increases, the costs of producing crops go up and relative prices associated with meat demands and food demand for wheat change. Thus, crop production will go down and there may be some substitution among competing crop enterprises. In general, increases in the nonfood CPI will lead to only small changes in food consumption. In the short run, increases in the nonfood CPI will have little effect on prices. In the longer run, however, crop prices can be expected to rise.

Crop production requires both direct energy inputs (for example, fuel for tractors) and indirect energy inputs (for example, fertilizer). Thus, higher energy costs are associated with increased crop production costs. As with increases in the nonfood CPI, increases in energy costs will mean reduced crop production and higher long-term crop prices.

Backward linkages. Three main influences in the macroeconomy reflect backward linkages from the agricultural sector. These linkages are evident in the CPI, endogenous deficits, and the effects on the balance of trade.

Food prices, represented by grain and livestock prices, are determined endogenously within the agricultural sector. Grain prices are determined at the farm level, and these influence the production of livestock and, hence, retail livestock prices. The set of prices is then converted into an index of food prices—which is one component of the overall CPI. The food-CPI linkage is important everywhere that the CPI enters the macroeconomic model. These linkages occur in any equation for which variables, such as income, are deflated by the CPI as well as equations in which the CPI enters as a separate explanatory variable.

The agricultural sector is also linked to the macroeconomy through agricultural program expenditures. Unlike many of the nonfarm components of the budget, government storage programs and deficiency payments are fixed legislated expenditures, usually in dollar terms. The outcome for prices, production, private storage, and other variables endogenous to the agricultural sector thus determines the level of government spending on agriculture and its contribution to deficits. As government expenditures rise, the gross national product (GNP) increases; and this enters into consumption, investment, and so on. The multiplier effects then lead to further increases in the GNP and in taxes.

The level of agricultural exports is a third linkage. *Ceteris paribus*, an increase in agricultural exports can be expected to increase the value of the dollar. Since the increase in exports leads to an increase in GNP, this is captured by including the GNP of the United States in the exchange rate equation.

International monetary linkages. In addition to the above linkages between the agricultural and domestic macroeconomic sectors, there are possibly important linkages between U.S. monetary policy and the policies of foreign banks. To the extent that such an interdependence exists, it represents another linkage between the domestic macroeconomic sector and agriculture. If, as U.S. monetary policy changes, the responses in the rest of the world affect foreign GNP, exchange rates, or prices, this will translate into shifts in the export demand curve faced by U.S. agricultural producers. Monetary interdependence is widely thought to exist in fixed exchange rate regimes, but one of the arguments advanced by proponents of flexible exchange rates includes "monetary independence." The presence of currency substitution suggests, however, that this argument is invalid.

Under fixed-rate regimes, such as the monetary system set up by the Bretton Woods Agreement, central banks are compelled to intervene in currency markets to maintain a fixed exchange value of their domestic currency vis-à-vis foreign currencies. Under flexible rates, no such intervention is necessary; although monetary authorities may still engage in intervention to affect the foreign exchange value of domestic money, such actions become discretionary. The monetary interdependence result follows from the observation that, under fixed-rate regimes when one country follows a particular monetary policy (say, an expansionary one), if that policy creates pressure on the rate of exchange with another currency, a response is called for by central banks abroad. For the present example, foreign monetary authorities are compelled to engage in a similar expansionary monetary policy when they observe a tendency for their currency to appreciate. Thus, the country beginning the process is said to have "exported" its inflation. When exchange rates are flexible, no such obligation exists on the part of central banks; only if they act to maintain exchange rates within a certain band (for example, by following the U.S. lead and inflating their currency)—in a "managed float"—can inflation be exported by other countries.

Some have argued in recent years that the monetary independence argument for flexible exchange rates involves an untested assumption about the portfolios of moneyholders.[53] If monetary independence is to hold, it must be assumed that the country in question is an insular economy, at least as far as money demand is concerned. Moneyholders must not substitute foreign currency holdings when the domestic currency becomes less desirable and vice versa. If this does not hold, currency substitution implies that the effects of domestic monetary policy are exported even under perfectly flexible rates.

This exporting of monetary policy and resulting loss of independence can occur in two ways. Each scenario follows an essentially monetarist treatment of the effects of monetary policy, with short-run effects on real variables such as income. First, suppose that foreign monetary authorities target a growth rate for foreign currency consistent with objectives for unemployment, interest rates, or some other variable or mix of variables, on the basis of their expectations of the demand for that currency. In the case of substitution between currencies, such a targeted growth rate is also conditional on expected money growth abroad. If the United States engages in some unanticipated monetary policy, say, expansion, there will be an increase in the demand for the foreign currency if expansionary policies in the United States are expected to depreciate the value of the dollar. The upshot is that the foreign monetary authorities will have underanticipated money demand, and their monetary policy will then be more restrictive than was desired. Independence from U.S. policies of the operation of foreign monetary policy is thereby lost.

A second possibility is that the foreign authorities will be able to recognize the unanticipated shift in U.S. monetary policy quickly. In that case, they may attempt to maintain the value of their currency rather than allow it to appreciate. They will accommodate the U.S. money growth by responding with the same policy. Money will no longer be as tight in the foreign country, but the result will be an even greater increase in the world money supply. This is precisely the phenomenon that has been blamed for the rapid worldwide inflation of the 1970s.[4]

Currency substitution has interesting implications for the agricultural, domestic macroeconomic, and international sectors. In particular, a new linkage of agricultural and nonagricultural variables is introduced. The direct effect of monetary policy on agriculture through exchange rates and interest rates is straightforward. Under currency substitution, however, domestic monetary policy also affects money growth abroad and real variables such as income. These feedback effects from U.S. money supply to foreign currencies work alongside the direct effects through financial markets—the changes in the growth rates of foreign currency will affect foreign income. Foreign income, in turn, is an important variable in the demand for U.S. agricultural exports in that increased income abroad will lead to greater consumption through an income effect. Either of the currency substitution scenarios described above can cause this income effect.

Whether foreign monetary policy turns out to be more or less restrictive than originally intended, U.S. agricultural exports can either fall or rise relative to the monetary independence outcome. The magnitude of foreign income effects and the resulting change in export demand will depend on the extent to which economic agents abroad failed to anticipate the change in monetary

223

policy following the change in U.S. policy. As long as any part of the change in money growth is unanticipated, the effects on income and other variables will be real.

The offsetting changes in money growth rates required in the presence of currency substitution and monetary interdependence can be said to sterilize the effects of the unanticipated money shocks from abroad. It is important to distinguish our use of the term *sterilization* from the conventional interpretation with respect to reserve flows. It is usually taken to mean that the central bank intervenes in the currency market. This could involve buying its currency for either bonds or foreign exchange, and hence reducing its money stock. Sterilization in this sense would involve an offsetting expansion of domestic money so as to maintain previous growth targets. There is no clear reason for such an operation, however, since as long as capital is mobile, the sterilization operation will restore the currency to a situation of excess supply. The so-called sterilization of the effects of intervention in exchange markets does, indeed, leave the total money stock unchanged; but the excess currency supply is also unchanged.

Sterilization involves a different concept in the present study. We assume that the central bank targets the growth rate of some monetary aggregate, which is based on desired levels of unemployment, interest rates, and so on. This will involve some forecast money demand, both by domestic resident and foreign holders of the currency. Since the foreign demand, in the presence of currency substitution, will be a function of the policies of foreign banks, these will also have to be forecast. When there is some unanticipated shift in monetary policy abroad, then there will be a shift in money demand that leaves the original target either too restrictive or too easy in comparison with the levels of money growth consistent with original goals.

It will therefore be necessary to adjust monetary growth to accommodate or sterilize the unanticipated change in money demand. To the extent that monetary authorities are able to make this adjustment and to the extent that moneyholders do not perceive this as a shift in policy but merely a response to the policies of other central banks, there will be no real effects. More likely, there will be shocks in real variables, such as income and the real rate of interest, as the unanticipated money growth is discovered by moneyholders. To incorporate this effect in the most general way, we could add a set of reaction functions measuring monetary interdependence to the model. This would complete the linkage between U.S. monetary policy and domestic agriculture operating through effects on foreign income. As interdependence becomes important, foreign GNP and other variables become endogenous to the model.

Although theoretically satisfying, the empirical significance of currency substitution has yet to be either demonstrated or rejected conclusively. Some supporting evidence has been presented,[5] but a recent study finds that changes in the rate of return to holding foreign currencies seem to have little effect on the demand for domestic money.[56] Related empirical work illustrates the role of increases in worldwide liquidity in explaining the inflation of primary commodity prices.[57] Currency substitution exacerbates this growth in liquidity and therefore the growth in commodity prices. Although empirical determination of the real effects of currency substitution remains an open question, its presence introduces another linkage between monetary policies and agricultural markets.

The most recent effort at conceptualizing and empiricizing most of the linkages described above deals with a detailed agricultural sector (crops, livestock, dairy, and poultry) and a small demand-side macromodel.[58] This effort is an improvement over previous studies because it endogenizes the international sector (exchange rates) and direct links from the macroeconomy to agriculture (for example, interest rates on inventories and price/wage inflation on agricultural supply through variable costs) and the influence of certain key agricultural policies.

The present study takes this recent work a step further by condensing and improving upon its agricultural component and substantially altering the international and macroeconomic components. Furthermore, a behavioral determination of exchange rates has been introduced, and a more detailed monetary sector subcomponent has been constructed.

Model Structure

The questions posed at the opening of this discussion dictate a model structure that concentrates on the effects of macroeconomic and agricultural sector policies. For this reason, the model advanced here has been designed with policy analysis in mind. The version of the model specified is not intended to serve as a forecasting tool. At this juncture, the model is only a preliminary attempt to assess the effects of policy changes and of other exogenous shocks in one sector on each of the three components. In particular, it must be able to assess the effect of (1) sectoral policies on agriculture, (2) the resulting endogenous variables in the agricultural sector on the general economy, (3) fiscal and monetary policies on the general economy, and (4) the resulting general economy endogenous variables on the agricultural sector. This is accomplished by treating endogenously the links among U.S. agriculture, the U.S. general economy, and the international economy.

Previously developed conceptual frameworks and empirical analysis provide the building blocks of an integrative framework that attempts to capture the interrelationships among agriculture, the domestic economy, and the international economy. These interrelationships establish a dynamic pattern of feedback effects among prices, outputs, and incomes in the different sectors. Only a general equilibrium representation of these interrelationships allows

225

the full effects of the agricultural sector, general economy, and trade policies to be analyzed.

Structure of the Macroeconomy. At least three specifications could be advanced for the macroeconomy component: (1) new classical and monetarist, (2) Keynesian, and (3) neo-Keynesian. In (1), price determination occurs in the flex-price or auction markets with relative prices set by a neoclassical general equilibrium market; the general price level closely follows the rate of monetary expansion. Expectations are rational, the Phillips curve is vertical, and a monetary exchange rate approach is taken to explain the balance of payments. The Keynesian framework is well known and need not be repeated here. The third framework follows a fixed–flex price determination.[59] The macroeconomic representation of (3) contains a number of customer markets. In these markets, prices are sticky because of contracts that set prices (on the basis of economic forces in some previous period) and, thus, disequilibrium output adjustments are required.

Macroexternalities or overshooting can be imposed upon the agricultural sector under (2) and (3), but no externalities are admitted by (1). The model advanced in the present study for the macroeconomy component can be described as a demand-side neo-Keynesian sticky-price framework. Its fixed-price character comes from the specification that prices adjust slowly to changes in excess demand through an expectations-augmented Phillips curve. The principal subcomponents of the specified structure are aggregate consumption, aggregate domestic investment, domestic monetary sector, Phillips curve relationship, domestic income sector, and government finance sector.[60]

Aggregate domestic demand is composed of equations for private consumption expenditure, private fixed-capital investment, change in inventories, and government expenditure. Interest rates influence private expenditures. Aggregate supply is represented by price and wage equations. Nonagricultural prices are determined as a markup over wages (adjusted for productivity) and material costs. A price expectation formation process, based upon expected money growth, is used to construct an expectations-augmented Phillips curve to explain nonfarm price-wage relationships. These equations provide the key relationships determining prices, wages, and real income. The general price level, which also enters the wage equation, is a weighted average of nonfarm prices and food prices. A conventional money demand equation and changes in reserve movements are used to determine short-term and long-term interest rates.

The specification of the macroeconomy component pays particular attention to a framework that easily handles fiscal and monetary policies as well as agricultural policies. As a result, the framework incorporates a series of links with the agricultural sector and a series of important policy instruments—both monetary and fiscal. A high degree of interaction exists between the subcom-

FIGURE 1

Macroeconomic and International Components Flows

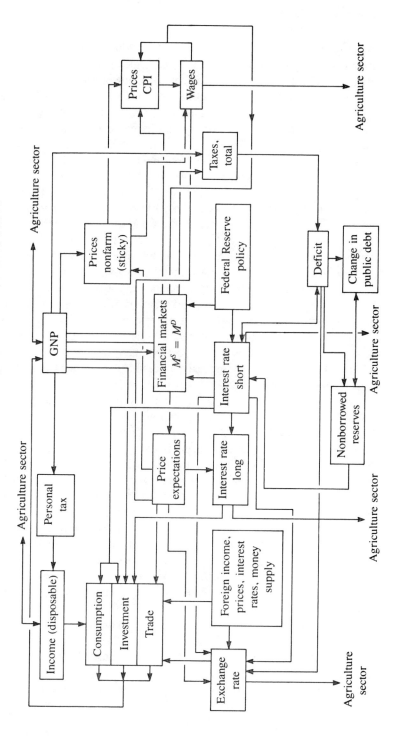

ponents of the macromodel (see figure 1).[61] Within the income-determining subcomponent, aggregate income and its elements (consumption and investment) are linked in such a way that changes in any of the elements bring about changes in income through the GNP identity and through multiplier effects appearing in the individual equations of consumption and investment. An increase in aggregate income flows into the monetary sector through an increase in aggregate demand. It leads to an increase in the total demand for money and an increase in the yield on bonds as demand for credit for new investment increases. As the gap between current and potential income closes, employment tends to rise, as do wages and prices. Linkages with the international economy component (see figure 1) lead to an increase in imports and appreciation in the exchange rate as the domestic demand for money rises, provided that the domestic money supply remains fixed. For the financial sector of the model, an increase in nonborrowed reserves tends to reduce short-term interest rates and, consequently, long-term interest rates.

The government finance sector includes an equation determining total tax collections by the federal government, which is affected by changes in nominal GNP. Increases in tax collections help finance the deficit and also reduce disposable income, which is endogenously determined by income and taxes. Two different formulations with respect to nonborrowed revenues and changes in government debt outstanding make it possible to construct two scenarios for financing government deficits.

Because of the importance of monetary policy, the change in policy regimes from controlling interest rates to controlling the money stock is reflected in the specification of the monetary-financial sector. A monetary policy shock has a number of effects. If the shock assumes the form of an increase in money growth rates, for example, short-run interest rates will decrease because of increases in nonborrowed reserves of commercial banks and relative credit availability. The decrease has spillover effects on the long-term instruments and tends to drive the long-term bond rate down. This tends to increase investment, GNP, and so on. As noted earlier, it also affects the exchange rate directly and indirectly (through changes in short-run interest rates). It creates inflationary expectations to the extent that part of the shock (increase in this case) is considered to be permanent. Those expectations feed directly into the price level through the expectations-augmented Phillips curve.

The monetary sector of the macroeconomy component and the associated actions of the Federal Reserve Bank's accommodation-nonaccommodation of the government deficit/surplus (or sterilization-nonsterilization of foreign reserves) may be represented in many different forms. In the specification advanced here, three identities form the basis for the role of the Federal Reserve and the interaction among money creation, deficit spending, and government debt holding. These identities are

$$G - T = \Delta B_d + \Delta B_{cb} + \Delta B_f \quad \text{(government deficits)}$$
$$CA + KA + ORT = 0 \quad \text{(current account)}$$
$$\Delta B_{cb} - ORT = \Delta MB \quad \text{(monetary base)}$$

where

G = government expenditures
T = taxes (net transfers to public sector)
ΔB_d = net change in domestic holdings of government bonds
ΔB_{cb} = net change in the Federal Reserve Bank's holdings of government bonds
ΔB_f = net change in foreign holdings of government bonds
CA = current account
KA = capital account
ORT = official foreign reserve transactions
ΔMB = change in the monetary base (high-powered money)

Note that G and T are part of the demand model of the macroeconomy model; and CA, KA, and ORT are as defined in the balance of payments equations appearing in the international economy component. The government deficit equation is defined as the government budget constraint, and the budget surplus/deficit is financed through bond purchases/sales by the U.S. Treasury.

Two extreme cases illustrate the workings of the government deficit identity. If, on the one hand, the entire deficit is publicly financed, then the change in Federal Reserve bond holdings is zero; investors finance the deficit by accepting additional government securities. On the other hand, if the Federal Reserve engages in open-market operations creating money by buying bonds, complete monetization of the deficit could occur. This increases the stock of high-powered money and Federal Reserve holdings of government securities. Thus, the money supply, rather than the supply of bonds held by the public, is increased, and the deficit is financed by the creation of money.

At the same time, there is a constraint on the operations of the central bank that holds under fixed or flexible exchange rates. This is a condition on the international transactions of the United States reflected by the current account identity. Under fixed exchange rates, official reserve transactions are dictated by the other two balances and are needed to offset excess demand or supply for dollars without exchange rate movements. Under floating rates, the exchange rate adjusts in a manner consistent with this identity, and there is no need for official reserve transactions.

The final identity relates to the creation of high-powered money or monetary base. The difference between the change in bond holdings by the Federal Reserve and the official reserve transactions is the change in high-powered money. In the more general case, the first term, representing the monetization of the debt, creates money, since the Federal Reserve's open-market operations involve the purchase of bonds that are paid for by increasing its liabilities to the banking sector. To the extent that bonds are acquired through official reserve transactions and then sold to the general public through the opposite open-market operation, however, the change in monetary base is offset.

Our money supply process reflects the Federal Reserve Bank's latest operating procedures with respect to controlling the monetary aggregates through control of the bank's nonborrowed reserves. Conceptually, a change in nonborrowed reserves because of open-market operations by the Federal Reserve will tend to change the federal funds rate since banks will have to secure the necessary reserves to cover reserve requirements. This change in the federal funds rate will subsequently spread through the system and change the rates across the whole maturity spectrum.

The model specification is based on the assumption that the Federal Reserve conducts monetary policy in a discretionary fashion. Note, however, that other possible frameworks can be advanced, as will be demonstrated later. Discretion of the Federal Reserve is exercised in terms of whether or not and to what extent it conducts open-market operations.

The model of the monetary process does not treat bank behavior explicitly. Instead, it moves directly from the federal government finance sector to the interest rates. Modeling the market for reserves is a tedious process and is not necessary for our purposes. In any event, the monetary equilibrium can be summarized by two equations:

$$G - T - ORT = \Delta B_d + \Delta B_f + \Delta MB$$

and the equilibrium condition in the money market. The interest rate is determined by the money market equilibrium condition. Changes in the interest rate directly affect private expenditure decisions in the rest of the domestic economy and a number of relationships in the international and agricultural economy components.

Note that the government deficit equation can be decomposed to permit the endogenous variables of the agricultural sector to be jointly determined with the government finance sector. When particular conditions in agricultural markets make it necessary to include some expenditures in agricultural policies, that portion of government spending is no longer exogenous. Thus, agricultural markets feed back directly into the domestic macroeconomy—this situation does not exist with either exogenous government spending or with the typical "satellite" model approach to the agricultural sector.

Structure of the International Economy. For reasons of simplicity and variable parsimony, the structure of the international economy was specified to involve six endogenous variables and a large number of exogenous variables.[62] The specification revolves around the balance of payments equation.

Exports and imports are disaggregated into agricultural and nonagricultural components. The exchange rate is determined by an asset market equilibrium framework. The detailed specification of the identity for U.S. transactions with the rest of the world (in terms of U.S. dollars) is given by

$$CX*PC + OX*\frac{PW}{E} - LM*PPL - OM*PW*E + KA + ORT = 0$$

where

CX = real quantity of crop exports
PC = index of crop prices in U.S. dollars
OX = real quantity of other exports
PW = index of world prices (using the same weights as for exchange rate)
E = index of exchange rate (defined as number of U.S. dollars required to purchase a unit of foreign currency) given by the Federal Reserve Board's bilateral ten-country weighted index
LM = real quantity of livestock imports
PPL = index of livestock import prices in U.S. dollars
OM = quantity of other imports

and KA and ORT are as defined in the section "Structure of the Macroeconomy." Note that, given the model specification, the current balance, CA, is determined by

$$CA = CX*PC + OX*\frac{PW}{E} - LM*PPL - OM*PW*E$$

Crop exports, CX, and crop price, PC, are aggregates of the export quantities and prices of wheat and feed grains. Similarly, livestock imports and prices, LM and PPL, refer to aggregates for beef. Livestock imports are treated exogenously, but wheat and feed grain exports are determined endogenously. The demand portion of this endogenous determination is specified as a net rest-of-world excess demand function. The key price variable is the U.S. farm price adjusted for any export subsidy. The exchange rate measured in U.S. dollars per unit of foreign currency enters the specifications as a separate explanatory variable. Because there are substitution possibilities in both the production and the consumption of those grains in other countries, the export demand will have cross-price as well as own-price arguments. The effects of shifts in foreign income, of production shifts in other countries, and of seasonal conditions are incorporated in the specification.

The import demand of nonagricultural products implicitly assumes that the supply of imports to the United States is nearly infinitely elastic. The export equation is regarded as a reduced-form equation of a supply of and demand for U.S. exports.[63] Although the response to income changes is considered to be fairly immediate, the specification allows for delayed adjustments in the case of price changes.

231

In the exchange rate–asset market determination, increased money stock exerts upward pressure on the exchange rate through the log differential between the U.S. money stock and the world money stock indexes. Interest rate effects operate through a constructed measure for domestic excess demand for credit.[64] The relevant causal flows in figure 1 show that the international sector's real part (imports and exports) feed directly into the income determination sector (with opposite signs). The exchange rate affects both imports and exports and, thus, these effects spread throughout the model via changes in aggregate demand. Note, also, that changes in the wage-price combinations affect the international sector via the changes in the U.S. wholesale price index that enter both export demand and import demand equations.

Structure of the Agricultural Economy. The agricultural sector is specified as a series of supply and demand equations with price playing the key equilibrating role; hence, governmental intervention aside, this sector is specified as a series of flex-price markets. Agricultural crop production is disaggregated into wheat and coarse grains (soybeans, cotton, tobacco, fruits, vegetables, and other crops are not included in this condensed version of the agricultural sector model).[65] Demand equations are specified for domestic food demand, private storage demand, government storage demand, and government export disposal. Planted acreage equations representing planned supply are expressed as functions of expected market prices, government policies regarding target and loan rates and diversion payments, and input costs. The input costs are related to general economy movements in wages, interest rates, and material costs. Yields are explained by seasonal conditions, technology, current output prices, and current input costs.

Livestock products are disaggregated into beef, pork, and poultry (eggs, fluid milk, and manufactured milk products are not included in this condensed version of the model). Domestic supply is influenced by expected and past output prices, by feed costs, and by costs of nonfarm purchased inputs. Allowance is made for cyclical response behavior, particularly in the cattle and hog subsectors. Domestic supply plus government-determined import volumes are equated with domestic demand to determine prices.

The structure of the agricultural sector represented here is decomposed into two main blocks of grain equations and three blocks of livestock equations. These blocks are related to the international and macroeconomy sectors through forward and backward linkages (figure 2). Each grain block (see the "Agricultural Sector" estimated component in my earlier paper)[66] includes behavioral equations for acreage planted, yield per planted acre, domestic utilization, and inventories. Production is computed as the product of acreage and yield. Domestic utilization is divided into two components: (1) livestock and residual demand and (2) industry or food demand.

Inventories are either publicly controlled (government-owned stocks, in-

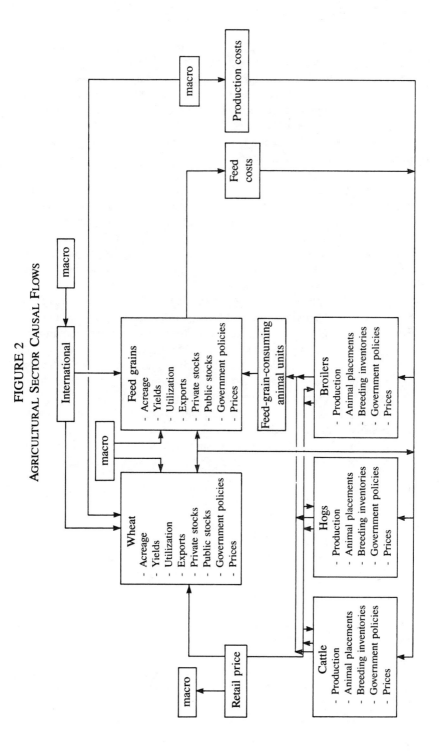

FIGURE 2
AGRICULTURAL SECTOR CAUSAL FLOWS

233

ventories tied to outstanding CCC loans, and stocks in the farmer-owned reserve) or privately owned. The government-owned and CCC inventories are aggregated into a single inventory position, whereas farmer-owned reserve and privately owned stocks are each modeled separately. This makes it possible to incorporate the different characteristics and rules governing control of the different types of stocks.

Since the planting decision is inextricably tied to the choice of participation in farm programs, an appropriate specification must incorporate the tradeoff between compliance or noncompliance with government programs that depend on acreage reductions as well as the tradeoff between expected returns on all potential crop choices. Traditional acreage equations included in the past models do not fully incorporate these tradeoffs. Acreage planted for each crop is presumed to depend on (1) the difference between expected returns from noncompliance and compliance with acreage programs for the crop under consideration, (2) acreage that can be planted under full program compliance, and (3) lagged acreage.

Since both yields and acreage crop allocation emanated from a common decision model, each yield equation is specified to be a function of the same expected profit variables as the acreage equations, the diversion requirement, a time trend (which measures technical progress), and a number of indicator variables representing incidents of bad weather. The comparative static characteristics of the acreage and yield equations indicate, inter alia, that an increase in their own target price will result in a reduction in acreage planted and that an increase in the diversion requirement can result in an increase or decrease in acreage planted.[67]

As noted above, the domestic consumption of feed grain is divided into feed and other uses. Both are determined endogenously. Domestic wheat consumption is divided into food consumption and other uses, but only food consumption is determined endogenously. Domestic demand for feed grains is specified to be a function of the inventories of cattle on feed, pigs on feed, and broilers on feed. "Cattle on feed" is specified as a function of lagged placements of cattle on feed, "pigs on feed" is equal to the pig crop for the preceding two quarters, and "broilers on feed" is determined by the hatch of broiler chicks in the preceding period. Feed grain consumption increases with the number of animals on feed. Per capita demand for feed grains in other uses is specified as a function of real per capita income, the real price of corn, and a time trend. Domestic per capita food demand for wheat is a function of the real price of wheat, an index of real food prices, and real per capita income.

Inventory equations are used to complete the grain blocks and determine the price of each crop. Inventories are separated into three components: stocks controlled by the government (CCC inventories plus government-owned stocks), the farmer-owned reserve, and other privately held stocks. In general, a measure of the expected profitability of holding stocks will be the main determinant of stockholding. The specifications for the inventory positions reflect the various constraints imposed on release and entry in the publicly controlled stocks.

Quantity of stocks demanded by the private sector (by both the producers and the users) depends on transactions and precautionary motives (a large part of this is due to the seasonability of production) and, to some extent, on speculation. All motives are conditioned by the cost of holding stocks. Expected commercial sales for domestic food and feed and for export are important determinants of transactions and precautionary needs. Speculative demand is influenced by the farm price relative to expected farm price. It is also presumed that the farm price relative to loan price and quantity of stocks demanded by the government sector has an influence.

Interest rates represent a major component of the cost of inventory holding. The interest rate plays an important role in the inventory equations but one that differs from equation to equation. Although interest is expected to enter in the private stock equations with a negative coefficient, for instance, it should have a positive coefficient in the equations for the farmer-owned reserve. The reason is that, although private stockholders must forego the interest on their asset, in some years participants in the farmer-owned reserve received an interest subsidy in the form of interest-free loans. Thus, higher interest rates correspond to increased subsidization from participation in the farmer-owned reserve and, therefore, to increased net entries into the farmer-owned reserve.

Quantities demanded by the government sector include government-owned stocks and those placed in either the CCC nonrecourse loan scheme or the farmer-owned reserve scheme. To a large extent, government stocks are a residual, with the government playing a passive role. Farmers place stocks with the government when the farm price is close to the loan price, and they redeem loans only as the farm price moves above the loan price. Again, the government is loath to release its own supplies until prices rise above the loan price; and, in the case of the farmer-owned reserve, such prices are prespecified and are well above the loan price.

The livestock sector includes blocks of equations for beef, pork, and broilers. The qualitative structure of each block in the meat sector is the same. The meats are disaggregated to reflect different consumption patterns over time, different income elasticities, and different production processes (for example, length of time on feed). Per capita meat demand is modeled in price-dependent form as a function of own-quantity, the price of substitute meats, and income. Prices and income are measured in constant dollars, and income is per capita. A nonagricultural price index representing the price of substitute nonfood items is also included in the meat demand equations.

Supply behavior in the cattle sector is disaggregated into equations explaining the closing inventory of beef cows, the gross number of placements of cattle on feed, and the production of beef. Disaggregation of the cattle sector facilitates the capture of some of the dynamics associated with biological production lags and interactions between cattle and feed prices. Our model is similar to one proposed elsewhere,[DX] except that, for simplicity, we have only one cattle price. The cattle-breeder and fed-cattle activities are treated as distinct operations with different decision makers.

Decisions to hold cows and heifers reflect a balancing of the expected returns of retaining them for breeding and selling feeder calves some seven to nine quarters ahead (nine-month gestation and twelve-to-eighteen-month yearlings) or selling the animals for current-period slaughter. The closing inventory of beef cows is expressed as a function of expected farm price of beef reflecting the breeding option, current farm price of beef reflecting the slaughter option, and the cost of nonfeed purchased inputs for beef cows when running a breeder-cow operation.

The gross number of placements of cattle on feed is expressed as a function of the number of feeder calves and the expected profitability of cattle feeding. Profitability is influenced by the expected farm price of beef and the costs of the feeder calves as measured by the current farm price of beef; the feed cost for beef cows, which in turn depends on the cost of feed grains as measured by the farm price of corn and the farm price of soybean meal; the cost of nonfeed purchased inputs for cattle on feed, which are functions of the wage rates, market interest rate, and general economy material and services prices. Production of beef comes from gross number of placements of cattle on feed in previous periods, cull beef and dairy cows, and other nonfed cattle slaughter. The previous period's closing inventory of beef cows and the previous period's closing inventory of dairy cows act as proxies for the potential supply of cull beef and dairy cows. The farm price of beef and the feed cost for beef may have two effects: on the one hand, they may encourage feeding of animals to heavier weights and, on the other, they may encourage withholding of breeding stock. The latter effect stems directly from the dynamics of beef cow inventory.

As with the cattle sector, the representation of the hog sector is highly aggregated. It is specified to allow for cyclical responses of pork production to changes in the final product price and costs. Equations are given for the closing inventory of breeding sows, market hogs, and production of pork.

The decision to retain breeding sows or send them for slaughter is based on a comparison of their current sale value and the expected returns from the sale of hogs in the future. Algebraically, the closing inventory of breeding sows is negatively related to the farm price of hogs; to the expected feed cost for hogs, which in turn depends on feed grain and soybean prices; to the cost of nonfeed purchased inputs for hogs; and, positively, to the expected farm price of hogs. The number of market hogs is a mirror image of the sow equation with the addition of the previous period's sow inventory. Production of pork depends on the beginning inventory of market hogs with adjustments for hog and feed costs as they affect the final market weight. Equations presuming the same kind of causal influences as for the beef and pork sub-components are specified for poultry production, broiler chicks hatched, and broiler hatchery supply flocks.

The supply equations for both grains and meats contain a cost of nonfeed purchased inputs to reflect costs of inputs, most of which are purchased from the nonfarm sector. Specifically, for each activity, the nonfeed purchased input price variable is a weighted average of wage rate paid for hired labor; market interest rate paid for financing working capital, machinery, and build-ings; index of raw material prices paid for energy and fertilizer; and index of nonfood prices paid for services and materials not included above and equip-ment. This cost measure provides a direct link with performance of the gen-eral economy.

Model Validation and Simulation Experiments

The estimated model used for policy analysis has been interpreted and evalu-ated in a more detailed study.[69] Since the models representing each of the three components (macroeconomy, international economy, and agriculture) have been constructed over the past few months, very few validation exercises and simulation experiments have been conducted. The validation exercises have focused on the ex post forecasting properties of the model. The flex–fixed price specification or, equivalently, the differential response of markets to changes in money supply has also been investigated. The results of this investigation enable us to determine the degree of money nonneutrality in the short run. To assess the verifiability of the model, we have also examined some of its stability properties with respect to the estimated parameters in the entire sample. Furthermore, we have investigated the stability of the parame-ters over some major distinguishable regimes that define the nature and struc-ture of linkages between the agricultural sector and the macroeconomy and international economy.

The simulation experiments, only some of which are reported here, are pairwise comparisons. In all of these comparisons, the macromodel is com-bined with the international model as one submodel, and the agricultural sector representation is treated as one submodel. First, the within-sample simulations are performed for each of the two submodels as separate struc-tures. These are then compared with the joint simulation of the two submodels running in tandem. Each of these simulations was performed to check that the model tracks the data well and that no apparent specification errors exist.

Some of the simulation experiments focus on evaluating the effects of two alternative scenarios, one corresponding to a "tax period" and another to a "subsidy period." First, a situation such as the 1981–1983 period is recreated

237

with a strong dollar, expansionary fiscal policy, falling energy prices, and tight money. This is compared with the 1973–1975 regimes of a weak dollar accompanied by easy money and rising energy prices. Each is analyzed to determine the extent to which the macroeconomic and international environments affect agricultural markets.

Two versions of the model are used for the above simulations. First, only the forward linkages are included. This set of simulations will be analogous to most econometric models with an agricultural sector; agriculture appears only as a satellite. Second, the backward linkages from the agricultural sector to the rest of the economy are incorporated. This set of simulations enables us to evaluate the extent to which ignoring backward linkages, *ceteris paribus*, has affected previous models and the results derived therefrom.

Finally, simulation experiments are undertaken with different agricultural policies. The above simulations are conducted with all of the agricultural policy instruments set at present levels. Possible alternatives that might come out of the 1985 farm bill, such as reduced price supports, are examined. The goal here is to compare the effects of alternative policies under different macroeconomic environments. (This work is still in progress.)

Validation Exercises. The macro/international submodel performs reasonably well, according to the within-sample simulations. For these experiments, the agricultural submodel and the estimated linkage equations are excluded. Overall, prediction errors are well within acceptable bounds. The in-sample tracking properties of the model were assessed using a Gauss-Newton simulation provided by the Time Series Processor (TSP Version 4.0). The algorithm is sufficiently flexible to handle nonlinear simulations and uses the sum of squared derivations for each equation as its criterion function. The sample period chosen covers the years 1979 to 1983. As reported elsewhere, the model appears to track observed data well, even for variables that are difficult to predict, such as the money supply or the exchange rate.[70]

The dynamic stability properties of the complete model have been investigated from a number of perspectives. First, we have investigated the local, component stability of each of the two submodels: macro/international and agricultural. For each submodel, the analytical stability properties of the linearized versions have been derived. In each instance, all of the relevant characteristic roots satisfied the conditions for stability. We have also investigated the dynamic properties of the linearized version of the complete model that incorporates the linkages between the macro/international and the agricultural sector submodels. Here again, the analytically derived characteristic roots satisfy the conditions for stability. As yet, however, we have not investigated the global stability properties of the model—that is to say, the model in its original nonlinear form. We have investigated the dynamic paths of the two nonlinear submodels separately as well as the complete nonlinear model over

238

three-year horizons. The model has been shocked with wide ranges of exogenous variables, as well as initial conditions, and it has generated dynamic paths composed of internally consistent values. On the basis of these results, we have concluded that the nonlinear version of the model is sufficiently stable, at least for the three-year horizons needed for the simulation experiments.

A major issue of validation concerns the fixed–flex price specification of the model advanced in this study. Without the fixed-price sector, anticipated money is nonneutral in the short as well as in the long run. Moreover, if we disregard unanticipated money, we have no overshooting and need not account for macroeconomic linkages in the design of any agricultural policies. This suggests that it is indeed imperative to determine whether or not the fixed–flex price specification is appropriate.

An eclectic approach may be used to distinguish between the fixed- and flex-price assumptions for a specified model.[71] This involves estimating both a fixed–flex model and flex–flex model and making several comparisons. Ad hoc comparisons are necessary because the nonnested hypothesis testing procedures are only asymptotically valid, and their behavior is quite uncertain for complex models of the type considered here. The plausibility of the two sets of parameter estimates, their relative success in simulation, and their ability to predict outside of the sample must be evaluated. These comparisons could be conducted to supplement any formal statistical testing. A particularly important comparison would involve the predictive performance of the two competing models, especially for the flex-price markets.

A simpler approach can be pursued to discriminate between the fixed–flex versus the flex–flex specification. This approach has already been used to test for the importance of overshooting.[72] As is well known, no overshooting occurs with the purely flexible price model; it takes some price inflexibility to generate overshooting. This earlier work focuses on the sensitivity of food and nonfood prices to anticipated money growth.[73] In this analysis, the rate of change of the nonfood consumer price index is taken as the growth rate of prices that are potentially generated in fixed-price markets, while the rate of change in the U.S. Department of Agriculture index of prices received by farmers is used to measure the potentially flex-price markets.

Variation in these two rates of change have been explained in terms of anticipated money growth, distributed lags of the gap between potential and actual income, oil price inflation, the differential of wage and productivity growth rates, and a lagged dependent variable.[74] When the coefficients across the two equations were compared, it was found that the lagged dependent variable had a large significant coefficient in the nonfood price inflation equation and an inconsequential coefficient in the food equation. Moreover, anticipated money growth caused a much greater response in food inflation than for nonagricultural goods. In fact, the estimated coefficient exceeded

239

one, corresponding to overshooting of food prices following money growth. By contrast, the coefficient in the other equation was significantly less than one, implying sluggish response to anticipated money growth. These results strongly support the specification that prices in the nonfood sectors adjust more sluggishly to changes in money growth than do food prices.

In conjunction with the money demand equation, the above results lead to the conclusion that overshooting of food prices results from the nonneutrality of money in the short run. Note also that, with the growth in money, individual willingness to hold real balances is augmented. Specifically, since the demand for money is negatively sloped, individuals are willing to hold more real balances if the interest rate falls because it is the opportunity costs of storing wealth in the form of real balances. With a fall in interest rates, it would be possible for less of the excess money to be spent on food, more money balances would be held, and the resulting price increase in the food market would be reduced.

This reasoning illustrates the importance of interest rates in the overshooting scenario. Although money demand is found to be interest elastic, it does not always follow that interest rates can adjust to make individuals willing to hold an increase in real balances. Interest rates may not be flexible, for example. Such was the case prior to October 1979, as the Federal Reserve operated monetary policy so as to peg or target nominal interest rates and maintain market interest rates within a specified range. As a result, money supply was allowed to vary widely. With the switch to targeting of reserves in managing money growth, nominal interest rates became a flexible price.

When interest rates are fixed and the real balances are initially at their long-run equilibrium level, money growth pushes food prices up sharply. Of course, if interest rates can vary, the overshooting is spread into two markets— interest rates will fall somewhat and food prices will rise less. Then, as nonfood prices gradually adjust to a new equilibrium level, there is again a reduction in food prices, accompanied now by a rising interest rate. Again, if it is assumed that the structure of the markets is unchanged by any developments during the adjustment phase to money growth, the long-run equilibrium occurs with the price level twice its original level and all quantities and interest rates back to their original levels.

The extent to which the overshooting causes real price changes in flexprice markets depends both on the interest elasticity of the money demand and on the degree of flexibility of interest rates. Overshooting is inversely related to both the demand elasticity and the ease of adjustment of interest rates. This means that prior to October 1979, when interest rates were pegged, overshooting was more severe in food markets. After that time, interest rates became flexible and, other things being equal, the effect of overshooting on food prices was lessened. It has been shown that the degree of overshooting in a particular flex-price market is decreasing in the number of additional flexprice markets in the system.[75]

This reasoning does not imply that the degree of instability in food prices will necessarily fall with the introduction of flexible interest rates. Instead, it simply means that the linkage between the interest rate or financial markets and food commodity markets will be smaller as a result of flexible interest rates. If interest rates are shocked significantly, however, the interaction of the linkage parameters with the large variability in interest rates could, in fact, imply more instability in food prices after the introduction of flexible interest rates.

Empirical implications of the above proposition have been examined in the context of the model by evaluating the parameter and linkage stabilities over the principal regimes of macroeconomic environments facing agriculture.[76] In a context of the number of flexible price markets in the macro/international economy, three principal regimes can be distinguished for the sample period employed to estimate the complete structure. The regime during 1965–1972 was one of fixed exchange rates and pegged interest rates; during 1973–1979 it was one of partly flexible exchange rates and target interest rates (the exchange rates are viewed as partly flexible because the U.S. government pursued a "dirty float" policy of exchange rate manipulation); and during 1980–1983 exchange rates as well as interest rates were flexible.

For each of these regimes, the equations in the model that involve interest rates or the exchange rate were reestimated. The results obtained in the form of significant shifts in the parameter estimates support the hypothesis of reduced overshooting in food markets. Because the results are too detailed to present here, only a few of the regime equations estimated will be highlighted.

One of the more interesting sets of parameter shifts occurred for the money demand equation. Prior to 1979 and for the sample as a whole, the lagged dependent variable in the money demand equation had a rather large coefficient reflecting slow adjustment in money balances over time. For the flexible interest rate period, that coefficient is much smaller and corresponds to more rapid adjustment of money balances. The response to increased opportunity costs of holding money was more rapid adjustment to interest rate changes. The increase in the interest rate elasticity of money demand for the post-1979 period is also consistent with this result.

Another set of interesting results for parameter and linkage stability occurred for the breeding stock equations of the livestock sector. For both cattle and hog inventories, the equations for the entire sample during the 1965–1983 show the inventory-reducing effects of increasing interest rates and feed costs. Distributed lags on both variables feature negative coefficients in both equations. When these linkage equations are estimated using only observations prior to 1979, however, the effects of interest rates (nominal) become insignificant and positive, reflecting the fact that at that time nominal interest rates were not a major determinant of inventory decisions. This is due in part to the lack of variation in nominal interest rates during the period 1965–1979. By contrast, there is significant evidence that food markets responded to the change in flexible interest rates during the last sample regime (1980–1983). For cattle inventories, in particular, the last few distributed lagged coefficients are larger in magnitude, negative, and statistically significant, although the first several are positive. Similar results were obtained for the hog inventory equations. The results for the latter equations, however, were complicated by the technological changes that occurred for hog production over the sample period under investigation.

"Tax" and "Subsidy" Simulation Experiments. To provide some flavor for the preliminary simulation results of the model, consider the scenario that corresponds to the economic environment in 1981–1983. For this scenario, the model describes the likely path of general prices, wages, income, agricultural prices, and inventories; it also describes income over a three-year period under bountiful harvests, tight monetary policy with no changes in fiscal policy, and a flexible exchange rate policy with no changes in agricultural sector programs.

The initial price-depressing effect of the bountiful harvest will be exaggerated by secondary effects. The tight monetary policy causes a rise in real interest rates. These, in turn, depress nonfarm inventory investment and fixed investment. After a period of steady adjustment, there are reductions in real income, employment, and consumption expenditure, including expenditure on food (more so for income-elastic beef). At the same time, the high interest rates encourage greater capital inflow, which, together with the fall in imports caused by the slowdown of real income growth, causes appreciation of the exchange rate. In addition, the higher interest rates induce the private sector to hold smaller grain inventories. After extended lags, the forces of lower rates of price increases reduce the rate of decline in real money balances and modify pressures on nominal interest rates.

Effects on the livestock sector are more complex. The fall in crop prices, by reducing animal feed costs, raises expectations about the future profitability of animal production. Although this means greater supplies of poultry, eggs, and dairy products in the next quarter, the initial effect for beef and pork is the reverse since animals are retained for breeding rather than sent for slaughter. Those animals intended for slaughter will be fed to attain heavier weights. In due course, however, the fall in income associated with the tight monetary policy causes a shift to the left of the food demand curves. After some quarters, the decline in the price of meat may exceed the effect of the decline in feed cost on expected livestock profitability. In the longer run, livestock prices will fall.

Developments stemming from the tight monetary policy and the fall of agricultural commodity prices are deflationary. Low commodity prices work through to lower food prices, the full effect taking up to two quarters. In turn, the expected prices used in the wage-bargaining process are reduced. Slower real income growth also exerts a downward force on the growth of nonfarm prices. The reduced rates of wages and nonfarm prices offer some relief to nonfarm costs, but of course high interest rate costs are still incurred.

After some quarters, a set of countervailing forces emerges to affect the agricultural sector. First, as wage and nonfarm prices fall in the general economy, the costs of agricultural production tend to fall. Second, particularly for the more income-elastic livestock products, the revival of real income stimulates demand. Third, where the initial response was to reduce production, the forces of supply and demand raise prices to more attractive levels. In the case of the cattle and hog industries, there is a process of dampened cyclical adjustment because of the short-term perverse response of supply to increased profitability as inventories of breeding animals are accumulated.

For the scenario corresponding to 1973–1975, dynamic paths at the other end of the spectrum were generated. Farm incomes were observed to be substantially above present levels, and inventories were significantly lower. Repeating the macroeconomic experience of those years leads to rapid growth in the U.S. and worldwide money supply, lower rates of interest, and exchange values of the dollar significantly below present levels. These phenomena lead to increasing export sales and reduced inventories. These developments are, of course, tempered by supply response, especially in the case of wheat, where excess supply capacity is an important constraining influence on price increases.

In one of these simulation experiments, we allowed exports to rise at the same growth rate that they did during the early 1970s. For this rate of growth in exports, along with the 1973–1975 fiscal and monetary policies, the cropland base would have to rise significantly. For corn and grain sorghum, for example, acreage in the neighborhood of 100 million acres would be necessary. Given rises in both prices and output, farm incomes would obviously improve considerably. Initially, there would be some liquidation in livestock breeding herds, especially cattle, that would help to moderate increases in the price of meat at the wholesale and retail levels. Later, within the three-year simulation horizon, breeding inventories begin to rebuild and meat prices jump substantially.

In the simulation experiments that have been conducted thus far, the large-scale model provides an internally consistent set of results.[77] In all instances, increases in the real rate of interest and the exchange value of the dollar have distinct negative effects on commodity prices, and the expected money growth rate has a positive effect on these prices. The latter variable causes the long-run equilibrium commodity price path to move in a corresponding direction. Hence, if a very restrictive monetary policy is put in place, the long-run equilibrium commodity price falls, but there is a corresponding rise in the real rate of interest and the exchange value of the dollar. Because of slower adjustments in other markets of the macroeconomy, short-run com-

243

modity prices overshoot the new long-run equilibrium commodity price. With an expansionary monetary policy, all three of these effects run in the opposite direction.

The comparative dynamic simulation experiments conducted with the model show that, under the current 1981 Food and Agriculture Act, macroeconomic policies can easily dominate the *short-run* effects of agricultural policies on the price and income paths for U.S. agriculture. Money is neutral in the long run, and thus agricultural sector policies can be expected to have a more significant influence on resource allocation to the U.S. agricultural sector. Agricultural sector policies that provide incentives for overallocation of resources to agricultural production simply make the sector especially vulnerable to macropolicies that impose implicit taxes by lowering the long-run equilibrium of commodity prices; in the short run, they also overshoot these equilibrium prices in a downward direction. This is, in fact, the reason for the current financial crisis in U.S. agriculture. Agricultural policies can be set at extreme levels for the model described here in order to counteract extreme taxations as well as excessive implicit subsidizations.

Concluding Remarks

To the extent that money is nonneutral in the short run, analysis of agricultural market dynamics must take into account not only real demand and supply forces and the effects of sectoral governmental intervention, but also the macroeconomic policies of the federal government. The fixed–flex price dichotomy of the U.S. economy implies that money is in fact nonneutral. Because some goods and services do not respond to changes in demand in the short run,[78] analysis of commodity markets requires an explicit treatment of monetary factors and the linkages with the macroeconomy. The prices of most other goods are sticky, whereas the prices of agricultural commodities, in the absence of governmental intervention, are free to respond to fluctuations in demand and supply.

Since the general price level is not free to respond fully in the short run, changes in nominal money supply are also changes in the real money supply and therefore induce changes in the real interest rate; these changes in turn induce changes in relative prices. As a result, changes in the money supply will lead to overshooting in flex-price markets. Since 1973 exchange rates have by and large been flexible; hence, changes in the money supply should lead to changes in the value of the dollar that are more than proportionate to the change in money supply. Only when the dollar is "overvalued" ("undervalued") will investors rationally expect a future rate of depreciation (appreciation) that is sufficient to offset the interest rate differential so that the interest rate parity condition holds and investors are willing to hold foreign currency. In the short run, the exchange rate overshoots its long-run equilibrium. This quite obviously happened from 1980 to 1982 when the Federal Reserve adopted a stringent monetary policy. The resulting higher nominal interest rates did not reflect higher expected inflation, as they did in the 1970s, but, rather, represented higher real interest rates. As a consequence, the dollar appreciated sharply.

In the "tax" and "subsidy" simulation experiments conducted in this analysis, overshooting was found to occur in U.S. feed grain and food grain markets. This overshooting is a direct implication of the fixed–flex price framework. This framework was formally tested, and the empirical results corroborate the differential response of nonfood market prices and food market prices to changes in anticipated money growth. Factors affecting commodity price overshooting were shown to be the number of fixed-price markets, the speed of adjustment of those prices, and the interest rate elasticity of money demand.

Nonmonetization of large federal government deficits can be interpreted as a restrictive monetary policy. Such a policy leads to increases in the real rate of interest and the exchange value of the dollar and to decreases in the long-run equilibrium price path of feed grain and wheat. Because of slower adjustment in other segments of the macroeconomy, commodity prices in the short run add insult to injury by overshooting the new long-run equilibrium commodity price. With a highly expansionary monetary policy, all of these factors run in the opposite direction.

The simulation results reported in this paper demonstrate that macroeconomic policies can easily dominate the short-run effects of agricultural policies on the price and income paths of U.S. agriculture. The implicit taxes resulting from overshooting that are imposed on U.S. agriculture are modified by the current form and shape of U.S. agricultural policy. In particular, price supports imply downward inflexibility of some commodity prices, which in turn cause the macroeconomic policy tax on agriculture to show up as an unexpected increase in the cost of maintaining price supports and the various forms of government stockholding. Overshooting agricultural commodity markets in the downward direction places some of the implicit tax on the private sector and some on the public sector. Because of the form of current U.S. agricultural policies, the overshooting effects of expansionary monetary policies are asymmetric. Much, if not all, of the subsidy accrues to the private sector.

Because money is long-run neutral, agricultural sector policies in the long run have a more significant influence on resource allocation to the U.S. agricultural sector than do macroeconomic policies. The sector policies that provide incentives for overallocation of resources to agricultural production quite obviously make the sector especially vulnerable to macroeconomic policies that impose implicit taxes via overshooting. Such sector policies, when combined with macroeconomic policies that "subsidize" U.S. agriculture, must by definition lead to a financial crisis for both private and public sectors if and when macroeconomic policies begin to impose "taxes" via overshooting on agriculture. The dynamic path composed of a subsidy period followed by a tax period during which sector policies provide incentives for overallocation of resources to agricultural production can be expected to create crises.

The implications of this study for the 1985 Food and Agriculture Act must, of course, focus on the overshooting phenomenon. If macroeconomic policies were appropriately designed, there would be no need for the sector-specific policies to address the implications of overshooting for the U.S. food and agriculture system. If we assume that no significant changes will take place in the design and implementation of fiscal and monetary policies, the normative justification for governmental intervention in food and agriculture continues to be excessive instability and the nonexistence of a complete set of markets for risk transfer. As noted in the introductory comments, this market failure provides an efficiency justification for governmental intervention to reduce the degree of inherent instability in agricultural markets.[79]

For the objective of risk reduction or, equivalently, the management of instability in food and agriculture markets, flexible storage and conditional target price policies are appropriate.[80] Such policies are designed to reduce risk, meet minimal food security goals, achieve an adaptable farm sector, minimize Treasury cost, and minimize the probability of political failure. The augmentation to the degree of instability by the phenomenon of overshooting can and should be recognized and taken into account in setting the flexible storage and target price policies. If we fail to condition agricultural programs on monetary and fiscal policies, we can expect crises of the type that generated the payment-in-kind program and the unexpected imposition of huge Treasury costs. In essence, the flexible storage and target price policies are concerned with the distribution of tax and subsidies across the private and public sectors. Aside from the need to manage inherent instability, during periods of "subsidy overshooting," the flexible storage and target price policies would impose a self-regulating tax on agriculture. For periods of "tax overshooting," the conditional policies would involve a self-regulating subsidy to agriculture.

In the actual implementation of agricultural policies, there are other goals to consider as well, such as income distribution, reasonable food prices, preservation of the family farm, and conservation of resources.[81] The flexible storage-price and target-price policies outlined above do not address these specific objectives. As argued by numerous analysts, the conservation-of-resources objective can be handled through land-retirement programs, while the preservation of family farms and the redistribution of income are most effectively dealt with through direct subsidies to the "family farm" component of the trifurcated farming sector. The most efficient means of implementing the direct-payment scheme is through negative income taxes. Additional improvements in the adaptable farm-sector objective can be obtained by eliminating the current tax shelter provisions of investments in agricultural production. This would reduce the bias in resource allocation to agricultural production. It should also be noted that the conservation-of-resources objective would be enhanced by conditional storage and target prices that specifically address the overshooting phenomenon emanating from macroeconomic policies. Overshooting that arises from restrictive monetary policies gives farmers little incentive to maintain the quality of their land resource. Insulation from the spillover effects of monetary policy would most certainly help to improve the conservation of agricultural resources.

These recommendations are prescriptive; their applicability depends on the specified goals of public policy for food and agriculture. Political feasibility or the positive aspects of governmental intervention in food and agriculture are not explicitly addressed by the analysis in this paper. It should be pointed out, however, that the implementation features of any designed food and agriculture policy must also be evaluated in terms of their effect on the probability of political or governmental failure.

Notes

1. Coming into the 1981 crop year, substantial quantities of stocks already existed in the farmer-held reserve. The addition in stocks from the 1981 and 1982 record crops were considered excessive relative to the stabilizing and food-security objectives for the farmer-held reserves. With the accumulation of public stocks of more than 1 billion bushels of wheat and more than 2.5 billion bushels of feed grains and the associated escalation of U.S. Treasury outlays, strong criticism surfaced; and some stopgap, crisis-driven policy provisions were enacted.

2. The U.S. Treasury exposure of carrying public stocks became unbearable in the early 1970s. This was the direct result of the U.S. government holding price supports above market equilibrium prices. Under these circumstances, the "Soviet grain deal" appeared as a savior for the policy disequilibrium that existed. See Gordon C. Rausser, "Macroeconomic Environment for U.S. Agricultural Policy," American Enterprise Institute Occasional Paper (Washington, D.C., November 1984). The U.S. government liquidated public stocks and thus exposed the economy to the risk of large increases in the price of agricultural commodities. From the standpoint of officials who are struggling to contain inflation, governmental stocks were liquidated prematurely and thus failed to provide the stabilizing influence that taxpayers had supposedly been paying for so long.

3. See G. Brandow, "Policy for Commercial Agriculture, 1945–1971," in L. Martin, ed., *A Survey of Agricultural Economics Literature* (Minneapolis: University of Minnesota Press, 1977); and Bruce L. Gardner, "Policy Options for Grains" and other papers in Gordon C. Rausser and Kenneth R. Farrell, eds., *Alternative Agricultural and Food Policies and the 1985 Farm Bill* (Berkeley: University of California, 1984), pp. 81–99.

4. Richard E. Just and Gordon C. Rausser, "Uncertain Economic Environments

and Conditional Policies," in Rausser and Farrell, eds., *Alternative Agricultural and Food Policies*, pp. 101-32.

5. Gordon C. Rausser and Eithan Hochman, *Dynamic Agricultural Systems: Economic Prediction and Control* (Amsterdam: North Holland, 1979).

6. John Maynard Keynes, "The Policy of Government Storage of Food Stuffs and Raw Materials," *Economic Journal*, vol. 48 (September 1938), pp. 449-60.

7. See, for example, H. S. Houthakker, *Economic Policy for the Farm Sector* (Washington, D.C.: American Enterprise Institute for Public Policy Research, 1967).

8. Barry P. Bosworth and Robert Z. Lawrence, *Commodity Prices and the New Inflation* (Washington, D.C.: Brookings Institution, 1982), chap. 4.

9. This is a primary reason why the international debt crisis of the 1980s has potentially important implications for U.S. agricultural exports. In particular, it causes some countries (such as Argentina, Brazil, Thailand, and Turkey) to price their agricultural exports competitively on current spot markets, and causes other countries (for example, Mexico) to reduce their imports.

10. Popular pressure frequently compels countries to take such measures as windfall profit taxes, price controls, rationing, export embargoes, and even confiscation.

11. If we take into account only physical capital, not land, the U.S. agricultural sector is more than twice as capitalized as manufacturing on a per worker basis.

12. G. Edward Schuh, "U. S. Agriculture in an Open World Economy," testimony presented before the Joint Economic Committee of the U.S. Congress, May 26, 1983, Washington, D.C.

13. For a formal demonstration of this result, see Kostas G. Stamoulis, "United States Agriculture in a World Context: Policy Considerations" (Draft Ph.D. diss., University of California, Berkeley, 1985).

14. Rausser, "Macroeconomic Environment."

15. Ibid.

16. Dale E. Hathaway, "Food Prices and Inflation," *Brookings Papers on Economic Activity* (1979), pp. 63-116. D. Gale Johnson, "Postwar Policies Relating to Trade in Agricultural Products," *A Survey of Agricultural Economics Literature*, ed. Lee R. Martin, vol. 1 (Minneapolis: University of Minnesota Press, 1977), pp. 295-325.

17. Bosworth and Lawrence, *Commodity Prices and the New Inflation*, chap. 4.

18. Colin Lawrence and Robert Z. Lawrence, "Global Commodity Prices and Financial Markets: Theory and Evidence" (New York: Columbia University, 1985, processed).

19. Robert J. Gordon, "The Impact of Aggregate Demand on Prices," *Brookings Papers on Economic Activity* (1975), pp. 613-62.

20. See Arthur M. Okun, "Inflation: Its Mechanics and Welfare Costs," *Brookings Papers on Economic Activity* (1975), pp. 351-401.

21. Rudiger Dornbusch, "Expectations and Exchange Rate Dynamics," *Journal of Political Economy*, vol. 84 (December 1976), pp. 1161-76.

22. J. A. Frankel and G. A. Hardonvelis, "Commodity Prices, Overshooting, Money Surprises and FED Credibility," National Bureau of Economic Research Working Paper no. 1121 (Cambridge, Mass., May 1983), p. 4.

23. Robert J. Gordon, "Alternative Responses of Policy to External Supply Shocks," *Brookings Papers on Economic Activity* (1975), pp. 183-204.

24. Gordon, "The Impact of Aggregate Demand."

25. Michael Bordo, "The Effects of Monetary Change on Relative Commodity Prices and the Role of Long-Term Contracts," *Journal of Political Economy*, vol. 88 (December 1980), pp. 1088–109.

26. M. Mussa, "Sticky Prices and Disequilibrium Adjustment in a Rational Model of the Inflationary Process," *American Economic Review*, vol. 71 (December 1981), pp. 1020–27.

27. J. J. Rotemberg, "Sticky Prices in the United States," *Journal of Political Economy*, vol. 90 (1982), pp. 1187–211.

28. R. A. Meese, "Is the Sticky Price Assumption Reasonable for Exchange Rate Models?" *Journal of International Money and Finance*, vol. 3 (1984), pp. 131–39.

29. Carl Van Duyne, "Food Prices, Expectations, and Inflation," *American Journal of Agricultural Economics*, vol. 64 (August 1982), pp. 419–30.

30. See, for example, Luther Tweeten and Steve Griffen, *General Inflation and the Farming Economy*, Oklahoma State University Agricultural Experiment Station Research Report P-732 (1976).

31. For example, David A. Lins and Marvin Duncan, "Inflation Effects on Financial Performance and Structure of the Farm Sector," *American Journal of Agricultural Economics*, vol. 62 (1980), pp. 1049–53.

32. For example, E. Melichar, "Capital Gains versus Current Income in the Farming Sector," *American Journal of Agricultural Economics*, vol. 61 (1979), pp. 1058–92.

33. Bruce L. Gardner, "On the Power of Macroeconomic Linkages to Explain Events in U.S. Agricultural Economics," *American Journal of Agricultural Economics*, vol. 63 (December 1981), pp. 871–78.

34. R. E. Lombra and Y. P. Mehra, "Aggregate Demand, Food Prices, and the Underlying Rate of Inflation," *Journal of Macroeconomics*, vol. 5 (Fall 1983), pp. 383–98.

35. Robert Mundell, "Capital Mobility and Stabilization Policy under Fixed and Flexible Exchange Rates," *Canadian Journal of Economics*, vol. 29 (November 1963), pp. 301–11; Robert Mundell, "The International Disequilibrium System," *Kyklos*, vol. 14 (1961), pp. 154–72 (adapted in R. Mundell, *International Economics* [New York: Macmillan, 1968]); and J. Marcus Fleming, "Domestic Financial Policies under Fixed and under Floating Exchange Rates," *International Monetary Fund Staff Papers*, vol. 9 (1962), pp. 369–79.

36. See William Branson, "Asset Markets and Relative Prices in Exchange Rate Determination," *Sozialwissenschaftliche Annalen*, vol. 1 (1977), pp. 69–89; Pentti J. K. Kouri and Michael G. Porter, "International Capital Flows and Portfolio Equilibrium," *Journal of Political Economy*, vol. 82 (1974), pp. 443–68; and Carlos Alfred Rodriquez, "The Role of Trade Flows in Exchange Rate Determination: A Rational Expectations Approach," *Journal of Political Economy*, vol. 88 (December 1980), pp. 1148–58.

37. See Peter Hooper and John Morton, "Fluctuations of the Dollar: A Model of Nominal and Real Exchange Rate Determination," *Journal of International Money and Finance* (April 1982), pp. 85–93.

38. R. C. Fair, "A Model of the Balance of Payments," *Journal of International Economics*, vol. 9 (1979), pp. 25–46.

39. G. Edward Schuh, "The Exchange Rate and U.S. Agriculture," *American Jour-

nal of Agricultural Economics, vol. 56 (1974), pp. 1-13.

40. See the studies by Robert G. Chambers and Richard E. Just, "A Critique of Exchange Rate Treatment in Agricultural Trade Models," American Journal of Agricultural Economics, vol. 61 (1979), pp. 249-57; and "Effects of Exchange Rate Changes on U.S. Agriculture: A Dynamic Analysis," American Journal of Agricultural Economics, vol. 63 (1981), pp. 32-46.

41. Paul R. Johnson, Thomas Grennes, and Marie Thursby, "Devaluation, Foreign Trade Controls and Domestic Wheat Prices," American Journal of Agricultural Economics, vol. 59 (1977), pp. 619-27.

42. Sun-Yi Shei, "The Exchange Rate and United States Agricultural Product Markets: A General Equilibrium Approach" (Ph.D. diss., Purdue University, 1978).

43. Robert G. Chambers and Richard E. Just, "An Investigation of the Effect of Monetary Factors on U.S. Agriculture," Journal of Monetary Economics, vol. 9 (1982), pp. 235-48.

44. See Jeffrey A. Frankel, "On the Mark: A Theory of Floating Exchange Rates Based on Real Interest Differentials," American Economic Review, vol. 69 (1979), pp. 610-22; and Robert A. Driskill, "Exchange Rate Dynamics: An Empirical Investigation," Journal of Political Economy, vol. 89 (1981), pp. 357-71.

45. See H. S. Houthakker and Stephen P. Magee, "Income and Price Elasticities in World Trade," Review of Economics and Statistics, vol. 51 (1969), pp. 111-25.

46. See Maury E. Bredhal, William H. Meyers, and Keith J. Collins, "The Elasticity of Foreign Demand for U.S. Agricultural Products: The Importance of the Price Transmission Elasticity," American Journal of Agricultural Economics, vol. 61 (1979), pp. 58-63; Philip C. Abbott, "Modelling International Grain Trade with Government Controlled Markets," American Journal of Agricultural Economics, vol. 61 (1979), pp. 22-31; and Paul R. Johnson, "The Elasticity of Foreign Demand for U.S. Agricultural Products," American Journal of Agricultural Economics, vol. 59 (1977), pp. 735-36.

47. See A. C. Zwart and K. D. Meilke, "The Influence of Domestic Pricing Policies and Buffer Stocks on Price Stability in the World Wheat Industry," American Journal of Agricultural Economics, vol. 61 (1979), pp. 434-47; and Johnson, World Agriculture.

48. Dean T. Chen, "The Wharton Agricultural Model: Structure, Specification, and Some Simulation Results," American Journal of Agricultural Economics, vol. 59 (February 1977), pp. 107-16.

49. Robert G. Chambers, "Agricultural and Financial Market Interdependence in the Short Run," American Journal of Agricultural Economics, vol. 66 (February 1984), pp. 12-24.

50. A. F. McCalla, "Impact of Macroeconomic Policies upon Agricultural Trade and International Agricultural Development," American Journal of Agricultural Economics, vol. 64 (December 1982), pp. 843-49.

51. Ronald McKinnon, "Currency Substitution and Instability in the World Dollar Standard" (Stanford, Calif.: Stanford University, July 1981, processed).

52. See Shun-Yi Shei and R. L. Thomson, "Inflation and Agriculture: A Monetarist Structuralist Synthesis" (Extended version of a paper presented at the Annual Meeting of the American Agricultural Economics Association, Washington State University, July 19 to August 1, 1979); and Shei, "The Exchange Rate."

53. McKinnon, "Currency Substitution and Instability."

54. Ibid.

55. Ibid.

56. Dallas S. Batten and R. W. Hafer, "Currency Substitution: A Test of Its Importance," *The Federal Reserve Bank of St. Louis Review,* vol. 66 (August/September 1984), pp. 5–11.

57. Enzo R. Grilli and Maw-Cheng Yang, "Real and Monetary Determinants of Non-Oil Primary Commodity Price Movements," in G. Storey, A. Schmitz, and A. Sarris, eds., *International Agricultural Trade: Advanced Readings in Price Formation, Market Structure, and Price Stability* (Boulder, Colo.: Westview Press, 1984).

58. This work of John W. Freebairn, Gordon C. Rausser, and Harry de Gorter is described in "Government Intervention and Food Price Inflation" (Paper presented at the American Economics Association meeting in Washington, D.C., December 1981); "Food and Agriculture Sector Linkages to the International and Domestic Macroeconomies," in Gordon C. Rausser, ed., *New Directions in Econometric Modeling and Forecasting in U. S. Agriculture* (New York: Elsevier North-Holland, 1982), chap. 17; and "Monetary Policy and U.S. Agriculture," in G. Storey, A. Schmitz, and A. Sarris, eds., *International Agricultural Trade: Advanced Readings in Price Formation, Market Structure, and Price Stability* (Boulder, Colo.: Westview Press, 1984).

59. See John R. Hicks, *The Crisis in Keynesian Economics* (Oxford: Basil Blackwell, 1974); Arthur M. Okun, "Inflation: Its Mechanics and Welfare Costs," *Brookings Papers on Economic Activity* (1975), pp. 351–401; and idem, *Prices and Quantities: A Macroeconomic Analysis* (Washington, D.C.: The Brookings Institution, 1981).

60. For the endogenous variables for each of these subcomponents, see Rausser, "Macroeconomic Environment."

61. Ibid.

62. Ibid.

63. As described by Morris Goldstein and Moshin S. Khan, "The Supply and Demand for Exports: A Simultaneous Equations Approach," *Review of Economics and Statistics,* vol. 60 (1978), pp. 275–86.

64. For further details, see Rausser, "Macroeconomic Environment."

65. A more detailed version of this model—which includes soybeans, soybean meal, soybean oil, eggs, fluid milk, and manufactured milk products—is available. See Freebairn, Rausser, and Gorter, "Government Intervention," "Food and Agriculture Sector Linkages," and "Monetary Policy."

66. Rausser, "Macroeconomic Environment."

67. These results and others are derived in H. Alan Love, Gordon C. Rausser, and John W. Freebairn, "The Effectiveness of Government Policy in Controlling Agricultural Output" (Paper presented at the summer American Agricultural Economic Association meetings, Cornell University, August 1984).

68. See Lovell S. Jarvis, "Cattle as Capital Goods and Ranchers as Portfolio Managers: An Application to the Argentine Cattle Sector," *Journal of Political Economy,* vol. 82 (1974), pp. 489–520; John W. Freebairn and Gordon C. Rausser, "Effects of Changes in the Level of U.S. Beef Imports," *American Journal of Agricultural Economics,* vol. 57 (1975), pp. 676–88; and Enrique Arzak and Maurice Wilkinson, "A Quarterly Econometric Model of the United States Livestock and Feed Grain Markets

251

and Some of Its Policy Implications," *American Journal of Agricultural Economics,* vol. 61 (1979), pp. 297-308.

69. Rausser, "Macroeconomic Environment."

70. Ibid.

71. Ibid.

72. Kostas G. Stamoulis, James A. Chalfant, and Gordon C. Rausser, "Monetary Policies and the Overshooting of Flexible Prices: Implications for Agricultural Policy" (Department of Agricultural and Resource Economics, University of California, Berkeley, 1985, processed).

73. As defined by Robert J. Barro in "Unanticipated Money Growth and Unemployment in the United States," *American Economic Review,* vol. 67 (1977), pp. 101-15; and "Unanticipated Money Output and the Price Level in the United States," *Journal of Political Economy,* vol. 86 (1978), pp. 549-80.

74. Stamoulis, Chalfant, and Rausser, "Monetary Policies and the Overshooting."

75. Ibid.

76. Rausser, "Macroeconomic Environment."

77. Ibid.

78. Namely, the customer goods defined by Okun, "Inflation: Its Mechanics and Welfare Costs"; or the fixed-price goods defined by Hicks, *The Crisis in Keynesian Economics.*

79. There are other potential solutions to the excessive instability for which, unfortunately, there is very little empirical information. In fact, it can be argued that, if the government withdrew from all forms of intervention, other institutional or market solutions would emerge to address the excessive instability. Whether these institutions would offer a profile of benefits and costs that would be superior to governmental intervention is unclear.

80. Just and Rausser, "Uncertain Economic Environments and Conditional Policies."

81. Gordon C. Rausser and William E. Foster, "Agricultural Policy: A Synthesis of Major Studies and Options for 1985" (Paper presented at the National Conference on Food, Agriculture, and Resources: Policy Choices, 1985, Washington, D.C., December 4-6, 1984).

Commentary

Robert G. Chambers

Professor Rausser's paper and the econometric model that he details represent what I think is the most ambitious attempt to investigate the linkages between the agricultural sector and the rest of the economy that I have yet encountered. All agricultural economists interested in macroeconomic phenomena owe Professor Rausser and his associates a debt of gratitude for their painstaking efforts. That does not mean that we should accept their results uncritically, however. The issues at hand are too important to place too much faith in any large-scale modeling effort without an equally painstaking analysis of the structure and logic of such a model. For as Professor Rausser has noted elsewhere, large-scale models have some well-known pitfalls. So if my remarks seem somewhat critical, they should not be interpreted as a criticism of Rausser. Rather, they indicate the importance I attach to the issues he addresses. Indeed, there are few people who are better equipped to carry out this type of analysis than Gordon Rausser.

With respect to the paper itself, it seems to me that it contains three basic parts: an introduction, an explanation of the conceptual framework, and a section on model specification. In the introduction Professor Rausser seems to be advancing the working hypothesis that much of the recent history in U.S. agricultural markets can be explained by developments that are at least partly external to the sector. In particular, he augments the traditional stylized facts of U.S. agriculture (inelastic demand and supply, asset fixity, rapid technical change, and competitive market structure with the Hicksian fix-flex price hypothesis) in an attempt to gain some insight into recent market developments. This section shows how Professor Rausser has predetermined the rest of his analysis.

In reading Professor Rausser's paper, I find that it is sometimes easy to lose track of the forest for the trees. The trees are the various equations and the associated discussion, and the forest is the fix-flex price hypothesis. The paper and its analysis lives or dies by the validity of this assumption. If it is false, the paper really has little new to say.

Understandably, much of the discussion concerning the conceptual framework revolves around a taxonomy of models and results dealing with various aspects of exchange rate adjustment, monetary policy effects, relative price flexibility, and other pertinent issues. An important portion of this discussion concentrates on several studies that have focused on the fix-flex price hypothesis. What is lacking is a reasonably clear discussion of what causes agricultural prices to adjust.

As we know from the classic paper by Arrow, there is no neoclassical theory of price determination. The usual equilibrium mechanism is not a theory but an assumption, as are all of the excess-demand (excess-supply) price adjustment rules. And almost all of the theoretical explanations lying behind the models cited rely on some monopolistic or monopolistically competitive theory of price determination. How these fit with the stylized facts of agriculture (competitive market structure) is an open question. My point is that there is a gap here that must be filled—we have no true theory of agricultural price determination, and the theories of price determination that are being advanced are almost totally geared to the stylized facts of the manufacturing and service sectors and not to agriculture. Thus, for this paper, at least, the fix-flex price remains an assertion. Like all assertions, it could be wrong. But the price of it being wrong in this model is particularly high.

The importance of fix-flex prices is perhaps best illustrated by an example. One of the results that Professor Rausser has emphasized in his current discussion is the tendency of flexible prices to overshoot their steady-state values in their short-run adjustment if there are some fix prices in the system. Although the possible phenomenon of overshooting would go a long way toward explaining Cochrane's stylized description of agricultural price behavior in *Farm Prices: Myth and Reality*, it is an inherent characteristic of many models of comparative dynamic adjustment. Therefore it is not a surprising result, given the fix-flex price assumption, but it can have important implications from a policy perspective. But if this model is to be truly valuable, we need more information and better explanations of why agricultural prices are not sticky and manufacturing prices are.

Like all good econometric models at this level of aggregation, Professor Rausser's model rests on a skillful mixture of bald assertion, strong implicit theorizing, and good common sense. Fortunately, Professor Rausser seems to have relied most heavily on the latter two.

That doesn't mean, however, that I agree with him on all aspects of the model. Let me preface my next remarks by stating that I am somewhat skeptical about the value of large-scale models. Several times in his paper Professor Rausser seems to criticize what he terms the "satellite approach" of previous modeling efforts. Instead he proposes closer attention to what he calls "backward linkages" that feed developments in the agricultural sector back into the macroeconomy. Such efforts are worthy, but I want to caution against what I see as a potentially Ptolemaic approach on Professor Rausser's part. By my count, he has roughly 110 equations—about 30 are for the macro portion of the model, the rest for the agricultural sector. Although one might argue that the laws of comparative advantage dictate that agricultural economists should not build macromodels (with this I wouldn't argue), we want to be sure that we do not get the earth of the macroeconomy orbiting the moon of agricultural economy in our nonsatellite modeling efforts.

In building any model, one must ask many questions. Paramount among these are: What do I want to use it for? and What will best help me achieve that goal?

Professor Rausser clearly points out that the model is not designed as a forecasting tool but instead is designed principally for policy analysis. Now anytime people say their econometric model isn't designed to forecast, I become nervous and wonder whether the model really fits the data at all, or whether we're just getting their version (perversion) of reality. Fortunately, however, this model appears to fit reasonably well and I don't think we have to be concerned on that count.

But there is a broader issue involved here: What do we gain by the construction of such large-scale models? As it stands, they are basically linear, theoretical models with (we hope) plausible numbers attached to them, which are used for comparative static and comparative dynamic analysis. But when you get right down to it, we cannot tell whether an unexpected result is really important or whether it is the result of a flaw in model specification. When we use relatively simple models that we understand thoroughly, we obviously sacrifice a good deal of reality because of our inability to think clearly in much higher dimensions, but we can be fairly sure about the consequences of what we are doing. Because of the inherent misspecification problems connected with all large-scale models, there seems to me to be real pressure to obtain plausible—that is, expected—results. How many times have you heard an econometrician say that he dropped a variable because its sign contradicted theoretical expectations when it is obvious that he did not have a clear theoretical model in mind? More than just the signs have to be consistent with theory—a lot else is involved. And, as we know, most aggregation theorems are virtual impossibility theorems.

In considering how to make these models more capable of addressing their goals, we have to recognize that they are prisoners of their past. Thus, they can only use observations from a relatively long time series to tell us anything. If models of this sort are to be really useful, they need a stable policy environment. Unfortunately, these models are often incapable of depicting structural change. As an example, the Rausser model is probably quite good at depicting the implication of lowering target prices or loan rates. How good do you think it would be at depicting the elimination of all programs? My guess is probably not very good, for this is really asking the model to forecast outside of the data sets. It is just in times like these, when there is a great deal of uncertainty about the future policy environment, that the so-called Lucas critique of econometric models is most forceful. Models presume stable functional relationships between variables, but stable is not exactly the term that I would use to describe some of the more radical proposals that one hears

255

bruited about. Thus, as a policy tool for rapidly changing times, all such models must be used with extreme care.

With these comments in mind, consider now some details of the model. First, the overall model seems, at best, tenuously stable. By my count, there are at least five or six dynamic equations with lagged dependent variables whose coefficients are not significantly different from one. The most blatant example appears to be the cow-and-heiffer inventory equation. I have seen two estimated equations for this relationship. The first, which was reported in earlier versions of the paper but which is not included in this one, had a lagged dependent variable with an estimated coefficient greater than one. In the surrounding discussion, Professor Rausser says that lagged dependent variables are included to model slow adjustment. But his original estimated equation for this relationship tells us that the adjustment desired today essentially took place yesterday. If we recognize the implausibility of this result, the current version reports an equation with the coefficient on the lagged dependent variable *forced* to be one and with a longer distributed lag on the other explanatory variables. (Here it may be appropriate to recall my earlier comment about the tremendous pressure on econometricians to obtain plausible results in such models.)

On balance, the only departure from the traditional Keynesian model in the specification of the macromodel is the inclusion of the fix-flex price mechanism. Professor Rausser refers to this as a neo-Keynesian model, and although it is probably not appropriate to argue about definitions, the current model takes relatively little account of recent developments in the microeconomic foundations of macromodels in the Keynesian mode. Nowhere is this more clear than in the specification of the aggregate investment equations that are modeled as relatively standard functions of income and interest rates in a quasi-flexible accelerator form. Accordingly, they basically ignore the developments on investment theory and modeling since the 1960s (q theory, expectations, and the like).

In closing, I want to reiterate that, on balance, I find this an excellent piece of work. Furthermore, Professor Rausser and his associates have attempted to go where no (or at least very few) agricultural economists have gone before. Many (including myself) have argued for years that someone should try to do just what they have attempted, and it is easy (but not exactly sporting) for one who has not attempted it to point out apparent missteps.

Commodity Market Stabilization in Farm Programs

Brian D. Wright

Many of the important interventions in agricultural markets in the United States are undertaken in the name of stabilization, broadly defined. In this paper I consider the past performance and future potential of market-stabilizing measures as components of an agricultural policy structure, concentrating on wheat and corn. In doing so, I draw on evidence from these grain markets, augmented by insights from some modeling exercises.

To put the discussion in perspective, the following brief, broad-brush sketch of relevant characteristics of these grain markets may be helpful.[1] In both wheat and corn, U.S. yields and production are on a long-term upward trend associated with a secular decline in real price, obscured, in the 1970s, by violent fluctuations. Domestic consumption of wheat is quite stable and slowly increasing; domestic corn consumption is more responsive to price fluctuations. A substantial share of both crops is exported. This has always been true for wheat but is a phenomenon of the past two decades for corn.

In corn but not in wheat, domestic yield fluctuations related to weather and pests are important sources of aggregate market disturbance, and in both crops variations in acreage controls have been major influences on supply. But the most important source of market disturbance has been the instability of export demand, reflecting yield disturbances overseas and exchange rate fluctuations. These international disturbances have been magnified by the behavior of major market participants, who suppress domestic food and feed price fluctuations and rely on adjustments in quantities traded to equilibrate the home market. Because of the suppression of internal price response in other countries, the export demand for wheat and corn appear to be quite inelastic, although one would expect that in a free international market demand for U.S. exports would be very sensitive to price.

Of course, the domestic market itself has not been free of government intervention. In what follows I assess the roles of the principal policies in market stabilization and consider the appropriate stabilization measures for current conditions and those anticipated in the future.

Principal Market-stabilizing Measures for Corn and Wheat

One pillar of stabilization policy since the 1930s has been the nonrecourse loan. Although its provisions have changed over the years, the loan is essentially a short-term marketing loan (for less than one year) made by the Commodity Credit Corporation (CCC) to an eligible farmer, with his crop as collateral. The amount of the loan is the value of the crop calculated at the loan rate. If the farmer defaults on the loan, the crop is forfeited to the CCC, which forgives the interest due. If the farmer redeems the loan, he pays interest, but at a rate below market levels.

A second pillar of policy has been acreage reduction, which has been applied over the years in various guises to limit supply. Compliance, when not mandatory, has been encouraged by direct payments and by the fact that it has generally been a condition of eligibility for loans and other measures for supporting producer prices.

In the 1950s, after the Korean War boom, loan rates were maintained, against the wishes of the administration, at levels well above world market prices. The supply-reducing effects of acreage allotments were overwhelmed by yield increases, and accumulation of stocks ensued, with exclusion of farmers from competition in the world market.

In the 1960s policy moved toward a greater market orientation. Loan rates were lowered, and a third pillar of policy—an additional subsidy that places a floor under the producer price at a level above the loan rate—was introduced. In the 1960s such a subsidy came initially in the form of a price support payment, then as a certificate payment for wheat. In the 1970s government-financed deficiency payments were introduced for corn and wheat (but not for soybeans); the payment equaled difference, if positive, between a target price and the higher of the market price and the loan price.

Recent years have seen two major innovations in policy. The first is the farmer-owned reserve (FOR), introduced in 1977. It is a three-year loan for grain previously placed under a nonrecourse price support loan. The loan rate is above the rate for the prior loan. The grain cannot be sold without penalty till a higher release price is attained, and it must be sold if a still higher call price is reached.

A second recent innovation is the payment-in-kind (PIK) program of 1983, under which farmers were offered payments in grain (up to 80 percent of established yield) as an incentive to reduce the acreage planted. A principal attraction of this program seems to have been that its expenses, which were very real, would not appear in the budget. Unlike the FOR, the PIK has been discontinued and is not considered in this paper as a candidate for continuing policy.

The four major continuing policies are nonrecourse marketing loans, the

FOR, deficiency payments, and acreage controls. When used in combination, these instruments have such strong interactions that it is very difficult to discuss their effects on the market separately. But in the interests of simplicity I first outline loan-based policies and then the other measures individually before considering them in concert.

Nonrecourse Loans and the Farmer-owned Reserve

The idea of a nonrecourse loan program has appeal to farmers and consumers simultaneously. From the farmers' standpoint the loan rate affords downside price protection. By providing liquidity, it affords participating farmers more flexibility in timing the marketing of their grain when prices are low; and, like a put option, it places a price floor under the price of the grain under loan. (The effective floor may not be exactly at the relevant loan rate, for a number of technical reasons.) Nonparticipating farmers also gain price protection from the program, to the extent that acquisitions by the CCC at the loan rate support the market price for all holders of grain.

Consumers obviously have an interest in avoiding food shortages and inflation. A government-controlled ever-normal granary is very plausibly capable of dampening price increases by judicious release of stocks to consumers.

Perceptions of the advantages of the FOR may be quite similar to those outlined above. For producers the higher loan rate has additional appeal, and constraints on selling below the release price are offset by farmers' expressed satisfaction in the perception that ultimate disposal of stocks above that price is at the discretion of farmers, not the CCC. For consumers the release and call prices may add confidence that the really high prices seen in the early 1970s will be avoided. Policy makers who read the history of that decade as evidence of an important and highly nonlinear macroeconomic cost of inflation would greatly appreciate such a result.

These advantages of the storage-based programs are obvious, but are they real? If they are, it must be true, first, that the programs change the responsiveness of stockholding to fluctuations in available supply and that the nature of this change stabilizes the market in a meaningful fashion and, second, that the effects of such stabilization benefit both consumers and producers. I now consider each of these questions in turn.

Effects of CCC Nonrecourse Loans and the FOR on Aggregate Storage Behavior. The loan program and the FOR encourage storage indirectly through the effects of an interrelated set of instruments including the loan rate, interest subsidies, eligibility rules, storage payments, and release and call prices. A naive observer might infer the effectiveness of these measures from

FIGURE 1

Effect of a Price Floor on Market Price and Storage

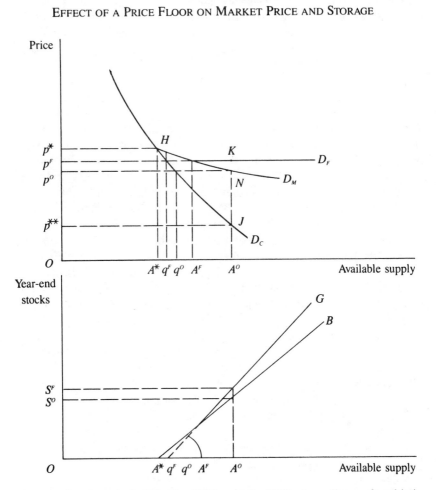

the quantity of stocks held by the CCC or in the FOR. A modicum of sophistication might direct attention to the responsiveness of those stocks to shortages and gluts.

Unfortunately the amount of stocks held in government programs is not necessarily a reliable indicator of the effect on aggregate storage. Private storers respond to the presence of such programs by storing less on average and by altering their acquisition and drawdown rules.

The main features of the theory of the net effects of public storage are illustrated in figure 1. In the top panel the consumption demand curve, D_C has a low price elasticity, consistent with the facts for agricultural staples such as wheat. This means that relatively small increases in available supply can lead to much larger proportional declines in price, if all supply is consumed. If

260

there is no storage, for example, and supply and consumption increase from A^* to A'' because of a large harvest, price falls from P^* to P^{**}, and producer revenue declines from an amount represented by rectangle P^*HA^*O to rectangle $P^{**}JA''O$.

Let us now assume that when the available supply is A'', the government decides to support price through unlimited offers to purchase stocks at a floor price P^f. To maintain the price at P^f, the government purchases all supply above q^f. The government storage behavior is indicated by the dashed line in the lower panel from q^f, to G, with a slope of 45 degrees. Of supply A'', the government stores S^f, equal to $(A'' - q^f)$. Revenue is then represented in the top panel by rectangle $P^fKA''O$. The floor price scheme has increased price, in relation to the case with no storage just described, by $P^f - P^{**}$ and revenue by the area P^fKJP^{**}.

These effects describe the naive view of a price floor. But profit-maximizing arbitrage, which ensures that marginal costs of storage are not less than the rate of price increase, implies that, in the absence of government storage, private storage behavior would follow a curve roughly like OA^*B in the lower panel. (For simplicity the observed nonlinearity of storage costs is ignored here.) If supply is A'', storage is S'' and consumption is q'' in the lower panel, and the top panel shows that price is then P'' and revenue is the area $P''NA''O$. So the approximate effect of the price floor is to increase price by only $(P^f - P'')$ and revenue by area P^fKNP''.

The proportion of public storage that merely replaces discretionary private stocks is greater than the average slope of A^*B between A^* and A''. If we can estimate that slope, we can consider it a lower bound on the degree of slippage between total government stocks and their net addition to total stocks, at a given supply. Note that if the government stores less than the private market would store, slippage is 100 percent. It would be lower if the two kinds of storage were imperfect substitutes. In the limiting case of zero substitutability, government storage is viewed as a reduction in available supply, and the slippage rate is again the private marginal propensity to store.

I use two methods to estimate the degree of substitution of public for private stocks in the U.S. wheat and corn markets. The first uses a numerical model of profit-maximizing private storage developed in collaboration with Jeffrey Williams of Brandeis University.[2] Using my best guesses of the relevant market parameters,[3] the model shows a degree of slippage of about 0.81 for wheat and a little less than 0.7 for corn, at levels of available supply sufficiently high that private discretionary storage would have been positive in the absence of the government program. Thus for wheat one extra bushel of government storage adds only about one-fifth of a bushel to total storage; for corn it adds one-third.

The second, quite different method uses data for the postwar years to estimate the linear relation between total ending stocks, available supply, CCC

261

stocks, and FOR stocks. The coefficients on CCC and FOR stocks indicate their net contribution after slippage. For wheat the results are quite striking. The best estimate for the entire postwar period (crop years 1950–1951 to 1982–1983) is that the degree of slippage is 82 percent for CCC stocks, close to that derived by the numerical model.[4] The FOR has no measurable net effect at all: slippage is complete. If the sample is reduced to the period starting in crop year 1967–1968, when the support policy had become more market oriented and CCC stocks had declined from the huge levels accumulated in the late 1950s, the net contribution of CCC stocks becomes negligible. Slippage in recent years appears to have been virtually complete both for the FOR and for CCC stocks acquired through forefeiture of nonrecourse marketing loans and through additional purchases in the 1979–1980 crop year to alleviate the cutoff of Soviet exports.

If it is true that government programs have not increased total stocks in the more recent period, aggregate storage behavior should be consistent with the slope of about 0.81 generated by the numerical model assuming only competitive private storage, and it is. When ending stocks are regressed on available supply and time, the coefficient is 0.84. The data for the linear regression include periods when available supply is so low that private storage is close to minimum working levels and therefore relatively unresponsive to marginal supply fluctuations. One might therefore have expected a downward rather than upward bias on the slope estimate for the relevant range of supply (that is, the range where price supports might be effective). Nevertheless the difference (0.81 versus 0.84) is remarkably small.

Another obvious check on the appropriateness of the numerical model might be a comparison of mean discretionary storage generated in the model with the mean discretionary storage observed in the grain market. In the parameters assumed above, mean wheat storage is only about half of that observed in the wheat market. Mean storage in the model, however, is quite sensitive to the variability of the underlying market disturbance, which does not change the slope of the storage rule significantly but shifts the intercept (point A^* in the lower panel of figure 1). The variability of the composite market disturbance due to yield fluctuations and export disturbances cannot be estimated with any precision over the time period of interest. The assumed coefficient of variation of 22.5 percent of domestic use is in the neighborhood of my best guess, given that yields and exports are exogenous.[5] But an increase in variability sufficient to generate observed mean storage is certainly plausible. Fortunately this issue does not affect the slope of the private storage rule that determines the marginal substitutability for public storage, which has been confirmed by the econometric results presented above.

For corn the extent of slippage at the margin appears to be much less. My econometric estimates range from 20 to 40 percent for CCC stocks and from 25 to 60 percent for the FOR. (Recall that the numerical model suggests slippage of nearly 70 percent.) Further inferences about the effects of public storage of corn are complicated by the dynamics of its use as animal feed. Hog production and beef production follow cycles that interact with corn market conditions in ways not captured in this analysis.

Nevertheless, it is clear that stocks of both major grains held by the CCC or in the FOR are substantially larger than the net increase in storage caused by these programs. The effect on market stability is less than meets the eye because private competitive storage would fill a large part of the void if government storage programs were rescinded. Indeed, government stocks of wheat appear to be so highly substitutable for private stocks that they do not affect total storage unless, as in the early 1960s, they dominate the market. There is no serious doubt that corn and wheat markets can operate satisfactorily without government storage programs, as the soybean market essentially does now. Consumption and prices might be somewhat less stable in the corn market, but the stability of the wheat market might be less affected, assuming acreage control policy is not changed.

Is an increase in stability advantageous to consumers and producers? This is a second question that must be answered to establish the desirability of CCC price supports and the FOR, and to it I now turn.

Effects of Market-stabilizing Price Supports on Consumers and Producers. In the United States agricultural products in their unprocessed form constitute only a minor share of the consumer's budget and tend to be viewed as necessities rather.than luxuries. One consequence is that shifts in demand from income fluctuations are not nearly as important for agricultural markets as they are for many other goods and services. Other determinants of domestic agricultural demand, such as tastes and demographic structure, are sufficiently predictable that any changes are usefully categorized as trends rather than disturbances. Market disturbances tend to come from unforeseen fluctuations in domestic or foreign production of the commodity or relevant substitute products or from the arbitrary behavior of governments. What are the implications for the commodity market?

There are at least two quite different ways of looking at this question. One focuses on the long-run or "comparative statics" effect on prices, expenditures, and revenues in the market in question; the other focuses on the effects of a policy change on the welfare of market participants. Both are discussed more fully in Wright and Williams.[6] Here I concentrate on the principal results.

Long-run perspective. From the long-run viewpoint, if a price support scheme successfully stabilizes consumption, several fairly clear-cut implications emerge:

1. Stabilization of consumption reduces or at most maintains the mean

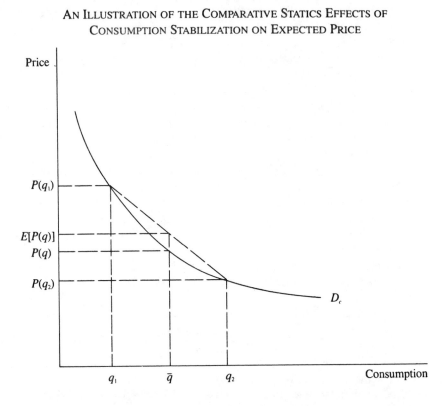

price for the normal (nonconcave) consumer demand curve shape. The result is easily understood from figure 2, in which D_c is the consumer demand curve if quantity consumed is a random variable q that equals q_1 or q_2, each with a probability of one-half; expected price is $E[P(q)] = 1/2 \, [P(q_1) + P(q_2)]$. If consumption is stabilized at $\bar{q} = E[q] = 1/2 \, [q_1 + q_2]$, the mean price is reduced from $E[P(q)]$ to the constant price $P(\bar{q})$. Stabilization of consumption results in a fall in mean price if demand is convex, as in the constant elasticity case, and no change if it is linear. This result does not apply, of course, if the government program *reduces* as well as stabilizes mean consumption, as is the case with aid measures that effectively divert products to a noncompeting market or other measures that destroy "surplus" production.

    2. If consumer demand has its normal (nonconcave) curvature, producers with stable production have lower revenue in the long run when consumption is stabilized by a storage scheme that does not reduce supply. Their mean revenue is positively related to the mean price, which falls with stabilization, as in 1 above.

    3. If private speculators are ready to supply storage services competi-

tively in a way that maximizes their expected profits, government schemes that partially stabilize consumption by increasing total storage must lose money in the long run. By adding stocks when private competitors would not, they are undertaking trades that cannot be expected to cover costs over the long run.

4. The more responsive producers are to prices, the less significant is the consumption-stabilizing effect of a given price floor, and the more moderate are the distributional consequences. In the presence of private storage, responsive supply adds to the stability of the free market by cutting back production when stocks are high and prices are low and increasing output when stocks are low and prices are high. It follows that a given price floor will be effective less often, and contribute less additional stability, when supply elasticity is higher.

Then there a few of those "two-handed" results that are obligatory for card-carrying economists:

5. When the disturbance is in domestic production, the effect of a consumption-stabilizing price support on long-run mean producer revenue increases as the curvature of consumption demand (domestic plus export) decreases. For typically inelastic demand, two popular demand specifications, the linear and the constant elasticity cases, have opposite effects on mean revenue, positive and negative respectively.

6. The change in the long run in consumer welfare is also determined by the curvature of consumption demand. If the demand curve is linear, mean consumer welfare typically falls, but it increases if the demand curve has constant elasticity. Given typical U.S. budget shares of agricultural commodities, this result is virtually independent of consumers' aversion to risk, conventionally defined.[7]

The problem with results 5 and 6 is that the curvature of the consumption demand curve is very difficult to determine empirically. We do not know whether the demand for major U.S. agricultural products is better represented by a linear or by a constant elasticity specification. It is therefore not possible to know whether stabilization increases or decreases the welfare consumers can expect to obtain in the long run from a floor price consumption stabilization program using a buffer stock. For producers the results imply that expected revenues are likely to fall in the long run unless the market disturbance is mainly domestic and the (unknown) consumer demand curvature is quite low.

Dynamic welfare effects. The foregoing results are of interest because they help us to understand how a floor price scheme affects a commodity market in the long run, but they do not tell us how a change in stabilization policy affects consumers and producers. The introduction of a floor price or an increase in its level increases the demand for the commodity and its price when the floor price is first effective, regardless of its long-run effect on mean price. Figure 3 shows the effect on the expected price path in the numerical

265

FIGURE 3

EFFECT OF THE INTRODUCTION OF A PRICE FLOOR IN A LOW-PRICE YEAR ON THE EXPECTED TIME PATH OF PRICE

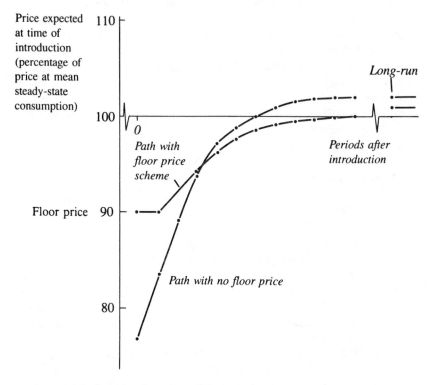

market model of a price floor introduced when the market price is low.[8] In the first four periods price expected at time 0 is increased by the price floor, even though the greater stability associated with the increase in storage reduces the mean price in the long run. For current consumers, this early price rise decreases the welfare benefits of stabilization relative to the long-run results. Consumers who enter the market after the market has converged to a (stochastic) steady state gain or lose in accordance with the long-run analysis discussed above, assuming they are not linked to earlier cohorts by gifts or bequests that are sensitive to the welfare of earlier consumers.

For producers the early price effects increase revenues in the short run. The curve *AB* in figure 4 shows the expected gain in revenue to producers and to holders of initial stocks associated with the price effects shown in figure 3. Curve *CD* shows the revenue effects if the price floor is introduced in a year when the price is well above the floor and there are negligible carry-over stocks; and the first revenue effect comes one or more harvests later.

But neither the long-run revenue effects indicated to the right of figure 4

266

FIGURE 4

EFFECT OF INTRODUCING A PRICE FLOOR ON REVENUE EXPECTED IN
FUTURE PERIODS

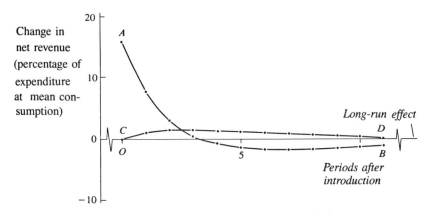

nor the short-run changes farther to the left correctly indicate the benefits of stabilization for any generation of producers. Any anticipated changes in revenue flows are reflected in the price farmers are willing to pay for fixed assets, particularly land. Therefore at the time of announcement of a stabilization policy change, the implications of future revenue gains and losses are capitalized in the wealth of current holders of land and commodity stocks, who are the only production-side entities to benefit significantly from the policy change. Later entrants into farming, who have to pay the market price for land, neither gain nor lose except perhaps through increased gifts or bequests from earlier landholders. In the long run price stabilization policy cannot change the welfare of U.S. farmers. Their net welfare in farming will be entirely determined by the income they could receive in off-farm employment regardless of policies in place. It is well recognized that in the long run farmers are all dead. The corollary is that in the long run they feel no pain from changes in farm policy.

What of those who own land or commodity stocks at the time when stabilization policy changes? They enjoy an immediate change in their wealth, equal to the current price effect on the value of their stocks plus the net discounted value of the expected changes in future revenues from their land. The initial demand-boosting effect of an increase in the price floor means that this wealth change is greater than the capitalized value of the long-run change in mean revenue. Of course if the long-run effect on revenue is sufficiently negative, wealth might still fall.

When the floor price falls, the effects are reversed. Although landholders do not gain from any scheme that existed before they purchased land, their land value, and so their wealth, will change if price supports are reduced or

FIGURE 5

DISTRIBUTIONAL EFFECTS OF INTRODUCTION OF A PRICE FLOOR WHEN
PRICE IS LOW

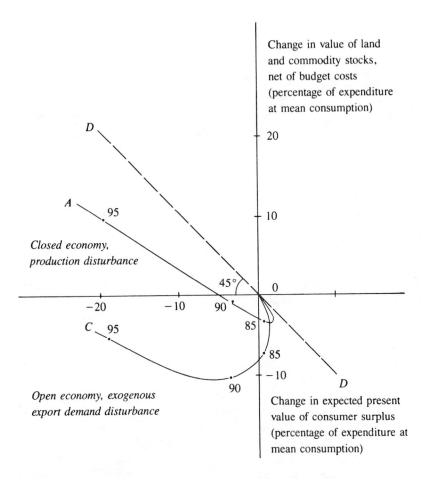

Change in value of land
and commodity stocks,
net of budget costs
(percentage of expenditure
at mean consumption)

Closed economy,
production disturbance

Open economy, exogenous
export demand disturbance

Change in expected present
value of consumer surplus
(percentage of expenditure at
mean consumption)

eliminated. In this case near-term expectations of decumulation of stocks or reduced accumulation imply a decrease in their wealth greater than the purely long-run revenue expectations would indicate.

Alternative possibilities for the transfer of wealth to current owners of land and commodity stocks when a price support scheme is introduced in the numerical model are illustrated in figure 5, which refers to the same case presented in figures 3 and 4. Curve *OA* shows that when market disturbances stem from domestic production, at a low support price consumers gain and initial owners of land and commodity stocks lose, results consistent with the long-run effects discussed above. At higher support levels the value of these assets, net of the capitalized program costs, increases. But the gain is much less than the discounted loss to consumers present and future, and the difference, the vertical distance from OA to the diagonal OD, is the net social cost of the transfer, sometimes called the dead-weight loss. In the language of the late Arthur Okun, it is the leakage from the bucket transferring wealth from consumers to producers, and here the bucket loses half its contents, wasted as excessive interest expenses and storage costs, as it makes the trip. In this case it is possible to show that the same expected transfer could be achieved much more efficiently by setting a much lower floor and destroying any quantities acquired at the floor.

The efficiency of transfer is much worse if the market disturbance comes from outside the market, for example, from fluctuations in export demands that are not responsive to price.[9] Then the transfer possibilities are indicated by curve OC. The transfer is so inefficient that both consumers and initial owners of stocks and land lose from the scheme.

This case is very important, for most of the aggregate market disturbances in wheat, and an increasing share of the disturbances in corn, originate overseas. Who gains from stabilization in this case? The answer is the large overseas importing country with a price-insensitive domestic market, which tends to find itself buying less or selling more when prices are low and buying more when prices are high. Stabilization through storage reduces the average cost of such internationally destabilizing market behavior. The net gain to the destabilizing foreigner in this example is the full vertical distance between curves OC and OA in figure 5.

Introduction of a positive supply response would moderate these distributive effects, but the qualitative lessons remain valid. These examples assume that the consumption demand curve has constant elasticity, which means that the curve is convex, its slope becoming less steep as consumption rises. If instead the demand curve had the same slope at the mean but were linear, initial landholders and asset owners would do better and consumers worse.[10] As explained above, we do not know which curve is more realistic. But in either case the crucial lesson for an agricultural sector increasingly exposed to the international market is that when substantial disturbances originate overseas, domestic price supports are very inefficient (ignoring the welfare of foreigners).

The fact that stabilization favors market destabilizers indicates a moral hazard problem, similar to that seen in the subsidization of other kinds of insurance. The program reduces the private incentive to take market-stabilizing actions. In the context of current U.S. policy, this is an important point. Major world grain market customers, most prominently the Soviet Union and other centrally planned economies, fix the domestic price of grain and absorb variable production through imports in lean years and perhaps by exports in the rarer good years. If their excess demand is large enough to affect price significantly, this amounts to a costly strategy of buy high and sell low. But U.S. efforts at market stabilization make it less costly for these unreliable customers. The Russian "great grain robbery" of 1972 not only was a particular instance of inappropriate export subsidization but was symptomatic of the wider but less obvious problem that all domestic market stabilization efforts can make policies that destabilize the international market more attractive, or less costly, to their proponents.[11]

Deficiency Payments

Deficiency payments are an alternative to price supports as a means of placing a floor under producer prices. In recent years they have been imposed on top of price support loans in wheat and corn, with the result that grain stocks are effectively supported at the loan rate (complemented by the FOR) while the grain output of eligible producers is supported at the higher target price.

From a policy standpoint, deficiency payments have two crucial advantages over price supports. The first is that the payments do not directly reward and encourage large, unstable foreign market participants as price supports do. The second is that their effect on producers' revenue, and so on land value, is unambiguous, whereas the effects of price supports are more complex and depend in part on currently unidentified characteristics of consumer demand, as discussed above.

The operation of deficiency payments is simplicity itself. If production elasticity is negligible, the payments directly affect only producer income and land values. All market transactions, including storage, are untouched by the scheme. The major costs of the scheme and who pays are easy to determine, a fact that may not appeal to the beneficiaries.

If production is responsive to the extra expected incentive of deficiency payments, storage will also be indirectly affected. The complementary market-stabilizing interaction of private storage and responsive supply is blunted by deficiency payments, somewhat reducing the efficiency of transfers. Nevertheless, if the efficiency costs of revenue raising to finance the scheme are reasonable, the net social cost of the transfer achieved should be less than for an equal expected transfer to landholders through price supports imposed in the presence of other distorting taxes.

In short, if the government in its wisdom wishes to help the current holders of land in a way that stabilizes producer prices, raising the target price on which deficiency payments are calculated is a surer and more efficient means than price supports. Of course deficiency payments are no more capable than price supports of raising the welfare of future entrants into farming, for all expected benefits will be capitalized in the value of land, broadly defined to include all fixed assets used in farming.

Acreage Controls

Because of the observed inelasticity of export demand, especially for wheat, acreage controls can raise mean revenue from exports by reducing mean supply.[12] They can also increase price stability in a manner similar to the effect of a higher (one-year-lagged) production supply elasticity. When carry-over stocks are large, acreage reductions can raise prices from depressed levels; when shortages develop, controls can be rescinded.

Generally economists emphasize the inefficiency associated with the yield-increasing response to such controls. But the numerical model reveals that destruction or other disposal of already produced output can be more efficient than price supports. Although I have not conducted an analysis of acreage controls, I should expect them to be more efficient than destruction.

Against these advantages are some drawbacks. Implementation decisions tend to be arbitrary rather than determined by rules, and they can be disastrously destabilizing (for example, wheat in 1972). In the longer run the supply response from other countries must be expected to reduce the market share of the United States. History shows that major primary commodity suppliers that are heavy-handed in export curtailment do not remain major suppliers.

Another perceived disadvantage of acreage controls is the lag between their imposition and the direct market effect. In a market with storage, however, acreage controls will, upon adoption, increase current prices to bring them into equilibrium with the increased future price and the market carrying costs.

Recent Policy Packages for U.S. Major Grains

For soybeans the sole instrument of market stabilization is a (low) loan rate. In markets for wheat, corn, and other products, however, four policies—nonrecourse loans, the FOR, deficiency payments, and acreage controls—form frequently modified, complex policy packages with multiple and interrelated instruments.

Target prices, generally above loan rates, increase land values at the expense of the public budget, but any requisite compliance with acreage restrictions moderates this effect. Price support loans, in this context, may increase carry-over somewhat, but substantial offsetting reductions in private storage reduce the effect of CCC acquisitions. In the presence of target prices, loans are most relevant for producers who, because they do not comply with eligibility requirements, cannot participate in the FOR or deficiency payments or, for that matter, the loan program. These include a majority of all domestic producers. Increases in loan rates probably increase land values. They very likely raise the wealth of foreign importers with unstable demand. To the

271

extent that they put a floor under market prices, price supports also reduce budget costs of deficiency payments. Similar comments apply to the FOR, except that its effectiveness is perhaps more questionable and the complications of its operations have led to charges of inefficient administration.

In the long run the major source of stabilization has been acreage restrictions, which, like storage programs, affect the revenues of nonparticipants by raising the market price. Given the surprisingly inelastic export demand for wheat and corn, these restrictions raise export revenues, at least in the short run. One way to characterize current policy would be as exploitation of the export market through variable supply control, tempered by incentives to increase the stability of the international market by increasing average storage, accompanied by deficiency payments to compensate producers for an overvalued exchange rate and to encourage voluntary compliance with acreage reductions. The participation-nonparticipation, compliance-noncompliance decisions have not been fully worked out in practice, but they certainly depend on the parameters of this policy package.

A Prescription for the Current Distress

The policies I have been discussing have little relevance for our short-run problem of farmer problems. The major current source of farmers' problems is not disturbance of prices and yields of individual commodities but the unprecedentedly high real interest rates and the associated overvaluation of the dollar.

The macroeconomic game is being played under new rules. Farmers are caught in a deadly squeeze between real interest costs so high that they could not have been foreseen and low dollar prices for exportables. Although trade-weighted exchange rate movements have differed markedly among commodities, the problems are not commodity-specific. Rather, the distress cuts across product lines and is concentrated on those who entered farming or expanded operations within the past decade, at times when reasonable judgment would have ruled out current conditions as incredible.

If the objective is to relieve distress, the policy should be distress-oriented, not commodity-oriented. Direct emergency credit relief as an explicitly short-term, one-time program to combat dislocations caused by high interest costs makes a great deal of sense. After all, similar measures have relieved pressures on banks and debtors from much less judicious international loans.

Credit relief could be complemented by retention, in the short run, of deficiency payments to cushion producers against an exchange rate almost universally regarded as above its long-term equilibrium level. These payments make more sense than support prices fixed in domestic dollars that, under a market disturbed by fluctuating exchange rates, command more foreign resources when stocks are being withdrawn from the market and the dollar is high and less when stocks are being released for export.

In a time of budget stringency, the blend of credit relief and producer price protection is essentially a political decision. The government has not felt obligated to protect other small businesses from unpredictable increases in interest costs, although it has protected steel and automobiles from exchange rate movements. If the main short-term objective is to reduce the number of failures of good farms and of rural banks and suppliers, direct credit intervention is the essential ingredient.

Policy for the Longer Term

High real interest rates are probably an unusual aberration that will not very long persist, but fluctuations of income and prices will no doubt endure as perceived problems of the agricultural sector, causing continued pressure for public intervention in farm prices. But a government role in price insurance makes less sense now than in the past. First, income sources of farm families are now more diversified between farm and off-farm earnings, making total income less sensitive to farm prices. Second, as public restrictions on agricultural commodity options, futures, and combinations of the two are progressively relaxed, a range of sophisticated private hedging instruments becomes available to farmers and other traders. More generally, proponents of government insurance of price or income risks carry a heavy burden of proof, because the historical record, which is extensive, is almost uniformly negative, even for countries in which the lack of development of private financial markets makes the case for government intervention more plausible than it can be in the United States. Unless the insurance carries a large subsidy or a high opportunity for default, farmers generally do not buy it, and that is a sufficient argument against providing it.

Given its dominant role in world grain trade and aid, another type of insurance may be desirable. As the experience of the early 1970s showed, relatively small shortfalls of world grain production below the trend can, given the insulation of large portions of the world grain market from price effects, lead to large and disruptive price rises that threaten the lives and health of millions of the world's poor. Since similar world shortages are bound to recur, retention of a moderate-sized emergency wheat reserve under government control, which can be drawn down only to feed those excluded from market participation by high prices in times of dire emergency, is a relatively cheap insurance measure. There are some grounds for the conjecture that the existence of such a stock may also reduce the chances that disruptive "speculative bubbles" will form. At this stage in our understanding, such dangerously disruptive phenomena cannot be ruled out as impossible in rational private commodity markets. Since price controls (perhaps in the form of export controls, as in the Nixon soybean embargo) are to be expected in the

273

United States in emergency situations, especially if no special reserves are available, operation of such a reserve under strict and explicit guidelines may not significantly reduce private storage incentives. Indeed, since the United States cannot avoid some kind of involvement when famine threatens almost anywhere in the world, a clear policy of this type would probably increase the efficiency of the market by increasing the confidence of private market participants.

If price supports are to be a continuing part of agricultural policy in spite of the arguments against them, deficiency payments, with target prices adjusted below the current loan rates, would provide protection against major price declines. Price support loan programs are not appropriate for internationally oriented markets. Economists do not yet have the information to determine their true effects on the wealth of producer-landholders, but they may well be much less than the budget cost or even negative, and the efficiency of any transfer achieved is unacceptably low. The FOR has rather similar characteristics, given the presence of private storage. Further, as currently administered, it locks farmers into holding for a long time an asset the value of which is presumably highly correlated with that of the growing crop and production assets. Grain, especially if stored off-farm, is a highly diversifiable asset, and this restriction on farmers' portfolios must, needlessly, partly offset the price-stabilizing aspects of the program.

Acreage controls have several advantages. They can provide significant, medium-term stabilization, with some short-run (within-year) effect through the linkage of spot and futures markets. Their well-known efficiency cost is probably overemphasized in relation to less obvious costs of other programs. Further, they can probably raise the mean revenue from exports because of the observed inelasticity of short-run export demand, especially if the effect is small enough to be discreetly disguised as a byproduct of stabilization measures.

Conclusions

Given the current development of futures markets and options, the increasing sophistication and flexibility of other financial institutions, and the increasing integration of farm and nonfarm labor and financial markets, governmental market stabilization to protect producers against short-term commodity-specific price risks is becoming increasingly redundant. If short-term hedging services are left to the private market, acreage restrictions can provide a reserve of protection for producers in case low producer prices persist over several seasons, but they should be used sparingly. No other direct commodity-specific price interventions are justified in the long run, but if they cannot be avoided, deficiency payments are preferable to price support loans or the FOR. These storage programs have ambiguous distributional effects and encourage disruptive behavior by foreign market participants. If the induced storage is a moderate proportion of total storage, its effects are substantially offset by private storage reductions. If price supports are so high that storage under the program dominates the market, the programs can be quite wasteful as transfer mechanisms.

Although the government should largely withdraw from the business of stabilizing privately diversifiable, short-term, idiosyncratic commodity price risks, solid arguments can be made for a government role in two other stabilization tasks. First, since sharp shifts in macroeconomic policies have caused great distress through unforeseeable adverse movements in real interest rates and exchange rates, a good case can be made for one-time credit market intervention to reduce farm failures, and a fair case can be made for some current subsidization through deficiency payments to compensate for an overvalued exchange rate. In the longer run farmers can directly or indirectly acquire considerable protection through futures markets for financial instruments and foreign exchange. Public policy should aim to make these markets as flexible, accessible, and liquid as possible, on the one hand, and to refrain from a repetition of the current macroeconomic disruptions, on the other.

Second, maintenance of a moderate-sized, government-controlled, and publicly financed emergency food reserve of wheat and perhaps some feed grains is desirable and not very expensive. Such reserve should be drawn down only in clearly defined conditions of famine or panic. This policy, like a strategic petroleum reserve, is necessary because of the expectation that price controls will be imposed in times of dire need and the consequent lack of adequate incentive for storage by the private market.

Finally, it should be clearly understood that in a country like the United States any measures that increase or stabilize revenues of farmers will not improve the attractiveness of farming in the long run. Rather they will be capitalized upon introduction as an increase in the wealth of current landholders and in the price of entry for future farmers. In the long run the welfare of farmers in the United States will be determined by the fortunes of the rest of the economy.

Notes

1. Greater detail and some caveats are contained in Brian D. Wright, "An Assessment of the United States Farmer-Owned Reserve and Commodity Credit Corporation Storage as Market Stabilization Policies," American Enterprise Institute Occasional Paper (November 1984).

2. Brian D. Wright and Jeffrey C. Williams, "The Welfare Effects of the Introduction of Storage," Quarterly Journal of Economics, vol. 99, no. 1 (February 1984), pp. 169–92; and idem, "The Incidence of Market-stabilizing Price Support Schemes," Yale Economic Growth Center Discussion Paper No. 466 (December 1984).

3. Consumption demand elasticity is constant at -0.2 for wheat, -0.5 for corn.

Supply elasticity is 0.3 for both, and the real interest rate is 5 percent. Storage costs are constant at 2.5 percent of the price that would occur with no market disturbances. The standard deviation of the market disturbance is 12.5 percent of mean consumption for corn and 22.5 percent for wheat. These parameter choices are explained and defended in Wright, "An Assessment of Market Stabilization Policies."

4. The estimated equation is

$$WSTOCKS = -466.8 + 0.82\,WSUPPLYD + 0.22\,WCCC - 0.009\,WFOR - 1.41\,TIME$$
$$\qquad\qquad\quad (19.1) \qquad\qquad (6.0) \qquad (-0.17) \qquad (-1.06)$$

$$R^2 = 0.987$$
$$D.W. = 1.30$$

where $WSTOCKS$ is ending wheat stocks, $WSUPPLYD$ is domestic supply (production plus carry-in stocks less exports), and $WCCC$ and $WFOR$ are CCC and FOR stocks of wheat. The numbers in parentheses are t-statistics. Use of aggregate supply including exports gives fairly similar but less precise results, and correction for serial correlation has negligible effect on the coefficients. A more extensive discussion of the econometric work reported here is presented in Wright, "An Assessment of Market Stabilization Policies."

5. A market disturbance was constructed by taking proportional deviations from a five-year moving average of yields, multiplying by a five-year moving average of acreage, and subtracting deviations from a five-year moving average of exports.

6. Wright and Williams, "Incidence of Market-stabilizing Schemes."

7. Ibid.

8. For the illustrations in figures 3, 4, and 5, consumer demand has constant elasticity of -0.2, supply elasticity is zero, and the standard deviation of the market disturbance is 7.5 percent of mean consumption. In the low-price year illustrated, supply (net of minimum working stocks) is assumed to be 120 percent of mean output. In the high-price year it is 90 percent of mean output.

9. In the case illustrated, mean export demands are zero. The foreign market participant enters the market randomly as a price-insensitive importer or exporter, depending on its domestic harvest outcome.

10. Wright and Williams, "Incidence of Market-stabilizing Schemes."

11. James Trager, *The Great Grain Robbery* (New York: Ballantine Books, 1975); and U.S. General Accounting Office, *Russian Wheat Sales and Weaknesses in Agriculture's Management of the Wheat Export Subsidy Program* (Washington, D.C., 1973).

12. Wright, "An Assessment of Market Stabilization Policies."

Commentary

Larry Salathe

I find Brian Wright's paper both interesting and extremely challenging. Its conclusions seem to stem from a mixture of empirical analyses and considerable personal judgment. The empirical analyses are derived from what Wright describes as a profit-maximizing storage model for wheat and corn. The model assumes certain supply and demand elasticities and an aggregate market disturbance distribution. Wright states:

> I do this [calculate the distribution of the market disturbance term] by taking a three-year moving average of acres planted, and multiplying this by the proportional disturbance in yield after extracting an exponential trend . . . and divide by a three-year moving average of the sum of domestic use plus exports.[1]

He then goes through a fairly lengthy discourse of why this procedure may be invalid. No rationale is given for why the procedure is even reasonable. But if we assume that it is reasonable, we find that the storage rule generated by these assumptions corresponds fairly well to a simple regression of total storage on total available supply. Wright then concludes, "There is nothing in any of the evidence considered so far to suggest that public storage intervention in the wheat market has changed storage behavior at all in this period."[2]

Let us go a step further. Wright's model tells us that if the supply and demand elasticities were known with certainty, as well as future interest rates, the strength of the dollar, other factors affecting the wheat and corn markets, and the distribution of the market disturbance, a given quantity would be held in storage by the private sector. But we as economists cannot agree on the magnitudes of such parameters. Given the assumptions above, does the model adequately predict the behavior of the private sector in our dynamic and uncertain world? Wright does provide a clue. He states:

> But the model results do differ from observed data in another, important dimension. Average storage generated in a long time series simulation of the model is 13.4 percent of total supply for wheat, compared to 22.6 percent in the sample 1967/68–1982/83, if supply and storage are defined as net of minimum stocks, which equal 340 million bushels in the sample. For corn, the difference is even more dramatic, 4 percent versus 11.7 percent.[3]

The views expressed herein are those of the author and may not reflect those of U.S. Department of Agriculture or the Economic Research Service.

Thus, if we assume that Wright's model is reasonable, we must conclude that government storage was extremely effective in raising the total stocks of both wheat and corn. Wright overlooks this evidence, however, and suggests that the model's failure to portray history with reasonable accuracy is probably due to its inadequate treatment of acreage control provisions. At this point I can only ask, Why was the model presented in the first place? and Is it reasonable to place any confidence in the model's results and use those results as a basis for analyzing past government storage programs? I think not.

So where do we go from here? It seems to me that there is ample evidence from a number of independent studies that government storage programs stabilized prices during the 1950s, 1960s, and early 1980s.[4] During the 1970s government stocks were drawn down to minimal levels as export expansion generally kept prices above release levels. This drawdown of government stocks and the consequent lack of adequate stocks to fill any shortfall in production at home or abroad caused farm prices to be much more unstable in the 1970s than in previous decades. Price instability was a major reason for the development of the farmer-owned reserve program. Empirical studies suggest that the program, as administered in combination with the Commodity Credit Corporation (CCC) loan program, by itself probably failed to reduce price variability significantly. It did expand stocks and has raised commodity prices and farm income, but it also increased government outlays for agricultural commodity programs.[5]

As economists we find it very difficult to evaluate policies or programs that have price stabilization as their stated goal. We often hear the argument that price stability will improve the welfare of all market participants by providing a more stable environment for all—a market environment in which production, marketing, and consumption decisions can be made independently of random and chaotic fluctuations in prices. Yet we have no quantitative measure of the extent to which price stability improves the ability of markets to function efficiently. On the opposite side of the ledger is the cost of these programs measured down to the last dollar and cent. This is certainly true of government storage programs since they have come into being. The costs stare us in the face while we search for quantitative measures of the benefits.

At this point we might throw up our hands in despair and recommend that government storage programs be scrapped since we know they cost money but we cannot measure their benefits. We could go a bit further, however, and attempt to measure the extent to which farm prices and incomes are affected by government storage policies. That seems to be worthwhile. But government storage and price support policies are not independent, even though the movement to target prices in the 1970s was an attempt to reduce the degree to which farmers' incomes were directly affected by government storage policies. To evaluate government storage policies, we must thus make further assumptions

278

about price and income support policies. Past studies commonly assume that both government storage and price support policies would be discontinued simultaneously, but I doubt that such a dramatic change in policy would occur. It seems much more likely that a dismantling of farm programs will occur piecemeal.

Let us examine the more likely scenario: elimination of government storage programs while our current price and income support policies are retained. Currently, farmers who participate in acreage reduction programs are eligible to receive deficiency payments. Those payments to each producer equal the payment rate times the planted acreage of the program commodity times the farm program yield. The payment rate is the difference between the announced target price and the greater of the market price for a portion of the marketing year and the announced loan rate (support price). History indicates that the support price or loan rate generally sets a floor for market prices. It is likely that eliminating the floor, especially given current market conditions for both corn and wheat, would lower market prices and, since not all farmers participate in acreage reduction programs, lower farm incomes. Government outlays would probably increase in the short term because the inelasticity of agricultural commodities makes it cheaper to support prices through government acquisition than through direct payments to support incomes. In the long term, however, lower CCC grain storage and handling costs could offset the increase in outlays resulting from larger deficiency payments.

Some economists argue that our current government storage and price support policies impede our ability to compete in world markets and stabilize the markets of our competitors, who also enjoy the benefits of our stabilization policy. I agree. When support prices are set above their long-term equilibrium level, they undoubtedly give our competitors an incentive to expand production. They further encourage our own farmers to use additional inputs and expand acreage at a time when there is already excessive production. This is the box we find ourselves in when we attempt to raise rather than to stabilize prices. Of course, hindsight makes much more readily apparent whether our policies stabilize or raise prices. We thus need to make our price support and government storage policies flexible and conditional on market forces.

Another question is whether less costly or more effective means can be found to stabilize farm prices and incomes. Wright suggests that acreage controls may be a more effective way to stabilize farm prices, but the marketing year 1983–1984 for corn dramatically demonstrates the inability of such controls to do so. Let me provide some background. At the beginning of the 1982–1983 marketing year, corn stocks totaled nearly 2.2 billion bushels, over a billion bushels more in than the previous year. Given prospects of even greater stocks by the end of the 1982–1983 marketing year, the administration announced the payment-in-kind (PIK) program in January 1983. Farmers responded by placing nearly 32 million acres of corn in conserving use. But

279

what happened? Along came the drought and prices jumped from $2.68 for 1982–1983 to $3.20 for 1983–1984; they are forecast to average about $2.70 per bushel for 1984–1985. Thus acreage control provisions, rather than being price stabilizing, are price destabilizing. The reason should be clear. A cutback in acreage can be coupled with equal probability with poor or good yields. Acreage controls might provide some price stability if weather, both at home and abroad, could be forecast with reasonable accuracy. But weather has a mind of its own, and it is thus unreasonable to expect that acreage control provisions by themselves can be managed to stabilize prices.

Another alternative suggested by Wright is to have the government purchase commodities on the open market and dispose of such purchases through noncommercial markets or outright destruction. The result, he argues, would be lower government outlays since storage and handling costs would be minimal. Let us assume, however, that the purpose of government storage is to reduce price instability. Obviously, if purchases are destroyed or sold through noncommercial outlets, the goal of reducing instability is meaningless—government stocks will not be available to enter the commercial market when poor weather reduces supplies at home or abroad. If price enhancement is the goal of government storage policies, however, disposal of government purchases through noncommercial outlets makes good sense at least from a budgetary standpoint.

Finally, we could turn to the private sector. An abundance of evidence suggests that private stockholding would expand if government storage programs were discontinued.[6] But ample evidence also supports the conclusion that total carry-over of stocks would decline if government storage programs were discontinued. I believe this to be true, and it seems to be consistent with Wright's model results.

Past history provides us with some insight into why the private sector will not hold large stocks of farm commodities to help offset future shortfalls in production. Over the past half-century, for example, farm prices have declined in real terms, and quite dramatically, and they continue to do so. The reasons are twofold—the income elasticity for food is low, and productivity continues to be steadily improved. From the viewpoint of the private sector, commodity prices must on average increase from year to year to cover both storage costs and a reasonable return on investment. Given current interest rates and storage costs, the prices of wheat and corn would have to increase from year to year by about $0.60 and $0.50 per bushel, respectively. This simple fact alone suggests that the private sector would not be willing to hold stocks considerably greater than minimum pipeline levels, especially given the prospects for export growth for the foreseeable future. Since the elimination of government storage programs would probably result in lower carry-over stocks, commodity prices would be more variable if government storage programs were totally eliminated.

The real question seems to be, To what degree should commodity prices be stabilized? A related question is, To what degree should farmers' incomes be stabilized? We should not overlook the fact that volatility in food prices may be as much of a policy issue as volatility in farm prices. As economists we again cannot provide an answer. We can determine with reasonable accuracy the stocks that would be needed to maintain prices within some bounds; but, since we do not have any measure of the benefits of price stability, we certainly cannot determine what level of price stability is optimal. All we can do is to examine the costs of stabilizing prices within various ranges and make a decision. Maybe our current government storage programs are too costly. As an economist I cannot provide an answer, but I am confident that policy makers will decide despite our inability to quantify the benefits of price stabilization.

Finally, it is probably worthwhile to indicate who benefits from price stability even though we cannot measure the benefits. Wright concludes that price stabilization will increase the wealth of those holding land at the time the price stabilization policy is introduced. If the policy stabilizes prices, the risks of farming decline; higher land prices may result as additional resources are attracted to or held in agricultural production. This, however, is likely to be a very small and short-term effect. As the past couple of years indicate, stabilizing prices does not ensure a bullish market for agricultural land. Consumers probably receive some benefits from price stabilization since the probability of shortages and extremely high prices is lower. Food-processing firms probably also benefit since more stable supplies and prices could result in more efficient use of processing facilities and improved management decisions. For the same reasons livestock producers probably also benefit from grain price stabilization and government storage policies.

In conclusion, government storage programs, as in biblical times, have a role in ensuring adequate supplies and stabilizing commodity prices. The question of whether the costs outweigh the benefits continues to be debated, especially during a period of budget austerity. Government stocks of 300 to 500 million bushels of wheat and 700 million to 1 billion bushels of corn would seemingly provide a fairly large degree of price stability at a reasonable cost to society. The degree to which government stocks stabilize prices is also influenced, however, by the rules governing the accumulation and dispersal of such stocks. Government storage programs must operate in conjunction, and not at odds, with market forces, or such programs will tend not to meet the objective of stabilizing prices. This is the lesson that the past few years have taught us. We can use government storage programs to raise prices above their long-term market-clearing level, but budget outlays soon become excessive. Raising prices is more effectively accomplished through acreage and production controls than through the accumulation of government stocks.

Notes

1. Brian D. Wright, "An Assessment of the United States Farmer-Owned Reserve and Commodity Credit Corporation Storage as Market Stabilization Policies," American Enterprise Institute Occasional Paper (January 1985), p. 30.

2. Ibid., p. 31.

3. Ibid., p. 32.

4. Frederick J. Nelson and Willard W. Cochrane, "Economic Consequences of Federal Farm Commodity Programs, 1953–72," *Agricultural Economics Research*, vol. 28, no. 2 (1976), pp. 52–63; and Daryll E. Ray and Earl O. Heady, *Simulated Effects of Alternative Policy and Economic Environments on U.S. Agriculture*, CARD report 46T (Ames: Center for Agricultural and Rural Development, Iowa State University, 1974).

5. William H. Meyers and Mary E. Ryan, "The Farmer-owned Reserve: How Is the Experiment Working?" *American Journal of Agricultural Economics*, vol. 63 (1981), pp. 316–23; Larry Salathe, J. Michael Price, and David E. Banker, "An Analysis of the Farmer-owned Reserve Program, 1977–82," *American Journal of Agricultural Economics*, vol. 66 (1984), pp. 1–11; and Jerry A. Sharples and Forrest Holland, "Impact of the Farmer-owned Reserve on Privately Owned Wheat Stocks," *American Journal of Agricultural Economics*, vol. 63 (1981), pp. 538–43.

6. Bruce L. Gardner, *Consequences of USDA's Farmer-owned Reserve Program for Grain Stocks and Prices*, GAO Report to Congress CED-81-70, vol. 2 (June 26, 1981); Richard E. Just, *Theoretical and Empirical Considerations in Agriculture Buffer Stock Policy in the Food and Agriculture Act of 1977*, GAO Report to Congress CED-81-70, vol. 3 (June 26, 1981); and Salathe, Price, and Banker, "Analysis of the Farmer-owned Reserved Program."

Farm Programs and Structural Issues

Daniel A. Sumner

The number of farms currently operating is less than half what it was three decades ago. The remaining farms (2.2 million) are diverse but on the whole much larger by any measure than the farms of the 1950s. The total agricultural output of the country has increased while the number of large farms has increased and the number of small and very small farms has fallen dramatically. The structure of agriculture remains a topic on the farm policy agenda, where it has been for decades.

This paper examines the structural consequences of farm programs to provide further background to the policy debate leading to the 1985 farm bill. A number of arguments are presented, and considerable evidence is discussed, in an attempt to relate structural characteristics of farming to the effect of farm programs. The programs considered are the basic price support, output control, and storage programs for the major farm products. No attempt is made to analyze all the government policies and programs that affect farms. The structural characteristics considered include farm size distributions as measured by inputs, outputs, and sales; diversification and specialization across commodity outputs; off-farm employment; and farmland ownership and farm financial status.

Farm programs may affect these characteristics, mostly in indirect ways. They may affect the level of prices, the variability of prices, and capitalization into farm asset values. They may also affect expectations of future output and the potential for farm expansion.

The paper briefly critiques some often stated reasons for interest in industry structure and attempts to frame a useful definition of the family farm. The major portion of the paper considers the effects of commodity policy on endogenous structural characteristics. The effects of past and potential commodity programs on distributions of structural characteristics across farms are also considered, and program changes that may occur in 1985 are given special emphasis.

After an outline of the policy issues, some of the economic reasoning

James D. Leiby and D. Arthur Sparrow provided extraordinary assistance throughout this project. This report also benefited from general research and editorial assistance from E. Frazao, P. Henderson, M. Kowalski, E. Newton, and M. Pereira.

related to farm structure is considered. Several authors have concluded that commodity programs encourage farm consolidation and specialization, in part by reducing the riskiness of farming. The effects of commodity programs are diverse, and no complete or rigorous analysis is attempted. The economic reasoning developed raises doubts, however, about any strong effects of farm programs on structural variables. It is not clear, for example, that programs reduce the riskiness of farming over the horizon relevant for major farm decisions.

The basic approach is to derive distributions of endogenous measures of farm or enterprise size and other structural characteristics from individual firm choice. The observed industry structure is a distribution of choices by individual firms, which arrive at different solutions because of different fixed inputs, prices, production parameters, or random influences on their behavior. This conceptual approach is used to critique some previous studies of farm structure and to guide the formulation of empirical analysis of structure. The empirical sections consider specific commodities and policies, as well as discussing part-time farming and other issues.

Empirical evidence on policy and structure is also inconclusive. For specific commodities and for farming as a whole, farm programs do not seem to have had a definite effect in any direction. Farm programs have not been major factors in past structural changes and are not likely to be major factors in the future.

Why Study Size and Structure?

Among the policy issues related to the size and structure of farms are the size of rural populations and incomes; industrial concentration and monopoly power; the allocation of people or workers among farm and nonfarm occupations and other issues related to costs of mobility; the efficiency of farm production and the cost of farm products; the biases of government policies (mainly designed for other purposes); and the moral or political value of family farms. These issues have varied degrees of relationship to the distributions of various measures of farm size and structure. Some are really matters of land-to-labor ratios; others relate to the demand for and supply of factors of production in agriculture and hence to incomes and mobility. The distribution of farm size, or the "structure of agriculture," has often been a central focus of discussion for those interested in the more basic issues listed.

Even if farm size itself were not a policy issue, the effect of policy on farm structure would be. Policies designed for other purposes may have unintended effects on the competitive position of farms of a certain type. Informed policy judgments require the analysis of indirect and unintended effects of government actions.

Much policy rhetoric is devoted to the indirect contributions of "family

284

farms." Without investigating the specifics of these contributions more deeply I note that policy encourages attention to the effect of economic events and policy changes on family farms. This concept of a family farm is important enough to warrant some further discussion and the proposal of a working definition.

One of the uses of economic analysis is to provide an early warning of potential changes in the economy. Private sector and public sector decision making depends on the ability to forecast changes in the farm economy. Therefore, even without other interests we want to be able to predict the effect of policies on size and structure.

The Family Farm

The political rhetoric and real policy—at least some of it—attempt to focus government benevolence on family farms.[1] The Food and Agriculture Act of 1977 required the secretary of agriculture to report annually on the status of the family farm, and the subsequent reports contain a wealth of useful information on farm structure.[2] To understand policy discussions, we must understand the way policy participants, policy analysts, and those in the industry use the term.

The concept of a family farm seems to be based on excluding some farms. Family farms are those that are (1) not so small in the use of family labor and management, or in gross or long-run net returns, that they are not primarily business enterprises; and (2) not so large that they are business enterprises owned or operated by more than just a few closely associated families that devote significant time to farm activities.

In a recent National Planning Association (NPA) report, Luther Tweeten proposed a more restrictive set of ideals for a family farm, about which he says there is some agreement:[3] the family members make most of the farming decisions, supply most of the labor, derive most of their income from farming, and receive an income and rate of return comparable to those in the nonfarm sector.

This definition, however, does not seem to be applicable across a variety of commodities and regions.[4] It is revealing that one member of the Food and Agriculture Committee of the NPA, a Washington wheat farmer, immediately took exception to Tweeten's definition. The points he made were good ones. First, it is an old-fashioned, or perhaps just a midwestern, idea that on a family farm the family must provide most of the labor. Such a rule does not apply to wheat farms in Washington, to the fruit and vegetable industries of California, or to the tobacco industry of North Carolina, where even relatively small operations would not satisfy that requirement. In flue-cured tobacco, some of the crop is harvested by machine and some by hand. It seems ironic that of two otherwise identical farms, Tweeten would classify the farm with the large machinery investment as a family farm. This bias toward capital intensity seems narrow and inappropriate for a wide range of U.S. farms. Second, many farm families with large farms earn more net income from nonfarm sources than from farming—at least in some years. Among younger families especially, it is common for farm wives to have careers and for husbands to take some work off the farm; so even if the husband is a "full-time" farmer, it is not unusual for off-farm income to be larger than farm income. The implicit limitation on the occupation of the spouse of a farmer seems an odd criterion. Finally, the condition that the family farms cannot leave the family poor or that family farmers cannot, by definition, have made mistakes that imply low returns, seems odd indeed. The one condition that remains unchallenged relates to family management.

In developing a definition I want to avoid what I like to call the Corn Belt bias. I do not want my definition to exclude labor-intensive enterprises important in many commodities in favor of the capital-intensive grain and livestock farms that dominate the Midwest. I also do not want to exclude small farms—even those operated by farmers who work significant amounts of time off the farm—that are operated as businesses and that make significant contributions to the economic well-being of the farm families.

A working definition that I have found useful is this: a family farm is a business enterprise producing primary crop or livestock products that under normal conditions (1) generates returns based on the resources controlled by a single extended family or at most two or three families, (2) provides income to support not more than a very few owner-operator families, and (3) provides at least half of one full-time-equivalent employment for family members.

No capital bias is contained in this definition, nor is there a presumption that farming is the dominant income-producing activity of the family. I believe this definition captures the intent of policy makers and can be useful to analysts as well. It is not, however, an operational, empirical definition. The criteria of gross sales, acres, or asset value that determine membership in the class of family farms would vary by region or commodity and by the degree of operator ownership of farm inputs.

In numbers of farms, the important exclusions are the farms with small gross revenue. At the upper end nonfamily corporations and some very large farms that produce significant shares of total sales of some commodities would be excluded.

Commodity Programs and Farm Structure: The Economic Reasoning

Farms and farmers are diverse, and it is sometimes implicitly assumed that farms are different because farmers have chosen the "wrong" size. The basic underlying notion of this paper is that the distribution of size and other structural variables among farms is the result of economic choices by farmers.

Therefore, farms differ because farmers differ and because the underlying economic constraints and incentives differ among farms. Input demand functions, supply functions, or revenue functions relate these measures of size to input and output prices, levels of fixed factors, and technological parameters. Farm commodity programs affect the size distribution of farms and other structural distributions by affecting the basic factors that determine the optimal sizes of the firms in the industry. In the longer term the entry or exit of farms and farmers may also be affected by programs.

Six years ago Gardner noted that the accepted result of studies of commodity programs and farm structure was that farm programs increase average farm size.[5] He also reasoned that the basis for this conclusion was weak, since neither applied economic theory nor careful empirical analysis had established any consistent link between the programs and the structural characteristics of American agriculture. Despite considerable research in the interim, Gardner's comments still characterize the state of knowledge about the effects of commodity programs on farm structure.

A 1980 survey by Spitze et al. contains a detailed and useful account of the potential effects of commodity programs on small farms.[6] Their three general findings were that relative benefits varied according to commodity, region, eligibility, and participation; that short-run or direct benefits were indeed proportional to size; and that long-run effects either were neutral or benefited larger farms.[7] Spitze et al. note that it is well known that the basic commodity programs are not appropriate tools for addressing rural poverty or for improving the competitive positions of the smallest farms.

For farm commodity programs the basic unit of account is the physical commodity, not the farm itself. Therefore, higher price supports, benefits, deficiency payments, or disaster payments will generally be proportional to output or normal output. Farm commodity programs are commercial policies that affect farm people through their farm business. Whatever the shortcoming of these programs may be, it is not that they fail to eliminate low net incomes or wide disparities in gross income among farms. These points are well known and are not subject to serious debate. The discussion of farm programs as though they were poverty programs is due either to ignorance or to an attempt to mislead.

Asset Values. Rausser, Zilberman, and Just have emphasized their belief that "the distributional effects of agricultural production policies can be explained seriously only through their indirect effects on asset markets."[8] The rates of return on farmland, other physical capital, and farmers' time and talents are determined in part by farm prices. These rates also affect the entry and exit of individuals into farming. Price supports and other programs affect farmers' net incomes by affecting the rates of return and the values of assets owned by farmers. Long-run expectations of programs affect the asset values because

287

they affect expected rental rates for farm-specific inelastic resources. An increase in the margin between the gross revenue and the cost of variable inputs is capitalized into the prices of the more inelastically supplied inputs. Since some of those inelastic resources are owned by farmers, farmers gain from the programs. Farmers lose from elimination of the programs whenever they own resources that would be worth less without a price support or other program. The most direct observation of this phenomenon is in the capital value of tobacco quotas.

Differences in the proportion of farm assets owned by farmers operating farms of different size and organization would seem to lead to differential gains, by size, from the programs. A further complication, however, is that ownership of farm assets may be only partly related to farm operation. The different effects of policy on size or structure must come through differential effects (the price of output available to farms of different sizes or different structure) or through asset ownership patterns that are linked to structure. For example, if small farms face a relatively lower cost of owning than of renting farm land, then policies that benefit firms that own rather than rent also benefit small farms in relation to large farms.

Price and Income Variability. Programs are often assumed to affect farm structure indirectly by reducing the riskiness of farming. For example, Spitze et al. state that "it is generally agreed that price supports, when effective, reduce price and income uncertainty."[9] They then proceed to examine the potential effects of reduced uncertainty on farm organization and operation. These include less diversification, ex post mistakes, and less borrowing. They assert that these factors help larger farms. The basic reasoning has two steps: (1) price supports reduce risk over the relevant range of the horizon for investment decisions; (2) lower risks allow some farms to acquire the borrowed capital to expand, small farms to be sold, and large farms to grow even faster. Johnson, Ericksen, Sharples, and Harrington also see risk as leading to larger farms and cite this increased size as a standard result.[10] More new technology, more specialization, and more outside credit are all attributable to price supports and associated programs. But Lin et al. argue that large farms are more vulnerable to price risk than small farms because they have higher ratios of debt to equity and of cash costs to total revenues.[11] Recent analysis from the economists at the U.S Department of Agriculture (Harrington, Reimund, Baum, and Peterson) has considered the effect of the commodity programs in the context of simulations of representative farms.[12] These simulations showed huge falls in real net worth (even with the programs) over the period of the simulations using the base-case scenario. But the net worth of farmers falls without price supports, especially for the most supported crops and for the farms with lower equity. The authors emphasize the role of variability of prices and income in determining the structure of farming. In the

288

context of naturally unstable prices, they see the commodity programs as having three basic effects in various subsectors of agriculture: the programs stimulated growth and consolidation by allowing farmers to face less risk and therefore have access to more debt at lower market interest rates because the government assumes some of the risk; they reduced the proportion of forced sales of farm land by eliminating the lower tail of the commodity price distribution; and (combined with the first two effects) they encouraged high and rising land prices, increased the mean of farm prices, and also directly increased the rental rate on farm land and the capital value of farm assets.

The reasoning behind the so-called risk effects may be flawed, however. Many farm decisions, especially those that affect structure, have several-year horizons. For these decisions—say, leasing additional land, adding to the dairy herd, or borrowing for machinery investments—the relevant price or income risk is not year-to-year variability over (for example) the four years of a farm bill. The horizon may more realistically be a decade or more.

The major risk facing a farmer making structural investments is that the long-term price path or income path may make a discrete change or fall more quickly than anticipated. This is just the sort of risk that farm programs do not address. Price supports and associated policies can smooth out short-run movements in prices, but they can do little to alter long-term trends or changes in underlying supply or demand conditions.

The recent history of commodity programs is ample testimony to the stress that changes in economic conditions can place on farm programs. Budget costs have risen, export markets have been lost, and many poorly planned policy changes have taken place. It can be argued that farm policies have encouraged inappropriate expectations and slowed market adjustments. It may just be too difficult to make consistent policy in an inconstant world. Thus the programs may have added an element of risk.

Commodity programs also affect the distributions of prices among farms. Price differences among farmers may in turn have a significant effect on the distributions of size and structure. Consider a program that offers a guaranteed price to all producers of some commodity. This program reduces the differences of output price among these farmers and thus provides additional benefit to those who would otherwise get lower prices for their output. If output differences among farms are due (in part) to differences in the price received, reducing price differences would reduce output or size differences.

In some farm industries farmers must search for the market for their output. Some of the advantages of good management derive from success at selling for above-average prices. Even competitive markets have some differences in price that allow the astute manager to gain from the careful and rapid gathering and processing of information. In these industries good marketers will operate larger firms. Federal dairy policy, for example, provides for blend prices and order-wide pooling. This may reduce year-to-year variability, but it also reduces the gains to the best, or most lucky, price searchers.

The implication is that commodity programs may have more effect on higher moments of the distributions of structural characteristics than on their central tendencies. The commodity programs may benefit farmers less able to cope with market variability and more willing to accept potential program changes. Year-to-year price variability may be reduced, but variation among program participants is also reduced.

Costs of Production and Returns to Farming. In 1981 Miller et al. reported that for field crops, "as farm size increases, per unit costs decline at first and then are constant over a wide range of sizes" and that "further growth . . . will not likely improve . . . production efficiency." They also note that "farmers tend to enlarge their operations in search of higher incomes" and that with only minor size economies, "society can consider many issues related to farm size separate from questions of [farm produce] costs." They distinguish between two sources of farm growth: increases in farm size that lower operating costs per unit of output and keep the farm in business or make it more efficient and increases in size that just allow more total profits, thereby increasing the income of the farmer.[13] This distinction is, at the very least, misleading. The problem is in the definition of opportunity costs. If we allow that farming is a competitive industry, it "purchases" farmers in an essentially competitive market of occupational choice. The returns to farm operators are those necessary to keep agriculture a healthy sector of the economy.

Particularly good managers will operate larger farms and make more income as a return on their superior skills. Without this higher income, however, these people would often not be farming at all.

From the view of the industry, farm operators are a productive input that must be attracted from other occupations. To have an input used in farming, factor payments must be attractive. This is true for land, operating capital, and farm operators.

Consider the effect of policies that penalize large farms in relation to small farms. To take an extreme case, consider a policy that held that Corn Belt grain farms could not have more than $140,000 in gross income in 1981. This amount is large enough to exhaust all the economies of size found by Miller et al. These economies, however, include returns to operator talent as a fixed cost after imputing a cost to the labor use of the farm. When farm operators are mobile in and out of farming, farmer talent is a partially variable input to the farming sector.

Policies that attempt to restrict farm growth are not a free lunch even if economies of size are unimportant. At best such policies encourage a reallocation of management talent, with managers less able to operate larger farms (or with lower off-farm opportunities) replacing effective managers of large operations who are attracted out of farming. If the policy is binding, it means that

290

the aggregate marginal cost or supply curves of farm output will generally shift up. Farm output is then more expensive. Only if no large farm operators move out of farming would output prices remain unchanged.

Evidence on Structure and Commodity Programs

Empirical analysis of the effect of the commodity programs on the structure of agriculture requires considerable caution. First, by all accounts the effects are mostly indirect and may be small over some intermediate term. Econometric work often has a difficult time capturing even large effects; so separating the effects of the programs from other influences on structure is not easy. Program changes over time or program differences among similar commodities or among states are required to see variation in the explanatory variable. The problem is that other factors are expected to have a more direct influence than policy variables.

To test hypotheses directly or even to illustrate the implications of programs for structure requires a search for data that contain both variation in structural variables and variations in farm programs while other factors do not change. Such conclusive natural experiments have not been found.

The Sales Distribution over Time. The number of farms has been falling for fifty years while the distribution of farms by size (by any measure) has been shifting up. Table 1 summarizes some evidence on sales classes for the past two decades (unadjusted for inflation). The number of farms has fallen by about 50 percent during this period.

In 1982 about 5 percent of the farms, with about half the gross receipts, had sales over $200,000; 1 percent of the farms, with 30 percent of the receipts, had sales over $500,000. About one-quarter of all farms had sales between $40,000 and $200,000 and about 40 percent of all cash receipts. The smallest 70 percent of the farms sold less than $40,000 each and accounted for about 12 percent of all sales.

Government payments follow the distribution of farm numbers and gross receipts. Because the largest farms tend to produce commodities without significant direct payments, the over $500,000 class accounted for only 7 percent of payments and less than $10,000 per farm. The $100,000–200,000 class received a slightly higher percentage of payments than of receipts; that was also true in 1978. All the smaller categories received higher shares of payments than of cash receipts.

Table 2 allows a comparison between sales categories adjusted for price levels in 1969 and in 1978.[14] Since farm output prices approximately doubled during this decade, 1969 categories were adjusted accordingly. To create comparable sales categories, some different grouping was done than in table 1. The $40,000–199,000 category includes the $20,000–39,000 and the

TABLE 1

NUMBER AND PROPORTION OF FARMS BY SALES CLASS AND DISTRIBUTION
OF CASH RECEIPTS AND GOVERNMENT PAYMENTS, 1965–1982

				Sales Class ($000s)			
	500+	200–499	100–199	40–99	20–39	10–19	<10
1965							
Number (000s)	n.a.	n.a.	36[a]	125	280	464	2,451
% of farms	n.a.	n.a.	1.1[a]	3.7	8.4	13.8	73.0
% of receipts	n.a.	n.a.	24.6[a]	18.7	20.1	17.7	18.9
Receipts per farm ($000s)	n.a.	n.a.	288.1[a]	63.1	30.2	16.1	5.7
% of government payments	n.a.	n.a.	6.0[a]	12.6	19.8	25.4	36.2
Government payments per farm ($000s)	n.a.	n.a.	4.1[a]	2.5	1.7	1.4	0.4
1969							
Number (000s)	4	11	32	155	304	369	2,125
% of farms	0.1	0.4	1.1	5.2	10.1	12.3	70.8
% of receipts	13.8	7.5	9.8	21.2	20.2	13.0	14.5
Receipts per farm ($000s)	1,953.0	339.9	160.2	72.0	34.8	18.5	3.6
% of government payments	3.0	3.3	6.5	18.3	22.7	18.7	27.5
Government payments per farm ($000s)	30.7	11.0	7.6	4.5	2.8	1.9	0.5
1975							
Number (000s)	11	38	96	316	315	314	1,431
% of farms	0.4	1.5	3.8	12.5	12.5	12.5	56.8
% of receipts	22.0	14.0	16.5	24.8	11.4	5.7	5.6
Receipts per farm ($000s)	1,825.2	330.7	155.7	71.2	32.9	16.5	11.4
% of government payments	7.0	7.9	13.0	28.6	17.3	10.1	16.1
Government payments per farm ($000s)	5.2	1.7	1.1	0.7	0.4	0.3	0.1
1978							
Number (000s)	17	60	135	347	292	295	1,290
% of farms	0.7	2.5	5.5	14.2	12.0	12.1	53.0
% of receipts	26.6	16.8	18.1	21.8	8.3	4.2	4.2
Receipts per farm ($000s)	1,817.1	328.1	156.4	73.6	33.4	16.6	14.1

TABLE 1 (continued)

	Sales Class ($000s)						
	500 +	200 – 499	100 – 199	40 – 99	20 – 39	10 – 19	< 10
% of government payments	5.7	12.5	19.8	34.9	13.1	5.3	8.7
Government payments per farm ($000s)	10.1	6.3	4.4	3.1	1.4	0.5	0.2
1982							
Number (000s)	25	87	186	393	273	281	1,155
% of farms	1.0	3.6	7.7	16.4	11.4	11.7	48.2
% of receipts	30.1	19.0	19.3	19.2	6.1	3.1	3.2
Receipts per farm ($000s)	1,804.6	326.4	155.7	73.4	33.4	16.6	19.2
% of government payments	7.0	15.2	22.9	33.2	10.3	4.2	7.2
Government payments per farm ($000s)	9.8	6.1	4.3	3.0	1.3	0.5	0.2

n.a. = not available.
a. $100,000 and over.

SOURCE: U.S. Department of Agriculture, Economic Research Service, *Economic Indicators of the Farm Sector: Income and Balance Sheet Statistics, 1982* (Washington, D.C., 1983).

$40,000–100,000 categories in 1969 dollars. It includes the $100,000–200,000 and the $100,000–200,000 categories in 1978.

During the 1970s the number of farms producing over $200,000 in 1978 dollars rose by more than 60 percent. The number producing between $40,000 and $200,000 remained about the same while the other numbers fell. This group of middle-sized farms received over half the direct payments in 1978 and about 40 percent in 1969. They thus increased their share of government payments by fifteen percentage points while holding steady—at about 40 percent—their share of cash receipts.

In 1965 farm output prices were about 40 percent of 1982 prices. Therefore we can compare $40,000 sales at 1965 prices with $100,000 sales at 1982 prices. Between 1965 and 1982 the number of farms selling over $100,000 (in 1982 prices) rose from 160,000 to about 300,000. The percentage of farms rose from 5 percent to 12 percent, and the share of receipts rose from 43 percent to 68 percent. Between these years the share of government payments rose from about 20 percent to 45 percent while payments per farm fell from

TABLE 2

NUMBER AND PROPORTION OF FARMS BY SALES CLASS AND DISTRIBUTION
OF CASH RECEIPTS AND GOVERNMENT PAYMENTS, REAL 1978 DOLLAR
VALUES, 1969 AND 1978

	Sales Class ($000s)				
	200+	40–199	20–39	10–19	< 10
1969					
Number of farms (000s)	47	467	362	372	1,695
% of farms	1.6	15.3	12.3	12.7	58.1
% of receipts	31.1	41.2	13.0	6.8	7.7
Receipts per farm ($000s)	695	93	37	19	5
% of government payments	12.8	41.0	18.7	11.1	16.4
Government payments per farm ($000s)	10.3	3.3	1.9	1.4	0.7
1978					
Number of farms (000s)	77	482	292	295	1,290
% of farms	3.2	19.7	12.0	12.1	53.0
% of receipts	43.3	39.9	8.3	4.2	4.2
Receipts per farm ($000s)	660	97	33	17	4
% of government payments	18.2	54.7	13.1	5.3	8.7
Government payments per farm ($000s)	7.1	3.4	1.4	0.5	0.2

SOURCE: Based on table 1, with 1969 prices received by farms equal to 0.5 prices received in 1978.

$7,000 to $5,000 (in 1982 prices). Farms have been growing in size in the past two decades, but there is no indication that government payments are fundamental to this growth.[15]

The Potential for Emergence of a Bimodal Distribution of Farm Structure. Among the influential "stylized facts" about the structure of agriculture is the supposed emergence of a bimodal distribution of farm size and structure. The stylized fact has been stated in several forms. For example, Tweeten states that "the farming industry is gradually evolving into a dual economy. The commercial sector is comprised of a few large industrialized farms which account for most farm output. The non-commercial sector, comprised mostly of small part-time operators, accounts for a minor portion of farm output but for most farms in number."[16]

We clearly do not yet have a dichotomy based on sales. Let the approximately 1.4 million farms with less than $20,000 sales in 1982 be the category of noncommercial farms. They accounted for less than 10 percent of all sales and about 60 percent of all farms (table 1). The "few" commercial farms constitute the remaining 1 million farms, which produce close to 95 percent of all output. This second category does not contain a few farms by any useful criterion. Further, if we use sales as the horizontal axis in the histogram or frequency table, we note that these two categories are not separated. (It is difficult to build up a histogram using published data from the Agriculture Department or the Census Bureau because the sales categories do not have equal sales differences.) There are more farmers in the smallest equal-sized commercial category ($20,000–40,000) than in other equal-sized sales category groups (say $120,000–140,000). This distribution is thus not bimodal; it is unimodal but strongly skewed.

The notion of the "vanishing" middle derives from the following underlying "observations," which are partially true and partially mistaken:

• Small farms—those that are part-time in that the operator and possibly other earners make essentially full-time salaries at nonfarm occupations—are not significantly hurt by lack of farm profitability. A mistaken idea is that the number of these farms is holding steady or falling slowly and is rising in relation to "commercial" farms.

• Large farms—those that generate enough cash flow and returns that they support several families of owners or managers—have succeeded and will continue to succeed in spite of the failures of government programs and economic problems in farming. The number of these farms will continue to grow slowly or remain constant as they acquire resources from middle-sized farms.

• The assumed decline in the middle-sized farms, essentially full-time businesses run by owner-operators who provide management and some physical labor, is based on the assertion that they are being outcompeted by the more efficient large farms. It is assumed that as a group these farms cannot generate high enough returns to farmers' time and talent to allow them to attract and keep farm operators from other occupations. The number of these farms falls as they sell or lease land to large farms and as the operators take full- or part-time jobs out of farming. Few of these farms will "grow" into large farms.

A finding that large and small farms were more successful than middle-sized farms would mean that an evolution to a bimodal distribution is under way. The sales facts in table 2 do not support these notions, for several reasons. First, the sales distribution of farms operated part-time has considerable variance and is strongly skewed to the right. The mean sales by these part-time farms have been shifting up. This means that there will be no clean

295

break between small and middle-sized farms. Second, family farms have been growing. The ratio of net farm income to gross farm income has been falling dramatically as purchased inputs have replaced farm-supplied inputs. In the late 1940s and early 1950s, net farm income was approximately 40 percent of gross farm income. It fell gradually until the late 1970s and early 1980s, when it fell below 20 percent. Thus the gross sales needed to maintain a constant net income have doubled in thirty years. In addition, the net farm income necessary to compete with off-farm occupations has risen in real terms, and farm output prices have fallen in relation to the consumer price index. The result is that for a net income of $30,000 from farm operations, the average farmer must generate sales of at least $150,000 during the recent period.[17]

The Distribution of Production and Government Payments among States and Commodities. It is well known that commodity programs affect some segments of agriculture and neglect others. The amount of government payments is not a sufficient statistic to reveal the effects of farm programs on a region or commodity, but government budget costs have become an important factor in the discussions of farm programs.

Measured by cash receipts from marketings, California is the largest agricultural producer in the country, with an average of close to $14 billion of output per year from 1979 to 1982. Iowa and Texas rank next, producing about $10 billion. Illinois, Minnesota, and Nebraska produce about $7 billion. The differences among states in direct government payments in relation to cash receipts are dramatic. In 1982 Texas received 18 percent of the payments while Kansas and Nebraska each received 8 percent. California farmers received 4 percent of the payments although they generated 10 percent of all farm marketings while Texas generated 7 percent. Texas leads in government payments, averaging close to $400 million per year during the period 1979 through 1982. During this period the plains states (including Kansas, Nebraska, North and South Dakota, and Oklahoma) were major recipients of government payments. Iowa, Illinois, and Minnesota, all Corn Belt states, also received significant payments.

The geographic pattern of government payments follows from the geographic pattern of production of specific commodities, the pattern of government commodity programs, and the pattern of participation in the programs. The cotton, wheat, and feed grain programs have long accounted for the majority of direct payments from farm programs. The tobacco, dairy, and certain other programs have tended to raise market prices without significant direct payments to producers. California agriculture has relied relatively less on feed grains and wheat than the midwestern states and has had low participation rates. The fruit, vegetable, egg, milk, and beef industries either have not had federal commodity programs or (like milk) have not had direct payments. Texas has been a major producer of each of the three commodities with large

296

TABLE 3

DISTRIBUTION OF CASH RECEIPTS AMONG COMMODITIES, 1952-1982

	Livestock		Crops					
	Dairy	Other	Food grains	Feed crops	Cotton	Tobacco	Other crops	Total
1952								
Millions of dollars	4.6	13.6	2.6	2.3	2.9	1.1	5.4	32.5
Percentage of total	14	42	8	7	9	3	17	100
1962								
Millions of dollars	4.9	15.3	2.5	3.0	2.6	1.3	6.9	36.5
Percentage of total	13	42	7	8	7	4	19	100
1972								
Millions of dollars	7.1	28.5	3.5	5.9	1.8	1.4	13.0	61.1
Percentage of total	12	47	6	10	3	2	21	100
1982								
Millions of dollars	18.4	51.8	11.5	18.2	4.9	3.3	36.5	144.6
Percentage of total	13	36	8	13	3	2	25	100

SOURCE: Agriculture Department, *Economic Indicators.*

payments, and Texas producers—like others in the plains states—have had high participation rates.

In 1982 the total value of farm marketings was about $145 billion (table 3). About half of this was for livestock output, where only the dairy industry, which produced about $18 billion, has a major program. Of the $75 billion of crop production, corn, wheat, cotton, and tobacco were the largest commodities with effective programs. Vegetables, fruits, and soybeans are the major

297

TABLE 4
FARM LAND TENURE, BY STATES, 1974–1982
(percent)

	Full Owner	Part Owner	Tenant
California			
1974	70	18	12
1978	71	17	12
1982	73	15	11
Iowa			
1974	51	29	20
1978	48	29	23
1982	46	33	21
North Carolina			
1974	62	25	12
1978	54	32	14
1982	56	32	12
Texas			
1974	59	27	14
1978	57	29	14
1982	60	27	13
Wisconsin			
1974	68	26	6
1978	62	31	7
1982	59	32	9

SOURCE: *U.S. Census of Agriculture*, various years.

crops without commodity programs that generate direct payments of changes in market price. Overall, the dairy industry, with a total of about 50 percent of crop output (and about one-fourth of livestock output), is covered by the effective commodity programs.

The program benefits may vary with market conditions and policy changes. In 1978, for example, 39 percent of direct program payments went to the feed grain program and another 32 percent to the wheat program. Cotton accounted for only 4 percent of payments. In 1982, however, 20 percent went to feed grains, 19 percent to wheat, and 23 percent to cotton. Of course, direct payments are only one measure of programs' effects. Tobacco quota owners, for example, benefit by about $800 million per year from the quota program even though direct payments are zero. Beef producers are protected by import restrictions, although feed grain programs increase the prices they pay; and dairy and sugar prices are held up by quotas on imports.

The pattern of government payments not only depends on the geographic distribution of production but also affects that distribution. Without the availability of program payments, the pattern of cotton, wheat, and feed grain production would probably be different. It is a difficult task, however, and beyond the scope of this paper to attempt to project a geographic structure of production without the programs.

The shares of major commodities have changed somewhat over time. Feed grain production has gained while cotton has lost an equal amount. In 1982 crops other than those with the major commodity programs gained up to 25 percent of all sales, and livestock sales (other than dairy) lost.

Land Tenure. Farms in the United States combine inputs from many sectors. Farmers do not typically produce the inputs they use. Increasing proportions even of labor and land are acquired in the "rental" market. Farmers who own all the land that they operate tend to be smaller, and they are a falling proportion of all farms in Iowa, Wisconsin, and North Carolina (table 4). To expand farms, operators rent land and buy other inputs from off the farm. The land ownership pattern varies somewhat among states, but no particular relationship with commodity programs is evident from the distribution by state or by commodity.

Farm Programs, Characteristics of Farmers, and Off-Farm Employment

Schooling and Age Patterns. Table 5 shows the age and education distributions of farmers in 1978. Most farmers are middle-aged, and most are high school graduates. Younger farmers are much better educated than older farmers; almost half of those under thirty-five have post–high school training, compared with about 30 percent of those over thirty-five. Only 10 percent of young farmers did not complete high school, compared with over 40 percent of those over sixty-five.

Farmers with less than high school educations generally operate small farms, although the available categories from the census do not allow detailed sales breakdowns for higher sales levels (table 6). Part-time farming is significant for those with higher education, but they still tend to have more gross sales per farm. Farm programs will be better understood by farmers with more education and experience, but they may also be better able to manage without the wealth transfers the commodity programs entail.

Off-Farm Work. Off-farm employment may be subdivided into seasonal

TABLE 5

EDUCATION OF FARMERS BY AGE GROUP, 1978

(percent)

Education	<35 Years	35–64 Years	65+ Years	Total
Not high school graduate	6.9	82.1	11.0	100.0
	10.5	31.4	42.8	28.3
High school	20.0	75.0	5.1	100.0
	41.4	39.2	27.1	38.7
Higher education	27.3	66.1	6.6	100.0
	48.1	29.4	30.1	32.9
Total	18.7	74.1	7.3	100.0
	100.0	100.0	100.0	100.0

NOTE: The upper entries of each pair read across, the lower entries down.

SOURCE: *U.S. Census of Agriculture* (Washington, D.C., 1978).

TABLE 6

VALUE OF AGRICULTURAL PRODUCTS SOLD, BY EDUCATION OF FARM

OPERATOR, 1978

(percent)

Education	<$20,000	$20,000–39,999	$40,000 or more	Total
Not high school graduate	80.4	8.9	10.9	100.0
	31.7	24.7	16.9	28.3
High school	68.1	10.9	21.0	100.0
	36.8	42.1	44.7	38.7
Higher education	68.7	10.1	21.2	100.0
	31.5	33.2	38.4	33.0
Total	71.8	10.0	18.2	100.0
	100.0	100.0	100.0	100.0

NOTE: Differs from schooling distribution in table 5 because of nonreporting. The upper entries of each pair read across, the lower entries down.

SOURCE: *Census of Agriculture*, 1978.

jobs, part-time year-round jobs, and full-time jobs. Seasonal off-farm work is strongly affected by the seasonal pattern of the commodities that have a comparative advantage on each farm, but the availability of seasonal off-farm jobs also affects the farm activities that are undertaken. Part-time year-round work supplements work on farms that do not make full use of the farmers' time or talents. A farmer may be diversifying his earning sources, or he may not find it profitable to operate a farm large enough to offer himself full-time employment. Farmers with little access to capital, little managerial expertise, or particularly good off-farm opportunities may find part-time off-farm work an optimal allocation of time. Most farmers who work off the farm find that their relative potential earnings make off-farm occupations more attractive as a full-time activity. These farmers are "part-time on the farm" and full-time off it. Many occupations offer only full-time jobs or significantly higher wages for full-time work. Farms may be established around the full-time off-farm job so that the major activities may be carried out either on weekends or after work. Some part-time farmers hire on-farm workers to leave their own time available for work off the farm.

In the United States in recent years, over one-half of all farmers work off the farm, and a little over half declare something other than farming as their principal occupation. According to census data, close to 90 percent of those without off-farm work say that their principal occupation is farming, while over 90 percent of those working 200 days or more per year off the farm declare that something other than farming is their principal occupation. Off-farm work itself is bimodal, with about 35 percent of all farmers working more than 200 days off their farms. About 10 percent each are in the intermediate categories of 1–99 days and 100–199 days of work off the farm per year. Off-farm work increased only slightly between 1969 and 1978. The data for major farm states and commodities indicate little change between the 1978 and the 1982 censuses of agriculture.

Table 7 describes patterns of off-farm work in the United States by farm type. In 1978 about half of all cash grain farmers and about 75 percent of all dairy farmers reported that they did not work off the farm. Less than 10 percent of the dairy farmers reported more than 200 days off the farm, compared with 30 percent for the grain farmers. Only a third of the cotton farmers worked off the farm, but most of those worked full-time off their farms. In 1978 tobacco farmers were most likely to work off the farm and had off-farm work patterns similar to those of the cash grain farms in both 1969 and 1978.

The 1982 patterns by state tell much the same story as those by commodity. In Iowa, for example, 46 percent of all farmers—but only 25 percent of dairy farmers—worked off the farm. In California 62 percent of all farmers and only 16 percent of dairy farmers worked off their farms. The pattern in North Carolina was very similar to that in California. In these states 57 percent of all farmers and only 18 percent of the dairy farmers worked off the farm.

TABLE 7

OFF-FARM WORK, BY FARM TYPE, 1969 AND 1978

(percent)

Days Worked Off Farm	Cash Grain	Tobacco	Cotton	Dairy
None				
1978	46.8	40.0	67.9	74.5
1969	55.5	57.7	68.5	69.5
1–99 days				
1978	14.9	12.7	9.9	13.4
1969	18.1	13.9	15.0	15.0
100–199 days				
1978	8.2	12.2	3.4	4.2
1969	7.7	8.8	5.2	4.3
200 days and over				
1978	30.2	35.0	18.9	7.9
1969	18.7	19.7	11.4	11.2

SOURCE: *U.S. Census of Agriculture* (Washington, D.C., 1969, 1978).

The Effects of Programs on Farming as a Part-Time Job. Off-farm work patterns indicate the suitability of farming as a moonlighting occupation. About one-third of all farmers spend over 200 days at another occupation. Significantly higher proportions of farmers than of other workers combine more than one occupation. Farming as self-employment allows flexibility that may be difficult to arrange for employees. Further, part-time wage jobs tend to pay less per hour after standardizing for workers' characteristics.

Some farm types strongly discourage this part-time involvement. Chief among these are dairy farms, which have the lowest incidence of full-time off-farm work. Farm programs that require large time investments to understand will discourage the part-time farmer from participating. Farm types that can be maintained with just a few hours per week for most of the year and that do not have great economies of total size offer the best opportunities for part-time farming. Further, tax advantages may be associated with part-time farming for high nonfarm earners.

Commodity programs have only a minor influence on the long-term propensity of a worker to farm part-time. By increasing output and input prices and asset values, they make the total cash flow in farming higher but do not directly affect the complementarity with off-farm work. This major phenomenon of the structure of agriculture in the United States seems to lie mostly outside the influence of the commodity programs. No major effect of the programs across commodities is noticeable in the data. Part-time farming occurs across the country and also across commodity lines irrespective of the effect of programs. Participation in programs is also about the same on full-time and part-time farms.

The Effects of Programs on Moonlighting off the Farm. "Full-time" farmers who do some work off the farm make up the second category of off-farm work by farmers. Of those that are principally farmers, about 30 percent work part-time off the farm. Spouses and other family members are likely to have other employment as well.

Off-farm work by farmers depends partly on the characteristics of farms and farmers. Among the factors that contribute to moonlighting off the farms are the seasonality of the demand for farm labor, the seasonal variability of farm income, the year-to-year variability of farm income, the year-to-year variability of the demand for farm labor, the uncertainty of returns to farm investments, the diminishing returns to farm labor or management given limitations on invested capital or specific managerial talent, and the adjustment costs entailed in expanding or reducing farm activities.

Commodity programs may reduce the year-to-year variability of farming. If they do, the incentive for off-farm work to benefit from diversification of income sources is reduced, and the gains from off-farm work are reduced. Higher costs of farm land due to the capitalized value of price supports could also encourage part-time off-farm work to help finance farm expansion. Each of these factors may be related to farm commodity programs, but the linkage is not direct.

The Effect of Commodity Programs on Structure in Specific Industries

Two general issues have directed the early discussions of the 1985 farm bill: government budget costs and international competitiveness. The programs for the major field crops—wheat, corn, and cotton—have been plagued by both significant costs to the taxpayers and prices that reduce international competitiveness.

Two other major programs avoid one of the two problems faced by the wheat, corn, and cotton industries. The dairy industry has successfully kept imports out and has not been a major exporting industry. The dairy program has also kept domestic prices above world market levels but has recently been costly for taxpayers. The tobacco program has long avoided significant budget costs by operating a largely self-financing cartel, but increased imports and reduced exports have troubled the industry recently.

In this section the relationship between the commodity programs and the structural variables is examined for each of these industries. These case studies allow some judgments across a variety of regional areas, program types, and industry structures.

The Effect of Programs for Food and Feed Grains. The programs for the grains are the most important of all U.S. crop programs. They affect a large group of geographically and economically diverse farmers. Wheat and corn programs are used here as representative of the policies affecting the grains. Since these programs are voluntary, participation affects the distribution of effects. They have recently consisted of several major instruments: (1) price supports with nonrecourse loans; (2) a farmer-owned reserve, with payments for storage and low-interest-rate loans; (3) target prices, with deficiency payments to producers based on the differences between target prices and market prices; (4) the setting aside of acreage, crop-specific acreage reductions, and paid acreage diversion contracts to control output; and (5) disaster payments for loss in output from natural or economic emergency (this program was limited to producers without access to federal crop insurance).

The provisions of the policies are on a per acre or per output unit basis. Thus their direct effect depends on differential participation and is directly neutral with respect to size or structure within these commodities. Payment limits have not been effective. The effects on structure follow from effects on diversification, returns to assets, ownership, location, or other characteristics of the farm or farmer.

Wheat. Wheat production occurs across the nation, but about two-thirds of the acreage is in the great plains from Montana to Texas. Wheat is the major crop on many farms in the plains and in the Northwest and is a supplementary crop on many other farms. Moreover, double cropping of wheat with soybeans is an important and expanding pattern in the South.

Participation rates in the wheat program differ among regions, with participation rates higher in the plains than in the other regions. In 1978 over 80 percent of wheat acreage in the plains participated. The South has smaller wheat acreage per farm than other regions and also has the lowest program participation rates. Less than 20 percent of the southern base acreage participated in 1982, compared with 56 percent participation in the plains.[18]

Table 8, adapted from Johnson and Short, shows structural information about farm size on participating and nonparticipating wheat farms in 1978.[19] In most states participating farms are larger in wheat acreage, harvested cropland, and grain sales. In North Dakota participants and nonparticipants are quite similar. In several states participants grow more wheat but have lower total farm sales.

304

TABLE 8

SIZE AND STRUCTURE OF WHEAT-PRODUCING FARMS, SELECTED STATES, BY
PROGRAM PARTICIPANTS AND NONPARTICIPANTS, 1978

| | Wheat | | Average Sales ($ thousands) | | |
| | Acreage | Harvested cropland | | | |
States	(average)		Grain	Livestock	Total
Kansas					
Participating	219	372	26.3	31.5	59.3
Nonparticipating	182	329	23.3	32.7	57.5
Minnesota					
Participating	127	404	38.1	15.3	59.7
Nonparticipating	80	306	29.9	20.4	54.9
North Dakota					
Participating	275	524	31.2	11.2	47.6
Nonparticipating	292	534	32.8	11.1	49.1
Oklahoma					
Participating	253	339	18.1	28.8	53.0
Nonparticipating	178	258	13.7	22.1	40.6
Washington					
Participating	565	563	79.4	10.0	107.5
Nonparticipating	350	542	59.0	25.4	137.1

SOURCE: Johnson and Short, "Commodity Programs."

A national crop acreage distribution, derived from 1978 census data and published by Johnson and Short, shows that about half the production for participants and 45 percent for nonparticipants is from farms of more than 1,000 acres of cropland.[20] At the lower end, 7 percent of participants' output and 15 percent of nonparticipants' output is from farms with less than 250 acres. Over half the nonparticipants and 31 percent of the participants operate these smaller farms.

These statistics indicate that wheat program participants operate larger farms that may be somewhat less diversified than those of participants. Further, the state totals indicate that the differences between the two groups is not due solely to the geographic distribution.

Wheat programs have raised the direct receipts of wheat producers as well as the price of wheat. This connection between programs and price increases is especially obvious if target prices are considered the effective supply price. Participants received significant deficiency payments of over $400 million in 1981 and 1982; so the target price has been effective. Disaster payments were in the range of $200 million in 1980 and 1981, and payments through the farmer-owned reserve grew from $75 million to close to $300 million from 1980 to 1982. Overall these payments were close to $800 million or $0.28 per bushel in 1978, 1981, and 1982, using figures from the Agriculture Department.[21] These payments affect size and structure, as producers differ in their propensity to participate in the program or as the indirect effects of the program affect producers differently. Of course, since restriction of supply increases the market price, nonparticipants are also affected by wheat programs.

Variability in wheat yield is high in nonirrigated regions, but because wheat is widely dispersed geographically, national yields have been more stable than regional yields. The coefficient of variation (C.V.) of real price deviation from trend has been about 18 percent in the past three decades; the C.V. of yield deviations from trend has been about 17 percent in the same period, and that of production about 30 percent. The programs may have dampened this variation, but it has still been substantial. The program has also added an element of policy risk to the variability faced by wheat producers. Changes in wheat policy have occurred with each farm bill and sometimes more often.

Corn. Corn production in the United States is centered in the north-central region, which produces about two-thirds of the acreage. The other important production regions are the plains and the South. About half the corn enterprises are small (less than 50 acres), and over 25 percent of the production occurs on farms with less than 100 acres of corn.

Participation in corn programs has been attractive to farmers with a small share of the nation's corn acreage (less than 30 percent of the national base participated in 1982). The plains states led in participation rate with 46 percent of the acreage enrolled, compared with 27 percent in the north-central and only 10 percent in the South.[22]

Table 9 shows that participants operate larger corn enterprises, have more cropland, and sell more grain than nonparticipants in all the states included. In Iowa and Nebraska, however, higher livestock sales by nonparticipants make average total sales larger on the nonparticipating farms.

Nationally, participating corn farms are much more likely than nonparticipants to have large crop acreage. About half the participants but over 70 percent of the nonparticipants have less than 100 acres of cropland. These small farms account for 20 percent of the production of participating farms and 30 percent of the production of nonparticipants. At the upper end, the 20 percent that have over 500 acres produce half the output of participants.

TABLE 9

SIZE AND STRUCTURE OF CORN-PRODUCING FARMS, SELECTED STATES, BY
PROGRAM PARTICIPANTS AND NONPARTICIPANTS, 1978

| | Corn | | Average Sales ($ thousands) | | |
| | Acreage | Harvested cropland | | | |
States	(average)		Grain	Livestock	Total
California					
Participating	203	1,112	187.7	155.2	527.8
Nonparticipating	82	427	45.6	208.5	371.0
Illinois					
Participating	148	295	46.7	23.8	71.4
Nonparticipating	138	259	43.5	21.4	65.7
Iowa					
Participating	135	243	31.3	40.0	72.5
Nonparticipating	124	211	26.8	48.6	76.0
Nebraska					
Participating	178	328	39.9	49.5	90.9
Nonparticipating	148	284	28.0	80.5	111.4
Ohio					
Participating	75	195	25.8	19.8	47.6
Nonparticipating	62	152	20.1	18.0	39.8

SOURCE: Johnson and Short, "Commodity Programs."

Among nonparticipants 9 percent have over 500 acres; they produce 40 percent of the sales of this group.

Corn farms tend to be diverse. Many produce soybeans along with corn, and about 44 percent were classified as cash grain farms in 1978. About 29 percent are primarily livestock farms, 13 percent are dairy farms, and 7 percent are primarily producers of other field crops. In the South tobacco, cotton, and peanuts are major crops grown with corn.

The effect of the corn program on structure is indirect. The price support system may allow less diversification and more production in marginal regions. Since program returns are capitalized into land prices and since rents reflect those prices, landowners would suffer a loss from having no program. The potential changes in the program may encourage some diversification in asset holding and more part ownership and tenancy.

The Effect of Cotton Programs on the Structure of the Cotton Industry.
Cotton programs in the United States have a history similar to those of the
other major commodities.[23] The program has evolved away from acreage
allotments and price supports to a standard program including a loan rate (set
at low price support levels), a target price with associated deficiency payments, acreage reductions for program eligibility, and disaster payments and
crop insurance. No farmer-owned reserve is available. In both the early 1970s
and the early 1980s, direct government payments to cotton producers made up
a significant share of producers' revenue. From 1974 through 1980 these
payments ranged from 2 to 7 percent of total income. In 1982 they rose to 16
percent before jumping to about 40 percent with the 1983 payment-in-kind
(PIK) program. Disaster payments have been made to participating producers
in each year since they were instituted.

Cotton production is spread across the southern part of the United States,
with the Mississippi delta, the southern plains, and the far West being the
major producing areas, each with about 30 percent of national production.
The size of cotton enterprises as well as other structural characteristics varies
among regions. Yields are low in Oklahoma and Texas, high in the irrigated
West, and about the national average in the Southeast and delta regions. The
number of farms harvesting cotton has fallen dramatically while production
has shown no particular trend since the late 1960s.[5] The share of national farm
sales from cotton has fallen from 9 to 3 percent. Cotton acreage per farm that
produces cotton has just about doubled since the early 1970s, and yields have
risen. Texas has the most cotton producers—about 23,000 in 1978—and had
280 acres per farm. California had some 4,000 producers in 1978, close to
400 acres per producer, and three times the yield of Texas cotton farms.
Nationally the number of farms growing cotton fell from 200,000 to 38,000 in
the thirteen years from 1969 to 1982. Most of the remaining farms get over
half their gross income from cotton sales.

Participation in the cotton program has varied over time and also varies
significantly by region. Payments, therefore, though proportional to production for participants, are not necessarily proportional to overall production. In
1984 participating farms constituted about 70 percent of the national acreage
base but over 80 percent of Taxes acreage and about 30 percent of California
acreage. Smaller farms are more likely to participate, and high-yielding irrigated farms of the West are less likely to do so. Almost all plains cotton
producers participated in the program in 1978, and 61 percent of western
cotton acreage was enrolled. Table 10 shows that about half of all farms that
grow some cotton produce less than 100 acres of cotton. Less than 10 percent
of the cotton acres are grown on those farms, and half of the cotton acres are
on the 12 percent of farms with over 500 acres of cotton. The largest 15
percent of the standard industrial classification (SIC) cotton farms have more
308

TABLE 10
DISTRIBUTION OF ACRES AND FARMS FOR COTTON, 1978

Cotton Acres[a]	Percentage of Farms	Percentage of Acres	Crop Acres[b]	Percentage of Farms
1–49	29	3	1–49	23
50–99	17	5	50–99	16
100–249	26	17	100–249	19
250–499	16	24	250–499	26
500–999	9	26	500–999	11
1,000+	3	25	1,000–1,999	3
			2,000+	1

a. For all farms growing cotton.
b. All standard industrial classification (SIC) cotton farms.
SOURCE: *Census of Agriculture*, 1978.

TABLE 11
DISTRIBUTION OF COTTON DEFICIENCY PAYMENTS, BY SIZE OF FARM, 1978 AND 1982
(percent)

Total Cropland Acres	1978 Participating Acreage	1978 Participating Producers	Total Cropland Acres	1982 Participating Acreage	1982 Participating Producers
<70	4.8	40.1	1–99	6.9	50.7
70–219	11.8	25.6	100–259	9.5	17.2
220–499	18.7	16.6	260–499	15.0	12.5
500–1,499	39.1	14.4	500–999	26.9	12.0
1,500–2,499	13.5	2.3	1,000–1,499	16.1	4.3
2,500+	12.4	1.0	1,500–1,999	8.9	1.7
			2,000–2,499	4.7	0.7
			2,500+	12.2	0.9

SOURCES: Agriculture Department, *Cotton;* and Lin, Calvin, and Johnson, *Farm Commodity Programs*.

than 500 acres of all cropland. Table 11 shows information about program participation by size of farm. In 1978 about 17 percent of the participants in the cotton program had more than 500 total crop acres, compared with 15 percent of the SIC cotton farms with over 500 acres of cropland. Although the samples of farms are not strictly comparable, participation rates apparently do not vary dramatically by size.

The program for cotton does not directly affect size. Its provisions influence participating farms proportionally. Acreage set-asides, Commodity Credit Corporation (CCC) loans, and deficiency or disaster payments are all proportional to quantities sold. The effects on industry structure are thus second-round effects.

Among the second-round effects are those related to price and income variability, relative gains among regions, and the capitalization of benefits into land prices and other inelastic resources. Simulations by Harrington et al. and Smith, Richardson, and Knutson have attempted to project the effect of commodity programs on selected cotton farms.[24] Harrington et al. simulate the programs' effects for representative cotton farms in the Texas high plains and the delta region of Mississippi. They find that for farms in each of the land tenure–equity situations, net worth is significantly lower without the programs. Net cash income falls and is negative for the Mississippi farm without full equity in land. The probability of survival falls to 70 percent in Texas and 94 percent in Mississippi for the farms with part ownership, part equity. The simulations by Smith, Richardson, and Knutson consider more detailed program parameters. They examine the value of participation to the success of Texas cotton farms of different size and structure. In general, the farms all gain from participation and, since almost all Texas cotton farms did participate, this is a sign that the simulations are realistic. Participation provides relatively more benefit to the middle-sized farms. The authors note that their simulations do not provide direct information on what the success of firms would be if the programs did not exist, because the underlying distributions would be different.

Cotton programs provide significant transfers to producers across size ranges. No clear differential effects on structure are evident from the rough data available.

The Influence of the Program on the Structure of Tobacco Farming. This section considers the issues and analysis discussed above in light of the size, diversification, asset ownership patterns, resource use patterns, and other characteristics of tobacco enterprises and farms that grow tobacco in the United States. The major policy option for tobacco is substantial deregulation of the industry.[25]

The numbers, sizes, and organization of tobacco farms would probably change if the program were removed, but these changes would not be dramatic, at least when compared with the consolidation that has taken place in the past twenty years (table 12). Lease and transfer of quota (and recently the legal sale of quota) removed major barriers to tobacco farm consolidation.

TABLE 12

NUMBER OF TOBACCO FARMS AND OF ALL FARMS, 1954–1982

(thousands)

	Farms Growing Tobacco				All Farms			
	Ky., all	N.C., burley	N.C., flue-cured	S.C.	U.S., all	Ky.	N.C.	S.C.	U.S.
1954	136	14	136	35	512	193	268	124	4,782
1959	119	13	98	24	417	151	191	78	3,711
1964	96	11	77	18	331	130	148	56	3,158
1969	91	9	55	11	276	125	119	40	2,730
1974	71	6	38	7	198	102	91	29	2,314
1978	74	6	32	5	189	102	82	27	2,258
1982	74	7	23	4	179	102	73	25	2,241

SOURCE: Census of Agriculture, various years.

TABLE 13

DISTRIBUTION OF FARMS BY VALUE OF TOTAL SALES, 1982

(percent)

	SIC Tobacco Farms[a]			SIC Cash Grain Farms[a]		
	Ky.	N.C.	S.C.	Ky.	N.C.	S.C.
Sales (dollars)						
<2,500	18.0	7.9	4.7	11.2	30.9	27.5
2,500–4,999	21.6	11.3	6.7	9.9	18.2	15.6
5,000–9,999	23.6	15.6	10.4	15.5	16.6	16.5
10,000–19,999	19.1	17.1	14.5	16.7	12.5	14.2
20,000–39,999	11.5	16.2	17.1	17.3	9.1	9.7
40,000–99,999	5.3	19.1	25.3	17.0	7.6	9.5
100,000–249,999	0.9	10.5	16.9	9.1	3.7	5.1
250,000–499,999	0.1	1.9	3.6	2.7	1.1	1.4
500,000+	—	0.3	0.8	0.6	0.3	0.5

a. If production of a particular product accounts for 50 percent or more of the total value of sales of a farm's agricultural products, it is classified as SIC.

SOURCE: Census of Agriculture, 1982.

311

Mechanization of harvesting, bulk-curing, and other technological changes have allowed expansion of the quantity of tobacco that could be grown by a single-family farm, especially of flue-cured tobacco. These factors also increased the relative efficiency of larger farms with greater access to managerial expertise and lower interest rates for financing capital investments and quota purchase or lease. Compared with these factors, the elimination of price supports and quotas would have little effect on the size of tobacco farms.

Size barriers in the current program. Lease and sale of the legal right to grow and sell tobacco is currently limited to single-county markets. Since no single firm controls a large part of the quota available in any major tobacco county, this restriction has not had a major effect on farm consolidation. Tobacco is the least land-intensive crop grown in the region, and most farmers have many more acres of other crops and are more diversified than required by law. Some economists have argued that the tobacco program keeps farms small.[26] This argument seems to be based on a mistaken assumption that quotas are not readily transferable.

Changes in policy and farm size. Given the expected geographic movement of the industry, farms currently located in prime tobacco counties—the larger tobacco farms—would be in a position to expand tobacco production either by increasing the size of their farms or by reducing their production of other crops. This is a mechanical second-round effect tending to increase size. The elimination of quota rents would eliminate wealth and income for some farmers and an implicit or explicit cost for all farmers. At the same time, the price of tobacco would fall, offsetting the cost saving from the growers' viewpoint. For those growers who produce in less suitable growing areas, the price fall would more than offset the cost saving.

In the short run the price fall implies that there would be smaller farms if sales are used as a measure of size. This conclusion assumes a vertical supply curve where output is unchanged. In studying the effects of policy, we should be careful in choosing a measure of size and be aware of the built-in effects of the measure chosen.

Tobacco enterprises typically have fewer acres than those for most other field crops, but the sales distributions are much more similar to those of all U.S. farms and to other farms in tobacco states. Table 13 shows the percentage of tobacco farms in each sales class and, for comparison, the distribution of all grain farms in three states where tobacco is important. Tobacco farms in the flue-cured states of North Carolina and South Carolina tend to be much larger than the burley farms of Kentucky. Note that there have been no significant differences in programs to account for these differences in size distribution.[27]

The program has changed in one major respect related to structure. In 1961 for flue-cured and in 1971 for burley tobacco, lease and transfer of

312

production rights was allowed within county boundaries. Recently about half the flue-cured crop and about one-quarter of the burley production rights have been leased. Before 1961 the flue-cured allotment could be exchanged only by renting or selling the farm on which the tobacco was to be grown. Lease and transfer made consolidation of production cheaper by eliminating the restriction on where in the county the tobacco could be grown; but the evidence does not suggest that the years just after the legalization of lease and transfer (1959 to 1964) showed a major increase in the continuing structural change in this industry. For burley the legalization of lease and transfer occurred between the 1969 and the 1974 censuses. Overall, the evidence is weak in its support of the hypothesis that this major program change had major effects on structure. The other major change in the program from the 1960s and 1970s was the shift from acreage allotments to poundage limits. There the effect on yields was dramatic. The long upward trend in flue-cured yields stopped in 1964, and yield growth has been near zero since poundage became the limiting factor. For burley the same shift occurred in 1971, and again the slope of yield growth dropped to zero.

Price variability and tobacco structure. Some increase in the variability of tobacco prices would occur in the absence of a program. The price variability of tobacco—given its storability and the relatively high elasticity of demand—is distinctly limited. It has often been argued that price variability implies more risk and smaller enterprises, more diversification, and smaller farms. One argument is that credit markets limit the availability of loans to farmers because of the riskiness of the investment and the debt-equity ratio of the investor.

A program may reduce tobacco price variability without reducing the risk relevant to investment decisions. Year-to-year yield and price variability implies fluctuations in returns that may be compensated for by the maintenance of some liquidity. They are not typically a source of default. The risk associated with public program changes may be much more relevant to rapid and unpredicted changes in net worth. Program risk may then be much more relevant to lending and investment decisions.

Moreover, in the long run the characteristics of a program may affect the characteristics of the human capital attracted into an industry. A tobacco industry with no program would be more likely to attract entrepreneurs willing to innovate in marketing and other decisions. These may be people that optimally operate larger farms to use their managerial abilities. The more flexible the industry, the more this tendency results in larger farms. Thus applying the variability argument to tobacco leads to mixed conclusions.

The Influence of Federal Dairy Policies on Structure. Federal policies regulate four aspects of dairy markets: cooperative marketing, geographically distinct markets, price supports, and import quotas. In addition to these federal regulations, several states, especially California, have enacted their own price regulation for milk that does not move in interstate commerce. In 1982, 81 percent of all U.S. fluid grade marketings were regulated by federal market orders, and 17 percent were regulated by states alone.[28]

Prices are supported by federal purchases of butter, nonfat dry milk, and American cheese. Since manufactured products are easily transported and the Minnesota-Wisconsin market has the major share of the manufactured milk products, manufactured milk prices are similar to the Minnesota-Wisconsin price in all markets. Fluid milk prices in federal orders are above this rate by a differential that depends on distance from the upper Midwest.

The price received by most producers is an average or blend price based on the number of pounds sold for manufacturing or fluid use either in the total market or by the individual handler. The blend price may be modified by the imposition of several forms of output quotas, called base plans. Under 1983 legislation producers could contract with the Department of Agriculture to reduce production from 5 percent to 30 percent below their base levels of production in 1982.

Dairy production is a major farm industry throughout the country. Although milk for manufacturing is centered in the upper Midwest, high transport costs imply that fluid milk production occurs roughly in proportion to population. Thus California, New York, Pennsylvania, and Texas are also major dairy states. Among farm commodities dairy production ranks second nationally in value of sales and ranks in the top five farm commodities by value of sales in more than forty states.

In all regions farms that produce milk for sale are predominantly dairy farms. Over 90 percent of milk production is from farms that get most of their revenue from milk sales. For these farms milk sales account for over 90 percent of total revenue. Dairy farms are also the least likely of all major farm types to have the operator working off the farm. This is true of California, where 62 percent of all farmers but only 16 percent of dairy farmers work off the farm during a year. In Wisconsin 65 percent of nondairy and 21 percent of dairy farmers work off their farms.

Table 14 shows the distribution of dairy farms with ten or more cows by herd size for the United States and selected states in 1978 and 1982. Included in the total are Kentucky, North Carolina, California, Wisconsin, New York and the states in the Southeast. Dramatic differences are evident among states in the numbers of cows per farm. In California in 1982 60 percent of the dairy farms had herds larger than 200 cows. In Wisconsin two-thirds of the herds were smaller than fifty cows. Kentucky is similar to Wisconsin, and 40 percent of the herds of Texas have more than 100 cows.

In general, price supports, classified pricing schemes, import quotas, and producer taxes act only to alter the price received by producers. That

TABLE 14

DISTRIBUTION OF FARMS WITH TEN OR MORE MILK COWS, BY HERD SIZE,
1978 AND 1982

(percent)

	10-19	20-29	30-49	50-99	100-199	200-499	500+
United States							
1982	12.6	15.7	31.9	28.7	7.9	2.2	1.1
1978	15.7	18.8	32.7	24.5	6.2	1.7	0.4
Kentucky							
1982	10.0	3.9	7.6	29.1	35.2	12.8	1.3
1978	10.3	7.1	6.9	35.4	27.7	11.7	0.8
North Carolina							
1982	10.8	8.4	16.2	41.6	19.1	3.6	0.2
1978	17.1	9.5	17.1	37.2	16.3	2.7	0.1
Texas							
1982	9.5	5.0	10.7	34.5	27.8	11.3	1.2
1978	9.7	5.1	16.1	35.0	25.2	7.9	1.0
California							
1982	3.0	1.7	3.5	10.6	21.2	38.2	21.7
1978	3.3	2.9	5.0	13.5	24.1	34.2	17.1
Wisconsin							
1982	10.0	17.3	40.4	28.0	3.9	0.4	0.0
1978	13.4	21.4	40.8	21.7	2.4	0.2	0.0
New York							
1982	4.4	10.0	33.8	40.3	9.7	1.6	0.1
1978	6.2	11.6	37.9	35.6	7.6	1.1	0.1

SOURCE: *Census of Agriculture*, 1982.

price may differ among markets but not among producers within a particular market. Base plans, may, however, vary the prices received among producers within a market as well as among markets. One of the effects of dairy policy is to reduce price dispersion among producers.

There is a tendency for firms to shrink as the price of milk falls with a more market-oriented policy. Without other restrictions a reduced price support will also imply exits of dairy farms. The effects of falling price on other parameters of the distribution of existing firms, however, are not so clear.

Entry or exit of firms can also cause the average herd size to fall even as existing dairies expand. Farms with high reservation prices for entry or exit may have small entry or exit sizes. Therefore, as small firms enter at high prices, the average size may move in an opposite direction from the average size of firms that are continuously producing. This may cause the variance of the size distribution to rise. We have no direct evidence about this phenomenon for dairy farms. Leiby finds growth rates proportional to size among southern dairies and smaller dairies associated with farmers with less schooling and experience.[29]

The existence of a base plan usually means that a producer no longer faces a price that is independent of his product. The essence of a class I base plan is that a producer is assigned a quota of milk for which he receives a higher price than for milk sold beyond the quota. Average revenue and marginal revenue will equal the class I price up to the level of the base, but marginal revenue is less than average revenue past the base amount.

The offering of premiums for reduced production—as allowed by the Dairy and Tobacco Act of 1983—has an effect very similar to that of base plans in that such premiums employ a base for the determination of reduced production. It is useful to view these plans as a discrete shift of the marginal costs of production. If the output price should fall below that implied by the base, all producers would desire to contract to the level of output implied by the shifted marginal cost curve.

Several issues, however, cloud the effects described above. The most important of these concerns expectations about future policy. If producers anticipate changes in policy, they may react before the new policy is implemented. When a base reduction plan is instituted, for example, if producers expect that mandatory base plans or quotas are to be imposed in the future, their response may be to expand current production to build a future base. The perceived stability of policy also affects the response to policy. With costs of changing output, the costs of adjusting to a temporary policy change may outweigh the benefits of the change. The stability of policy may also directly influence the structure of the industry. Producers may diversify.

The total supply of milk for manufacturing is the sum of grade B and the surpluses of fluid grade milk. The surplus is determined by the combination of the manufacturing support price and the class I price. The elimination of both classified pricing and price supports would alter these markets substantially. Price would fall in both fluid and manufacturing markets as the price support was eliminated. Fluid quantities would expand along the fluid demand curve; manufacturing quantities would fall. Since grade B milk does not compete with grade A milk in fluid markets and since high transport costs are associated with fluid milk, grade A producers in some regions may be insulated from the full effect of the removal of classified pricing and price supports.

The federal government has recently purchased up to 30 percent of the output of manufactured dairy products. The national share of manufactured dairy products would fall, and fluid quantities and share would rise, with elimination of price supports and classified pricing. Seasonal surpluses in chiefly fluid markets would also increase, further reducing output in the areas that specialize in milk used for manufacturing.

As noted in table 14, herd size is much smaller in the areas that produce mostly manufacturing milk. Thus a regional shift away from these markets might increase aggregate herd size while herd sizes in each region remained unchanged or fell slightly. In the dairy industry these regional differences are a major structural factor.

If transportation barriers for fluid milk between the upper Midwest were low (as they might be if reconstitution were permissible), the milk price in regions that produce mostly grade A milk would fall in relation to regions producing grade B. This implies that the market share of the grade A regions would fall. That is, the decline in the size of the grade A markets would be greater than the size of grade B markets.

Substantial movement to market orientation in the dairy program would have mixed effects on size and structure in the industry.

Implications of Policy Changes in 1985 and Beyond

Among the major general changes suggested for farm commodity policy in 1985 have been (1) substantially more market orientation with low federal budget costs and competitive world prices of farm output—that is, a movement away from effective target prices, loan rates, or supply controls—and (2) a basic structure like recent farm programs but with severe and tightly enforced direct payment and loan limits per farm. This would imply a free market for large farms but nonrecourse loans or deficiency payments for farms with low gross sales output. The idea of the second suggestion is to move federal budget outlays for farm programs to a low level while providing some subsidy to small farms. A third option is to fine-tune the existing programs by changing their parameters and perhaps building in some adjustment features to help the programs adapt to economic conditions.

The proposals to limit government budget liability per farm from commodity programs can be equivalent to eliminating programs in its market effects. As a minor transfer to individuals who own resources used on small farms, such limits are probably less harmful than a more thorough deregulation, but the program would still not function effectively as income maintenance for the rural poor.

The option of a movement toward reducing the market effect of programs or essentially eliminating them has been seriously discussed for several commodities. After considering current and past structural patterns and attempting to isolate the indirect effects of structure, we still cannot confidently assert the general effect of such a deregulation on size distributions or other structural variables.

With a fall in the effective price of several supported commodities, some output reduction and reallocation among commodities would be expected. Crop producers in the plains states might be especially affected since they are usually participants in voluntary programs. The fall in land values and other asset prices would hurt some and help others, but there seems to be no particular structural bias in these effects.

A final word about the effects of program risk: farmers and others currently operate in an environment of substantial uncertainty about how the "rules of the game" might change. The elimination of programs would not necessarily eliminate this state of unease, because programs that are ended may be started again. Policies that have predictable and stable real effects seem to have substantial merit even if they are flexible in their operation.

Notes

1. Don Paarlberg, "Purposes of Farm Policy," and Ronald D. Knutson, "The Goals of Agricultural and Food Policy," in "The Purposes of Farm Policy," American Enterprise Institute Occasional Paper (November 1984); and Dale E. Hathaway, *Government and Agriculture* (New York: Macmillan, 1963).

2. U.S. Department of Agriculture, Economics, Statistics, and Cooperative Service, *Status of the Family Farm: Second Annual Report to the Congress,* Agricultural Economics Report no. 434 (September 1979).

3. Luther Tweeten, *Causes and Consequences of Structural Change in the Farming Industry,* NPA Report no. 207 (Washington, D.C.: National Planning Association, 1984).

4. See also Edward G. Smith, James W. Richardson, and Ronald Knutson, "Impact of Farm Policy on the Structure of Agriculture in the Texas High Plains," Agricultural and Food Policy Center, Texas A&M University, n.d.

5. Bruce L. Gardner, "Public Policy and the Control of Agricultural Production," *American Journal of Agricultural Economics,* vol. 60 (1978), pp. 836–43.

6. R. G. F. Spitze, A. S. Walter, D. E. Ray, and J. G. West, *Public Agricultural Food Policies and Small Farms* (Washington, D.C.: National Rural Center, 1980).

7. See also E. M. Babb, "Consequences of Structural Change in U.S. Agriculture," in U.S. Department of Agriculture, *Structure Issues of American Agriculture,* Agricultural Economics Report no. 438 (November 1979); Harold O. Carter and Warren E. Johnston, "Some Forces Affecting the Changing Structure, Organization, and Control of American Agriculture," *American Journal of Agricultural Economics,* vol. 60 (1978), pp. 738–48; Thomas A. Miller and Jerry A. Sharples, "Issues Concerning the Level of Price and Income Support," in Agriculture Department, *Structure Issues;* C. L. Schultze, *The Distribution of Farm Subsidies: Who Gets the Benefits?* (Washington, D.C.: Brookings Institution, 1971); and B. F. Stanton, "Perspective on Farm Size," *American Journal of Agricultural Economics,* vol. 60 (1978), pp. 727–37.

8. Gordon C. Rausser, David Zilberman, and Richard E. Just, "The Distributional

Impacts of Agricultural Programs," in Walter J. Armbruster, ed., *Proceedings from Perspectives on Food and Agricultural Policy Research Workshop* (Oak Brook, Ill.: Farm Foundation, 1982).

9. Spitze et al., *Public Policies and Small Farms.*

10. James D. Johnson, Milton H. Ericksen, Jerry A. Sharples, and David H. Harrington, "Price and Income Policies and the Structure of Agriculture," in Agriculture Department, *Structure Issues.*

11. W. Lin, J. Johnson, and L. Calvin, *Farm Commodity Programs: Who Participates and Who Benefits?* Agricultural Economics Report no. 474 (September 1981).

12. David H. Harrington, Donn A. Reimund, Kenneth H. Baum, and R. Neal Peterson, *U.S. Farming in the Early 1980s: Production and Finance Structure*, Agricultural Economics Report no. 504 (September 1983).

13. See Thomas A. Miller, Gordon E. Rodewald, and Robert McElroy, *Economics of Size in U.S. Field Crop Farming*, Agricultural Economics Report no. 472 (July 1981).

14. For a related table, see B. F. Stanton, "Changes in Farm Structure: The United States and New York, 1930–1982," Cornell Agricultural Economics Staff Paper no. 84-23, Department of Agricultural Economics, Cornell University, September 1984.

15. See also J. B. Penn, "The Structure of Agriculture: An Overview of the Issue," in Agriculture Department, *Structure Issues.*

16. Tweeten, *Causes and Consequences*, p. 19.

17. See also Stanton, "Changes in Farm Structure."

18. U.S. Department of Agriculture, Economic Research Service, *Wheat: Background for 1985 Farm Legislation*, Agriculture Information Bulletin no. 467 (September 1984).

19. James D. Johnson and Sarah D. Short, "Commodity Programs: Who Has Received the Benefits?" *American Journal of Agricultural Economics*, vol. 65, no. 5 (December 1983).

20. Ibid.

21. Agriculture Department, *Wheat.*

22. U.S. Department of Agriculture, Economic Research Service, *Corn: Background for 1985 Farm Legislation*, Agriculture Information Bulletin no. 477 (September 1984).

23. U.S. Department of Agriculture, Economic Research Service, *Cotton: Background for 1985 Farm Legislation*, Agriculture Information Bulletin no. 476 (September 1984).

24. Harrington et al., *U.S. Farming in the Early 1980s;* and Smith, Richardson, and Knutson, "Impact of Farm Policy."

25. Daniel A. Sumner and Julian M. Alston, "The Impact of Removal of Price Supports and Supply Controls for Tobacco in the United States," in *Research in Domestic and International Agribusiness Management* (New York: JAI Press, 1984), vol. 5, pp. 107–64.

26. Tweeten, *Causes and Consequences.*

27. See Sumner and Alston, "Impact of Removal"; and U.S. Department of Agriculture, Economic Research Service, *Tobacco: Background for 1985 Farm Legislation*, Agriculture Information Bulletin no. 468 (September 1984).

28. U.S. Department of Agriculture, Economic Research Service, *Dairy: Background for 1985 Farm Legislation*, Agriculture Information Bulletin no. 474 (September 1984).

29. James D. Leiby, "Determinants of Farm Growth: The Case of Southern Dairies" (Ph.D. dissertation, North Carolina State University, 1985).

Commentary

B. F. Stanton

The central focus of attention for this segment of the program is the effects of federal farm programs on the structure of agriculture. The question posed is, Would the structure of American agriculture have been different if the commodity and other federal programs of the past fifty years had not existed or had been substantially different? As Sumner clearly points out in his paper, "A search for data that contain both variation in structural variables and variations in farm programs while other factors do not change [produced nothing]. Such conclusive natural experiments have not been found." His careful review of existing published literature, the time series data he has studied over the past three decades, and the patterns of change he found on wheat, corn, cotton, tobacco, and dairy farms led to this summary statement: "For specific commodities and for farming as a whole, farm programs do not seem to have had a definite effect in any direction. Farm programs have not been major factors in past structural changes and are not likely to be major factors in the future."

Reasons for Structural Change

If it is agreed that farm programs have had little or no effect on structural change in American agriculture, it is important to recognize the important forces that have led to these changes. My list includes the following:

- adoption of new technology both within and outside agriculture and associated economies of size
- changes in markets and access to those markets
- physical resources available to farmers and production alternatives consistent with those resources
- opportunities for off-farm employment

It is not necessary to lecture to this audience about the effect of new technology on structural change in agriculture. The broiler industry, large tractors in crop farming, and the use of electronics in processing and warehousing all speak to the kinds of transformation that occur at every level from input supply to farming to agricultural processing and distribution. Government has helped through research to produce some of the new technology and through extension to encourage its testing and adoption. In an industrialized economy structural change can be rapid, and the associated obsolescence of plant and equipment is readily obvious.

In any brief review of the reasons for structural change, the importance of changing markets and access to them is sometimes forgotten. Technology may be the primary agent of change, but the ability to buy and sell products is fundamental. The advent of regional, national, and international markets as well as vertical and horizontal integration has encouraged specialization, geographical shifts in production, and major capital flows in the food and agricultural industry. The movement of perishable products today throughout the great common market that is the United States could not have been imagined fifty years ago at the time of the New Deal.

The rate of structural change also depends on the quality of the physical resources used in agriculture, their alternative uses, and off-farm employment opportunites for labor. Clearly, in the 1930s the exodus from agriculture, particularly in the eastern third of the country, was slowed by a lack of alternatives both for land and for labor. In the 1950s economic opportunities outside agriculture hastened structural change. The return of cropland to pasture and of pasture to forest was sometimes dictated by the principle of opportunity cost. In my home state farm numbers were more than cut in half, and harvested cropland was reduced by 50 percent between 1950 and 1970. Structural change came in one generation because the combination of technology, markets, available resources, and opportunities outside agriculture dictated such change.

In this setting an impressive array of well-intentioned federal programs was launched, from overseas grain shipments to less-developed countries to domestic price support programs and market orders. Some agricultural commodities were protected by tariffs and quotas at the same time that we tried to expand overseas markets for others.

Intent of Government Programs

It is my hypothesis or assertion that one of the underlying and unstated purposes of most government programs in agriculture has been to *slow* structural change rather than to encourage it. The Food and Agriculture acts of 1977 and 1981 both contain a specific section and policy statement on family farms. In 1981 that statement ran as follows:

> Congress reaffirms the historical policy of the United States to foster and encourage the family farm system of agriculture in this country. Congress believes that the maintenance of the family farm system of agriculture is essential to the social well-being of the nation and the competitive production of adequate supplies of food and fiber. Congress further believes that any significant expansion of non-family owned, large scale corporate farming will be detrimental to the national welfare . . . It is the policy and the express intent of Congress that no such program be administered in a man-

TABLE 1

AVERAGE SALES PER U.S. FARM, BY TYPE, 1982

Type of Farm (SIC)	Number of Farms	Average Sales per Farm (dollars)
Poultry and eggs	41,953	240,281
Cotton	21,041	149,264
Horticultural specialties	29,176	130,144
Vegetables and melons	30,684	127,828
Dairy	164,472	110,226
Fed beef, hogs, sheep	287,693	99,069
Fruit and tree nuts	84,304	68,589
Cash grains	576,369	58,509
General farm, crop	58,457	55,124
Sugar, potatoes, peanuts, and other field crops	100,771	45,618
General farm, livestock	29,825	42,295
Tobacco	131,281	21,195
Animal specialties	65,004	20,044
Beef cattle raising	618,270	18,353

SOURCE: *U.S. Census of Agriculture, 1982.*

ner that will place the family farm operation at an unfair economic disadvantage.[1]

In my view this is a direct, clear statement. There is also plenty of room for argument about what constitutes a "family farm" or "unfair economic disadvantage." Sumner has given us a flexible definition of family farms that neatly includes a substantial component of both part-time and full-time commercial farms today. Such a definition is consistent with the language of the 1981 law. The unwritten intent, I believe, is to maintain as much of the status quo as possible. After all, it is a good system; it is competitive; let us keep as much of it in place as we can for as long as possible.

The agricultural legislation and policies of most Western countries during the past fifty years have had two underlying themes. One is to provide farm families with incomes equivalent to those in other segments of society; the second is to ensure an adequate and safe food supply for all the people in the country. To these ends a complex combination of measures has been produced, which at one end of the spectrum has tried to keep small farmers on the land and at the other has encouraged the consolidation of holdings into

TABLE 2

U.S. Farms with $500,000 Sales or More, by Type, 1982

Type of Farm	Percentage of Total	Number
Fed beef, hogs, sheep	20.6	5,740
Cash grains	14.6	4,052
Poultry and eggs	13.3	3,687
Dairy	11.2	3,105
Beef cattle raising	8.3	2,303
Fruit and tree nuts	6.7	1,857
Horticultural specialties	5.4	1,492
Vegetables and melons	5.1	1,409
Sugar, potatoes, peanuts, and other field crops	4.9	1,377
Cotton	4.1	1,145
General farm, crop	3.4	949
Animal specialties	1.2	341
General farm, livestock	0.7	204
Tobacco	0.5	139
Total	100.0	27,800

Source: *Census of Agriculture, 1982.*

efficient mechanized units. Quotas and tariffs barriers have been used to protect local production from foreign competition. Price supports, production subsidies, and supply controls have all been used to raise minimum family incomes while meeting some government budget constraint. *The net effect of these programs in retrospect has been to try to keep as many people as possible in farming but to ensure that they have some minimum level of income.* The Europeans and Japanese in particular would be quite willing, I think, to agree that this has been their conscious intent. They have given farmers incentives through prices and income to stay in agriculture and to modernize and at the same time have tried to keep as many people as possible on the land.

Current Distributions in the United States

Perhaps this rather elementary historical review and set of assertions is unnecessary in examining the influence of government programs on structural change in the United States. It does provide some perspective. An examination of three tables garnered from the 1982 census of agriculture adds one further

TABLE 3

DISTRIBUTION OF U.S. FARMS OF FIVE COMMODITY TYPES,
BY SIZE, 1982

	Poultry and Eggs	Cotton	Dairy	Cash Grain	Tobacco
Total sales ($ billions)	10.1	3.1	18.1	33.7	2.8
Number of farms	41,953	21,041	164,472	576,369	131,281
Farms by sales class (%)					
Less than $5,000	18	9	2	17	38
$5,000–9,999	2	9	2	11	22
$10,000–19,999	3	12	6	15	17
$20,000–39,999	5	15	15	17	11
$40,000–99,999	17	23	41	23	8
$100,000–249,999	31	18	27	13	3
$250,000 and over	24	14	7	4	1
Total	100	100	100	100	100

SOURCE: Census of Agriculture, 1982.

dimension to Sumner's comprehensive review of structural change by commodity groups. In table 1 are listed fourteen types of farms, using the standard industrial classification (SIC) established by the Department of Commerce. All farms regardless of size are included. They are ranked on the basis of average sales per farm. This table simply emphasizes that changes in technology and markets have had strikingly different effects on different commodities. Poultry and eggs are dominated by large commercial farms; at the other end of the distribution, tobacco and cattle operations include thousands of small, part-time farms.

Table 2 shows the distribution by type of farm of the 27,800 farms with $500,000 or more of sales in 1982, which produced 30 percent of aggregate sales. They are widely distributed geographically and across many commodities. Not surprisingly, 60 percent of the total number are included in the first four categories: fed beef, hogs, and sheep; cash grains; poultry and eggs; and dairy.

Table 3 compares the size distributions of five of these types of farms. The poultry and egg industry has received minimal government intervention over the years. The contrast between the days when nearly every commercial farm had a farm flock and the egg money was the domain of the farmer's wife

325

and the present day of caged layers and the industrialized broiler industry constitutes a vast change in structure. By far the majority of the eggs and the poultry meat, not only in the United States but also in other rich countries of the world, is produced and marketed through an integrated industrialized system.

For contrast one can look at the distribution of farm size where tobacco is the principal crop. It is hard to think of a type of farming for which government programs have been more important or regulation has received more attention. Clearly the majority of tobacco farms are still small, part-time operations, as Sumner has helped us understand. In my view government programs have *slowed* structural changes here just as they have wherever production quotas have been established around the world. In contrast, consider cotton, for which government programs have been in place in a variety of forms for many years. Larger farms now predominate; major shifts in areas of production have occurred over the past fifty years. Large Commodity Credit Corporation (CCC) or payment-in-kind (PIK) payments to individual cotton farmers regularly capture headlines when complaints about current farm programs are registered.

The key point to recognize in table 3 is the amount of diversity that exists in the size distributions of farms that have experienced different kinds and amounts of government programs. Similarly, these distributions by region of the country or by state exhibit striking differences, as Sumner points out, such as the contrast of dairy farms in Wisconsin and California. It is the resources available, technology, markets, and employment opportunities that explain most of these differences. Government programs have tended to slow the process of structural change, but in most cases their net effect has been modest in relation to the other forces.

All these statements simply update and support the clear exposition on this topic by Bruce Gardner in 1978: "Compared to the policy environment prior to, or most likely in the absence of, government institutions that now exist, historical policies have probably tended to retard the rate of structural change."[2]

I agree. Why then the continuing notion by other analysts cited throughout Sumner's paper that commodity programs and federal policy have provided "unfair" advantage and encouraged large farms at the expense of smaller ones? I believe it has recently been tied up with the effects of two other types of public policy: (1) federal programs for credit emergency loans and disaster relief; and (2) changes in federal tax legislation.[3] Undoubtedly publicity about the size of government payments received by some of the largest farms, when the payment limit provisions have been set aside, has contributed as well.

In the last half of the 1970s CCC stocks were low; farm real estate values rose faster than the rate of inflation; credit was easy to obtain; crop disaster payments and low-interest emergency loans were commonplace; an atmosphere of market growth for U.S. agriculture seemed all-pervasive. Federal tax policy encouraged investment. In this environment Farmers Home Administration (FmHA) credit was extended in large chunks to farmers who would normally not have qualified for loans. Other lenders happily shifted questionable parts of their portfolios to government-guaranteed paper. Not surprisingly, some of the farmers who took on these large loans as well as full advantage of investment tax credits are now unable to meet their interest and debt payments.

Davenport, Boehlje, and Martin, two lawyers and one economist, concluded a major section of their study in 1982 as follows:

> Were agriculture less tax favored than it is, land prices would undoubtedly be lower; there would be less need for sophisticated financial and tax advice; holding periods for farm assets would likely be less; there would likely be a higher proportion of owner-operators in farming; there would be fewer high bracket taxpayers in farming; and farmers might even be younger on the average. These results are remarkable because however beneficial or detrimental one may think that these results are, they have never been an explicit policy goal.[4]

In conclusion, I believe we should all thank Sumner for his careful review of the literature and the evidence he has brought together on the indirect effects of commodity policy and programs on farm structure. Let me underline again with him that it is impossible to separate out the independent effects of the major forces causing structural change. I agree with his central conclusion. Commodity programs in the aggregate have not speeded up structural change in farming or hastened the demise of small farms. On the contrary, they may have provided a small brake on the express train of new technology, particularly for a few commodities. Federal tax policy may well be a more fertile field in which to plant some needed seeds for change.

In my efforts to understand the causes of structural change in American agriculture and the rates at which change takes place in different locations and for different commodities, I am struck by the motivation of the people studying the same data sets. Some want to keep the status quo or preserve a particular way of life. Some are primarily concerned with efficiency and productivity. Still others fear the evils of monopoly control over resources and markets. All of us have some sense of what we think is right. Whatever our beliefs of what is best for society and for American agriculture, we do need to anticipate the rates at which the numbers of farms of various sizes for each of the commodity groups will change. If there is a smaller hand of government in the process, I think structural change will move forward a little more rapidly. But marshaling the evidence to make that case seems intractable.

Notes

1. Food and Agriculture Act of 1981, sec. 1608.
2. Bruce L. Gardner, "Public Policy and the Control of Agricultural Production," *American Journal of Agricultural Economics*, vol. 60 (1978), pp. 836–43, at p. 842.
3. Charles Davenport, M. D. Boehlje, and D. Martin, "The Effects of Tax Policy on American Agriculture," Agricultural Economics Report no. 480 (February 1982), p. 62.
4. Ibid., p. 30.

Bibliography

Boehlje, Michael, and Hoy Carman. "Tax Policy: Implications for Producers and the Agricultural Sector." *American Journal of Agricultural Economics* 64 (1982):1030–38.

Davenport, Charles, M. D. Boehlje, and D. Martin. "The Effects of Tax Policy on American Agriculture." Agricultural Economic Report no. 480 (February 1982), p. 62.

Dorow, Norbert A. "The Farming Structure of the Future: Trends and Issues." *Farm and Food System in Transition* (Michigan State University), no. 17 (1984).

Gardner, Bruce L. "Public Policy and the Control of Agricultural Production." *American Journal of Agricultural Economics* 60 (1978):836–43.

Lin, William, J. Johnson, and L. Calvin. "Farm Commodity Programs: Who Participates and Who Benefits?" Agricultural Economic Report no. 474 (September 1981), p. 74.

Tweeten, Luther. "Causes and Consequences of Structural Change in the Farming Industry." National Planning Association Food and Agricultural Committee Report no. 2, NPA Report 207 (1984), p. 71.

The Repercussions of U.S. Agricultural Policies for the European Community

Stefan Tangermann

The relationship between U.S. farm policies and European Community (EC) farm policies can probably best be described as reluctant affinity. There are many similarities, connections, and interactions between farming industries and agricultural policies on both sides of the Atlantic, but agricultural relations between the United States and the EC are far from being harmonious. As far as economic interactions are concerned, there are direct links in the form of bilateral trade flows, half-direct links resulting from export competition on individual third-country markets, and indirect links through both partners' influences on the level and stability of world market prices. In the area of commercial policy, there are again directly bilateral issues, such as talks about restrictions on corn gluten trade, bilateral issues that are dealt with in a multilateral framework (such as complaints filed in the General Agreement on Tariffs and Trade, or GATT), and more general issues such as agreement or dissent as to whether a new round of multilateral trade negotiations should be launched. This multiplicity of links between the United States and the EC means that there is nearly nothing that one of the two sides can do in its agricultural and trade policies without the other side's being in some way affected by it.

It is therefore not only worthwhile but indispensable to examine the relationship between the two and to analyze feedback when policy decisions are made. In at least some commodity sectors, the United States has apparently learned this lesson much earlier than the EC, but the EC, which has always had trouble establishing an internal balance among member countries, is gradually recognizing that its Common Agricultural Policy (CAP) also has repercussions beyond the EC.

This paper investigates the manner by which EC behavior conditions the external feedback from U.S. policies rather than the way in which the success of EC policies depends on U.S. reactions. I shall first briefly consider the basic structure of agricultural market and trade policies in both countries or regions and the major forces behind them in order to determine whether there

329

is any fundamental divergence between U.S. and EC farm and agricultural trade policies in philosophy or doctrine. Against this background I shall discuss some possible future developments of the Common Agricultural Policy to the extent that they may affect the agricultural stance of the United States. In the main part I shall investigate various alternative unilateral policy actions of the United States, also considering the way in which the EC may react to them and the implications of this reaction for the outcome of these possible U.S. policies.

Throughout I shall emphasize policies for grain, in particular wheat, because they are in many respects at the core of agricultural policy in both the United States and the EC. In many instances, however, more general conclusions can be drawn from what in a technical sense is a commodity-specific analysis.

Farm Policies in the United States and the EC: Is There a Divergence of Doctrines?

The grain market regimes of the United States and the EC are rather different. The CAP completely dissociates the European Community's grain markets from the world market. Variable import levies prevent any grain from entering the European Community below the threshold price; obligatory buying into public stocks at the intervention price puts a floor under domestic prices; variable export restitutions ensure that surplus production of the EC can compete with any other country's exports on any third country's market. The immediate consequence of this regime is that grain prices in the European Community are safely kept in the band between the threshold price (which is effective in an EC deficit situation) and the intervention price (which is effective in an EC surplus situation), regardless of fluctuations in the world market price.

The U.S. grain market regime is much more open. Grain prices on the U.S. market are equal to international prices and move up and down with them. Farmers who participate in commodity programs, however, and fulfill the requirements are guaranteed the target price through government loans or purchases and deficiency payments. These program provisions do not directly interfere with market prices. In that sense they are much more liberal than the EC regime. It is obvious, however, that, given the weight of the U.S. grain sector in the international grain economy, the U.S. grain programs heavily influence the level of international grain prices, or, to be more exact, that the U.S. loan rate effectively puts a floor under international grain prices and therefore under grain prices on the U.S. market. In this sense the U.S. loan rate is a means of price support that is effective in much the same way as the EC intervention price, though it works through a different mechanism. Nevertheless, the U.S. system can be described as more liberal than the EC regime, as the loan rate can be and has been more flexible, adjusting to changing world market conditions. Moreover, a major distinction between U.S. and EC grain policies (and a very topical issue) is the fact that the U.S. system does not provide for explicit export subsidies, whereas no grain is exported from the European Community without the payment of export subsidies. Hence the view appears justified that there are significant and basic differences between U.S. and EC policies. The widespread notion that there is a fundamental divergence between the EC and the United States with respect to policy attitudes may help us understand why U.S. and EC negotiators often find it so difficult to reach a consensus. Where an attempt at policy coordination is concerned, however, it may be better to look for common ground than to emphasize differences.

Government interference with agricultural markets is so heavy in the European Community that little scope remains for market forces, and in general the point remains valid that the CAP is a rather protectionist approach to agricultural and trade policy. How should we view farm policy in the United States? Is it really so much more open and more oriented toward free trade than the CAP? Consider the U.S. grain market regime. Even though U.S. market prices are equivalent to world market prices, producer prices in the United States may well be above market prices, as the provision of target prices and deficiency payments means that farmers participating in the program receive nothing less than the target price. If market prices are below target prices (as was the case for wheat in five years out of seven, from 1977 to 1983), deficiency payments are made for total eligible U.S. production, that is, for *both* export production and production for the domestic market. In other words, aggregate deficiency payments can conceptually be decomposed into one component that is equivalent to an export subsidy and another component that could be called a subsidy on production for the domestic market.

In technical implementation a deficiency payment (which is disbursed domestically) differs from an export subsidy (which is paid out at the border). From an economic point of view, however, this difference means nothing to the farmer. The major distinction between a deficiency payment and an export subsidy lies in their different effects on users of the product and on the government budget. As far as trade effects are concerned, there is only a small difference, and for farmers there is no distinction at all. The seemingly significant difference between the grain market regimes in the United States and the EC thus boils down, in principle, to a different choice of instrumentation. U.S. and EC grain regimes differ in more ways, however, than merely in choice of domestic or border measures. Some of the additional distinctions, it can be argued, are much more important indicators that U.S. grain policy is less rigid that the EC regime.

The most salient characteristic of U.S. grain policy in comparison with the EC regime is the comparatively low level of grain price support in the

331

United States. From the middle of the 1970s to the early 1980s, U.S. target prices for wheat have consistently been some 40 percent below EC intervention reference prices, so that the level of price protection granted to U.S. farmers was considerably below that of the European Community. This, after all, is the decisive point. The instrumentation of support policy is an important criterion for evaluating its openness, but the level at which support is given is even more important, as it determines the degree to which market forces are distorted. There is little point in arguing that U.S. grain policy is more liberal than the grain policy of the EC because it does not employ export subsidies, but there is much strength in the argument that price protection is much lower in the United States than in the European Community.

Recently the situation has changed dramatically, however, with the strong appreciation of the U.S. dollar. Against the Eurocurrency unit, or ECU (the monetary unit in which CAP prices are fixed), the dollar rose by some 90 percent between 1979 and January 1985. This significant rise of the dollar value has of course had a major impact on price relationships between the United States and the EC. At the current dollar exchange rate (one ECU is about 0.7 U.S. dollars; January 1985), the CAP intervention price for wheat in 1984–1985 stands at about $132 per metric ton, whereas the U.S. target price is $163.51 per metric ton ($4.45 per bushel). The U.S. target price has hence gone from some 40 percent below the intervention price to some 24 percent above the intervention price. This drastic change is of course due to monetary developments rather than to any change in U.S. farm policy. On the other hand, U.S. farm policy has not adjusted support prices to the rising dollar value. In any case, for the time being we cannot readily say that, because of a lower level of price support, the U.S. grain market regime is less protective than the EC system and that this difference reflects a more liberal trade doctrine on the part of the United States.

The difference between the United States and the EC in behavior vis-à-vis world market instability remains significant, however. The CAP stabilizes domestic market prices in the European Community completely and makes them absolutely insensitive to world market fluctuations. The EC market therefore cannot contribute to buffering world market instability. Moreover, there is no indication that EC stock policy for grains has contributed positively to stabilizing world markets. U.S. market prices, on the other hand, move up and down with international prices. U.S. grain utilization is thereby forced to adjust to changing scarcities on world markets. In addition, U.S. grain stocks, through the effects of the loan rate provision, increase with low prices and decrease with high prices. Both aspects taken together mean that the U.S. grain market system can make and has made major contributions to buffering instability in the world grain economy. By the same token, however, we must also consider that, with fixed U.S. loan rates, a strongly rising dollar exchange rate not only leads to declining U.S. exports but also pulls international grain prices upward (in currencies that are not pegged to the dollar) and thereby injects instability into the world market. In addition, adjustments in U.S. production controls that overcompensate have possibly added an element of instability to worldwide grain production.

What conclusions can be drawn from this comparison of U.S. and EC grain policies? On some counts the U.S. system is more open or liberal than the EC regime. It is not invariably so, however, and lately the situation has changed. Thus it would be difficult to argue that U.S. farm and agricultural trade policy fundamentally differs from the CAP in the philosophy or doctrine on which it is based. It is probably more appropriate to assume that farm policies on both sides of the Atlantic are pursued rather pragmatically, that they react to all sorts of domestic (and sometimes also foreign) political pressures, and that the problems involved with them and the attempted solutions have much in common.

I do not mean that agricultural policies in the United States and the European Community are identical. One obvious difference is that the CAP is a policy that applies to and is decided by ten different nations, whereas U.S. farm policy covers the whole of one large country. In other words it is much more difficult in the EC to reach decisions, to react to outside pressures, and to adjust policies to changing circumstances.

In conclusion, when we try to understand farm policy developments in the United States and the EC and to project them, we are probably well advised to assume that the same basic forces are at work on both sides, though a number of special factors must be considered in each case. In short, on both sides of the Atlantic, farm policies are dominated by producer interests. The major constraint to expanding agricultural protection on either side appears to be the burden that farm policy places on the public budget. Both the United States and the European Community have recently experienced rapidly and intolerably increasing budget outlays for farm price support. The reaction has so far in principle been similar on both sides, though again the technical instrumentation has differed. Measures that reduce supply at given prices have been introduced (milk in the United States and the EC) or intensified (grain in the United States) in place of measures that reduce the level of protection significantly. Although the statement is of course a gross simplification, there is some point in the proposition that, in both the United States and the European Community, the design of farm policy depends mainly on the delicate political balance between producer interests and budget availability.

Future Developments of the CAP

So many problems have accumulated in the CAP, many observers believe, that a reform of this policy is unavoidable. Will a reform actually come? Will

333

changes in the CAP, if they take place, make life easier or more difficult for the European Community's trade partners? The answers to these questions are of course bound to be highly speculative. The prediction of future policy developments is even more risky than the forecasting of stock prices or exchange rates. It should at least be possible to specify major policy options, however, and to assign rough probabilities to them.

During the past fifteen years, EC threshold prices for grains have usually been about 40 percent to 80 percent above world market prices, and EC intervention prices for grains have been about 20 percent to 60 percent above. From the EC's domestic point of view, producer prices for grain have at the same time declined in real terms. Over the past fifteen years or so, real producer prices have decreased by an average annual rate of slightly more than 1.5 percent on average in the EC member countries. Is there a reason to assume that the trend of EC grain support prices will differ in the future?

Indeed, there are good reasons to suppose that the EC has now reached a point where it is close to a fundamental reconsideration of its policies for grains and related products. The major reason is the fact that the grain market situation in the European Community has dramatically changed over the past fifteen years. EC grain production has grown by an average annual rate of about 2.3 percent over this period, whereas grain consumption in the EC has essentially been stagnant. As a result the degree of self-sufficiency in grains, on aggregate, which was below 90 percent in the European Community at the end of the 1960s, exploded to 115 percent in 1982–1983.

The European Community's bumper crop in 1984, which brings the degree of self-sufficiency to 125 percent, has caused concern in the EC, mainly because of its implications for the European Community's budget. Over the past ten years, expenditure on the EC grain market regime has grown by an average annual rate of 14 percent, slightly faster than the financial resources available for the European Community budget. In 1983, expenditure on the EC grain market regime amounted to 2.4 billion ECUs, more than 15 percent of overall expenditure on CAP market regimes. After the milk market regime, on which 4.7 billion ECUs were spent in 1983, the grain market is the most expensive sector in the CAP.

The rapidly growing financial problem of the European Community has recently increased the pressure for CAP reform very significantly. The reform endeavors have so far culminated in a number of decisions by the Council of Ministers for agriculture in March 1984. The most significan of these decisions was the introduction of a quota system for milk. There is now a strong tendency in some quarters to believe that the most pressing problems of the EC's milk market have been solved by the quota system. The implication, apparently, is that efforts to "reform" the CAP will now move on to other sectors. The grain market regime will obviously attract particular attention. In the grain sector the European Community seems now to have reached a situation similar to that of the EC milk market a few years ago.

We should not conclude, however, that the EC has not yet started to reconsider its grain policy. Indeed, some noteworthy policy developments have already taken place in this sector. The EC Commission, for example, has proposed on various occasions since 1981 that grain support prices in the EC be gradually brought in line with grain prices in main competing countries (later specified as the United States). This proposal has never been formally accepted or rejected by the council. Such a strategy for fixing EC grain support prices, if it were ever implemented, would of course dramatically change the situation.

Moreover, since 1982 the concept of a "guarantee threshold" has been introduced into the EC grain market regime. In essence it means that the European Community specifies an "acceptable" volume of grain production for each year. If actual EC grain production (defined as the average for the three most recent years) exceeds this "acceptable" volume, intervention prices for the next crop year will be increased less (or reduced more) than the "normal" support price change. The exact specification is such that for each million ton of excess production one percentage point is subtracted from the "normal" price change, up to a maximum of five percentage points; excess production is the excess of the three-year average over the guarantee threshold, reduced, if applicable, by the excess of substitute imports over fifteen million tons. There is thus a penalty for excess production.

The crux of the guarantee threshold, apart from the decision of its level, is of course the definition of the "normal" change in support price. The CAP provides no rule or mechanism for determining actual or, for that matter, "normal" annual changes of market regime prices. Actual price decisions are nothing other than the result of political bargaining. Just possibly the council (implicitly) first decides the politically desired net price change for grains, then adds to it the "penalty" resulting from the guarantee threshold, and finally by doing so determines what the "normal" price increase would have been.

If so, we may wonder about the true significance of the guarantee threshold for grains. It may trigger a dynamic political development that could extend well beyond original expectations, as we may see by examining the quantitative details and by looking for parallels with the story of EC milk policy.

The annual level of the guarantee threshold is set such that a predetermined level for 1990 is gradually approached. This 1990 level has been set at 126 million tons. This means that the "acceptable" volume of EC grain production grows at only 0.6 percent per year. We must compare this figure with past annual production growth, which was 2.3 percent. It is now already clear that, because of the bumper crop in 1984, the "penalty" will be at its maximum of five percentage points in 1985. Moreover, it is rather likely that the penalty will not again drop below its 5 percent maximum until 1990. The commission's own estimate of EC grain production in 1990 (published independently of the threshold proposal) is 137 million tons, that is, 11 million tons above the 1990 guarantee threshold. It is rather doubtful whether the European Community's agricultural policy makers have fully understood these quantitative implications of the guarantee threshold concept.

How will the council react to these implications in its price decisions in coming years? There will be strong pressure for relatively high overall price increases in 1985, in particular as a consequence of the political debacle over the milk quotas. If average price increases in 1985 are 5 percent or more, the grain sector might see a price freeze or even a slight price increase. The council, however, probably cannot politically stand to have grain prices lagging behind other price increases by 5 percent for several years in a row. The alternative outcome is probably best understood by looking at what in a similar context happened to EC milk policy.

For milk a guarantee threshold had also been adopted. It allowed for an annual increase of deliveries by 0.5 percent. Actual deliveries, however, continued to increase by 3 percent and more. The situation soon became untenable. In 1983 the EC Commission argued that CAP milk support prices would have to be lowered by at least 12 percent in order to compensate for the excess expenditure on the milk market regime that resulted from deliveries in excess of the guarantee threshold. This number—12 percent—eventually played a decisive role in the discussions about future EC milk policy that took place in the following months. Agricultural policy makers and farmers were horrified at the prospect of a 12 percent cut in the milk price. In the last analysis everybody formed the impression that the only alternative to a 12 percent price cut was the introduction of quotas. Because such a large price cut was considered impossible, quotas appeared preferable, and in the end the council decided to adopt them.

I do not mean that EC grain policy will necessarily include quotas or some other form of mandatory production control in the near future. For technical and administrative reasons, quotas are much more difficult to implement in the grain sector than in the dairy sector. The story of the introduction of milk quotas under the CAP, however, appears to show that guarantee thresholds can trigger decisive political dynamics. The lesson is that major changes in the EC grain policy may lie ahead. It is, however, difficult to forecast the direction that they may take.

The EC will probably show a tendency to pursue a restrictive grain price policy. Moreover, it may show a tendency to introduce producer coresponsibility levies on grain, which could help to finance surplus disposal. Acreage reduction programs may be considered, and more rigid intervention on products competing with EC grain will also have a significant political appeal in the European Community.

336

In the current phase it is particularly difficult to predict the direction of the EC's future grain policy. Hence I am on shaky ground when I consider, in the following section, how EC policies might react to changes in U.S. policies. In order to avoid complications, I shall base my analysis on the assumption that no drastic changes will take place in the EC grain market regime and that the CAP will respond to its domestic grain market problems chiefly by a more restrictive grain price policy in the future—that is, that real grain prices in the European Community will come down somewhat faster than they have in the past.

U.S. Farm Policy Changes and EC Reactions

On the basis of the scenario that I have just described for the CAP, I shall now focus exclusively on the way in which the CAP may deviate from this base line in reaction to given changes of U.S. policy, apart from known and routine operations.

Conceptually this approach may appear very clear. Practically, however, it involves major difficulties. It is not really obvious, for example, what is meant by "change" in U.S. policy, and hence it is not at all clear on which type of "unchanged" U.S. policy I implicitly based my CAP projection in the preceding section. A change in policy can really be defined and analyzed only against a definite background. Furthermore, the changes to be discussed would also of course have to be defined in equally explicit terms. For purposes of a general assessment, however, it is neither possible nor really necessary to be so accurate. I shall therefore remain deliberately vague regarding the quantitative implications of the policy changes discussed below. A qualitative definition must and will suffice.

The U.S. wheat program includes a number of measures that can jointly be used to influence U.S. market prices, producer prices, U.S. production, exports, stocks, world market prices, budget expenditure, and so forth. Generally speaking, three policy variables can be set: the loan rate, the target price, and the level of production control. Moreover, the United States could consider the introduction of explicit export subsidies. Apart from any other structural policy change, these instruments alone permit a large array of changes. Fortunately enough, however, some theoretically possible options appear to be irrelevant for actual U.S. wheat policy, at least for the time being.

In the present situation increases of the loan rate and/or the target price seem unlikely to be a real option for U.S. farm policy. If the policy does not remain unaltered, the only price changes that appear relevant are reductions of the loan rate and/or the target price. The case of production control is somewhat less unambiguous. Clearly there is a tendency, in a market situation such as that described above, to intensify production control in order to reduce output. On the other hand this can hardly go further than the 1983 payment-in-kind (PIK) program. Moreover, if we consider production in combination with price reductions, there may be a point in relaxing production control. Yet tightening production control (we should recall the 1981–1982 situation) would appear to be the more plausible option. It will therefore be the only one that I consider below. Furthermore, in a situation like the one that serves as a point of departure for this assessment there is certainly a reason to discuss the option of introducing export subsidies.

Considerations of relevance have reduced the number of options significantly, but if all combinations of individual instrument changes are included, the number is still large. I shall therefore discuss individual measures in turn, touching upon combinations of changes only in passing. Each of these four options (tightening of production control, reduction of the target price, introduction of export subsidies, and reduction of the loan rate) has different implications for the external aspect of the U.S.wheat regime. Let us see, then, how the EC might react to these different options.

In my discussion of possible EC reactions, I shall address mainly two types of arguments. One relates to the economic effect, the other to the political effect. U.S. policies influence world market prices and thus affect the amount of export subsidies that the EC must pay—that is, budget expenditure for the CAP. This effect may condition support price decisions in the EC, because the budget factor is an important constraint on the CAP. Politically, on the other hand, U.S. policies may serve as "good" or "bad" examples for the CAP. They may cause the European Community to feel under siege, and they may affect the position of the United States and the EC in the GATT. These political impacts, too, can have a significant bearing on decisions made under the CAP. Economic and political impacts may reinforce or counteract each other. The balance between the two will finally determine how the EC might react to different U.S. policy options.

Tightening Production Control. Let us assume that U.S. wheat output is reduced, through tightened production control, to such an extent that U.S. wheat exports actually decline by a significant amount. In this case the EC and other wheat-trading nations are directly affected. A decrease of exports from the United States, the dominant wheat exporter, would drive the world market price up until world import demand was curtailed to the new, lower level of export availability. The EC could then sell its wheat exports at higher prices. How would the EC react? Would it increase, decrease, or maintain the volume of its wheat exports?

In trying to answer this question, I must emphasize that the European Community is, in the first place, affected only through savings on export restitutions. The quantity available for export from the EC is not directly influenced, as the increase in the world market price is not transmitted to the domestic EC market because of the system of variable import levies and export restitutions. Budget savings in the EC, however, could trigger policy responses that could then produce changes in quantity and hence a shift in the demand for U.S. exports.

The CAP would probably not respond to a change in its budget situation. Budget relief would permit price supports to be given to farmers somewhat more generously under the CAP. Though this price support could in principle apply to all products covered by the CAP, it would probably result in a less restrictive price policy for grains, in particular because there is a guarantee threshold for grains. This statement may seem paradoxical; we might expect the guarantee threshold and the related price-fixing rule to make CAP grain price decisions independent of the actual budget situation. It must be recognized, however, that the EC is likely to have major difficulties with its guarantee threshold for grains in any case, as I noted above. If these difficulties do not cause production control measures to be adopted in the EC, there will be strong tendencies either to disregard the guarantee threshold for grains or to lift the threshold quantity. These tendencies will become the more pronounced and the more likely to be successful, the lower the expenditure on the CAP grain market regime. A reduction of expenditure, through increased world market prices, is thus likely to result in higher grain prices in the EC. In any case, such an indirect but positive link between world market prices and CAP support prices has been observed in the past.

The political impact would in this case reinforce the economic influence. Politically it would be easier to lift or to disregard the guarantee threshold in the EC if the United States tightened production control. If the United States reduced its exports through tightened production control, it would thus face increased export competition on the part of the European Community. Alternatively, to put it slightly differently, if the United States reduced its export supply it would, at the same time, see the demand for its exports decrease.

Reducing the Target Price. Rather than tightening production control, the United States could reduce its excess wheat supply by reducing the target price. In order to have a clear basis for comparison, let us consider the case in which the target price is reduced to such an extent that the resulting drop in U.S. wheat production is the same as under the option of tightened production control.

In purely economic terms such a reduction of the U.S. target price would affect the EC in exactly the same manner as an equivalent cut of U.S. exports through production control. The world market price would rise, and in the first round this increase would lead to budget savings in the EC. In the second round it could trigger a less restrictive price policy in the European Community. In contrast to these equivalent economic effects, there is, however, a noteworthy difference in political impact. The point is that EC grain policy may well be affected by (a) the level of subsidies paid to U.S. wheat growers

339

and (b) the level of the U.S. target price.

1. Although the U.S. administration maintains that no subsidies are paid on U.S. wheat exports, deficiency payments in an exporting country are obviously an implicit form of export subsidy. For the time being, U.S. deficiency payments appear to cause no major trouble under the GATT. The situation may change, however. The GATT Committee on Trade in Agriculture has recommended negotiations on several points, including greater discipline of subsidies affecting exports. The European Community will probably strive to formulate the terms of reference for these (possible) negotiations so that they cover not only EC export restitutions but also U.S. deficiency payments on exported produce. If such coverage does materialize, the negotiating position of the United States will depend on the extent to which deficiency payments on exported commodities are made in the United States. If the United States had essentially eliminated deficiency payments, as would be the case if the U.S. target price were reduced to the then-increased level of the world market price, the United States would be in a very strong position to put pressure on the EC to reduce or eliminate its export subsidies. In such a case it would be much more difficult for the EC to react to the increased world market price by stepping up its domestic price support. The same reduction of U.S. export supply is thus likely to cause less (if any) expansion of exports from the EC when it is implemented through a reduction of the target price than when it is brought about through production control at high target prices.

2. Since 1981 the EC Commission has repeatedly suggested that EC grain prices should be adjusted to the level of U.S. prices. Though there are some doubts as to which U.S. prices are actually meant, we can assume that, if this proposal of the commission is ever taken seriously, the level of U.S. target prices will be considered the guideline. It is difficult to imagine that EC farmers will in the long run agree to receive prices lower than those to which U.S. farmers are entitled. Thus there is an indirect and weak but potentially effective link between the U.S. target price and the EC support price for wheat. If the United States wants to exploit this link, it must make sure that its target price is as low as politically possible. For this reason, too, a given reduction of the target price is preferable to tightened production control. Reducing the U.S. target price may bring political pressure to bear on the European Community to reduce its support prices. This reduction would benefit the United States, since it would lessen export competitions from the European Community.

Introducing Export Subsidies. One possible way of dealing with excess production capacity is to subsidize exports as necessary to sell the production surplus on the world market. The EC has long tended in this direction. The United States has for about twenty years essentially abstained from outright subsidies on grain exports. (I am excluding disguised export subsidies through subsidized export credits, and so forth, from consideration.) There may, however, be a strong temptation to expand U.S. exports with help from explicit export subsidies (as opposed to the implicit subsidies, or deficiency payments). Moreover, the fact that the EC has long used its variable export restitutions to secure a higher share of the world market may lead many observers to believe that the United States should fight back by introducing export subsidies, too.

In many ways the introduction of export subsidies would have implications that are at odds with a reduction in the target price. On the one hand export subsidies would put pressure on the EC budget because they would depress world market prices and would lead to higher EC export refunds. In that sense the export subsidies would improve the chances for CAP reform, for lower support prices in the European Community, and for reduced EC exports. On the other hand the export subsidies would provide the EC with a "bad example" and would increase the credibility of EC export subsidies. Again the economic factors tend in a different direction from the political factors. It is interesting to consider which of the two would prevail.

There can be little doubt that the political implications of the "bad U.S. example" would strongly outweigh the economic consequences through pressure on the EC budget and that the introduction of outright export subsidies by the U.S. would nearly force the EC to declare what in its view would be a subsidy war. Clearly the economic consequences of depressed world market prices, resulting from U.S. export subsidization, would harm the EC and would thus strengthen the case for a CAP reform toward a more restrictive support policy. We must nevertheless bear in mind some important considerations. In 1982 expenditure on export restitutions for grains from the EC budget was about 1,000 million ECUs. If the subsidization of exports by the United States reached the point where world market prices for all grains were depressed by 10 percent, EC export restitutions for grains would be forced up by 100 million ECUs as long as the EC did not change its export volume. The increase in EC expenditure would have been a mere 0.8 percent of total agricultural expenditure in the European Community in 1982. Even such small expenditure increases clearly count when the EC budget has hit its absolute ceiling, as is currently the case. The experience of 1984, however, indicates that the budget ceiling is in practice much less binding than it would appear in theory, particularly if the EC is politically motivated to make money available for the CAP.

Precisely this point is important here. An outright subsidization of exports by the United States is very likely to create the political will to spend more on the CAP in the European Community. Until now member countries have held differing views as to how much finance should be made available for the CAP. If the United States entered into a significant scheme of export subsidization, however, it would provide EC member states with the "common external enemy" or with the feeling of being under siege that is required to unite interests in the European Community. There is probably no single more effective way of making sure that the budget for the CAP is expanded than by putting explicit and direct external pressure on the CAP. Thus the explicit subsidization of U.S. exports would be ineffective and not only in the sense that it would cost the U.S. Treasury much more money than it would the EC budget. U.S. export subsidies are, moreover, likely to be counterproductive inasmuch as they would counteract tendencies to adopt a more restrictive grains policy in the EC.

The counterproductive effects of U.S. export subsidies are likely to be even more pronounced in the long run. The U.S. negotiating position within the GATT would be greatly weakened, if not completely eroded, in the event that the United States meanwhile introduced subsidies on its own grain exports. So far the United States has a strong point when it argues that the EC has not adjusted its grains policy to its changed market balance and that the EC cannot subsidize grain exports without limits. Once the United States adopts the same type of policy, it will lose in any argument of this type. The EC could counter any criticism by accusing the United States of the same sin, and it could continue to subsidize its exports without even having a bad conscience.

Reducing the Loan Rate. Another way of dealing with excess capacity in U.S. wheat production is to reduce the loan rate. This option would have the direct effect of causing more wheat to be exported rather than to be taken on stock. This option, too, would of course cause world market prices to decrease, forcing the EC to pay higher export subsidies. The resulting burden on the EC budget would enhance chances for CAP reform and would induce the European Community to adopt a more restrictive support price policy. In this sense the economic impact of this option would be favorable for the United States. Again, however, the political force tends in a different direction.

A reduction of the loan rate without a decrease in the target price means that the implicit subsidization of U.S. exports through deficiency payments increases. This effect is by far less visible than the introduction of explicit export subsidies. For this reason it would have a much lower political impact on the EC, and it would probably not be regarded as U.S. retaliation against EC export subsidies in the European Community. On the other hand, if the European Community finally came around to regarding U.S. deficiency payments as a different form of export subsidization, and if the EC was successful in having them included for consideration in GATT talks on export subsidies, the U.S. position would weaken in direct proportion to the widening of the gap between the loan rate and the target price. In any case, a reduction of the loan rate would trigger less dramatic reactions by far in the European Community than would the introduction of U.S. export subsidies.

342

By comparison with the current situation—in which the U.S. dollar is extremely strong—a reduction of the loan rate may actually be a necessary condition for ensuring that the EC does not increase its wheat exports significantly. The increasing dollar value has meanwhile led to a situation that may make it possible for the EC to export wheat at zero export restitutions, which would appear to change the atmosphere in the EC grains policy significantly. Claude Villain, the director general for agriculture in the EC Commission, is on record as having noted that in this changed world market the EC no longer feels obliged to constrain its wheat exports to 14 percent of the world market. So far, according to his argument, the EC has unofficially considered 14 percent as its "equitable share" of the world market and has voluntarily constrained its exports to this level. Now, however, it no longer feels the need to honor this self-imposed obligation. Hence an inflexibly high loan rate in the United States has provided the European Community with both the economic incentive and the political justification to expand its wheat exports. A reduction of the loan rate to at least a market-clearing level would prevent this reaction from the EC.

Reducing Both the Target Price and the Loan Rate. A combined option may have merits, both from the domestic U.S. point of view and with regard to EC reactions. The target price could be somewhat reduced but could still remain above the level at which markets would clear without government interference, and the loan rate could be reduced so that it would not become effective in "normal" years but would still function as a "safety net" in periods of weak world market demand. Domestically, within the United States, this option would make it possible to keep government expenditure under control without putting too much pressure on farm incomes.

With regard to EC response, this option may receive even higher marks than a pure reduction of either the target price or the loan rate. World market prices would remain at a lower level than if target prices were reduced more strongly. Hence the economic pressure on the European Community through its budget would continue to be effective. On the other hand, U.S. wheat production would be subsidized to a lower extent than if only the loan rate were reduced. There would thus be increasing political pressure on the EC to bring down the level of protection granted to its grain producers. The combined reduction of target price and loan rate may therefore be well worth considering.

My discussion has so far been in purely comparative, static terms. Yet policies must be pursued in a dynamic environment. What options can be followed when market conditions change from year to year? Without going into any details I can say that a strategy of support and target prices that are continuously adjusted to a changing market situation may well be a possibility. Such a policy on the part of the United States would put the EC in a rather difficult situation, as the European Community has never managed to adopt such flexibility. Should the United States follow such a strategy, it could well serve as a good example for the EC. Because such a U.S. strategy has the potential to induce the EC to adopt a similar policy, it could possibly contribute importantly to the stabilization of international markets through better adjustment of national policies.

Conclusions

U.S. and EC grain policies, different as they are often said to be, have much in common. Lately they have both come under major economic and political stress. Difficulties on both sides of the Atlantic will affect the way in which these policies will be reconsidered during the next few months. The CAP for grains will have to change soon if the European Community wants to avoid running into unmanageable problems on its domestic grain market and in international trade. The United States is considering different options for its grain policy in preparing the 1985 farm bill. The reconsideration of policy on one side of the Atlantic is linked with the simultaneous reconsideration of policy on the other side to a greater extent than observers often realize. The option that is finally adopted in the United States will have a major impact on future developments in the CAP. CAP repercussions may likewise significantly influence the outcome of U.S. policy decisions.

If we rank U.S. grain policy options according to the extent to which they would be counterproductive—in the sense that they would finally lead to an increase of EC exports and hence to an erosion of the demand for U.S. exports—the following picture emerges. Most counterproductive would be the introduction of outright export subsidies in the United States, as it would politically support the continuation or even the intensification of current EC policies, with their tendency toward increasing grain surpluses in the European Community. Tightening production control in the United States would be less counterproductive, but reducing the target price would be even better because it would put more pressure on the EC to bring down its grain prices. A reduction of the loan rate might stand between these latter two options. The optimal solution, from the standpoint of avoiding EC export expansion, might be a simultaneous reduction of the loan rate and the target price, since this measure would combine economic and political pressure on the CAP.

Commentary

Timothy Josling

Tangermann has provided us with an excellent overview of the political and economic linkages between U.S. policy, particularly in the grain sector, and that of the European Community. As I have no fundamental disagreement with his analysis, it may be more useful for me to elaborate on some of Tangermann's ideas than to give a critique of them. In particular, I would like to explore the notion of policy interdependence in agricultural markets and, by extension, the possible impact on other countries of the combined effect of U.S. and EC changes in farm policies.

The United States and the EC are the superpowers of agricultural trade: their conflicts and their agreements profoundly influence the conditions of trade for other countries. As superpowers, they watch each other's moves carefully, perhaps tending to ascribe more rationality and consistency to each other's actions than in reality exists. In matters of agricultural trade, they exhibit a combination of self-assurance and vulnerability, of declared autonomy and concerned dependence.

The case for treating U.S. and EC policies as autonomous is clear-cut. We could then regard the EC as "just" another trading country in the world market; there would be little need to single out the repercussions of EC policy as a topic for discussion in a conference about U.S. agricultural policy. To be sure, the reaction of the EC, like that of other countries in the trading system, would have to be built into the qualitative analysis of U.S. farm policy changes—for example, into the estimates of the slope of the export demand curve facing U.S. products, but there would be little point in trying to analyze policy linkages as such. Other countries' policies are merely part of the environment.

This domestic-centered view of agricultural policy would find support in Europe, where a similar conference on EC policy options might include a cursory look at U.S. policy as a part of the economic environment in which the CAP must operate. Just as U.S. policy is dominated by the clash between rent-seeking groups and budget constraints, so European policy is driven by rent-seeking countries against the limit of common financial resources. Under such circumstances, it is not obvious why studying the impact of one country's policy choices on those of another country warrants more than a passing footnote.

Governments do not always seem to take such a limited view of policy independence. In agricultural policy, as in foreign policy, it is essential to sustain the notion that one country's actions do impinge upon those of another and not just through an impersonal change in the world price level. Successive U.S. administrations have spent a considerable amount of time trying to change EC policy in agricultural markets. They have defined ideological positions to elevate the matter above the mere issue of export earnings; they have engaged in export subsidy skirmishes in selected markets to send "warning shots across bows" of the European Community; they have formed coalitions with other countries to put pressure on the EC to mend its ways; and they have used the institutions of trade and economic policy (GATT and the Organization for Economic Cooperation and Development, or OECD) as additional places to lobby for changes in the CAP. These developments do not square with the notion of independent agricultural policies dictated by domestic circumstance.

The EC also behaves as if U.S. policy influenced its own actions and, to a lesser extent, as if it could influence U.S. policy. As Tangermann notes, the EC Commission has actually declared its intention to harmonize its own cereal prices with those in the United States—a task made immeasurably easier by the appreciation of the dollar. The European Community links U.S. energy policy with its own need to "complete" the CAP by putting limits on corn gluten imports and complains that its own export subsidies on grains respond to the indirect subsidies on U.S. products through the target price policy. The commission certainly thinks it worthwhile to lobby against the Wine Equity Act and to threaten retaliation for any limitations on access to U.S. markets.

In view of the apparent assumptions behind both domestic and trade policy, we might be forgiven a little schizophrenia. Domestic policy is sacrosanct, born of domestic concerns tempered only by the knowledge that other countries can influence the size of export markets and the levels of import supplies through their own (autonomous) policies. Trade policy in agriculture, however, assumes interdependence of national policies, with potential modification of behavior resulting from foreign pressure or mutual agreement—with national authorities being able to secure the compliance of domestic interests to the policy changes. The U.S. farm bill will set domestic programs for the next few years, but the next round of GATT talks will discuss modifications in such national policies to improve the trading system. The European Community has the greatest difficulty in securing agreement among the ten member states on even the most sensible cost-reducing measures in the CAP but agrees (or seems to agree) to a GATT document calling for talks leading to the removal of export subsidies (the key instrument in price support for a large part of European agriculture), negotiates export shares in the world wheat market, and promotes international commodity agreements that depend upon domestic supply control. To what extent do domestic agricultural policies lie in the international domain? The question needs to be resolved in the next few years.

346

TABLE 1
Outcome of Combinations of U.S. and EC Agricultural Policy Choice

	United States	
	Protectionist	Liberalizing
European Community Protectionist	Chance of trade wars	EC captures benefits of U.S. policy change
	Cartelization of trade	U.S. changes more costly
Liberalizing	United States captures benefits of EC policy change	Relaxation of trade tensions
	EC changes more costly	Major benefits to trading partners

SOURCE: Author.

Superpower status in agricultural affairs confers on the United States and the EC obligations that extend beyond the degree of actual or presumed interdependence. Whether they act independently or coherently, the superpowers' combined actions will greatly influence other countries and other areas of international trade, as can be illustrated in a simple tableau. For convenience, let us define U.S. policy as becoming either more liberal (lowering target prices, reducing loan rates, or removing supply control) or more protectionist (with mandatory quotas, export subsidies, and trade policy retaliation against other nations). The makers of EC policy in agriculture face a similar choice. The move toward guarantee thresholds, as Tangermann notes, together with the proposed harmonization of grain prices with U.S. levels, would represent a measure of liberalization. Export subsidy costs are pushing the European Community in this direction, though over the objection of some member states that stand to lose. By contrast, other actions being proposed will lead the EC to new heights of protectionism—introducing quotas on nongrain feed imports, unbinding the oilseed tariffs, taxing vegetable oil consumption, and extending domestic quotas from sugar and dairy to cereals and other products. The four combinations of U.S. and EC policy appear in table 1.

Increased protectionism in both the United States and the EC cannot be ruled out—indeed, it may be the most likely development in the absence of

347

firm decisions on both sides of the Atlantic. If protectionism means that the United States tries to recapture lost markets with export subsidies, and if the EC chooses to find the money to respond, then trade wars will persist, to the detriment of commercial and diplomatic relationships in other areas. If protection takes the form of acreage control in both cases, then the door will be open for trade agreements "respecting each other's market shares"—in other words, cartelization of presently competitive markets. Such arrangements are unlikely to be stable, but their superficial appeal (and their low budget cost) might keep them around until the reputation of the United States as a competitive supplier has been damaged.

The two asymmetric combinations of policy have less dramatic consequences for world markets. They are, however, significant in terms of policy change. If the EC moves in the direction of protectionism at the same time that the United States is attempting to liberalize its policy, some part of the benefit of the U.S. change is captured by the EC policy maker. As U.S. agriculture adjusts to market possibilities without the cushion of extensive government financial supports, the pressure on the EC to make similar changes is reduced. On the other hand, the United States will find it more difficult to liberalize if the EC can take advantage of the easier market conditions and can postpone policy adjustments. Similarly, if the United States were to move toward greater protection—say, through export subsidies—the EC would lose some of its own economic benefits from liberalization, making such a move less likely, though the act of liberalization of the CAP if it occurred could in turn make U.S. protectionism less costly.

Only increased liberalization on both sides of the Atlantic offers the prospect of a relaxation of trade tensions and major benefits to the conduct of world agricultural trade. Such benefits will not come easily when interest groups have grown accustomed to protection against market forces, but a time of budget stringency offers an opportunity to correct past policy errors and to form new expectations. The United States and the EC have come to dominate trade policy in temperate-zone agricultural products. If both moved in the direction of trade liberalization, through the modification of protectionist legislation in their agricultural policies, there is little doubt that the world trading system would itself be significantly improved in its ability to satisfy the needs of developed and developing countries.

How are my two themes connected? The extent to which domestic agricultural policy is influenced by goings-on abroad in effect changes the probabilities of the outcomes illustrated in table 1. Imagine, for example, that domestic policy was *not* measurably influenced by the actions of other nations. Assume a 70 percent probability that the United States will move to more liberal agricultural programs and a similar chance that the EC, also acting autonomously, will move to more protectionism. This scenario implies that there is a 49 percent chance that the United States will liberalize at a time when the EC is not doing so; a 9 percent chance that the EC will undertake liberalization alone; a 21 percent chance of double liberalization; and a 21 percent chance also of double protectionism.

Such probabilities would of themselves be interesting to policy planners in the United States, the EC, and elsewhere in terms of assessment of future policy costs. Let us now assume, however, that U.S. liberalization is much less likely in the context of increased EC protection, either increasing the chances of a drift to double protection or inducing the EC to join in the liberalization trend. The other asymmetric outcome may also be less likely, as policy makers react to the other superpower. Again, double protection or double liberalization may be the outcome. The result is likely to be a reduced probability that U.S. farm policies will be liberalized (they will be held back by EC protection) and reduced chances of further EC protectionism (as the EC is coaxed by the United States toward liberalization). Tangermann's paper well illustrates these tendencies for food grains, and similar analyses could be done for other commodities. It is important for us to explore the extent to which quasi-autonomous policies are interdependent, if only to gain perspective on the degree of dependency and the direction in which such dependency pulls national policies. Interdependence may of course also imply the need for explicit policy coordination at the international level, but that is probably best left for another decade.

Toward a Market Orientation: The Dilemma Facing Farm Policy in the 1980s

Todd E. Petzel

One of the key themes of the present administration has been the desirability of economic policies that emphasize market orientation wherever possible. There have been some dramatic instances of deregulation of certain industrial sectors, but the reality for the farm community has been a continuation of government programs that attempt to bolster sagging producer incomes while promoting distorted prices and a misallocation of resources. The traditional view supporting intervention can be briefly summarized:

- Farmers face extraordinary risks from price volatility associated with the unique nature of agricultural markets.
- This risk has the effect of discouraging investment and innovation in agriculture because of farmers' highly uncertain income streams.
- The importance of agriculture in the U.S. economy is unparalleled, and consequently programs that reduce the risks in farming have broad benefits to society.

There are, however, counterarguments, and now, as discussions concerning the philosophy and reality of the next farm bill grow heated, is an opportune time to evaluate the currently existing market alternatives by which the stated goals of the government may be achieved.

Private solutions to problems of volatility can take many forms, including insurance policies, futures and forward markets, and options markets. For problems of agricultural price risk, insurance programs have never played a significant role because of difficulties relating to the cyclical nature of agriculture and the lumpiness of claims. Unlike accident and fire insurance, which involve actuarial risk that may be estimated precisely, farm price insurance would expose the insurers to long periods of massive claims followed by periods of virtually no claims. Because the incidence and duration of such periods is highly variable and is subject to both domestic and international government policy shifts, the environment has not been conducive to the success of private sector insurance.

The most efficient private sector response to the question of price volatility has been the widespread use of futures markets. These markets have provided risk-shifting opportunities to farmers, merchants, and consumers for decades. Historically, the level of activity on these markets is an almost perfect reflection of the price volatility and risk. In the 1950s and 1960s, when farm prices showed only minor price changes, the volume in agricultural futures was modest. In the 1970s and 1980s, however, there has been a dramatic increase in agricultural price risk and an explosive growth of futures use by all commercial agricultural sectors. This enhanced participation indicates the risk-shifting value of these markets.

Most recently, the Commodity Futures Trading Commission (CFTC) has approved a pilot program for options on agricultural futures, promising to offer a significant private alternative to firms and individuals seeking price protection. Options are frequently compared with insurance programs in that the buyer pays a premium for the right, but not the obligation, to perform on the contract. A farmer wishing to avoid the possible damage of a significant drop in prices over his planning horizon, for example, would buy a put option that would give him the right to sell his product at the option contract price. If prices increased over the term of the option, the farmer would let the contract expire and would sell his product on the open market. If prices fell, he would exercise his option and would receive the contract price less the cost of the premium.

Several contract prices are available to traders of exchange-listed options so that they may tailor their portfolio to match their risk preferences. If soybean futures are currently about $6.25 per bushel, the farmer could choose a $5.75 put, which would offer no protection against the first $0.50 decline in price but could then protect him from further calamities. This strategy is analogous to having a high deductible on an insurance policy, and such policies of course have lower premiums than put options guaranteeing higher contract prices.

The risk-shifting features of options and futures are well known, but these private instruments cannot change the market price. The resolution of supply and demand is the ultimate discipline, and only market participants who manage their positions with futures and options will be protected from unexpected shifts away from the equilibrium. The voluntary decision to seek price protection or not is one of the key factors in farm management and will become even more important if the new farm bill actually moves toward increased market orientation.

Income stability and support, not necessarily in that order, have been the priorities of the various farm programs for more than fifty years. Sometimes stability is simply a byproduct of support. Domestic sugar prices, lifted by the competition-stifling features of import tariffs, have been insulated near twenty-one cents per pound for over two years while freely traded world sugar

351

has fluctuated between four and fourteen cents per pound. It is clear that domestic growers benefit from not facing high price volatility, but it is further obvious that the stability occurred because programs leading to such a distorted equilibrium virtually require administered prices. Sugar is certainly an extreme example, but it is an important one because it highlights the fact that futures and options markets could provide similar stability in prices offered by the government, but they could never give artificial support.

Government price protection programs can be seen as equivalent to put options; the government (read here "taxpayers") is the seller of options but receives no premiums to compensate it for the risk. If prices fall below the targets, farmers are protected and the agricultural budget explodes. If prices are above the targets, farmers participate in the free market, ignoring their implicit puts, and the administration and Congress quibble about who should receive the credit for keeping costs under control. Depending on the degree of support, these programs are either dear or cheap. In every case, however, the farmer is receiving an implicit benefit in terms of price insurance, whether it is effective or not.

The government programs to stabilize agricultural prices are too frequently evaluated by their effect on the government budget rather than by their economic cost. The sugar program can be seen as good because little sugar is put under loan and direct government outlays are minor. The cost to consumers, forced to pay prices insulated from foreign competition, is over $2 billion a year, but since this figure is not part of the government deficit, it is somehow less subject to criticism.

The visible problems come from agricultural commodities that the United States exports. For net import goods, trade barriers may be erected and the costs shifted to consumers and foreign producers. There is no such easy way out for exported products, as has become acutely evident in a strong-dollar world. Any support for these products has to be supplied by the government. Although the relative level of support may be considerably less than that received by net import products, the grain programs receive disproportionate political attention because of their impact on the government budget.

In searching for cheaper alternatives to existing programs, the last farm bill authorized the study of an insurance scheme to protect farm incomes that would be a joint project of the private and public sectors. That project's report estimated costs and benefits for Illinois farmers and argued that the idea had sufficient merit to warrant a pilot program. To the authors' credit they identify many bureaucratic and functional areas of potential difficulty, and in my opinion the major stumbling block would be in the area of administrative costs and control.

The idea of insurance is certainly appealing, but it leaves undetermined the appropriate level of support. At one extreme are the farm programs that try to peg support levels over the long term. At the opposite end are options and futures that offer price protection for at most a year or two around the current equilibrium. In the middle is the hypothetical income insurance plan that has payouts as a function of a moving average of the past few years' prices. The signals that farmers receive are considerably different across the plans, and I believe the major policy issue of the next farm bill should be our measure of commitment to free-market signals for agriculture.

If the commitment to the market is genuine, we may validly ask what the best means to achieve price protection around the equilibrium value is. A simulation of the agricultural options markets (I have presented one elsewhere)[1] suggests that considerable price protection may be achieved at a modest cost. The early trading records of cotton, soybeans, live cattle, and wheat options all suggest that the prices used in the simulation were fairly close to the mark. The biggest problem right now is increasing the trading volume in these instruments so that a large number of farmers can achieve the desired price protection.

The advantages of relying on the market are enormous. Prices and resource allocation are not distorted, and taxpayers are not subject to periodic shocks as agriculture experiences its ups and downs. One disadvantage is that farmers have shifted a large degree of price risk management onto the government, and with a market orientation they would have to acquire some new tools. American farmers, however, have always been resourceful and efficient, given the proper incentives, and they will undoubtedly acquire the necessary management skills in this area.

There will be a strong temptation in this farm bill to suggest that the country "ease" into a market orientation by gradually winding down the support programs and moving to the markets. Such a program would have attractions for both the interventionist and the free-market camps, but I believe that it contains the seeds of its own failure. If farmers continue to receive free implicit puts from the government, they will have no incentive to participate in the futures and options markets. Furthermore, the price distortions caused by any support program will cause serious pricing problems in the option market that will impair the efficiency of these developing instruments.

A hybrid solution would be government support rates well below forecast prices, combined with the private alternative of participation in the options and futures markets. The taxpayers would be giving farmers an insurance policy with a large deductible, and farmers could secure more protection from the private sector if they so chose. Price distortions would be considerably reduced, the benefits of income stability would go to those farmers who valued them enough to pay for them, and the options and futures markets would be allowed to demonstrate their effectiveness in an unfettered market. Whether the 1985 farm bill will do this job remains to be seen, but no other alternatives can meet the dual goals of market orientation and protection from price volatility.

353

The CFTC has done its part in removing a fifty-year ban on agricultural options trading and has thus made it easier to bring about market orientation in agriculture. It now remains for the administration and Congress to decide whether these markets will form the basis of risk management in agriculture or whether it will be business as usual, with a continuation of interventionist policies.

Automatic Adjustment Rules in Commodity Programs

Richard E. Just

Agricultural policies have been among the most volatile areas of U.S. government regulation over the past three and a half decades. Many times these changes have involved switching to a new set of controls for which experience is lacking. Although grain programs have continued to involve some type of price support, they have periodically involved no production control, allotments, voluntary diversion, or set-aside requirements. Price support has periodically been maintained by means of government acquisition, shipments under P.L. 480, a subsidized farmer-owned reserve, or direct payments such as certificates, deficiency payments, or the payment-in-kind (PIK) program. In addition to each of these major changes in the set of active policy instruments, the levels of instruments have been revised annually when they were in effect, and in some cases emergency revisions have been made more often. The wheat support price, for example, has changed by an average of twenty cents per bushel during the past two decades, with a downward adjustment in seven of twenty years that occasionally amounted to twenty-five cents or more per bushel. Throughout this period the support price was revised in every year except 1975.

This history of agricultural policy volatility is indicative of a haphazard and shortsighted approach to agricultural policy formulation. A study of the evolution of these policy changes reveals that revisions have for the most part been made because anticipated economic conditions did not materialize.[1] Rather, unanticipated changes in the economy, for example in trade conditions or crop yields, led to unacceptable Treasury costs or farm income levels.

With the commodity boom of the early 1970s, for example, governmental policy, which had long faced a problem of excess stocks, acted instead to liquidate stocks too rapidly and then exposed the economy to the risk of large increases in agricultural price. That is, from the standpoint of a policy maker trying to contain inflation, government stocks were liquidated too quickly and thus failed to provide the stabilizing influence for which taxpayers had so long been paying.

As a result of these conditions, which were apparently not well anticipated, Congress enacted legislation in 1977 designed to replenish stocks, once again, in the form of a farmer-owned reserve. This policy was perceived to have accomplished its objectives when the term of the legislation expired in 1981. Thus the 1981 Food and Agriculture Act was passed with few modifications from the 1977 legislation. Again, however, unanticipated economic conditions materialized. With substantial stocks in the farmer-owned reserve, the record crops of 1981 and 1982, along with deteriorating general economic conditions, led to another urgent need for policy revisions. In contrast to the conditions that led to the commodity boom of the early 1970s, the exchange rate had turned against U.S. exports, real interest rates were rising sharply, and money supply was very tight.

With over 1 billion bushels of wheat and 2.5 billion bushels of feed grains in public stocks of one form or another, Treasury costs became excessive, and again a short-run solution was considered. One such "solution" was the Farm Crisis Act of 1982, which, if it had passed, would have mandated controls on production. As an alternative, Congress chose the PIK program. Again, however, unanticipated conditions materialized. Treasury costs of the PIK program were almost an order of magnitude greater than anticipated, and commodity-program costs exceeded the total net income from farming.[2] Again, policies had to be modified in 1984, lowering target prices from adjustments prescribed by the 1981 act.

This brief review of the U.S. agricultural policy process reveals that policies have often been set in a shortsighted, "firefighting" manner. According to Spitze, "the goal of public policy [has been] to find a responsive, workable solution to urgent, difficult, hurting problems."[3] Examination of the dynamics of the policy process, however, reveals that the firefighting approach to policy formulation tends to produce policies appropriate for conditions that have led to current problems rather than conditions that may exist after new policies are enacted.[4]

Neglected Considerations in Policy Formation

This reactive rather than active approach to agricultural policy, with its frequent and often unanticipated revisions, invites consideration of some fundamental and largely neglected questions about the nature and effect of policy. Specifically, these examples suggest the need for formulating agricultural policies with more foresight, so that the levels and perhaps the set of policy instruments adjust automatically to changing economic conditions. If the timing of adjustment is built into agricultural legislation in response to a sufficiently broad range of economic circumstances, then perhaps policy controls can be more in tune with current rather than lagged economic conditions, and thus short-run crises may be fewer and more infrequent.

Cochrane and Ryan have warned that the establishment of agricultural

356

price and income supports four years in advance (as attempted by most recent major agricultural acts) can only bring trouble in a highly uncertain world.[5] If market conditions deteriorate, target prices or loan rates may prove to have been set too far above market-clearing levels and may thus cause unpredictably large Treasury outlays. On the other hand, if market conditions improve unexpectedly, a policy may fail to provide price and income support when the cost of doing so is low. If policy makers isolate farmers from market signals by not making policy instruments responsive to evolving conditions, they risk either large increases in Treasury costs or program ineffectiveness as the economy diverges from perceptions held at the time of policy formulation. As Nelson and Cochrane, for example, have shown, by holding farm prices inflexibly high from 1953 to 1965 incentives were provided for enough expansion of output to keep farm prices lower than they would have been from 1968 to 1972.[6] Johnson argues that "a price just 10 percent above the market clearing levels soon results in a substantial excess production that must either be stored, disposed of in some manner, or eliminated through output reduction."[7] He concludes, "After all the attention that had been given to the increased instability that emerged post-1972, it was wholly inappropriate that legislation with so much inflexibility had become the law of the land."[8] Because market conditions change, inflexible policies, even with piecemeal adjustment, can become a destabilizing influence or can promote economic inefficiency by artificially holding prices too far out of equilibrium before adjustments are finally made. Automatic adjustments in policies can permit smoother, more orderly adjustments in producer prices that more rapidly transmit at least some appropriate adjustment signals between consumers and farmers. As a result, policy formulation along these lines seems to hold possibilities for reducing the cost of disequilibrium usually attributed to agricultural policy.

Goals of Agricultural Policy

A fundamental problem that has impeded the study of automatic adjustment of policy instruments is that optimal adjustment cannot be determined until the policy criterion that defines optimality has been identified. If a study answers the question of optimal automatic adjustment of policies using inappropriate policy objectives, the results will be of no use. As stated in the enabling legislation, the general purpose of U.S. agricultural policy is "to provide price and income protection for farmers, assure consumers an abundance of food and fiber at reasonable prices, continue food assistance to low-income households, and for other purposes."[9] This statement of purpose is open to considerable interpretation, and many more specific goals have been suggested in the interpretive literature. Some of the commodity policy goals delineated there include increasing total farm income, reducing income disparity, stabilizing

357

markets, providing an adequate food supply, increasing efficiency, cutting program costs, preserving the family farm, promoting exports, and stabilizing the overall economy.[10] The specific agricultural policy instruments in U.S. policy (price support, production controls, and government storage), however, do nothing to offer family farms special advantages and in fact work against export promotion. Such commercial policies only work to stabilize the overall economy by stabilizing agricultural markets. Furthermore, pursuance of these policies has led not simply to an adequate food supply but to an overabundance of the commodities with heaviest policy control. Thus, by the revealed preferences of policy makers, the goals of preserving the family farm, export promotion, stabilizing the overall economy, and providing an adequate food supply do not appear important in commercial policy formulation.

The remaining goals, with one important exception, tend to be consistent with and indeed suggestive of the usual criterion of social welfare economics: the criterion that maximizes consumer welfare (as measured by consumers' surplus) plus producer welfare (as measured by producers' surplus) less government costs maximizes efficiency globally, minimizes government program costs ceteris paribus, and leads to economically efficient levels of stabilization in the agricultural sector.[11] The exception has to do with special consideration of farm incomes vis-à-vis other sectors of the economy. Therefore, a revealed preference analysis of commercial agricultural policies suggests that some modification of the usual criterion of welfare economics to give increased weight to producers may serve as a basis for examination of the potential for automatic adjustment rules in policy legislation.

In this departure from usual practices, we must recognize that the customary equal weighting in social welfare economics is based on the compensation principle, which assumes that nondistorting lump-sum transfers are always possible.[12] With this "ivory tower" assumption, even though a policy that maximizes the simple sum of surpluses might cause an extremely skewed income distribution, policy makers can simply transfer the benefits among groups without cost and without altering marginal economic behavior so that any desired redistribution of income can be attained. In this way, an increase in, say, consumer surplus can be made equivalent to an increase in benefits for producers so that equal weighting is appropriate.

Realistically speaking, however, nondistorting and costless lump-sum transfers are simply not possible. If government decides to transfer money from consumers to producers, then more consumers will attempt to become producers and will thus alter the economic behavior that would otherwise maximize the simple sum of surpluses. Similarly, consumption behavior would be altered by a change in after-tax income associated with the transfer. For this reason, policy analysis must consider specific mechanisms for accomplishing transfers together with their accompanying distorting effects if it is to have practical policy relevance.[13] In this context, the free-market competitive economy may not be the norm by which alternative policies should be judged. If not, then the occurrence of dead-weight social loss, according to economists' usual definition, does not imply that policy is inappropriate.

The traditional definition of dead-weight loss is the difference in the simple sum of producers' and consumers' surpluses from the maximum possible simple sum after considering government costs. If a production quota is preferable to the free market because of an unequally weighted policy criterion, and some other politically, as well as economically, feasible mechanism does not exist for attaining a higher level of the policy criterion, then the quota attains optimality even though it does not maximize an unweighted welfare criterion. If we adopt the notion that only elected policy makers have the right to determine the social welfare function (the policy criterion), then only a departure from the optimal level of the operative policy criterion can properly be termed a social loss. If we bear in mind these arguments, we see that economic analysis of policy choice and adjustment mechanisms in particular must focus on direct maximization of a policy criterion function reflective of any unequal weighting determined by various political factors. Also, because of problems of political feasibility, we must recognize that only a limited set of policy tools may be feasible in practice. For this reason, the present paper limits its consideration to the tools of price supports and production control that have demonstrated feasibility.

With these considerations in mind, I depart here considerably from most literature on optimal policy formulation. With the traditional equally weighted welfare criterion, the justification for policy intervention is based on market failure. In the context of agriculture, the primary candidates for sources of market failure are risk, imperfect capital markets, and concentration in input and output markets. Commercial agricultural policies, however, do not address concentration in input markets or correct imperfections in capital markets. Antitrust law addresses concentration in output markets much more effectively than commercial agricultural policies. Finally, policies that directly reduce risk, such as federal crop insurance, have filled only a minor role in the overall agricultural policy picture. With the weighted criterion considered here, however, the justification for policy intervention can be simply income transfer, say, from consumers to producers. The major tools of agricultural policy (price supports and production controls) primarily cause a transfer of income from consumers to producers. If risk rather than income transfer were the justification for intervention, any minimum price should be symmetrically offset by a maximum price. Except for the farmer-owned reserve, for which the release and call prices have never been very effective, this has not been the case. Thus, by the revealed preference of policy makers, the optimal formulation of agricultural policy must apparently be studied in the context of unequal welfare weights.

The existence of and variation in these welfare weightings are explained

359

by two considerations. First, they may reflect some normative concept of preference for a particular income distribution. In this context, preference for an equal income distribution would suggest that the weight for producers versus consumers should decline if producers' income improves relative to consumers' income and vice versa. Alternatively, some recent literature departs from the normative concept of a social welfare function in studying how policy choices are made in reality and explains how the unequal weightings of benefits are determined by political behavior and by bargaining among various interest groups and policy makers. In this literature, the weightings of different groups in policy selection can be viewed as a function of the lobbying power and effort of farm groups relative to consumer groups.[14] Because agricultural support has continued—albeit at sometimes reduced levels—even when farm incomes have been above the average income of nonfarmers, both of these considerations appear to be appropriate. Thus consideration of welfare weights appears necessary for future policy analysis even though inequities may be resolved.

Optimal Adjustment in the Set of Policy Instruments

First, consider the possibility that the *set* of policy controls should be altered from time to time, depending on current economic conditions. Such changes are certainly typified by the history of agricultural policy revisions in the United States. If these changes are warranted from time to time, then incorporating a rule in agricultural legislation defining circumstances when the set of active policy instruments changes would help provide farmers with appropriate production signals. If a farmer does not correctly anticipate a switch from production subsidies (deficiency payments) to production limitations (allotments or set-asides), for example, he may overinvest in machinery and fixed productive inputs, thus causing economic inefficiency.

The concept of automatic adjustment in the set of policy instruments is not new in U.S. agricultural policy. Under 1981 legislation, for example, the secretary of agriculture has explicit power to impose varying levels of set-aside requirements in each new production period, depending on the outcome during the previous crop year. Similarly, in the 1985 feed grain program, if the U.S. Department of Agriculture estimates that the corn carryout as of September 30, 1985, will exceed 1.5 billion bushels, the 1985 program will include a total acreage cutback of 5 percent to 20 percent and a combination of acreage reduction and paid diversion in addition to the target price and deficiency payment mechanism. Although these programs specify changes in policies for certain circumstances, they leave the secretary with considerable discretion, and these areas of flexibility can cause farmers serious uncertainty.

The conceptual work of Wallace some twenty years ago represents the first analytical attempt to investigate the choice of agricultural policy instru-

FIGURE 1

PRODUCTION CONTROLS VERSUS DEFICIENCY PAYMENTS

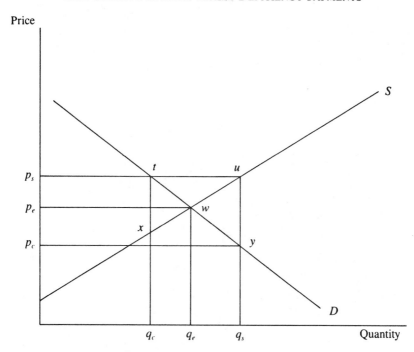

ments on economic grounds. On the basis of the standard supply-demand diagram, he examines the old Cochrane (production control) and Brannan (price subsidy) plans, concluding that the appropriate choice of policy instrument depends on the elasticities of supply and demand.[15]

Specifically, in the case of linear supply and demand, Wallace finds that the dead-weight loss areas with deficiency payments (area *uwy* in figure 1) and production control (area *twx* in figure 1) are just equal with equal slopes of supply and demand, but that production control causes greater net loss if demand elasticity exceeds supply elasticity, whereas deficiency payments cause greater loss if supply elasticity exceeds demand elasticity (at equilibrium). Gardner has recently extended this analysis by varying policy instrument levels to derive trade-off curves between producers' and consumers' surplus, as shown in figure 2.[16] By varying the maximum production control from equilibrium down to zero, he finds the curve that gives the frontier of producer-consumer surplus possibilities for production control. This curve terminates at the origin on one end because a production quota of zero causes complete loss of both producers' and consumers' surplus. It terminates at point *A* with a slope of −1 on the other end, because a maximum production

361

FIGURE 2

Welfare Possibilities Frontiers for Selected Policy Instruments

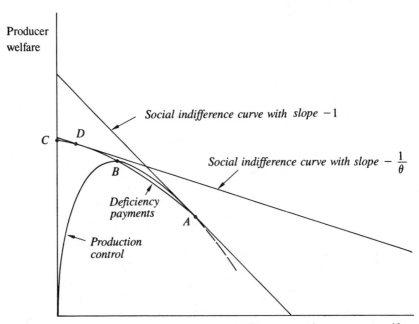

limit becomes ineffective when increased beyond free-market equilibrium output and because equilibrium output is the output level that maximizes the sum of producers' and consumers' surplus with the customary equal weighting. That is, with a social welfare function that equally weights producers and consumers, the social indifference curves have a slope of −1 and attain the optimal tangency with the surplus possibilities frontier at the free-market equilibrium output.

For purposes of comparison with the surplus possibilities frontier for production control, the corresponding surplus possibilities frontier for deficiency payments is derived by varying the target price upward from the equilibrium price, which thus moves the corresponding output upward from equilibrium. In this case, however, the government incurs expenditures for deficiency payments that must be considered in addition to the effects on producers' and consumers' surplus. Gardner argues that government costs are most conveniently combined with consumers' surplus, because consumers essentially constitute the tax-paying public that must finance government deficits. Thus the surplus possibilities frontier for deficiency payments in figure 2

362

is derived by varying quantity upward from equilibrium and observing the resulting trade-off between producers' surplus and consumers' surplus less government costs. This trade-off curve terminates on the vertical axis at point C, with negative slope throughout because increasing quantity by increasing price support continues to increase producers' surplus, whereas government costs rise faster than consumers' surplus until the two are just equal. The curve terminates on the other end at point A with slope -1, because the deficiency payment and government costs approach zero and the surplus trade-off approaches free-market conditions.[17]

The work of Wallace and Gardner is interesting from the standpoint of automatic adjustment because the conditions that determine whether a production control or a production subsidy are preferred can change. Thus automatic adjustment can be built into agricultural policy, for example, in order to switch from one control to the other when economic or political conditions so merit.

The selection of the optimal policy instrument shown in figure 2 depends on the weighting of producers' welfare relative to consumers' welfare. If this weighting, say, θ, is only slightly larger than 1, the indifference curve with slope $-1/\theta$ is steeper, and the highest point of tangency with a surplus possibilities frontier will occur on the production control curve. With larger relative weighting for producers, the indifference curve becomes less steep and the highest surplus possibilities tangency occurs on the deficiency payments curve, for example at point D.

Just shows that the maximum weighted welfare with production control is greater (less) than with deficiency payments if the slope of demand at equilibrium is greater (less) than the slope of supply at equilibrium multiplied by the welfare weight of producers relative to consumers.[18] This finding implies that the optimal choice of policy instrument changes with shifts in the slope of supply, in the slope of demand, or in the welfare weighting of producers relative to consumers.

In the context of this illustration, consider the possibilities for automatic adjustment of the set of policy instruments. Consider first the case of changes in the slopes (or elasticities) of supply and demand for a given welfare weight. If these slopes change in ways unanticipated at the time of policy formation but realized at the time of private decision making, then possibilities for improving welfare (as measured by the policy criterion function) may be lost without automatic adjustment.

Suppose the choice between production control and target prices with deficiency payments is made in formulating the 1985 farm bill, and an optimal choice of level is made in either case. Assume that conditions at the time lead to the optimal choice of a deficiency payment scheme. An unanticipated decline, say, in the value of the dollar during the ensuing time period of applicability of the legislation could then render the choice inappropriate. A decline in the exchange rate, for example, is customarily viewed as tilting the demand for exports clockwise while increasing it.[19] If demand tilts sufficiently, production control becomes the more appropriate policy instrument. Conversely, if production controls were chosen from the outset, an increase in the value of the dollar could cause deficiency payments to become a better choice. One interesting caveat here is that deficiency payment mechanisms have dominated U.S. agricultural policy in the recent strong period of the dollar. This phenomenon is consistent with arguments mentioned here suggesting that deficiency payments tend to be preferred to production controls with a strong dollar.

Similarly, an increase in petroleum (and fertilizer) prices, investment in expensive fixed-capacity machinery, or an improvement in market conditions for an unregulated crop could cause the supply curve for a regulated crop to rotate counterclockwise and upward. If these developments were unanticipated in policy formation, they could render a production control scheme inferior to deficiency payments even though it was preferred at policy-making time. Such considerations thus suggest that preferred policies could be developed by specifying conditions under which policy controls would automatically adjust from deficiency payments to production controls or vice versa.

Next consider changes in the welfare weighting of producers. This weight may change for one of two reasons. First, it may be an endogenous term that is associated with some normative preferences for certain income distributions. It may be viewed, for example, as a local approximation of the marginal rate of substitution between producers' and consumers' surplus in the criterion function. Thus a change in conditions that causes substantial improvement in producers' welfare relative to consumers' welfare could prompt the weight to decline, causing production control to replace deficiency payments as a preferred policy.

Alternatively, this weight may be determined exogenously (or at least more indirectly) by pressures of political interest groups on politicians. In this case, determination of a mechanism for evaluating changes in welfare weightings may be difficult. Furthermore, policy makers may be unwilling to commit themselves to particular weighting mechanisms when there is too long a planning horizon because the weighting mechanism is removed from the associated political-economic markets until it is reformulated. Moreover, policy makers may be unwilling to formulate or validate such a concept sufficiently to allow its use in specifying appropriate automatic adjustment because of the adverse political implications of revealing explicit responses to such pressures.

These considerations suggest that the possibilities for setting in motion an automatic policy adjustment mechanism with a long time horizon are weak. Recent farm bills, however, have been enacted with a four-year time horizon, suggesting that policy making on a four-year time horizon is viewed as sufficiently frequent to maintain activity in political-economic markets with interest groups. Automatic adjustment mechanisms for revising the set of policy instruments thus appear to hold potential within at least four-year horizons.

Optimal Automatic Adjustment of Policy Instrument Levels

Consider next whether the levels of given instruments should adjust automatically in response to changes in conditions unanticipated at the time of policy formation. The concept of automatic adjustment in agricultural policy instrument levels is not new. Under the Agricultural Adjustment Act of 1938, for example, the specific formula-regulated loan rate for corn was to be 75 percent of parity if the supply was not expected to exceed domestic consumption plus exports for the year and 52 percent of parity if the supply was expected to exceed domestic consumption plus exports for the year by 25 percent. To take another example, the 1973 act specified a procedure for adjusting initial target prices in 1974–1975 for wheat, feed grain, and upland cotton in accordance with measures of the cost of production. Similar specifications were provided in the 1977 act. Political intervention, however, never actually allowed these automatic adjustment formulas to operate. Target prices determined by the 1977 act, for example, were changed occasionally by legislative action throughout the life of the bill; also, target prices were never allowed to fall from the level of the previous year even though estimated production costs declined.

Another example of the automatic adjustment of policies for the major commodities was introduced for the 1966 upland cotton crop. A procedure was delineated in the 1965 act in which the loan rate for upland cotton was tied to a moving average of world prices and/or U.S. spot-market quotations compounded by a minimum level. This policy of automatic adjustment proved to be effective. As noted by Cochrane and Ryan, this procedure worked to reduce cotton loan rates significantly by comparison with loan rates in previous years and was successful as a means of regaining important export sales.[20] The policy provided the basis for eliminating the need for domestic mill and export subsidies.

Very little research on optimal automatic adjustment of price supports and production controls has yet been done. Most of the economic literature is confined to the traditional criterion of welfare economics that weights producers and consumers equally. Both price and production controls thus cause dead-weight loss. Because no intervention with one-sided controls, such as price supports and production controls, is preferred according to such a naive criterion, no automatic adjustments are appropriate. Nevertheless, the possibility of improving economic welfare by automatic adjustment is clear in a model with a weighted policy criterion.

365

Elsewhere I have shown that automatic adjustments in production controls are desirable beyond the time of policy making.[21] Automatic adjustments are appropriate in response to changes in both slope and location of supply and demand unanticipated at the time of policy making but anticipated at the time of production decision making. The production control level should automatically increase in response to an increase in demand, an increase in supply, an increase in the elasticity of demand, or an increase in the elasticity of supply. These results show that the benefits of automatic adjustment in the production control are greater when uncertainty at policy-making time about demand and production conditions at production planning time is larger. The benefits of automatic adjustment are also greater when demand and supply are more inelastic.

Turning to the case of automatic adjustment of target/support prices, I have considered automatic adjustment both before and after farm decision making. The results show that automatic adjustment of price supports or target prices to changes in either demand or production costs beyond production planning time does not improve policy performance if the support level is set optimally at production planning time. Producers can thus be fully aware of the target price level at the time of production planning even though the policy legislation specifies an automatic adjustment system. Nevertheless, information not available until production planning time must be used in setting the optimal support level.

Policy performance is improved by automatic adjustment of the support price to changes in demand conditions unanticipated at the time of policy making but realized at the time of production planning such that price support is higher with higher demand. The extent of the adjustment should be larger if the welfare weighting of producers is larger, the demand elasticity is larger, the supply elasticity is smaller, and the basic support level is lower. The extent of adjustment should also be larger (smaller) with higher volatility of demand if the support level under normal conditions is above (below) average free-market price.

These results imply that changes in major economic forces, such as the exchange rate, after the time of policy making but before the time of production planning should be incorporated into automatic adjustments in agricultural price support levels. As the value of the dollar advances during this period, a price support should decline and tend to balance supply with declining export demand—but only if the increase in demand is recognized at the time of production planning. This statement is intuitively plausible because an increase in demand lowers the marginal cost of providing price support assistance to producers. Thus, for example, when involvement of the Soviet Union in U.S. grain export markets changes sharply, price supports should be raised if the growing seasons have not yet begun, as they had not for many farmers with the January 1980 embargo (ignoring possible supply response after planting). When the Soviet Union enters U.S. markets in early summer, however, as it did with the bulk of its buying in 1973, no price support adjustment is appropriate (unless such adjustments were anticipated at planning time by producers).

The results also imply that policy performance is improved by automatic adjustment in the support price such that the support level increases with unanticipated changes in production costs if the welfare weighting of producers is small, supply elasticity is large, demand elasticity is small, and the basic support level is high; the support should adjust inversely to costs in the alternative case. If the support level should increase with costs, the extent of adjustment should be smaller (larger) with more volatile demand conditions when the normal support level is above (below) the average free-market price. In most agricultural problems, for example with grains, the demand elasticity is believed to be low, the supply elasticity with respect to conditions at production planning time is relatively high (because marginal land can easily be allocated from one annual crop to another), and the basic level of price support is high. These conditions imply that the price support level should respond positively to changes in production costs such as interest rates unanticipated at policy-making time but realized at production planning time. As for production controls, the gains from automatic adjustment of price controls are larger when conditions are less predictable at policy-making time and when supply and demand are more inelastic.

Specifically, the benefits of automatic adjustment are proportional to the variance of the vertical difference in supply and demand (at planned production) that can appear between policy-making time and production planning time. An increase in volatility of demand and production conditions thus implies that automatic adjustment of agricultural policy instruments should become more attractive. In particular, from the standpoint of the domestic economy, the increased integration of the agricultural economy with a macroeconomy that is experiencing wide swings in monetary policy with the accompanying volatility of interest rates suggests increased need for automatic adjustment in agricultural policy instruments. Similarly, from the standpoint of the world economy, one of the most significant changes in agricultural markets in recent times has been the increased integration with international markets and the accompanying increase in export demand elasticity and volatility. These changes also suggest that the need for automatic adjustment of policy instruments has intensified.

Some Empirical Results

To suggest empirically the magnitude of benefits possible with automatic adjustment, some econometric results from a study of the wheat, corn, and soybean markets that I made with Chambers merit consideration.[22] The model is cogent for this purpose because (1) wheat and feed grains have been among the most important areas of regulation of agricultural corps both in terms of value of production and size of federal budget allocated to regulation and (2) the model focuses on the role of exchange rates in international trade. Since Schuh's work was published, exchange rates (which also embody many of the broad effects of general monetary policy) have been regarded as one of the most important determinants of the strength of U.S. grain markets.[23] Indeed, much of the growing need for automatic adjustment has appeared because of volatile conditions of international trade. Automatic adjustment to fluctuating exchange rates has been regarded as the most likely antidote because econometric studies identify exchange rates as the major explanatory force behind volatile trade conditions.[24] Although the demand component of the model is well suited to the analytic purpose, the supply side is quite abbreviated, and the results should be qualified accordingly. In the discussion of these empirical results, we should bear in mind that the purpose of the exercise is to estimate the potential magnitude of benefits from automatic adjustment and to suggest the magnitude of some adjustment elasticities. The purpose is not to estimate the level of price support that "should" be used or to suggest that policies should be set according to an econometric model. Both the structure of the economy and the policy preferences may not be the same in the upcoming policy period as they were during the sample period used here (1969–1977).

Nevertheless, if the estimated parameters in a standard econometric model of supply and demand reflect the behavior of the economy, then they are sufficient to determine optimal automatically adjusting policy instruments and levels for a given set of policy preferences. Furthermore, the tendency to favor producers relative to consumers in the sample period can be estimated by revealed preferences. Thus the results described here estimate the benefits from automatic adjustment that could have been attained during the sample period. Specifically, suppose policy instruments were set at optimal *nonadjusting* levels during the sample period used for estimating the econometric model. Then the levels of policy instruments during the sample period are sufficient to estimate the policy preferences that correspond to observed policy choices. Using this approach, I estimated, in the context of the model discussed here, that wheat producers are weighted 8 percent more than consumers, with corn producers weighted 4 percent more.[25] Although the wheat and corn markets have supposedly been subject to heavy government intervention, the relatively small policy preference parameters are plausible when we note that demand is highly inelastic and supply is comparatively much more elastic in each case. In other words, a moderate price support level can cause a severe oversupply relative to free-market levels without greatly improving producers' welfare, whereas the high level of support represents roughly an even trade-off between a gain in consumers' surplus and a loss because of

TABLE 1

OPTIMAL SHORT-RUN AUTOMATIC ADJUSTMENT FORMULAS FOR WHEAT

Policy Instrument Set	Formula[a]	Benefits of Automatic Adjustment[b]
Production control	$q_c = .4642a$ (93)	1.19
Deficiency payment	$p_s = .1042a$ (108)	1.18

a. Note that

$$a = 30 + 328\ RPDI - 16.6\ SDR - .0614\ THPW - .0644\ WSTOCKW$$
$$\quad\quad (.624) \quad\quad (-.945) \quad\quad (-.475) \quad\quad (-.162)$$
$$\quad - .0308\ PL480 + .0154\ PWDL + 2.13\ PWXL$$
$$\quad\quad (-.060) \quad\quad (.001) \quad\quad (.135)$$

where numbers in parentheses are elasticities at sample means; jointly dependent variables are *PWDL*, lagged per capita demand for wheat, and *PWXL*, lagged per capita wheat exports (bushels per person); predetermined variables are *PL480*, P.L. 480 shipments of wheat (million bushels); *RPDI*, per capita disposable income divided by wholesale price index; *SDR*, exchange rate (*SDR* per dollar); *THPW*, threshold price of wheat (units of account per metric ton); and *WSTOCKW*, stocks of wheat in other major exporters (metric tons). Numbers in parentheses in the body of the table give percentages of free-market prices and quantities represented by controlled prices and quantities at sample means. q_c = bushels per person. p_s = 1967 dollars per bushel.
b. 1967 dollars per person.

SOURCE: Richard E. Just, *Automatic Adjustment Rules for Agricultural Policy Controls* (Washington, D.C.: American Enterprise Institute, forthcoming).

taxes required to support the producer price.

The interesting estimates describing optimal automatic adjustment of policy instruments and the benefits of automatic adjustment appear in tables 1 and 2. These results are (can be) as rich as the econometric model underlying the adjustment equations. In this case, these considerations are rich in terms of factors affecting demand but weak in terms of factors affecting supply.

The associated elasticities for adjustment are reported in parentheses in the footnotes of tables 1 and 2. In this case, the adjustment elasticities apply for both the optimal price support and production control levels. In the case of wheat, for example, a 1 percent change in the exchange rate should lead to a 0.945 percent automatic adjustment of any price support or production control. A 1 percent increase in world wheat stocks should cause an automatic 0.162 percent decline in any price support or production control. The policy controls can thus respond automatically to keep supply more in balance with demand and to reduce the probability of large unexpected drains on U.S. Treasury funds.

The magnitudes of elasticities of adjustment are one measure of the importance of each exogenous variable in determining appropriate automatic adjustments. Thus, the exchange rate, consumer income, the European threshold price of wheat, and world wheat stocks are the most important variables in declining order of importance for wheat, whereas consumer income, the exchange rate, hog numbers, cattle numbers, and cattle prices are the important variables for corn. Another important consideration, however, is how volatile each variable is. Because consumer income is very stable, it may not contribute much to determining automatic adjustments even though its elasticity is high. On the other hand, exchange rates and world stock levels (and livestock variables in the case of corn) are more volatile and thus should likely contribute more to needed automatic adjustments beyond policy-making time.

The Benefits of Automatic Adjustment

Consider next the benefits that can be derived from introducing automatic adjustment of policy instruments. Tables 1 and 2 report estimates of the benefits of introducing automatic adjustment. The optimum value of the policy criterion function, although I estimated it as well, is not reported here because it is subject to much larger errors in estimation; that is, calculation of the optimal value of the policy criterion requires knowledge of the supply and demand functions outside the range of observed data, whereas calculation of the benefits of switching to automatic adjustment (or to a free market) does not.[26] The benefits of automatic adjustment are remarkably similar with different policy instruments. The benefits are about $1.17–$1.19 per person for wheat and $1.09–$1.10 per person for corn, both in 1967 currency, regardless of the policy instruments used for control. Thus the results suggest that there is relatively little advantage in using production control versus deficiency payments, although production controls are slightly advantageous.

Upon first examination of these results, the benefits of automatic adjustment seem small. Nevertheless, the benefits of automatic adjustment are over $200 million (over $1.00 per person) in 1967 currency for both wheat and corn and amount to almost 10 percent of the value of the crop in the case of wheat.

In examining the benefits of automatic adjustment it is more interesting to compare the benefits of adjustment with the benefits of intervening at all. In this context, the results suggest that the benefits of government intervention, as measured by the policy criterion function, are lost unless automatic adjustment is employed. To see this point, note that the optimal value of the policy criterion with automatic adjustment represents an improvement of only thirty-two cents per person for wheat and sixteen cents per person for corn over free-market equilibrium.

TABLE 2
Optimal Short-Run Automatic Adjustment Formulas for Corn

Policy Instrument Set	Formula[a]	Benefits of Automatic Adjustment[b]
Production control	$q_c = 2.7890a$ (93)	1.10
Deficiency payment	$p_s = .1426a$ (108)	1.10

a. Note that

$$a = 18.0 - 297\ RPDI + .227\ CATTLE + .268\ HOG + .0474\ PCAT - 8.50\ SDR$$
$$(1.000) \quad\quad (.326) \quad\quad\quad (.465) \quad\quad\quad (.172) \quad\quad\quad (-.857)$$
$$- .0732\ WSTOCKC + 0.457\ RPS - .135\ PCDL + .320\ PCXL$$
$$(-.091) \quad\quad\quad\quad (-.091) \quad\quad (-.072) \quad\quad (.044)$$

where numbers in parentheses are elasticities at sample means; jointly dependent variables are *PCDL*, lagged per capita corn disappearance (bushels per person); *PCXL*, lagged per capita corn exports (bushels per person); and *RPS*, soybean price index (no. 1 yellow at Chicago) divided by wholesale price index; predetermined variables are *CATTLE*, number of cattle on feed (million head); *HOG*, number of pigs on feed (million head); *PCAT*, price of beef cattle, farm level (dollars per hundredweight); *RPDI*, per capita disposable income divided by wholesale price index; *SDR*, exchange rate (*SDR* per dollar); and *WSTOCKC*, stocks of corn in other major exporters (metric tons). Numbers in parentheses in the body of the table give percentages of free-market prices and quantities represented by controlled prices and quantities at sample means. q_c = bushels per person. p_s = 1967 dollars per bushel.
b. 1967 dollars per person.

SOURCE: Just, *Automatic Adjustment Rules for Agricultural Policy Controls.*

 With these values in mind, government intervention improves the policy criterion function only if automatic adjustment is introduced. The reason is that the policy instruments distort equilibrium levels too far when they do not adjust automatically to market conditions. The benefits of free-market equilibrium are substantially better than intervention without automatic adjustment, even given policy preferences biased toward producers. On the other hand, benefits with optimal automatic adjustment are somewhat better than with no intervention at all.

 Repeating this same exercise for corn reveals the same qualitative results. Again, free-market equilibrium provides more benefits, even in the context of a weighted policy criterion, than production control or deficiency payments without automatic adjustment. With automatic adjustment, net benefits are somewhat better than free-market equilibrium. Thus the benefits of automatic adjustment estimated in tables 1 and 2, whether large or not, appear to be crucial to successful operation of agricultural policy unless intervention is curtailed.

These results are based on an econometric model not developed particularly for the purpose of designing automatic adjustment rules. Nevertheless, the results (1) demonstrate the important principles that should govern the choice of automatic adjustment mechanisms and (2) give a first-cut look at the magnitude of some key adjustment coefficients and the benefits of using automatic adjustment. The results strikingly indicate that automatic adjustment is crucial in obtaining an improvement over the free market even with a policy criterion biased toward producers. Nonadjusting policy controls can become so distorting with unanticipated changes in economic conditions that losses from distortion more than outweigh any political benefits from redistributing income.

Implications of the Results

The agricultural sector suffers from substantial inherent instability resulting from the dependence of production on weather patterns; the inelastic nature of aggregate demand; rapid technological change; asset fixity; atomistic behavior; and the significant integration of U.S. agriculture into international markets influenced by supply and demand fluctuations in other countries, changes in trade policies, and variations in exchange rates. Furthermore, the inherent riskiness and uncertainty of the U.S. agricultural sector can be increased by unstable fiscal and monetary policies.

For U.S. agricultural policy, conventional wisdom has long held the view that unstable markets can and should be supported and stabilized by conscious economic policies of the federal government. The conventional view of government as able to improve the future of an economic system that is perceived to be well understood neglects the fact that past government policies have failed because such perceptions proved ultimately to be inappropriate. Failure of policies because of inappropriate anticipations by policy makers may, in fact, introduce more instability and uncertainty through the form and shape of governmental intervention than the instability or uncertainty that existed in the private sector prior to such intervention. In essence, policy makers must recognize and explicitly treat imperfections in their anticipations about the agricultural economy.[27]

Some of the empirical results cited here suggest that observed variations in supply and demand conditions for wheat and corn can cause the benefits of intervention to evaporate rapidly even in a fairly short time horizon (policy regime) if appropriate automatic adjustments are not built into the policy. In fact, overall benefits can be seriously reduced from free-market levels when automatic adjustments are not incorporated, even when the benefits are measured in terms of the biased political interests that the policy process may be attempting to serve.

372

The results suggest, for example, that moving from a free market to a controlled price or quantity causes a social loss of almost 10 percent of the value of the crop (for wheat) because of the inability of the market to adjust to short-run changes. Thus, any such control must be capable of gaining back that value and more in terms of the operative policy criterion regardless of its foundation. The results suggest that this is not the case with policy preferences estimated to fit observed policy choices in the 1970s. That is, with policy preferences estimated in the context of the deficiency payment regime of the sample period, the policy criterion explaining observed deficiency payments could have been better served by a free market, because unanticipated conditions did not materialize.

Comparison with Observed Agricultural Policy Adjustment

The results also suggest that revisions in policy instruments after commencement of the growing season are not needed (without risk aversion) if adjustments prior to production decision time are appropriate. Thus either production quotas or target prices can be finalized in time for farmers to make short-run production decisions with full knowledge of the policy instrument levels. This possibility suggests that some aspects of agricultural policy announcement need not differ too much from historical practice. Automatic adjustment could be achieved by the secretary of agriculture, for example, who could announce policy instrument levels just before the beginning of each growing season based on a specific adjustment formula authorized by Congress. Alternatively, if Congress gives the secretary significant discretion, he could determine a specific adjustment formula for announcing policy instrument levels just before production planning time. In fact, this raises the question of whether policy instruments have tended to be adjusted appropriately from year to year even if not by some legislated automatic formula.

Here the evidence is rather negative. First, when conditioning factors have been written into law, only a very limited set of factors has been considered. In one policy period, for example, the level of stocks was used. In another, the cost of production was used. Exchange rates or livestock numbers were never used. Alternatively, the set of conditioning factors should include all the determinants of supply and demand that may change substantially during the relevant time period to which legislation applies.

Next consider the adjustments in policy instrument levels across policy periods. For this purpose, first consider which variables should "explain" most of the appropriate adjustment in price support levels. Table 3 computes an index of importance for each variable affecting the automatic adjustment formulas of tables 1 and 2. This index is simply the coefficient of variation of the relevant variable during the sample period multiplied by the absolute

373

TABLE 3

IMPORTANCE OF VARIABLES IN AUTOMATIC ADJUSTMENT

Wheat		Corn	
Variable[a]	Importance	Variable	Importance
SDR	.0848	SDR	.0801
PWXL	.0520	RPDI	.0380
THPW	.0495	HOG	.0367
WSTOCKW	.0307	CATTLE	.0324
PL480	.0306	WSTOCKC	.0304
RPDI	.0277	PCOW	.0268
PWDL	.0001	PCXL	.0230
		RPS	.0068
		PCDL	.0048

NOTE: Figures in the cells are the coefficient of variation times adjustment elasticity. For variable definitions, see tables 1 and 2.

SOURCE: Just, *Automatic Adjustment Rules for Agricultural Policy Controls.*

elasticity of adjustment in tables 1 and 2. The coefficient of variation measures the percentage variation in the variable, and the elasticity converts that percentage into a percentage variation in the adjustment rule. The results of table 3 suggest that exchange rates should be the dominant force explaining price support adjustments during the sample period.

To investigate whether these adjustments are actually reflected in observed price support levels in the sample period, the deflated price support, *RWSP* or *RCSP*, was regressed on the respective set of explanatory variables. These regressions were somewhat disappointing in that no variable other than exchange rate was significant at any reasonable level when included in the regression with the exchange rate or with the exchange rate and other variables. The exchange rate, however, was highly significant for both wheat and corn, and its coefficient was quite stable regardless of which variables were included in the regression. For this reason, only the results with the exchange rate alone are reported here. The estimated equations are

$$RWSP = -1.54 + 3.24 \, SDR, \quad R^2 = .82, \, \bar{R}^2 = .79$$
$$(-2.70) \quad (5.19)$$
$$RCSP = -.633 + 1.85 \, SDR, \quad R^2 = .61, \, \bar{R}^2 = .55$$
$$(1.16) \quad (3.07)$$

where figures in parentheses are *t* ratios.

The disturbing aspect of these results is that the sign of the exchange rate coefficient for both wheat and corn is the opposite of that implied by optimal adjustment. According to these results, the real support price was reduced when the dollar was weak and export demand was strong, whereas it was increased when the dollar was strong and export demand was weak. Agricultural price supports thus did little to help farmers when the cost of so doing was low, but heavy supports were used when the cost of providing support was highest and the distorting influence was greatest.

It is worth noting that this support price–exchange rate relationship has tended to reverse itself in later years, so perhaps better adjustments have been attained as more experience with an "internationalized" market has been gained. Another explanation is that perhaps the producer welfare weighting changed drastically during the sample period. This possibility is somewhat plausible, because both support prices and exchange rates were low when farm incomes were high during the commodity boom. On the other hand, either support prices or exchange rates were high before and after the boom when farm incomes were low and political pressures from farm groups were greatest.

Considerations of this type suggest that a given automatic adjustment rule may not be appropriate for operation over a long period of time unless it is highly sophisticated. The success of automatic adjustment rules for policy instruments over long periods of time depends on appropriate conditioning of the rules. If the equilibrium rules do not prescribe an appropriate change for a sufficiently broad set of circumstances, the policy rule will require change sooner. The wider the set of adverse conditions to which automatic adjustment rules respond, however, the less likely and less frequent the required changes should be.

Optimal Sharing of Public and Private Risk

This paper has focused on automatic adjustment rules as a means of reducing short-run disequilibrium costs of policy controls while maintaining a goal of income transfer reflective of the agricultural policy controls used in practice. Automatic adjustment rules, however, have further possibilities for reducing market failure due to inefficient distribution of risk. That is, another important motivation for considering automatic adjustment in agricultural policy is the opportunity to attain an optimal sharing of policy risk incurred by farmers with the Treasury risk incurred by government (taxpayers) while transmitting sufficient market signals to producers to encourage appropriate long-term investment. Unanticipated changes in policy are an additional source of risk that may affect farmers adversely in three distinct ways. The first is a loss in well-being for farmers who prefer more certainty. The second is the incurring of higher production costs in order to maintain flexibility. If a farmer does not know whether production controls or deficiency payments will be used as a policy response to declining demand, for example, he must maintain the

375

flexibility to do either during the life of the investments he undertakes. The third adverse effect is a decline in demand by trading partners who find they cannot count on U.S. exports. Traders tend to withdraw from U.S. markets when they are dominated by policy risk and to seek out or even create alternative markets elsewhere.

With respect to the Treasury risk faced by government, it is a well-understood fact that a fixed loan rate or target price can place much of the risk of fluctuating prices on the government and is reflected in terms of Treasury cost exposure. If, however, the policy is designed with automatic adjustments so that both government and the private sector incur some of the losses when market conditions deteriorate, the risk of market price variation can be shared by government and the private sector. Events in recent years suggest that government is not a risk-neutral decision maker as it would have to be to justify shifting risk in farming entirely away from farmers through agricultural policy. Because U.S. agriculture bears a growing relationship to volatile world markets, the need for sharing risk between the public and private sectors has increased. Automatic adjustments provide an important means whereby this sharing can be accomplished.

These considerations suggest that automatic adjustment of agricultural policy instruments offers important opportunities for balancing Treasury cost risk with the private costs of policy risk while reducing the costs of disequilibrium caused by inflexible agricultural policies.

Notes

1. See R. E. Just and G. C. Rausser, "Uncertain Economic Environments and Conditional Policies," in *Alternative Agricultural and Food Policies and the 1985 Farm Bill*, ed. G. C. Rausser and K. R. Farrell (Berkeley: University of California, Giannini Foundation of Agricultural Economics, Division of Agriculture and Natural Resources,1984).

2. This point is made by Don Paarlberg in "Purposes of Farm Policy" (paper prepared for the American Enterprise Institute Agricultural Studies Project, Purdue University, 1984).

3. Robert G. F. Spitze, "Revisions of Existing Agricultural and Food Policy as an Alternative for 1985" (paper presented at the Texas Agricultural Forum, University of Illinois, April 12, 1984).

4. Just and Rausser, "Uncertain Economic Environments."

5. Willard W. Cochrane and Mary E. Ryan, *American Farm Policy, 1948-1973* (Minneapolis: University of Minnesota Press, 1976).

6. Frederick J. Nelson and Willard W. Cochrane, "Economic Consequences of Federal Farm Commodity Programs, 1953-72," *Agricultural Economics Research*, vol. 28 (1976), pp. 52-65.

7. D. Gale Johnson, "The Performance of Past Policies: A Critique," in *Alternative Agricultural and Food Policies and the 1985 Farm Bill*, p. 18.

8. Ibid.

9. U.S. Congress, Food and Agriculture Act of 1981.

10. Paarlberg, "Purposes of Farm Policy."

11. Richard E. Just, Darrell L. Hueth, and Andrew Schmitz, *Applied Welfare Economics and Public Policy* (Englewood Cliffs, N.J.: Prentice-Hall, 1982).

12. Ibid.

13. Gardner, "Efficient Redistribution through Commodity Markets," *American Journal of Agricultural Economics*, vol. 65 (1983), pp. 225–34.

14. Sam Peltzman, "Toward a More General Theory of Regulation," *Journal of Law and Economics*, vol. 19 (1976), pp. 211–40; Gary S. Becker, "A Theory of Political Behavior," Centre for the Study of the Economy and the State Working Paper No. 006-1 (University of Chicago, September 1981); James Buchanan, Gordon Tullock, and Robert D. Tollison, eds., *Towards a General Theory of the Rent-seeking Society* (College Station: Texas A&M University Press, 1981); and Gordon C. Rausser, "Political Economic Markets: PESTs and PERTs in Food and Agriculture," *American Journal of Agricultural Economics*, vol. 64 (December 1982), pp. 821–33.

15. T. D. Wallace, "Measures of Social Costs of Agricultural Programs," *Journal of Economics*, vol. 44 (May 1962), pp. 580–94.

16. Gardner, "Efficient Redistribution through Commodity Markets."

17. For further mathematical justification of these results, see ibid.

18. Richard E. Just, *Automatic Adjustment Rules for Agricultural Policy Controls* (Washington, D.C.: American Enterprise Institute, forthcoming).

19. R. G. Chambers and R. E. Just, "A Critique of Exchange Rate Treatment in Agricultural Trade Models," *American Journal of Agricultural Economics*, vol. 61 (1979), pp. 249–57.

20. Cochrane and Ryan, *American Farm Policy, 1948–1973.*

21. Just, *Automatic Adjustment Rules.*

22. Robert G. Chambers and Richard E. Just, "Effects of Exchange Rate Changes on U.S. Agriculture: A Dynamic Analysis," *American Journal of Agricultural Economics*, vol. 63 (1981), pp. 32–46.

23. G. Edward Schuh, "The Exchange Rate and U.S. Agriculture," *American Journal of Agricultural Economics*, vol. 56 (1974), pp. 1–13.

24. See Just and Rausser, "Uncertain Economic Environments."

25. Just, *Automatic Adjustment Rules.*

26. Just, Heuth, and Schmitz, *Applied Welfare Economics.*

27. See Just and Rausser, "Uncertain Economic Environments."

Commentary

Alan J. Randall

Todd Petzel has presented perhaps the single most important paper in agricultural policy of this year or any recent year. Why do I say that? I do not believe
options on commodity futures are likely to replace traditional farm programs
soon or are ever likely to replace them entirely. I do not even believe options
markets are likely to grow large enough to hedge prices for most farmers.

Petzel's paper is important because of its radical contribution to the
language, the semantics, of policy. I cling to the rather old-fashioned belief
that words matter. Words can be used to direct the way we conceptualize
issues, to define the terms of the debate, to narrow and circumscribe the
options that are seriously considered, and thus to predestine the outcome of
the policy process and preordain the ultimate solution. Interest groups can use
words in ways that further their own causes, and careless habits of language
can undermine our effectiveness as independent analysts.

For too long the argument has been that traditional farm programs are
needed because farming is a risky business, that this risk represents a market
failure, and that programs can reduce and control this risk. Unwary agricultural economists by tolerating this kind of rhetoric have helped to perpetuate
it.

Farming is a risky business, but risk is not market failure, and policy
seldom reduces risk. Risk is real and persists because the costs of reducing it
are substantial and, at the margin, may well be greater than the benefits.
Traditional programs merely transfer risk from U.S. farmers (but, ironically,
also from Canadian, Argentinian, and Australian farmers and from taxpayers
in the European Economic Community) to U.S. consumer-taxpayers and often
at the price of forbidding budgetary cost and stifling inefficiency.

Petzel demonstrates how, once explicit prohibitions were lifted, market
institutions sprang up to transfer some of the price risk of farming to investors
who were willing to accept it if they were rewarded sufficiently. These market
institutions appear to be working fairly efficiently and to be capable of expansion.

How much will these markets in options on commodity futures be used?
Obviously, current farm programs discourage the general use of the options. I
would hazard a guess that, even if the programs were to be summarily eliminated, farmer participation in these markets would be limited. Perhaps we
publicly employed agricultural economists, who surely are risk averse, tend to
overstate the risk aversion of agricultural producers.

378

Will the traditional farm interests be delighted with Petzel's contribution? I think not. Why? They do not really want protection at cost from price risk. They would not find it especially satisfying even if it were free. They want price enhancement, not mere reduction of price risk.

When Todd Petzel speaks of taxpayers who give every farmer in major commodity sectors an in-the-money put option, he has struck a blow for semantic sanity that should long be remembered. He offers a real opportunity to muck out the stalls of the agricultural policy debate once and for all and to separate the issue of risk management, for which the market can provide, from price enhancement, for which by definition it cannot. If you want risk management, go to Todd Petzel for relief from price risk and to my colleague Jerry Skees (with his work on crop insurance) for relief from yield risk. If the Petzel semantic revolution were to succeed and if you wanted price enhancement, you would have to ask for it by name.

Richard Just's case for automatic program adjustments is, in the present paper, not quite as clear or persuasive. The problem is that Just writes at length about why automated adjustment rules are needed and why the arguments against them are not especially convincing before he fully explains automated adjustment rules, how they would work, and what they would accomplish. Mechanistically, how do these rules work? We need to understand the levers, bells, and whistles. With automated adjustment rules, how much price variability and income variability remain? When Just tells us that, relative to traditional programs, his proposal would provide more price support in times of buoyant markets (when support is cheap) and less in times of depressed markets (when support is expensive), such questions instantly spring to mind. To evaluate his proposal fairly, we need some estimates of farm prices, farm income, commodity production, and crop acreage under such a regime.

Let us not allow these irritants to blind us, however, to the good aspects of Just's paper. Given the enormous efficiency costs that arise when farmers are insulated from market signals and the substantial budgetary risk entailed in current programs, it is good to know someone is talking about a program that would mitigate some of these problems without completely withdrawing the price risk transfer and price enhancement features of the existing arrangements. Just's proposal represents a serious attempt to combine an equitable sharing of risk between farmer and taxpayer with some continued transfers toward the farm sector.

Just performs a considerable service in calculating optimal adjustment rules and estimating their welfare effects. In so doing, he introduces a historically weighted welfare function that is used to identify optimal (in its own terms) adjustment rules, risk-sharing arrangements, and transfers. This device would establish some degree of entitlement to the benefits of farm programs and thus offers some protection for the farm sector at large. On welfare and political grounds, this approach makes good sense. (Pareto-safe compensation would make even better sense, a point I will not pursue further here.)

In a conference focused on the 1985 farm bill, should we be talking about these kinds of relatively radical policy redirections? Should we be talking about reliance on options markets, an individualistic alternative, or about automated adjustment rules, a technocratic alternative? Should we be talking about other relatively radical changes? Have not the viable options with respect to the 1985 farm bill already been narrowed and circumscribed so much that such changes have been eliminated?

I have two responses. First, the gestation period for meaningful policy innovation is rather lengthy. The policy process is such that, if everyone thinking about policy focused attention entirely on the immediate legislative period, significant policy redirections would be even less likely. It is important that, along with the pragmatists, some visionaries remain active in agricultural policy discussions. Second, 1985 is not an ordinary farm bill year. I suspect that quite a few wild cards are already in play; so it would be foolish for us all to assume that the menu of policy alternatives is restricted to marginal tinkering with established programs.

Let me mention some of the wild cards. First, established programs are making unusually large budgetary demands at a time of great concern with budget deficits. That alone will place farm programs under unusually intense scrutiny. Second, the interest groups paying some attention to agricultural policy are becoming more and more diverse. We have become accustomed to representations from interests as disparate as foreign policy and environmental quality. This year, in addition, we can expect vigorous representation from the farm supply and commodity marketing interests, who desperately want to see cropland back in production and commodities flowing to export markets. Third, certain agricultural programs may be influenced by social concerns that are not directly connected to agriculture. Tobacco programs, for example, may fall victims not to the budget cutters or to the free-market zealots but to that increasingly vocal pressure group of citizens who seek to regulate the life styles of their fellows. If tobacco programs fell victim to these forces, other agricultural commodity programs might come under more intense scrutiny. All in all, there is a nontrivial probability that the pragmatic individuals who focus upon marginal adjustments to established arrangements may be blindsided this year or next. Right now, I suspect that it might be pragmatic to pay some attention to proposals that would appear radical in more "normal" times.

Let me make a final comment on production controls and exports. Richard Just's observation that deficiency payments involve substantial deadweight losses may provide some reason to reconsider what I had planned to say at this point. I have decided to acknowledge that caveat, however, and to push on ahead. I agree with many other observers who have argued that it makes little sense for the United States, which desperately needs increased exports, to withhold agricultural commodities from world markets in order to support prices not only for ourselves but also for all other exporters. For this reason, we should hope to see the lifting of production controls. The current and persistent high real interest rates, however, give cause for concern. Other observers have worried about the effects of high real interest rates on exchange rates and thus on export demand for American commodities and on the debt service obligations facing American farmers. It may be important to note another effect of high real interest rates. Consider the standard conditions for optimal intertemporal allocation of resources. Combined with fully developed markets in assets and contingent claims, these optimal conditions encourage a belief that market forces can take care of conservation needs.

Consider the role of the real rate of interest in determining the optimal rate of soil depletion, the optimal age of timber at harvest, and optimal retention and replacement strategies for livestock breeding herds. Real interest rates at approximately double their historical levels suggest that what is now optimal would have been considered inefficient and excessively exploitative under more "normal" interest rate regimes. It is sobering to people like myself, who had some faith in intertemporal optimality, to realize just how sensitive conservation and exploitation decisions are to the fiscal and monetary policy strategies that are believed to influence the real rate of interest.

I would endorse a view that has frequently been expressed here: The major problems facing agriculture may be more sensitive to macroeconomic policy considerations than to sector-specific agricultural policy. At this point, consider again the venerable theory of second best. When there is in the system an immovable obstacle to efficiency, the best attainable solution may involve a departure from the a priori optimal conditions. Our present interest rate problems, which seem to have such pervasive negative effects, have resulted (I believe) from the simultaneous implementation of a near-optimal monetary policy and a substantially suboptimal fiscal policy. Which is the immovable obstacle? While there is any reasonable chance of introducing a sound fiscal policy it would seem desirable for the monetary authorities to stand firm. If there prove to be immovable obstacles to a sound fiscal policy, however, the second-best optimum may well involve a departure from optimal monetary policy.

Commentary

Anne E. Peck

Let me first reiterate Todd Petzel's main point: options markets and government price support programs are not substitutes. Programs tend to have fairly long-term goals, at least across crop years. Options markets, like futures markets, have relatively short time horizons and do not fundamentally alter the underlying marketing-clearing equilibrium. Thus markets cannot ultimately provide the same degree of price or income support that a government program can in any specific crop year.

The concept of substitution has yet another meaning as well. Option markets will not succeed if price support levels remain significantly above market-clearing prices and they are actively defended by government program activity. In this sense, options and price supports are indeed substitutes: you can have one, but you cannot have both. The appropriate question, then, is whether programs can be designed (or current programs altered) in ways to make the programs and market alternatives—futures or options—complementary. Thus the right question, as Just suggests in his conclusions, is whether programs can be designed to permit risk sharing between the government, the Treasury, and producers.

Just's objective, it is worth noting, was not in fact to design a program that was risk sharing in the sense of permitting options markets to play a role. Just's automatic adjustment scheme is in essence a government-operated duplicate of an exchange-traded options market. The basic question therefore seems to whether his proposal results in a sharing of risks and leaves producers with some management alternatives.

If this session has a key, it is flexibility. At first pass, the papers and their proposals do seem complementary. First, Just designs policies to adjust to some set of optimal criteria, leaving producers and the government sharing risks. Second, Petzel analyzes the options market's potential role in helping producers manage those risks. Unfortunately, appearances are deceiving. There is in fact little such complementarity in the papers' proposals. Adjustable policies in fact duplicate options markets and thus seem unlikely to leave open a complementary role for the markets themselves. It should be clear, however, that some complementary policies (for example, income transfers) would permit a true sharing of risk. With such policies, we would expect an options market to trade actively and to offer a useful pricing and risk management tool for producers, not to mention the extension of production credit by rural banks.

382

What precisely are Just's adjustable policies and why are they needed? He argues that adjustable policies are needed because previous policy has been seriously destabilizing. Grain embargoes are used as an example. That embargoes are destabilizing and can increase risks in the system cannot be doubted. Nearly everyone agrees that embargoes are bad: they disrupt markets and they disrupt policy plans. Even of they were "adjustable embargoes," they would still be bad. Embargoes are not the subject here, though they have indeed contributed to instability in the markets in which other policies must operate. Just's basic point, I think, is that markets are inherently unstable and prices are not easily predicted. Thus, any fixed set of policy instruments can have serious unanticipated consequences. Indeed, an otherwise well-intentioned stabilization attempt like the payment-in-kind (PIK) program can destabilize market prices in the end.

Just's solution is to introduce increased flexibility into announced policies. What is flexibility? Just's paper is not altogether helpful in this regard—that is, he never really states precisely what he means. He seemingly intends, however, to define flexibility in the following way: A policy is flexible if the extent of its market intervention varies to accommodate the circumstances emerging between its announcement and its implementation. If price supports were set as a fixed percentage of market prices when program provisions were announced, for example, the actual support price could adjust to changing market conditions until a prespecified date, say, at planting time. A somewhat more restrictive adjustable policy would be adjusted only between crop years. The adjustments would' be similarly responsive to market conditions and would follow a prescribed set of rules. For discussion purposes, the latter case is stressed, which leaves aside the relatively minor adjustments that might occur between the announcement and actual implementation.

Consider price supports, for example. Under the "old rules" and in the extreme, the price support for corn might be set at a fixed level, say $2.75 year after year after year. In contrast, the adjustable price support appears to be one that establishes a support price at a fixed percentage under or over each year's anticipated equilibrium price. The actual percentage Just uses seems to depend on welfare criteria, a relative weighting of producers' and consumers' interests. Its specific determination is an interesting exercise but one not germane to the present concerns.

Assume that welfare optimization results in a number of 8 percent, implying that the optimal support level is announced at 8 percent under the anticipated equilibrium price. Further assume, for simplicity, that the anticipated equilibrium price is the new crop futures price. Just might prefer an econometric model's estimate of equilibrium, but his own earlier work shows that these are quite similar to futures prices in their forecast reliability. In the present example, the adjustable rate of 8 percent is applied to a new crop corn futures price of $2.66, giving a support price of $2.45 for the next year.

Clearly, it is lower than the alternative, a fixed rate of $2.75, which is good, because the market is presumably above market-clearing levels.

Still, would an options market trade under these circumstances? Probably not. Combining recent volatilities and time premiums as illustrated in Petzel's paper, a put option written today on December 1985 corn futures is unlikely to be worth less than twenty-one cents (the 8 percent level). There is thus no opportunity for profits in a put at $2.65, but there is a positive probability for profits in a call. That is, even the adjustable policy creates a fundamental pricing asymmetry, and options are not likely to be active under such circumstances. Petzel provides some insightful examples of the effects of similar pricing asymmetries in the sugar options market in recent months. Although farmers are exposed to substantial year-to-year price risks, there is thus little hope that private markets will be available to cope with the risk.

If fully adjustable policies existed whereby targets moved sympathetically with futures prices until production decisions were near, there would clearly be some more scope for options markets, but consider what this statement means. Corn producers, to manage this risk, must take an options position in the fall when the program percentage is announced. For the sake of risk coverage, positions will of necessity be in an option maturing in the new crop year. Such a strategy seems unlikely to draw much interest, its time to expiration being at least fourteen months. That is, farmers have to buy put options in October 1984 that are written on the December 1985 future. The necessary option will be unlikely to be actively traded in practice, inasmuch as the underlying futures are likely to be inactively traded. Again, the proposed sharing of risks is simply not feasible, or, to state the matter somewhat less strongly, the sharing of risk does not permit or encourage the use of private market mechanisms to facilitate the management of risk.

There is good news here, however. According to Just's estimates, none of these considerations matters. The value of his optimum policy criterion (which is not defined in the paper) is reported in his tables 1 and 2 in the paper for the various policy scenarios. Careful inspection shows the values to differ by less than 2 percent among the free market solutions, old-fashioned rigid support price policies, and the proposed adjustable price supports. These results are an unusually strong argument for free markets, not for pure rigidity nor indeed for the equivalent of a government-operated options program. Adjustable and flexible are indeed key words. Still, new programs must permit the market prices to reflect underlying equilibrium—as, for example, do transfer payments geared to income concerns—where such payments do not alter the underlying fundamental supply and demand equilibrium. Such programs permit complementarity with market-oriented risk management strategies, thereby permitting producers much greater flexibility in their response to changing market conditions.

Finally, it is worth reemphasizing Petzel's point: options markets are not substitutes for any price support programs in the long run. That they could complement them is indeed a possibility, but this topic has not been addressed here.

Options are a truly interesting economic experiment. They may in fact have little opportunity to prove their value. If they do have the opportunity, furthermore, I fear they are being oversold to producers. The real value to producers of the new exchange-traded options markets will be in derivative instruments. Firms will be able, for example, more easily to provide producers or indeed banks (if there are any left) with downside pricing protection. Alternatively, instead of the standard, fixed-price forward contract, an elevator could offer a producer a minimum price contract tailored to the size and timing requirements of the individual transaction. Such contracts will of course be priced from the exchange market and elevators, and banks will hedge their risks there. The possibilities are great, so this new experiment may indeed have the opportunity to prove its worth.

Occasional Papers

published by
American Enterprise Institute
on
U.S. AGRICULTURAL POLICIES

1. *U.S. Agricultural Export Expansion Activities: An Evaluation and Analysis of Options for U.S. Wheat Exports*, Philip C. Abbott, Purdue University

2. *Recent Canadian Agricultural Policy and Its Relevance for the United States*, Richard R. Barichello, University of British Columbia

3. *Agricultural Policy and Soil Conservation: Implications for the 1985 Farm Bill*, Sandra S. Batie, Virginia Polytechnic Institute and State University

4. *Dairying and Dairy Policy in the 1980s*, Karen M. Brooks, University of Minnesota

5. *Automatic Adjustment Rules for Agricultural Policy Controls*, Richard E. Just, University of California, Berkeley

6. *The Incidence of Financial Stress in Agriculture* and *Agricultural Policy and Financial Stress*, Emanuel Melichar, Federal Reserve System, and Michael Boehlje, Iowa State University

7. *Two Papers: The Purposes of Farm Policy*, Don Paarlberg, Purdue University, and Ronald D. Knutson, Texas A&M University

8. *Alternatives for Managing Agricultural Price Risk: Futures, Options and Government Programs*, Todd E. Petzel, New York Coffee, Sugar and Cocoa Exchange

9. *Farm Policies and the Rate of Return on Investment in Agriculture*, Tim Phipps, University of Maryland

10. *Macroeconomic Environment for U.S. Agricultural Policy*, Gordon C. Rausser, University of California, Berkeley

11. *The U.S. Sugar Program under Price Uncertainty*, Andrew Schmitz, University of California, Berkeley

12. *Structural Consequences of Commodity Programs*, Daniel A. Sumner, North Carolina State University

13. *Effects of the Tobacco Program: An Analysis of Deregulation*, Daniel A. Sumner and Julian M. Alston, North Carolina State University

14. *U.S. Farm Policy Options and the European Community Response*, Stefan Tangermann, University of Göttingen, Federal Republic of Germany

15. *Effects of Federal Grain Programs on the Livestock Sector*, Richard M. Todd, Federal Reserve Bank of Minneapolis

16. *An Assessment of the United States Farmer-Owned Reserve and Commodity Credit Corporation Storage as Market Stabilization Policies*, Brian D. Wright, Yale University

AEI Occasional Papers are photocopied typescripts of analyses prepared for timely distribution during the process of policy formulation. They have not been editorially prepared for publication. Occasional Papers can be obtained from AEI's photocopying center at a price based upon a per-page copying charge and mailing rates. For information on orders, call toll free 800-424-2873 (in Washington, D.C., 202-862-5869) or write American Enterprise Institute, 1150 Seventeenth Street, N.W., Washington, D.C. 20036.